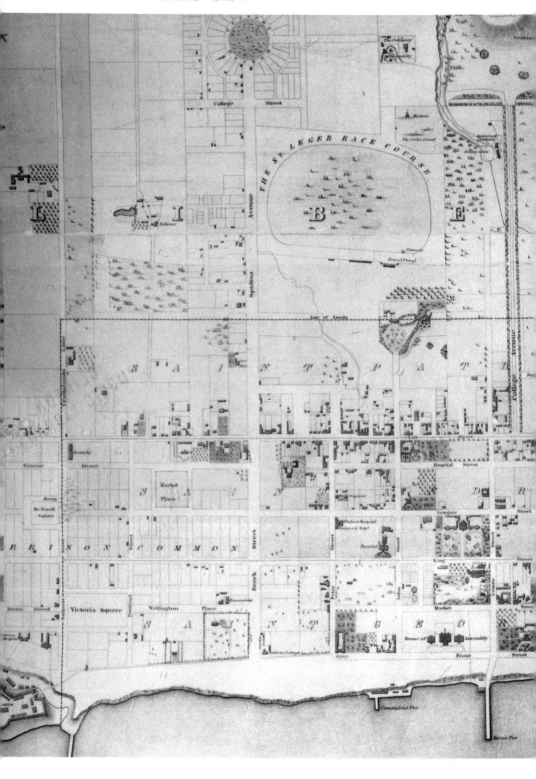

TORONTO OF OLD

HENRY SCADDING

TORONTO OF OLD

HENRY SCADDING

edited by Frederick H. Armstrong

Toronto & Oxford
Dundurn Press
1987

Design and Production: Andy Tong
Printing and Binding: Gagne Printing Ltd., Louiseville, Quebec, Canada

The publisher wishes to acknowledge the generous assistance and ongoing support of **The Canada Council The Book Publishing Industry Development Programme** of the **Department of Communications** and **The Ontario Arts Council.**

Care has been taken to trace the ownership of copyright material used in the text (including the illustrations). The author and publisher welcome any information enabling them to rectify any reference or credit in subsequent editions.

J. Kirk Howard, Publisher

Canadian Cataloguing in Publication Data
Scadding, Henry, 1813-1901
Toronto of old

Written by Henry Scadding
Previously published: Toronto: Oxford University Press, 1966.
Bibliography: p.
Includes index.
ISBN 1-55002-027-7

1. Toronto (Ont.) - Description. 2. Toronto (Ont.) - History. I. Armstrong, F.H. (Frederick Henry), 1926- II. Title.

FC3097.4.S27 1987   971.3'54102   C87-094965-9
F1059.5.T6857S27 1987

Dundurn Press Limited
1558 Queen Street East
Toronto, Canada
M4L 1E8

Dundurn Distribution Limited
Athol Brose, School Hill,
Wargrave, Reading, England
RG10 8DY

CONTENTS

ILLUSTRATIONS

Editor's Preface
To The Second Edition

For this second edition of my 1966 abridgement of Canon Henry Scadding's *Toronto of Old,* the introduction has been substantially revised to provide more explanations, and to update some sections in consideration of the many changes in the last twenty years. A fourth appendix has been added discussing some of the street name changes that have taken place since Scadding's time. Except for some minor corrections, the text and the other appendixes have been left as they were. For many of the people listed in the short biographies in Appendix III little is known; however, with the completion of most of the nineteenth century volumes of the *Dictionary of Canadian Biography* extensive biographies are available for many of the major figures mentioned by Scadding. For those who wish further information on early Toronto, a short bibliography has been added.

Helpful suggestions for textual revisions have been made by my colleagues in the Western History Department, James J. Talman and Peter F. Neary, by the late Archivist of Ontario, George Spragge, and by Mrs. Anne Barnard of Noble, Ontario. At Massey College in Toronto, Colin E. Friesen, the bursar; Desmond Neill, the librarian and Allyn Ridge, the assistant librarian have helped in many ways, as have Edward C.H. Phelps, John Lutman and Guy St.-Denis of the D.B. Weldon Library at the University of Western Ontario.

Department of History,   Frederick H. Armstrong
The University of Western Ontario
London, Ontario
September, 1987.

Editor's Preface
To The First Edition

The great length of the original 1873 edition of Henry Scadding's *Toronto of Old* made it necessary to abridge the text. In general, however, except for two large sections, the only parts that have been omitted dealt with matters that did not directly relate to Toronto, comparisons with England, for example, and long lists of people and commodities, as well as details of which Scadding had no personal knowledge. The chronicle of the harbour ('The Harbour: Its Marine, 1793-1863'), which was not a complete history, has been cut to about a quarter of its length mainly by leaving out passages that were not directly related to the city.

The two large sections that have been omitted in this abridgement are the Introduction dealing with the French Régime and the description of Yonge Street north of Hogg's Hollow (York Mills). For his Introduction Scadding did yeoman's service in his research on the French period of Toronto's past; but his findings have since been considerably amplified by Percy J. Robinson who wrote a detailed history of the city at that time in his *Toronto During the French Régime* (1933). As this work has recently been made available again by the University of Toronto Press, it was felt that Scadding's much shorter description could be omitted. The excursion up Yonge Street north of the city to Penetanguishene was dropped because it did not deal with Toronto proper; besides, it contained few matters of great interest today. One part of these chapters has been retained, however — the description of the Temple at Sharon and it can be found (with an appropriate note) in Chapter III, where Scadding discusses the activities of the Children of Peace in the city.

Scadding was a thorough and accurate scholar, especially so when one considers that he had no previous research to draw upon. A few minor changes have been made in his text, however: some dates have been corrected; the spelling of proper names has been altered to conform with present usage; and the punctuation has been modernized. I have added in square brackets: some first names to help distinguish people mentioned, modern street names where the original ones have been changed, dates where the period under discussion needed clarification, and the occasional explanatory phrase. In some cases two or more of Scadding's chapters have been combined to make a single chapter: an extra line-space in the text indicates where such a change has been made.

Two new appendixes are provided: a table of lieutenant-governors of Upper Canada and a list of biographies identifying many of the people mentioned by Scadding all, that is, about whom additional information could be found. (Virtually the only facts known about some people referred to are contained in Scadding's text.) Short notes have also been included on some of the major families of the city whose names appear frequently throughout the book. People mentioned who had no relation to Toronto in any way have been omitted from the biographical list, but where necessary their importance has been indicated in a footnote.

I would like to thank Edith G. Firth, Larry T. Ryan, and Michael Pearson of the Baldwin Room of the Toronto Public Libraries, and Anne M. Sexton and Edward C.H. Phelps of the Regional Room of the University of Western Ontario Library, who have been most helpful in the course of my research. Miss Firth has been kind enough to read the introduction and to make many useful suggestions for the biographies.

Middlesex College   F.H. Armstrong
The University of Western Ontario
London, Ontario
December, 1965

Editor's Introduction

I

When, in 1872-73, Henry Scadding arranged his many notes on the history of Toronto to form his monumental *Toronto of Old* he began a work that would become both the great classic of the early history of the city and the mine from which all future writers on old Toronto would draw much of their information. His intention, as he stated it, was merely to preserve many minor incidents of the city's past that would otherwise be forgotten. That the book should have attained a far greater importance, however, is not hard to understand. Scadding's father had been connected with the city from its earliest days, and Scadding himself had been a resident from the age of eight, over a decade before the Town of York became the City of Toronto in 1834. He knew York/Toronto as both town and city in all its features and byways; he watched it grow from a government-oriented village, important only as the site of the provincial capital of Upper Canada, into an industrial and commercial metropolis that dominated the new province of Ontario economically and socially, while retaining its political importance. In the eyes of his memory, Scadding could look beyond the commercial emporiums which had risen in the 1850s and 1860s to the village and countryside they had replaced, and he could recall the story of each lane and corner.

Scadding was equipped for his task, however, by more than a good memory and the fact that he had lived through a period of remarkable expansion. Not only had he witnessed the physical development of the city, but his social position enabled him to observe the inner workings of its government and the activities of the province's leaders. Son of Lieutenant-Governor John Graves Simcoe's estate manager, pupil and protégé of Bishop John Strachan, possessor of an independent income, and one of the best-educated men in the city of his time, Scadding was closely connected with the leading members of the Family Compact, a group that continued to play a leading role in Toronto's business and society long after it had ceased to dominate the city and province politically. Also, as Rector of Holy Trinity, one of the most important downtown churches in the city, he met the new leaders rising in Toronto society and was accepted into their social circles.

But *Toronto of Old* is much more than the recollections of a man who was an early inhabitant with good social connections. It is also the work of a polished writer who was able to grace his descriptions with charm and gentle humour and colour them with an appealing fondness for the city's early history without in any way affecting their accuracy. Finally, it is the product of scholarly research. In preparing his manuscript Scadding did far more than rely on his memory, for over the years he had kept a diary and made voluminous notes on the activities and growth of the city. In addition he had an exceptionally fine collection of documents and early printed matter material that is often cited in his text. His connections with so many of the early families must have been valuable in helping him acquire many manuscripts and letters that would otherwise have been destroyed. Besides the documents, he possessed a very complete library that included many descriptions of the city by early travellers, some of whom he must have met with and discussed their impressions. All these materials, which were used effectively in his many works, were willed by him to the Toronto Public Libraries (now Metropolitan Toronto Library), where they still form one of its most important collections. Scadding's non-Canadian books and papers were left to the University of Toronto and are now kept in the rare books collection of the University Library.

It is not surprising, then, that *Toronto of Old* became popular, going into a second edition in 1878 and consolidating Scadding's reputation as the great historian of the early years of the city. It eventually became a classic, and even before Scadding died in 1901 it was one of the basic sources on Toronto's history: John Ross Robertson of *The Evening Telegram* referred to it frequently in his six volume *Landmarks of Toronto*, which began to appear in 1894. Though never again reprinted, *Toronto of Old* has continued to hold its place as the most quoted work on the story of the city, and Scadding himself reigns without a rival as Toronto's finest historian.

II

The Scadding family were of old Devonshire stock, and when John Graves Simcoe purchased his five-thousand-acre estate at Wolford in that county in 1784, he appointed Scadding's father, John Scadding (1754-1824), as his property manager. Seven years later Simcoe was appointed first lieutenant-governor of Upper Canada, and in 1792 John Scadding followed him to North America. When Simcoe moved the capital from Niagara-on-the-Lake to York, Scadding senior, like most of Simcoe's associates, received a land grant near the new town, his property comprising 253 acres on the east side of the Don River stretching from Lake Ontario north to what is now Danforth Avenue. When Simcoe retired in 1796 John Scadding returned to England with him, leaving the property, which had been developed to an extent, under the management of George Playter, one of his neighbours. Back at Wolford, Scadding resumed the management of the estate, first for Simcoe and then after his death for his widow Elizabeth Posthuma Simcoe. About 1806, shortly before Simcoe's death, Scadding married Melicent Triggs (1768-1860), who presented him with three sons of whom Henry, born in 1813, was the youngest.

In 1817 or 1818, in spite of the fact that he was then well into his sixties, John Scadding decided to return to York and develop his property, possibly because he wanted to build up a patrimony for his sons. On this visit he had a more commodious home prepared for his family than his original cabin. Then, in 1821, he brought his wife and children out to the new world. Only three years later he was killed while superintending the clearing of his lands when a tree, which was being cut down, fell unexpectedly. His widow was left with the three sons to raise, fortunately with what was apparently an adequate income and a valuable piece of property located immediately adjacent to the growing town.

Certainly Henry's schooling did not suffer as a result of the death of his father, for he received as fine an education as was available in the Upper Canada of the period. His school experiences are so well described in his section on the Grammar School that we need not note them here except to say that at an early age he must have attracted the attention of the Rev. John Strachan, then still a schoolmaster as well as Rector of York. Another of his teachers was the Rev. Thomas Phillips, who later became first vice-principal of Upper Canada College. When that institution opened in 1830, Scadding was the first pupil to enroll, and he became the first head boy. In 1833 he graduated and was appointed a King's Scholar, an honour that enabled him to complete his education at St. John's College, Cambridge, where he received his B.A. degree in 1837. In 1850 he became an M.A. and in 1852 a D.D. was conferred upon him by his old university, an honour that he also received from Oxford in 1867.

On his return to Canada in 1837 Scadding was ordained a deacon by Bishop Mountain of Quebec and he then lived for a year in Montreal as tutor to the sons of Sir John Colborne, then the commander-in-chief of the British army in North America. In 1838 he moved to Toronto and was appointed a classical master at Upper Canada College; after he had been ordained a priest, he also became assistant minister at St. James' Church. When the Church of the Holy Trinity was opened in 1847, Scadding became the first incumbent, serving without a salary; at the same time he retained his post at Upper Canada College, where he sometimes acted as principal, until his retirement in 1862. In spite of chronic ill health he remained at Holy Trinity until 1875 when he retired and was appointed a canon by Strachan's successor, Bishop Alexander Neil Bethune.

In 1841 Scadding married Harriet, daughter of John Spread Baldwin, who was a brother of Dr. William Warren Baldwin; his wife was thus a member of one of the most prominent families in the city. J.S. Baldwin was one of the wealthiest merchants; in 1815 he and Jules Quesnel of Montreal had continued the business of Quetton de St. George when that pioneer of Toronto merchandising returned to France on the restoration. Three of Scadding's brothers-in-law were Anglican clergymen: the most famous of them was Maurice Scollard Baldwin who became Bishop of Huron (London). Unfortunately Scadding's marriage was of brief duration because Harriet died in 1843 at the age of twenty. Scadding, who never remarried, was left to raise their daughter Henrietta who had been born in 1842. In 1866 she married a second cousin, Robert Sullivan, a son of the second mayor of Toronto, and nephew of Dr. W.W. and J.S. Baldwin, who, like so many of the Baldwins and Sullivans, was a member of the bar. Her marriage, like that of her father, was of short duration for Robert died in 1870 leaving her with three children, and again like her father, she never remarried. She died at her home, 70 Spadina Road, in 1926.

Even though he had retired from Holy Trinity, Scadding continued to live at 10 Trinity Square, (renumbered 6 in 1889) just around the corner from his old church and rectory. It is a remarkably tall house, because Scadding had architect engineer John George Howard, the donor of High Park, add a third storey to the original 1860-61 house designed by William Hay, who had returned to Scotland after building St. Michael's College and St. Basil's Church, and making additions to Holy Trinity. From the upper windows of his third floor study, Scadding could look over much of the city and gradually see his view to the south partially blocked by the rising towers of commerce. The house may still be seen today between the east end of Holy Trinity and the Eaton Centre.

Scadding's retirement was far from inactive. Even as a master at Upper Canada College and Rector of Holy Trinity he had found time to engage in many outside activities. History and theology were, of course, among his major pursuits, but like most of the educated men of his time he was also interested in the advance of science and in 1849 was one of the founders of the Royal Canadian Institute. When he retired from Upper Canada College in 1862 he became its librarian, and in 1870 he was elected president and held that office for six years. As can be seen from his magnificent description of the Don Valley, one of the finest parts of *Toronto of Old* natural history was another of his favourite diversions, and like the great English naturalist Gilbert White (1720-93), to whom he refers, he particularly wanted to record the flora and fauna of his own region.

Scadding was also one of the founders of the York Pioneer and Historical Society in 1869, and was president from 1880 until he retired in 1898. Throughout these years his interest in research and writing continued. Aside from *Toronto of Old*, his most famous work was *Toronto, Past and Present, Historical and Descriptive* (1884), written in collaboration with John Charles Dent (1841-88) to mark the semi-centennial of the incorporation of the city. For this book Scadding prepared the history of the city up to 1834; Dent, whose death at the age of forty-seven prematurely removed one of Canada's best early historians, wrote the section after incorporation. Seven years later Scadding wrote the introduction for G. Mercer Adam's *Toronto, Old and New*, a book designed to commemorate the centenary of the founding of Upper Canada. This was Scadding's last participation in a major work, though he continued his interest in writing until his death on May 6, 1901. He was buried in St. James' Cemetery. A year after his death a tablet was erected to his memory on the south wall of Holy Trinity Church, opposite the plaque in memory of the founder.

III

The Toronto that Scadding describes is basically the town as it appeared before incorporation in 1834. There are some anecdotes and facts about the city in the years immediately following incorporation, but only a few passages relating to events after the 1840s. (Incidents dating from that period would be too familiar to a historian in the early 1870s and would be readily remembered by many of his readers.) Since the town, and later the city, was the centre of activities for Upper Canada, the leading figures of both capital and province tended to be the same. Scadding says much about the government of both units, and though his comments would have been clear to a reader of his day, circumstances have changed so much that some additional historical background may be useful for the present edition.

The province of Upper Canada was in existence for almost fifty years and geographically coincided with what is now southern Ontario. It was separated from the old province of Quebec (which became known as Lower Canada) by the Constitutional or Canada Act in 1791. In 1841 the two provinces were reunited as the Province of Canada and remained one political unit until they were again separated at Confederation in 1867. During this period Upper Canada was often known as Canada West and Lower Canada as Canada East; but the old names continued, particularly in popular usage. Toronto ceased to be the capital in 1841, and except for the years 1849-51 and 1855-59 was not a political centre again until 1867.

In the period before 1841, which interested Scadding most, the province of Upper Canada was not completely separated from the lower province, for the overall governor resided at Quebec, and some departments, such as the Post Office, had their headquarters there. On the other hand, difficulties of communication tended to give the upper province far more autonomy than the Constitutional Act had intended, especially as the governor soon came to report directly to the Colonial Office in England rather than through the governor in Quebec. As a result, and because of the differences between the French and the English, Upper Canada developed an identity of its own. There the upper classes at least came to regard the province as a replica of England separated geographically from the Motherland, and to an extent beleaguered by the threatening forces of French to the east and Americans to the south. Their attitude to the United States belied the vast amount of trade that was carried on with that nation; but it only became more entrenched when the Reformers began to demand American institutions.

Scadding's outlook typified the colonial prejudices of the period. He was connected with England by birth and the affiliation of his church, and his Anglophile sympathies seem to have been little changed by his long residence in Canada, or by the fact that he definitely regarded Canada as his home. When he wished to make an especially complimentary reference to some location or building, he almost invariably compared it with a similar place in the old country, and his text is full of extended literary and historical references to England (some of which have been deleted in this edition for want of space). He makes few references to the United States; when he does refer to that country, it is treated as any foreign nation.

Such an attitude was natural in emigrants from England, and could be found in Ontario until well after World War II. In fact one of the reasons for the separation of Upper Canada from Quebec in 1791 had been to ensure that the area would become English. This was considered only fair to the Loyalists who had opened up the province and were demanding the substitution of British laws and land tenure for the French system that had been confirmed by the Quebec Act in 1774. But in designing the new constitution the British authorities had in mind more than the creation of a little England in Canada. They wanted to set up an aristocratic government and a semi-established church that would prevent a recurrence of the democracy which they saw as the basic cause of the American Revolution. The idea of divide and rule was possibly also present in their minds.

The Constitutional Act turned these ideas into practice and set up a government that was carefully designed to foster a local oligarchy. At the head of state in Upper Canada was the lieutenant-governor, a man who unlike the ceremonial heads of state today possessed vast powers of patronage and appointment, and who even had complete control over certain funds which enabled him to ignore the popularly elected Legislative Assembly on occasion. The lieutenant-governor also controlled all appointments of members of the upper house or Legislative Council and the 'cabinet' or Executive council, neither of which was responsible to the elected lower house. Unlike the Legislative Councillors, the Executive Councillors were not appointed for life but held office only at the pleasure of the Crown; in practice, however, they were almost never replaced before 1839. In the absence of the governor this group ran the province, and could appoint an administrator or president from among its own numbers. Peter Russell, who held office from 1796 to 1799, was the best known of these civilian administrators.

Another class of appointments made by the governor were the legal officers of the colony, men who figure large in Scadding's pages. Over the district courts (which will be discussed below) was a Court of the King's Bench, set up by Simcoe in 1794, which consisted of the chief justice of Upper Canada and two puisné (associate) judges; this was only superior court in the province until a Court of Chancery was established in 1837. (The first vice-chancellor of the province was Robert Jameson, the husband of the famous English writer Anna Jameson.) In addition to these offices the Crown appointed the solicitor-general and attorney-general. To an extent a *cursus honorum* evolved whereby a man moved through these offices to the bench, as is exemplified by the career of Sir John Beverley Robinson who was made solicitor-general in 1815 attorney-general in 1819, and chief justice in 1829.

The special place of an aristocracy was in keeping with the idea of an oligarchy which had dominated the thinking of those who had drawn up the Constitutional Act; but the extent of its power was probably more than the British officials had expected. From the departure of Simcoe in 1796 until the arrival of Colborne in 1828 there was no outstanding man in the governship of the province. Peter Hunter was basically a military man who was kept busy with his other duties as commander-in-chief at Quebec; Francis Gore and Sir Peregrine Maitland were far from remarkable; and the various generals who held office as administrators during the War of 1812 came and went rapidly and were too busy pursuing their military activities to have much influence on the civilian government. On the whole the governors lacked the ability to control the officials who were, after all, unquestionably loyal, and were running the province generally along lines entirely approved by Britain. Even after Colborne arrived, and the British government decided that new men should be brought into the Councils, it was difficult for some years to effect much of a change in the composition of the governing bodies; for there was a shortage of able and educated men outside the ranks of the oligarchy.

It was these Tory groups, then, that virtually ran the province and became the centre of the much-maligned Family Compact. That the members of the compact administered the province in their own interests cannot be denied; but that they ran it badly can be argued. In a primitive community, where there was a shortage of able men, some type of oligarchy was almost certainly bound to emerge, especially when the constitution was designed to create one. But these men whose homes, activities, and relationships are referred to throughout Scadding's *Toronto of Old* generally ran the government with competence. They regarded themselves not as politicians but rather as semi-permanent administrators to whom the control of affairs was entrusted because of their social position and ability. In many ways they were a late example of eighteenth century government by enlightened despotism and for a province where the eighteenth century lingered in so many ways, their type of government was not a bad one. Their tragedy was that, when the province outgrew them, they attempted to hold on to power after the need for their type of "benevolent" aristocracy had passed. A new era had begun in which they were forced to fight political battles for which they were entirely unfitted by their whole outlook. Their eventual defeat by 1841 showed that the ideas of a state church and an aristocratic government which had been foisted upon Upper Canada in 1791 were not acceptable to a frontier province influenced both by new ideas from England and Jacksonian democracy to the south; yet their era was an important one in the evolution of Canadian politics.

Below the Councils was the popularly elected Legislative Assembly, a body that was originally subservient to the Councils' orders, but which from 1816 became progressively more independent-minded. After the election of 1824 it was Reform-oriented, after that of 1828 Reform-dominated. Here in the Legislative Assembly such notables as Marshall Spring Bidwell, William Lyon Mackenzie, Jesse Ketchum, and Dr. William Warren and his son Robert Baldwin called for popular control of the government and opposed administration supporters such as John Beverley Robinson and Christopher Alexander Hagerman. It was in the Assembly also that a new politically oriented Tory group began to appear, men who backed the administration-minded Compact and fought its battles. In this fight they were far from unsuccessful, for their tactics enabled the Tories to regain control of the Assembly in 1830 and, except for the years 1834-6, to hold control until the end of the Upper Canadian period. But the real struggle for popular or Responsible Government was not to begin until after 1841.

In all the debates in the Assembly, however, the participants were not divided into formal parties according to the modern sense but rather were split into fluid factions that followed a man as much as principle. The Tories generally backed the administration. The Reformers, however, were split into two groups, a fact that is too often overlooked. The majority generally, men like Bidwell, Peter Perry, W.W. and Robert Baldwin were moderates, and in the two Assemblies the Reform group controlled the moderates elected Bidwell as the Speaker and their leader. The other part of the Reform faction was led by William Lyon Mackenzie; this group became more radical as the years progressed and in the end was responsible for the abortive stupidity of the Rebellion of 1837. In this Rebellion the radicals destroyed themselves thus leaving the stage to the moderates, who were to go on to play one of the most constructive roles in Canadian history and to bring Responsible Government into force. For, though it is Mackenzie who popularly gets so much credit for our receiving the right to govern ourselves, there is little evidence that he ever understood the idea: it is the Baldwins, Louis H. LaFontaine, the moderate officials in England, and such governors as Sir Charles Bagot and The Earl of Elgin, who were to bring it into being.

In his handling of these political questions, when the fires that they had ignited were still smouldering, Scadding shows himself as both a moderate and very much a man of his age. On the one hand he was a member of the establishment, his father was a protégé of Simcoe, he himself was a protégé of Strachan (only recently deceased in 1873) and a clergyman of the quondam state church; on the other side Scadding was a very enlightened Victorian, a man imbued with the idea of progress who was ready to back the advance of Canada within the framework of the Empire. The advent of Responsible Government and the separation of church and state were therefore developments that he accepted. He also largely accepted the exaggerated place that Mackenzie was already being given for his part in the Reform movement. When one considers that he had watched Mackenzie fight his battles from the opposing side, Scadding's analysis of his character is not only a masterpiece of judgement but also a magnificent example of scholarly detachment. Scadding did not desert Strachan his old mentor, however; he minimized his bad points and concentrated on giving him great credit for the work he had done in building up his church. Basically, Scadding felt that society had passed beyond all the political controversies of Upper Canada and that the discord they once engendered was best put aside.

IV

To clarify parts of Scadding's narrative, mention must also be made of the structure of local government. Before 1850 the unit of local government in what is now Ontario was the district, not the county; but the early districts have no relation to the districts in Northern Ontario today. The original districts predated the founding of Upper Canada; for, as soon as the Loyalists settled in the western part of Quebec, it was necessary for the province to provide them with some system of local administration. As a result, in 1788 what is now southern Ontario was divided into four districts. Counties made their appearance in 1792 when it became necessary to divide the new province into ridings for election purposes; but the counties were merely electoral divisions and units of organization. As the province grew in population, the number of districts was gradually increased until by the 1840s there were twenty of them and they were to a large extent coterminous with the counties. Finally, in 1849, Robert Baldwin was responsible for an act that abolished the districts and transferred local government to the county, an act that still stands as the basis of local government in Ontario today.

The districts were administered by boards of magistrates, or justices of the peace, who were appointed by the governor for indefinite terms. These men met in Courts of Quarter Sessions of the Peace for their district under the presidency of a chairman whom they elected from among their own numbers. Originally, they met only four times a year (hence the name 'Quarter Sessions'), but as the population increased their meetings became much more frequent, though the year always continued to be divided into four terms. The J.P.s were subsidiary members of the aristocracy, and appointment to the office was generally regarded as a recognition of a man's social status. The courts both supervised local government and acted as a law court for minor cases though an appeal to the King's Bench was always possible. Each district also had certain permanent officials holding special posts, such as the clerk, treasurer, and sheriff. At the very bottom of the governmental structure, each township and town elected its own warden and some minor officials such as pathmasters or road superintendents; but these men had very little power.

The Town of York was situated in the Home District, one of the four original districts dating from 1788, though until 1792 it was called Nassau. Like the other early districts, it was gradually reduced in size until, with the formation of a separate district for Simcoe County in 1837, the Home District consisted only of what became the area covered by Toronto and the counties of York, Peel, and Ontario. The magistrates met at York, and they included many of the men Scadding refers to: Alexander Wood, D'Arcy Boulton Jr., James FitzGibbon, George Monro, and George Taylor Denison I. Under their supervision the Town of York had its local officials who were elected at a joint meeting of town and township held at the first of every year. These local officials often tended to be Reform in outlook, whereas the magistrates were always Tories.

In 1817 York and other two other towns became police villages and thus received a few extra powers of local government; but there was no drastic change in the municipal system until York was incorporated in 1834. Incorporation came about basically because the population had reached such a size that it was impossible for the magistrates to carry on the government. At the same time that it was incorporated, the name was changed back to Toronto, and the city was divided into five wards named after the patron saints of the British Isles, with St. Lawrence thrown in for Canada. Each ward elected two aldermen and two common councilmen, the difference between the two categories being that the aldermen had a higher property qualification, and that they alone sat on the new Court of Quarter Sessions for the city, which had been created because a separate court was necessary to preside over municipal legal cases. In the early years the Council chose the mayor from among the aldermen; the common councilmen had a vote but were not eligible for the office.

Before the Rebellion the City Council was as much a political arena as the Legislative Assembly, with the two factions alternating in control: Reform in 1834 and 1836; Tory in 1835 and 1837. After 1837, however, the Reformers disappeared and the City Council became virtually a non-political body (though Tory-dominated, much as it is still conservatively oriented today). The mayors naturally changed with the composition of the Council. Mackenzie was elected in 1834, but was overwhelmingly defeated in 1835 when he and his Reformers failed to solve the problems of the city. His Tory successor, Robert Baldwin Sullivan, retired after a year in office, though his mayorality had been much more successful. In sum, before the Rebellion the two political forces in the city were very evenly matched, and one of the most important effects of that uprising was to wipe out the local Reform party and turn the city even more into 'Tory' Toronto.

V

For most of the period on which Scadding concentrates the Town of York was socially little more than a village in which life focused upon the Legislature, with its committees, and the Garrison. Church and tavern were the two main social meeting-places. Though York had been founded by Simcoe in 1793, the population was only about 700 at the end of the War of 1812, and there was no great influx until the wave of English emigration in the mid-1820s. By 1828 there were 2,235 inhabitants; then the population soared to 9,252 in 1834 and to 30,775 by 1850. With this population explosion came vast social changes that turned the village of the 1820s into the city of the 1830s, and made the period one of the most important in Toronto's development.

Up to about 1828 the town was characterized by the almost complete lack of a middle class. Society was made up of people connected with the government, wealthy landowners, and a few merchants. Below them were a handful of less prosperous merchants and at the bottom of the social scale the workers and soldiers of the garrison. With the sudden growth of population this picture changed drastically. The upper class did not greatly increase in number; but with the growing prosperity of the town and its hinterland, many successful merchants began to appear and soon large stores lined both sides of King Street. Their proprietors dealt in a wide variety of merchandise, both wholesale and retail, and Toronto's economic influence began to be felt over a widening section of southern and southwestern Ontario.

The lower class grew even more rapidly. Some immigrants were employed in the new stores, others in the industries that were increasing in both number and size throughout the city. But there were those who failed to find any employment, and by the early 1830s Toronto was having to face the problems of rapid growth: an urban poor, the need for an organized system of relief, increasing numbers of taverns (licensed and otherwise) and a consequent increase in drunkenness, prostitution, and juvenile delinquency, all problems that were to hasten the course of incorporation.

With the city's growth also came new interests and amusements. Societies for almost every imaginable form of entertainment began to appear: sports, politics, culture, and mere fraternal get-togethers. A temperance movement began to grow in reaction to the drinking and it soon turned from temperance to advocating total abstinence. More variety in life was provided by visiting entertainments of many kinds, circuses, plays, and concerts dominating.

Under this wave the city's frontier aspects began to be submerged, and the government and the garrison ceased to have the importance that they had before 1830. When the seat of government was moved to Kingston in 1841 the change had little effect on Toronto. At the same time the city began to take on new characteristics, those for which Toronto was to become famous or notorious in the years that followed: its temperance, sabbatarianism, and, with the Reform faction shattered, rabid Toryism. Scadding's 'Toronto of Old' was thus turning into something else: a city with a transformed character; but a city that was also coming to realize that it had a past. It was because of the suggestions of his many friends who were interested in Toronto's past that Henry Scadding began his researches which were to lead to the writing of his great classic.

TORONTO OF OLD:

COLLECTIONS AND RECOLLECTIONS

ILLUSTRATIVE OF THE

EARLY SETTLEMENT AND SOCIAL LIFE OF THE CAPITAL OF ONTARIO.

By HENRY SCADDING, D.D.

TORONTO:
ADAM, STEVENSON & CO.
1873.

TO

THE RIGHT HONOURABLE

The Earl of Dufferin, K.C.B.,

GOVERNOR GENERAL OF BRITISH NORTH AMERICA,

A KEEN SYMPATHIZER WITH

THE MINUTE PAST, AS WELL AS THE MINUTE PRESENT,

OF THE PEOPLE COMMITTED TO HIS CHARGE,

This Volume,

TREATING OF THE INFANCY AND EARLY YOUTH

OF AN IMPORTANT CANADIAN CIVIC COMMUNITY

NOW FAST RISING TO MAN'S ESTATE,

IS

(BY PERMISSION GRACIOUSLY GIVEN,)

THANKFULLY AND LOYALLY DEDICATED

It is singular that the elder Disraeli has not included in his *Curiosities of Literature* a chapter on Books originating in Accident. It is exactly the kind of topic we might have expected him to discuss, in his usual pleasant manner. Of such productions there is doubtless somewhere a record. Whenever it shall be discovered, the volume here presented to the reader must be added to the list. A few years since, when preparing for a local periodical a paper of 'Early Notices of Toronto', the writer little imagined what the sheets then under his hand would finally grow to. The expectation at the time simply was that the article on which he was at work would assist as a minute scintilla in one of those monthly meteoric showers of miscellaneous light literature with which the age is so familiar; that it would engage, perhaps, the attention for a few moments of a chance gazer here and there, and then vanish in the usual way. But on a subsequent revision, the subject thus casually taken up seemed capable of being more fully handled. Two or three friends, moreover, had expressed a regret that to the memoranda given, gathered chiefly from early French documents, there had not been added some of the more recent floating folk-lore of the community, some of the homely table-talk of the older people of the place; such of the mixed traditions, in short, of the local Past of Toronto as might seem of value as illustrations of primitive colonial life and manners. It was urged, likewise, in several quarters, that if something in this direction

were not speedily done, the men of the next generation would
be left irremediably ignorant of a multitude of minute particulars relating to their immediate predecessors, and the peculiar conditions under which were so bravely executed the
many labours whereby for posterity the path onward has been
made smooth. For many years the writer had quietly concerned
himself with such matters. Identified with Toronto from boyhood, to him the long, straight ways of the place nowhere presented barren, monotonous vistas. To him innumerable objects
and sites on the right hand and on the left, in almost every
quarter, called up reminiscences, the growth partly of his own
experience and observation, and partly the residuum of discourse with others, all invested with a certain degree of rational,
human interest, as it seemed to him. But still, that he was sometime to be the compiler of an elaborate volume on the subject
never seriously entered his thoughts. Having, however, as was
narrated, once tapped the vein, he was led step by step to further explorations, until the result was reached which the reader
has now placed before him.

By inspection it will be seen that the plan pursued was to proceed rather deliberately through the principal thoroughfares,
noticing persons and incidents of former days, as suggested by
buildings and situations in the order in which they were severally seen; relying in the first instance on personal recollections
for the most part, and then attaching to every coigne of vantage
such relevant information as could be additionally gathered
from coevals and seniors, or gleaned from such literary relics,
in print or manuscript of an early date, as could be secured.
Here and there, brief digressions into adjacent streets were
made, when a house or the scene of an incident chanced to
draw the supposed pilgrim aside. The perambulation of Yonge
Street was extended to the Holland Landing, and even to
Penetanguishene, the whole line of that lengthy route presenting points more or less noteworthy at short intervals.[1]
Finally a chapter on the Marine of the Harbour was decided
on, the boats and vessels of the place, their owners and com-

---

[1] See Editor's Preface, page ix.

manders, entering, as is natural, so largely into the retrospect of the inhabitants of a Port.

Although the imposing bulk of the volume may look like evidence to the contrary, it has been our ambition all along not to incur the reproach of prolixity. We have endeavoured to express whatever we had to say as concisely as we could. Several narratives have been disregarded which probably, in some quarters, will be sought for here. But while anxious to present as varied and minute a picture as possible of the local Past, we considered it inexpedient to chronicle anything that was unduly trivial. Thus if we have not succeeded in being everywhere piquant, we trust we shall be found nowhere unpardonably dull: an achievement of some merit, surely, when our material, comprising nothing that was exceptionally romantic or very grandly heroic, is considered. And a first step has, as we conceive, been taken towards generating for Toronto, for many of its streets and byways, for many of its nooks and corners, and its neighbourhood generally, a certain modicum of that charm which, springing from association and popular legend, so delightfully invests, to the prepared and sensitive mind, every square rood of the old lands beyond the sea.

It will be proper after all, however, perhaps to observe that the reader who expects to find in this book a formal history of even Toronto of Old will be disappointed. It was no part of the writer's design to furnish a narrative of every local event occurring in the periods referred to, with chronological digests, statistical tables, and catalogues exhibiting in full the Christian names and surnames of all the first occupants of lots. For such information recourse must be had to the offices of the several public functionaries, municipal and provincial, where whole volumes in folio, filled with the desired particulars, will be found.

We have next gratefully to record our obligations to those who during the composition of the following pages encouraged the undertaking in various ways. Especial thanks are due to the Association of Pioneers [the York Pioneer and Historical Society], whose names are given in detail in the Appendix, and who did the writer the honour of appointing him their

Historiographer. Before assemblages more or less numerous, of this body, large abstracts of the Collections and Recollections here permanently garnered were read and discussed. Several of the members of this society, moreover, gave special *séances* at their respective homes for the purpose of listening to portions of the same. Those who were so kind as to be at the trouble of doing this were the Hon. W. P. Howland, C. B., Lieutenant-Governor; the Rev. Dr Richardson; Mr J. G. Worts (twice) ; Mr R. H. Oates; Mr James Stitt; Mr J. T. Smith; Mr W. B. Phipps (twice) . The [Royal] Canadian Institute, by permitting the publication in its *Journal* of successive instalments of these papers, contributed materially to the furtherance of the work, as without the preparation for the press from time to time which was thus necessitated, it is possible the volume itself, as a completed whole, would never have appeared. To the following gentlemen we are indebted for the use of papers or books, for obliging replies to queries, and for items of information otherwise communicated: Mr W. H. Lee of Ottawa; Judge Jarvis of Cornwall; Mr T. J. Preston of Yorkville; Mr W. Helliwell of the Highland Creek; the late Col. G. T. Denison of Rusholme, Toronto; Mr M. F. Whitehead of Port Hope; Mr Devine of the Crown Lands Department; Mr H. J. Jones of the same Department; Mr Russel Inglis of Toronto; Mr J. G. Howard of Toronto; the Rev. J. Carry of Holland Landing; Major McLeod of Drynoch; the Rev. George Hallen of Penetanguishene; the Ven. Archdeacon Fuller, of Toronto; Mr G. A. Barber, of Toronto; Mr J. T. Kerby, of Niagara; the Rev. Saltern Givins of Yorkville; the Rev. A. Sanson of Toronto; the Rev. Dr McMurray of Niagara; the Rev. Adam Elliott of Tuscarora; Mr H. J. Morse of Toronto; Mr W. Kirby of Niagara; Mr Morgan Baldwin of Toronto; Mr J. McEwan of Sandwich; Mr W. D. Campbell of Quebec; Mr T. Cottrill Clarke of Philadelphia. Mrs Cassidy of Toronto kindly allowed the use of two (now rare) volumes, published in 1765 by her near kinsman, Major Robert Rogers. Through Mr Homer Dixon of the Homewood, Toronto, a long loan of the earliest edition of the first *Gazetteer* of Upper Canada was procured from the library of the Young Men's Christian Association of

Toronto. The Rev. Dr Ryerson, Chief Superintendant of Education, and Dr Hodgins, Deputy Superintendent, courteously permitted an unrestricted access to the Departmental Library, rich in works of special value to anyone prosecuting researches in early Canadian history. To Mr G. Mercer Adam we are much beholden for a careful, friendly interest taken in the typographical execution and fair appearance generally of the volume.

The two portraits which, in no mere conventional sense, enrich the work, were engraved from miniatures very artistically drawn for the purpose, from original paintings never before copied, in the possession of Capt J. K. Simcoe, R. N., of Wolford, in the County of Devon.[2]

The circulation to be expected for a book like the present must be chiefly local. Nevertheless, it is to be presumed that there are persons scattered up and down in various parts of Canada and the United States who, having been at some period of their lives familiar with Toronto, and retaining still a kindly regard for the place, will like to possess such a memorial of it in the olden time as is here offered. And even in the old home-countries across the Atlantic—England, Scotland and Ireland—there are probably members of military and other families once resident at Toronto, to whom such a reminder of pleasant hours, as it is hoped, passed there, will not be unacceptable. For similar reasons the book, were its existence known, would be welcome here and there in Australia and New Zealand, and other colonies and settlements of England.

In an attempt to narrate so many particulars of time, place, person and circumstance, it can scarcely be hoped that errors have been wholly avoided. It is earnestly desired that any that may be detected will be adverted to with kindness and charity, and not in a carping tone. Unfairly, sometimes, a slip discovered, however trivial, is emphatically dwelt on, to the ignoring of almost all the points in respect of which complete accuracy has been secured, at the cost of much painstaking. Conscious that our aim throughout has been to be as minutely

---

2 These were portraits of Governor Simcoe and Chief Justice Osgoode.

correct as possible, we ask for consideration in this regard. A certain slight variety which will perhaps be noticed in the orthography of a few Indian and other names is to be attributed to a like absence of uniformity in the documents consulted. While the forms which we ourselves prefer will be readily discerned, it was not judged advisable everywhere to insist on them.

10 *Trinity Square, Toronto,*
June 4th, 1873

I

PALACE STREET TO THE MARKET-PLACE

In Rome, at the present day, the parts that are the most attractive to the tourist of archæological tastes are those that are the most desolate; quarters that, apart from their associations, are the most uninviting. It is the same with many another venerable town of the world beyond the Atlantic, of far less note than the old Imperial capital—with Avignon, for example; with Nîmes and Vienne in France; with Paris itself also to some extent; with Chester and York and St Albans, the Verulamium of the Roman period, in England.

It is the same with our American towns wherever any relics of their brief past are extant. Detroit, we remember, had once a quaint, dilapidated, primæval quarter. It is the same with our own Toronto. He that would examine the vestiges of the original settlement out of which the actual town has grown must betake himself, in the first instance, to localities now deserted by fashion and be content to contemplate objects that, to the indifferent eye, will seem commonplace and insignificant.

To invest such places and things with any degree of interest will appear difficult. An attempt in that direction may even be pronounced visionary. Nevertheless it is a duty which we owe to our forefathers to take what note we can of the labours of their hands; to forbid, so far as we may, the utter oblivion of their early efforts and deeds and sayings, the outcome of their ideas, of their humours and anxieties; to forbid even, so far as we may, the utter oblivion of the form and fashion of their persons.

The excavations which the first inhabitants made in the construction of their dwellings and in engineering operations, civil and military, were neither deep nor extensive; the materials which they employed were, for the most part, soft and perishable. In a few years all the original edifices of York, the infant Toronto, together with all the primitive delvings and cuttings, will of necessity have vanished. Natural decay will have destroyed some. Winds, fires, and floods will have removed others. The rest will have been deliberately taken out of the way, or obliterated in the accomplishment of modern improvements, the rude and fragile giving way before the commodious and enduring.

At St Petersburg, we believe, the original log-hut of Peter the Great is preserved to the present day in a casing of stone with a kind of religious reverence. And in Rome of old, through the influence of a similar sacred regard for the past, the lowly cottage of Romulus was long protected in a similar manner. There are probably no material relics of our founders and forefathers which we should care to invest with a like forced and artificial permanence. But memorials of those relics, and records of the associations that may here and there be found to cluster round them—these we may think it worth our while to collect and cherish.

Overlooking the harbour of the modern Toronto, far down in the east, there stands at the present day a large structure of grey cutstone.[1] Its radiating wings, the turret placed at a central point aloft, evidently for the ready oversight of the subjacent premises; the unornamented blank walls, pierced high up in each storey with a row of circular-heading openings, suggestive of shadowy corridors and cells within—all help to give to this pile an unmistakable prison-aspect.

It was very nearly on the site of this rather hard-featured building that the first Houses of Parliament of Upper Canada

---

[1] This was the 1840 jail that was long a landmark on the waterfront. The architect was John Howard who later gave High Park to the city.

were placed—humble but commodious structures of wood,[2]
built before the close of the eighteenth century and destroyed
by the incendiary hand of the invader in 1813. 'They consisted',
as a contemporary document sets forth, 'of two elegant Halls,
with convenient offices, for the accommodation of the Legislature and the Courts of Justice.' 'The Library, and all the papers
and records belonging to these institutions were consumed, and,
at the same time,' the document adds, 'the Church was robbed,
and the Town Library totally pillaged.' The injuries thus inflicted were a few months afterwards avenged by the destruction of the Public Buildings at Washington by a British force.
'We consider', said an Address of the Legislative Council of
Lower Canada to Sir George Prevost, 'the destruction of the
Public Buildings at Washington as a just retribution for the
outrages committed by an American force at the seat of Government of Upper Canada.'

On the same site succeeded the more conspicuous and more
capacious but still plain and simply cubical brick block erected
for legislative purposes in 1818 and accidentally burned in 1824.
The conflagration on this occasion entailed a loss which, the
Canadian Review of the period, published at Montreal, observes, 'in the present state of the finances and debt of the Province, cannot be considered a trifling affair.' That loss, we are
informed by the same authority, amounted to the sum of two
thousand pounds.

Hereabout the Westminster of the new capital was expected
to be. It is not improbable that the position at the head, rather
than the entrance, of the harbour was preferred as being at
once commanding and secure. The appearance of the spot in
its primæval condition was doubtless more prepossessing than
we can now conceive it ever to have been. Fine groves of forest
trees may have given it a sheltered look and at the same time
have screened off from view the adjoining swamps.

The language of the early *Provincial Gazetteer*, published by
authority, is as follows: 'The Don empties itself into the harbour, a little above the Town, running through a marsh,
which when drained, will afford most beautiful and fruitful
meadows.' In the early manuscript Plans, the same sanguine

---

[2] Recent research has indicated that these were actually brick buildings.

opinion is recorded, in regard to the morasses in this locality [Ashbridge's Bay]. On one, of 1810, now before us, we have the inscription: 'Natural Meadow which may be mown.' On another the legend runs: 'Large Marsh, and will in time make good Meadows.' On a third it is: 'Large Marsh and Good Grass.'

At all events, hereabout it was that York, capital of Upper Canada, began to rise. To the west and north of the site of the Houses of Parliament the officials of the Government, with merchants and tradesmen in the usual variety, began to select lots and put up convenient dwellings; whilst close by, at Berkeley Street or Parliament Street as the southern portion of the modern Berkeley Street was then named, the chief thoroughfare of the town had its commencing-point. Growing slowly westward from here, King Street developed in its course, in the customary American way—its hotel, its tavern, its boarding-house, its waggon-factory, its tinsmith shop, its bakery, its general store, its lawyer's office, its printing office, its places of worship.

Eastward of Berkeley Street, King Street became the Kingston Road, trending slightly to the north and then proceeding in a straight line to a bridge over the Don. This divergency in the highway caused a number of the lots on its northern side to be awkwardly bounded on their southern ends by lines that formed with their sides alternately obtuse and acute angles, productive of corresponding inconveniences in the shapes of the buildings afterwards erected thereon, and in the position of some of them. At one particular point the houses looked as if they had been separated from each other and partially twisted round by the jolt of an earthquake.

At the Bridge the lower Kingston Road, if produced westward in a right line, would have been Queen Street, or Lot Street, had it been deemed expedient to clear a passage in that direction through the forest.[3] But some way westward from the

---

[3] The name Kingston Road, or earlier the Road to Quebec, was originally applied to the section of King Street East that stretched east from Parliament to where King Street terminates at Queen, and also to the section of Queen Street stretching from that junction to where modern Kingston Road branches off.

Bridge, in this line, a ravine was encountered lengthwise, which was held to present great engineering difficulties. A road cut diagonally from the Bridge to the opening of King Street at once avoided this natural impediment and also led to a point where an easy connection was made with the track for wheels, which ran along the shore of the harbour to the Garrison. But for the ravine alluded to, which now appears to the south of Moss Park, Lot Street (or, which is the same thing, Queen Street) would at an early period have begun to dispute with King Street its claim to be the chief thoroughfare of York.

But to come back to our original unpromising standpoint.

Objectionable as the first site of the Legislative Buildings at York may appear to ourselves, and alienated as it now is to lower uses, we cannot but gaze upon it with a certain degree of emotion when we remember that here it was the first skirmishes took place in the great war of principles which afterwards with such determination and effect was fought out in Canada. Here it was that first loomed up before the minds of our early law-makers the ecclesiastical question, the education question, the constitutional question. Here it was that first was heard the open discussion—childlike, indeed, and vague, but pregnant with very weighty consequences—of topics, social and national, which at the time, even in the parent state itself, were mastered but by few.

Here it was, during a period of twenty-seven years (1797-1824), at each opening and closing of the annual session, amidst the firing of cannon and the commotion of a crowd, the cavalcade drew up that is wont, from the banks of the Thames to the remotest colony of England, to mark the solemn progress of the sovereign or the sovereign's representative to and from the other Estates in Parliament assembled. Here, amidst such fitting surroundings of state as the circumstances of the times and the place admitted, came and went personages of eminence whose names are now familiar in Canadian story. Never, indeed, the founder and organizer of Upper Canada, Governor Simcoe himself, in this formal and ceremonious manner, although often must he have visited the spot otherwise, in his personal examinations of every portion of his young capital and its environs; but here, immediately after him, however, came and went repeatedly in due succession President [Administrator] Russell, Governor Hunter, Governor Gore, General Brock, General Sheaffe, [Baron de Rottenburg,] Sir Gordon Drummond, Sir Peregrine Maitland.

Extending from the grounds which surrounded the buildings in the east, all the way to the fort at the entrance of the harbour in the west, there was a succession of fine forest trees, especially oak, underneath and by the side of which the upper surface of the precipitous but nowhere very elevated cliff was carpeted with thick green-sward, such as is still to be seen between the old and new garrisons,[4] or at Mississaga Point at Niagara. A fragment, happily preserved, of the ancient bank is to be seen in the ornamental piece of ground known as the Fair-green—a strip of land first protected by a fence and planted with shrubbery at the instance of Mr George Monro, when Mayor [1841], who also, in front of his property some distance further on, long guarded from harm a solitary survivor of the grove that once fringed the harbour.

In the interval between the points where now Princes [Princess] Street and Caroline [Sherbourne] Street descend to the water's edge was a favourite landing-place for the small craft of the bay—a wide and clean gravelly beach with a convenient ascent to the cliff above. Here on fine mornings at the proper season skiffs and canoes, log and birchbark, were to be seen putting in, weighed heavily down with fish, speared or otherwise taken during the preceding night in the Lake, bay, or neighbouring river. Occasionally a huge sturgeon would be landed, one struggle of which might suffice to upset a small boat. Here were to be purchased in quantities salmon, pickerel, masquelonge, whitefish and herrings, with the smaller fry of perch, bass, and sunfish. Here too would be displayed unsightly catfish, suckers, lampreys, and other eels; and sometimes lizards, young alligators for size. Specimens also of the curious steel-clad, inflexible, vicious-looking pipe-fish were not uncommon.

---

4 Old Fort York and the Stanley Barracks. The latter has now been demolished except for the Officers' Quarters which survives as the Marine Museum in the Exhibition grounds.

About the submerged timbers of the wharves this creature was often to be seen—at one moment stationary and still, like the dragon-fly or humming-bird poised on the wing; then, like those nervous denizens of the air, giving a sudden dart off to the right or left without curving its body.

Across the bay from this landing-place, a little to the eastward, was the narrowest part of the peninsula,[5] a neck of sand, destitute of trees, known as the portage or carrying-place, where, from time immemorial, canoes and small boats were wont to be transferred to and from the Lake.

Along the bank, above the landing-place, Indian encampments were occasionally set up. Here in comfortless wigwams we have seen Dr Lee, a medical man attached to the Indian department, administering from an ordinary tin cup nauseous but salutary draughts to sick and convalescent squaws. It was the duty of Dr Lee to visit Indian settlements and prescribe for the sick. In the discharge of his duty he performed long journeys on horseback to Penetanguishene and other distant posts, carrying with him his drugs and apparatus in saddle-bags. (When advanced in years and somewhat disabled in regard to activity of movement, Dr Lee was attached to the Parliamentary staff as Usher of the Black Rod.) The locality at which we are glancing suggests the name of another never-to-be-forgotten medical man, whose home and property were close at hand. This is the eminent surgeon and physician, Christopher Widmer.

It is to be regretted that Dr Widmer left behind him no written memorials of his long and varied experience. Before his settlement in York he had been a staff cavalry surgeon, on active service during the campaigns in the Peninsula. A personal narrative of his public life would have been full of interest. But his ambition was content with the homage of his contemporaries, rich and poor, rendered with sincerity to his pre-eminent abilities and inextinguishable zeal as a surgeon and physician. Long after his retirement from general practice,

---

[5] Toronto Island was a peninsula stretching out from the east until a series of storms in 1858 created the Eastern Gap.

he was every day to be seen passing to and from the old Hospital[6] on King Street, conveyed in his well-known cabriolet and guiding with his own hand the reins conducted in through the front window of the vehicle. He had now attained a great age, but his slender form continued erect; the hat was worn jauntily, as in other days, and the dress was ever scrupulously exact; the expression of the face in repose was somewhat abstracted and sad, but a quick smile appeared at the recognition of friends. The ordinary engravings of Harvey, the discoverer of the circulation of the blood, recall in some degree the countenance of Dr Widmer. Within the General Hospital a portrait of him is appropriately preserved. One of the earliest, and at the same time one of the most graceful lady-equestrians ever seen in York was this gentleman's accomplished wife. At a later period a sister of Mr Justice Willis was also conspicuous as a skilful and fearless horse-woman. The description in *The Percy Anecdotes* [1821-3] of the Princess Amelia, youngest daughter of George II, is curiously applicable to the last-named lady, who united to the amiable peculiarities indicated, talents and virtues of the highest order. 'She', the brothers Sholto and Reuben [Percy] say, 'was of a masculine turn of mind, and evinced this strikingly enough in her dress and manners: she generally wore a riding-habit in the German fashion with a round hat; and delighted very much in attending her stables, particularly when any of the horses were out of order.' At a phenomenon such as this, suddenly appearing in their midst, the staid and simple-minded society of York stood for a while aghast.

In the *Loyalist* of Nov. 15, 1828, we have the announcement of a medical partnership entered into between Dr Widmer and Dr Diehl. It reads thus: 'Doctor Widmer, finding his professional engagements much extended of late, and occasionally too arduous for one person, has been induced to enter into partnership with Doctor Diehl, a respectable practitioner, late of Montreal. It is expected that their united exertions will prevent in future any disappointment to Dr Widmer's friends,

---

[6] The ancestor of the present Toronto General Hospital.

both in Town and Country. Dr Diehl's residence is at present at Mr Hayes' Boarding-house. York, Oct. 28, 1828.' Dr Diehl died at Toronto, March 5, 1868.

At the south-west corner of Princes Street, near where we are now supposing ourselves to be, was a building popularly known as Russell Abbey. It was the house of the Hon. Peter Russell, and, after his decease [1808], of his maiden sister, Miss Elizabeth Russell, a lady of great refinement who survived her brother many years. The edifice, like most of the early homes of York, was of one storey only; but it exhibited in its design a degree of elegance and some peculiarities. To a central building were attached wings with gables to the south: the windows had each an architectural decoration or pediment over it. It was this feature, we believe, that was supposed to give to the place something of a monastic air, to entitle it even to the name of 'Abbey'. In front a dwarf stone wall with a light wooden paling surrounded a lawn on which grew tall acacias or locusts. Mr Russell was a remote scion of the Bedford Russells [the Dukes of Bedford]. He apparently desired to lay the foundation of a solid landed estate in Upper Canada. His position as Administrator, on the departure of the first Governor of the Province, gave him facilities for the selection and acquisition of wild lands. The duality necessarily assumed in the wording of the patents by which the Administrator made grants to himself seems to have been regarded by some as having a touch of the comic in it.[7] Hence among the early people of these parts the name of Peter Russell was occasionally to be heard quoted good-humouredly, not malignantly, as an example of 'the man who would do well unto himself'. On the death of Mr Russell, his property passed into the hands of his sister who bequeathed the whole to Dr William Warren Baldwin, into whose possession also came the valuable family plate, elaborately embossed with the armorial bearings of the Rus-

---

[7] The patents granting land stated that Peter Russell, as administrator, was granting so many acres to Peter Russell as a private individual, and they were signed by Peter Russell.

sells.[8] Russell Hill, long the residence of Admiral Augustus Baldwin, had its name from Mr Russell, and in one of the elder branches of the Baldwin family Russell is continued as a baptismal name. In the same family is also preserved an interesting portrait of Mr Peter Russell himself, from which we can see that he was a gentleman of portly presence, of strongly marked features of the Thomas Jefferson type. We shall have occasion hereafter to speak frequently of Mr Russell.

Russell Abbey became afterwards the residence of Bishop Macdonell, a universally respected Scottish Roman Catholic ecclesiastic whose episcopal title was at first derived from Rhesina *in partibus* but afterwards from our Canadian Kingston where his home usually was. His civil duties as a member of the Legislative Council of Upper Canada required his presence in York during the Parliamentary sessions. We have in our possession a fine mezzotint of Sir M. A. Shee's portrait of Bishop Macdonell. It used to be supposed by some that the occupancy of Russell Abbey by the Bishop caused the portion of Front Street which lies eastward of the Market-place [St Lawrence Market] to be denominated Palace Street. But the name appears in plans of York of a date many years anterior to that occupancy.

Russell Abbey may indeed have been styled the 'Palace', but it was probably from being the residence of one who for three years administered the Government; or the name 'Palace Street' itself may have suggested the appellation. 'Palace Street' was no doubt intended to indicate the fact that it led directly to the Government reservation at the end of the town on which the Parliament houses were erected, and where it was supposed the 'Palais du Gouvernment', the official residence of the representative of the Sovereign in the Province, would eventually be. On an official plan of this region, of the year 1810, the Parliament Buildings themselves are styled 'Government House'.

---

[8] Actually the estate was divided between Elizabeth Russell's cousins, Phoebe (Dr Baldwin's wife) and Maria Willcocks. Maria was unmarried when she died in 1834 and the whole estate passed into the hands of the Baldwin family.

At the laying out of York, however, we find from the plans that the name given in the first instance to the Front Street of the town was not Palace Street but King Street. Modern King Street was then Duke Street, and modern Duke Street, Duchess Street. These street names were intended as loyal compliments to members of the reigning family—to George the Third; to his son, the popular Duke of York from whom, as we shall learn hereafter, the town itself was named; to the Duchess of York, the eldest daughter of the King of Prussia. In the cross-streets the same chivalrous devotion to the Hanoverian dynasty was exhibited. George Street, the boundary westward of the first nucleus of York, bore the name of the heir-apparent, George, Prince of Wales. The next street eastward was honoured with the name of his next brother, Frederick, the Duke of York himself. And the succeeding street eastward, Caroline [Sherbourne] Street, had imposed upon it that of the Princess of Wales, afterwards so unhappily famous as George the Fourth's Queen Caroline. Whilst in Princes Street (for such is the correct orthography, as the old plans show, and not Princess Street as is generally seen now), the rest of the male members of the royal family were collectively commemorated, namely the Duke of Clarence, the Duke of Kent, the Duke of Cumberland, the Duke of Sussex, and the Duke of Cambridge.

On the green sward of the bank between Princes Street and George Street, the annual military 'Trainings' on the Fourth of June, 'the old King's birthday', were wont to take place. At a later period the day of meeting was the 23rd of April, St George's day, the fête of George IV [1820-30]. Military displays on a grand scale in and about Toronto have not been uncommon in modern times, exciting the enthusiasm of the multitude that usually assembles on such occasions. But in no way inferior in point of interest to the unsophisticated youthful eye half a century ago, unaccustomed to anything more elaborate, were those motley musterings of the militia companies. The costume of the men may have been various, the fire-arms only partially distributed, and those that were to be had not of the brightest hue nor of the most scientific make; the lines may not always have been perfectly straight nor their consti-

tuents well matched in height; the obedience to the word of
command may not have been rendered with the mechanical
precision which we admire at reviews now, nor with that total
suppression of dialogue in undertone in the ranks nor with
that absence of remark interchanged between the men and
their officers that are customary now. Nevertheless, as a military
spectacle these gatherings and manœuvres on the grassy bank
here were effective; they were always anticipated with pleasure
and contemplated with satisfaction. The officers on these occasions—some of them mounted—were arrayed in uniforms of
antique cut—in red coats with wide black breast lappets and
broad tail flaps; high collars, tight sleeves, and large cuffs; on
the head a black hat, the ordinary high-crowned civilian hat,
with a cylindrical feather some eighteen inches high inserted
at the top, not in front but on the left side (whalebone surrounded with feathers from the barnyard, scarlet at the base,
white above). Animation was added to the scene by a drum
and a few fifes executing with liveliness 'The York Quickstep',
'The Reconciliation', and 'The British Grenadiers'. And then,
in addition to the local cavalry corps, there were the clattering
scabbards, the blue jackets, and bearskin helmets of Captain
Button's dragoons from Markham and Whitchurch.

A little further on, in a house at the north-west corner of
Frederick Street, a building afterwards utterly destroyed by
fire, was born in 1804 the Hon. Robert Baldwin, son of Dr
William Warren Baldwin already referred to, and Attorney-
General in 1842 for Upper Canada.[9] In the same building, at a
later period (and previously in an humble edifice at the north-
west corner of King Street and Caroline Street, now likewise
wholly destroyed), the foundation was laid, by well-directed
and far-sighted ventures in commerce, of the great wealth
(locally proverbial) of the Cawthra family, the Astors of Upper
Canada, of whom more hereafter. It was also in the same house,

---

[9] Baldwin held the office of attorney-general of Upper Canada in 1842-3
and again from 1848 to 1851. His position was somewhat similar to that of
the prime minister today, except that he had a colleague with equal power
from Lower Canada.

prior to its occupation by Mr Cawthra senior, that the printing operations of Mr William Lyon Mackenzie were carried on at the time of the destruction of his press by a party of young men [1826] who considered it proper to take some spirited notice of the criticisms on the public acts of their fathers, uncles, and superiors generally that appeared every week in the columns of the *Colonial Advocate*—a violent act memorable in the annals of Western Canada not simply as having been the means of establishing the fortunes of an indefatigable and powerful journalist, but more notably as presenting an unconscious illustration of a general law, observable in the early development of communities, whereby an element destined to elevate and regenerate is, on its first introduction, resisted, and sought to be crushed physically, not morally; somewhat as the white man's watch was dashed to pieces by the Indian as though it had been a sentient thing, conspiring in some mysterious way with other things to promote the ascendancy of the stranger.

The youthful perpetrators of the violence referred to were not long in learning practically the futility of such exploits. Good old Mr James Baby, on handing to his son Raymond the amount which that youth was required to pay as his share of the heavy damages awarded, as a matter of course, by the jury on the occasion, is said to have added: 'There! Go and make one great fool of yourself again!'—a sarcastic piece of advice that might have been offered to each of the parties concerned.

A few steps northward, on the east side of Frederick Street, was the first Post Office, on the premises of Mr Allan who was postmaster [1801-28]; and southward, where this street touches the water, was the Merchants' Wharf, also the property of Mr Allan; and the Custom House, where Mr Allan was the Collector. We gather also from Calendars of the day that Mr Allan was likewise Inspector of Flour, Pot, and Pearl Ash; and Inspector of Shop, Still, and Tavern Duties. In an early, limited condition of society, a man of more than the ordinary aptitude for affairs is required to act in many capacities.

The Merchants' Wharf was the earliest landing-place for the

larger craft of the Lake. At a later period other wharves or long
wooden jetties, extending out into deep water, one of them
named the Farmers' Wharf, were built westward. In the shoal
water between the several wharves for a long period there was
annually a dense crop of rushes or flags. The town or county
authorities incurred considerable expense, year after year, in
endeavouring to eradicate them but, like the heads of the
hydra, they were always reappearing. In July 1821 a 'Mr Coles'
account for his assistants' labour in destroying rushes in front
of the Market Square' was laid before the County magistrates
and audited, amounting to £13 6s. 3d. In August of the same
year the minutes of the County Court record that 'Capt. [John
Simcoe] Macaulay, Royal Engineers, offered to cut down the
rushes in front of the town between the Merchants' Wharf and
Cooper's Wharf, for a sum not to exceed ninety dollars, which
would merely be the expense of the men and materials in
executing the undertaking: his own time he would give to the
public on this occasion, as encouragement to others to endeavour to destroy the rushes when they become a nuisance'; it
was accordingly ordered 'that ninety dollars be paid to Capt.
Macaulay or his order for the purpose of cutting down the
rushes, according to his verbal undertaking to cut down the
same, to be paid out of the Police or District funds in the hands
of the Treasurer of the District.'

We have understood that Capt. Macaulay's measures for the
extinction of the rank vegetation in the shallow waters of the
harbour proved to be very efficient. The instrument used was a
kind of screw grapnel which, let down from the side of a large
scow, laid hold of the rushes at their root and forcibly
wrenched them out of the bed of mud below. The entire plant
was thus lifted up and drawn by a windlass into the scow.
When a full load of the aquatic weed was collected, it was
taken out into the open water of the Lake and there disposed of.

Passing on our way, we soon came to the Market Square [St
Lawrence Market]. This was a large open space with wooden
shambles [sheds] in the middle of it, thirty-six feet long and
twenty-four wide, running north and south.

By a Proclamation in the *Gazette*[10] of Nov. 3, 1803, Governor Hunter appointed a weekly market day for the Town of York, and also a place where the market should be held.

'Peter Hunter, Esquire, Lieutenant-Governor, &c. Whereas great prejudice hath arisen to the inhabitants of the Town and Township of York, and of other adjoining Townships, from no place or day having been set apart or appointed for exposing publicly for sale, cattle, sheep, poultry, and other provisions, goods, and merchandize, brought by merchants, farmers, and others, for the necessary supply of the said Town of York; and, whereas, great benefit and advantage might be derived to the said inhabitants and others, by establishing a weekly market within that Town, at a place and on a day certain for the purpose aforesaid;

'Know all men, That I, Peter Hunter, Esquire, Lieutenant-Governor of the said Province, taking the premises into consideration, and willing to promote the interest, and advantage, and accommodation of the inhabitants of the Town and Township aforesaid, and of others, His Majesty's subjects, within the said Province, by and with the advice of the Executive Council thereof, have ordained, erected, established and appointed, and do hereby ordain, erect, establish and appoint, a Public Open Market, to be held on Saturday in each and every week during the year, within the said Town of York:—(The first market to be held therein on Saturday, the 5th day of November next after the date of these presents), on a certain piece or plot of land within that Town, consisting of five acres and a half, commencing at the south-east angle of the said plot, at the corner of Market [Wellington] Street and New [Jarvis] Street, then north sixteen degrees, west five chains seventeen

---

[10] This was the first newspaper to be published in Ontario—an official government paper published by the King's Printer. As it is referred to throughout the book in several ways *(Gazette, Upper Canada Gazette, Oracle, Gazette or Oracle, Gazette and Oracle, Oracle and Gazette)*, it should be noted that its full name was the *Upper Canada Gazette, or American Oracle* when it was founded in 1793. It was originally published at Niagara-on-the-Lake, was moved to York in 1798, and continued until 1849. Scadding's account of it will be found in Chapter VIII, pages 186 to 190.

links, more or less, to King Street; then along King Street south seventy-four degrees west nine chains fifty-one links,[11] more or less, to Church Street; then south sixteen degrees east six chains thirty-four links, more or less, to Market Street; then along Market Street north seventy-four degrees east two chains; then north sixty-four degrees, east along Market Street seven chains sixty links, more or less, to the place of beginning, for the purpose of exposing for sale cattle, sheep, poultry, and other provisions, goods and merchandize, as aforesaid. Given under my hand and seal at arms, at York, this twenty-sixth day of October, in the year of our Lord one thousand eight hundred and three, and in the forty-fourth year of His Majesty's reign. P. HUNTER, *Esquire, Lieutenant-Governor.* By His Excellency's command, WM. JARVIS, *Secretary.'*

In 1824 the Market Square was, by the direction of the County magistrates, closed in on the east, west, and south sides, 'with a picketting and oak ribbon, the pickets at ten feet distance from each other, with three openings or foot-paths on each side'.

The digging of a public well here, in the direction of King Street, was an event of considerable interest in the town. Groups of schoolboys every day scanned narrowly the progress of the undertaking; a cap of one or the other of them, mischievously precipitated to the depths where the labourers' mattocks were to be heard pecking at the shale below, may have impressed the execution of this public work all the more indelibly on the recollection of some of them. By referring to a volume of the *Upper Canada Gazette,* we find that this was in 1823. An unofficial advertisement in that periodical, dated June the 9th, 1823, calls for proposals to be sent in to the office of the Clerk of the Peace 'for the sinking a well, stoning and sinking a pump therein, in the most approved manner, at the Market Square of the said town (of York), for the convenience of the Public.'

Near the public pump, auctions in the open air occasionally

---

11 A chain—a jointed metal measuring line—is sixty-six feet in length; a link is 7.92 inches.

took place. A humorous chapman in that line, Mr Patrick Handy, used often here to be seen and heard disposing of his miscellaneous wares. With Mr Handy was associated for a time in this business Mr Patrick McGann. And here we once witnessed the horrid exhibition of a public whipping in the case of two culprits whose offence is forgotten. A discharged regimental drummer, a native African, administered the lash. The sheriff stood by, keeping count of the stripes. The senior of the two unfortunates bore his punishment with stoicism, encouraging the Negro to strike with more force. The other, a young man, endeavoured for a little while to imitate his companion in this respect, but soon was obliged to evince by fearful cries the torture endured. Similar scenes were elsewhere to be witnessed in Canada. In the *Montreal Herald* of September 16th, 1815, we have the following item of city news, given without comment: 'Yesterday, between the hours of 9 and 10, pursuant to their sentences, André Latulippe, Henry Leopard, and John Quin, received 39 lashes each, in the New Market Place.' The practice of whipping and even branding of culprits in public had begun at York in 1798. In the *Gazette and Oracle* of Dec. 1st, 1798, printed at York, we have the note: 'Last Monday William Hawkins was publicly whipped, and Joseph McCarthy burned in the hand, at the Market Place, pursuant to their sentence.' The crimes are not named.

In the Market Square at York, the pillory and the stocks were also from time to time set up. The latter were seen in use for the last time in 1834. In 1804 a certain Elizabeth Ellis was, for 'being a nuisance', sentenced by Chief Justice Allcock to be imprisoned for six months and 'to stand in the pillory twice during the said imprisonment, on two different market days, opposite the Market House in the town of York, for the space of two hours each time'. In the same year the same sentence was passed on one Campbell for using 'seditious words'.

In 1831 the wooden shambles were removed and replaced in 1832 by a collegiate-looking building of red brick, quadrangular in its arrangement, with arched gateway entrances on King Street and Front Street. This edifice filled the whole square, with the exception of roadways on the east and west sides.[12] The public well was now concealed from view. It doubtless exists still, to be discovered and gloated over by the antiquarian of another century.[13]

Round the four sides of the new brick Market ran a wooden gallery which served to shade the Butchers' stall below. It was here that a fearful casualty occurred in 1834. A concourse of people were being addressed after the adjournment of a meeting on an electional question when a portion of the overcrowded gallery fell and several persons were caught on the sharp iron hooks of the stalls underneath and so received fatal injuries.

The damage done to the northern end of the quadrangle during the great fire of 1849 led to the demolition of the whole building, and the erection of the St Lawrence Hall and Market. Over windows on the second storey at the south-east corner of the red brick structure, now removed, there appeared for several years two signs united at the angle of the building, each indicating by its inscription the place of 'The Huron and Ontario Railway'[14] office.

---

[12] By the whole square Scadding simply means the area east of Market Street, not the entire acreage set aside by Governor Hunter. By the 1830s the western part had been separated and was rented out to various commercial establishments. It was known as the Market Block.

[13] The well was evidently uncovered when part of the Market was rebuilt in 1904 and it probably still exists under the flooring.

[14] This was Toronto's first railway which began operations with a Toronto-to-Aurora run in 1853 and eventually reached Collingwood. In 1858 it was renamed the Northern Railway and is now part of the CNR.

II

FRONT
STREET
FROM THE
MARKET-
PLACE
TO THE
GARRISON
AND BACK
TO THE
PLACE OF
BEGINNING

The corner we approach after passing the Market Square was occupied by an inn with a sign-board sustained on a high post inserted at the outer edge of the footpath in country roadside fashion. This was Hamilton's, or the White Swan. It was here, we believe, or in an adjoining house, that a travelling citizen of the United States, in possession of a collection of stuffed birds and similar objects, endeavoured at an early period to establish a kind of Natural History Museum. To the collection here was once rashly added figures in wax of General Jackson and some other United States notabilities, all in grand costume. Several of these were one night abstracted from the Museum by some over-patriotic youths and suspended by the neck from the limbs of one of the large trees that overlooked the harbour.

Just beyond was the Steamboat Hotel, long known as Ulick Howard's, remarkable for the spirited delineation of a steam-packet of vast dimensions extending the whole length of the building just over the upper verandah of the hotel. In 1828

Mr Howard is offering to let his hotel in the following terms: 'Steamboat Hotel, York, U. C.—The proprietor of this elegant establishment, now unrivalled in this part of the country, being desirous of retiring from Public Business, on account of ill-health in his family, will let the same for a term of years to be agreed on, either with or without the furniture. The Establishment is now too well-known to require comment. N. B. Security will be required for the payment of the Rent, and the fulfilment of the contract in every respect. Apply to the subscriber on the premises. U. HOWARD, *York, Oct 8th, 1828.*'

A little further on was the Ontario House, a hotel built in a style common then at the Falls of Niagara and in the United States. A row of lofty pillars, well-grown pines in fact, stripped and smoothly planed, reached from the ground to the eaves and supported two tiers of galleries which, running behind the columns, did not interrupt their vertical lines.

Close by the Ontario House, Market [Wellington] Street from the west entered Front Street at an acute angle. In the gore between the two streets a building sprang up which, in conforming to its site, assumed the shape of a coffin.[1] The foot of this ominous structure was the office where travellers booked themselves for various parts in the stages that from time to time started from York. It took four days to reach Niagara in 1816. We are informed by a contemporary advertisement now before us that 'on the 20th of September next [1816], a stage will commence running between York and Niagara: it will leave York every Monday, and arrive at Niagara on Thursday; and leave Queenston every Friday. The baggage is to be considered at the risk of the owner, and the fare to be paid in advance.' In 1824 the mails were conveyed the same distance, *via* Ancaster, in three days. In a post-office advertisement for tenders, signed 'William Allan, P. M.,' we have the statement: 'The mails are made up here [York] on the afternoon of Monday and Thursday, and must be delivered at Niagara on the Wednesday and Saturday following; and within the same period in returning.' In 1835 Mr William Weller [of Cobourg] was the proprietor of

---

[1] The Gooderham Building, built in 1892, now occupies the site.

a line of stages between Toronto and Hamilton known as the 'Telegraph Line'. In an advertisement before us he engages to take passengers 'through by daylight, on the Lake Road, during the winter season'.

Communication with England was at this period a tedious process. So late as 1836 Mrs Jameson thus writes in the Journal at Toronto:[2] 'It is now seven weeks since the date of the last letters from my dear far-distant home. The Archdeacon [Strachan]', she adds, 'told me, by way of comfort, that when he came to settle in this country, there was only one mail-post from England in the course of a whole year, and it was called, as if in mockery, the Express.' To this 'Express' we have a reference in a post-office advertisement to be seen in a *Quebec Gazette* of 1792: 'A mail for the Upper Countries, comprehending Niagara and Detroit, will be closed', it says, 'at this office, on Monday, the 30th inst., at 4 o'clock in the evening, to be forwarded from Montreal by the annual winter Express, on Thursday, the 3rd of Feb. next.' From the same paper we learn that on the 10th of November the latest date from Philadelphia and New York was Oct 8th; also that a weekly conveyance had lately been established between Montreal and Burlington, Vermont. In the *Gazette* of Jan. 31, 1808, we have the following: 'For the information of the Public.—York, 12th Jan., 1808.—The first mail from Lower Canada is arrived, and letters are ready to be delivered by W. Allan, Acting-Deputy-Postmaster.'

Compare all this with advertisements in Toronto daily papers now, from agencies in the town, of 'Through Lines' weekly, to California, Vancouver, China and Japan, connecting with lines to Australia and New Zealand.

On the beach below the Steamboat Hotel was, at a late period [1835], a market for the sale of fish. It was from this spot that Bartlett, in his *Canadian Scenery* [1842], made one of the sketches intended to convey to the English eye an impression of the town. In the foreground are groups of conventional and altogether too picturesque fishwives and squaws: in the

---

2 This is Anna Jameson's famous *Winter Studies and Summer Rambles in Canada* which was published on her return to London in 1838.

distance is the junction of Hospital[3] Street and Front Street, with the tapering building between. On the right are the galleries of what had been the Steamboat Hotel; it here bears another name [City Hotel].

Bartlett's second sketch is from the end of a long wharf or jetty to the west. The large building in front, with a covered passage through it for vehicles, is the warehouse or freight depot of Mr William Cooper, long the owner of this favourite landing place. Westwards the pillared front of the Ontario House is to be seen. Both of these views already look quaint and possess a value as preserving a shadow of much that no longer exists.

The lot extending northward from the Ontario House corner to King Street was the property of Attorney-General Macdonell who, while in attendance on General Brock as provincial aide de-camp, was slain in the engagement on Queenston Heights [1812]. His death created the vacancy to which, at an unusually early age, succeeded Mr John Beverley Robinson, afterwards the distinguished Chief Justice of Upper Canada. Mr Macdonell's remains are deposited with those of his military chief under the column on Queenston Heights. He bequeathed the property to which our attention has been directed to a youthful nephew, Mr James Macdonell, on certain conditions, one of which was that he should be educated in the tenets of the Anglican Church, notwithstanding the Roman Catholic persuasion of the rest of the family.

The track for wheels that here descended to the water's edge from the north—Church Street subsequently—was long considered a road remote from the business part of the town. A row of frame buildings on its eastern side, in the direction of King Street, perched high on cedar posts over excavations generally filled with water, remained in an unfinished state until the whole began to be out of the perpendicular and to become grey with the action of the weather. It was evidently a premature undertaking, the folly of an over-sanguine speculator.

---

[8] This should read Market [Wellington] Street.

Yonge Street beyond, where it approached the shore of the harbour, was unfrequented. In spring and autumn it was a notorious slough. In 1830 a small sum would have purchased any of the building lots on either side of Yonge Street between Front Street and Market [Wellington] Street.

Between Church Street and Yonge Street now we pass a short street uniting Front Street with Wellington Street. Like Salisbury, Cecil, Craven, and other short but famous streets off the Strand [in London], it retains the name of the distinguished person whose property it traversed in the first instance. It is called Scott Street, from Chief Justice Thomas Scott whose residence and grounds were here.

Mr Scott was one of the venerable group of early personages of whom we shall have occasion to speak. He was a man of fine culture and is spoken of affectionately by those who knew him. His stature was below the average. A heavy overhanging forehead intensified the thoughtful expression of his countenance. We sometimes to this day fall in with books from his library bearing his familiar autograph.

Mr Scott was the first chairman and president of the Loyal and Patriotic Society of Upper Canada, organized at York in 1812. His name consequently appears often in the *Report* of that Association printed by William Gray in Montreal in 1817. The objects of the Society were 'to afford relief and aid to disabled militiamen and their families: to reward merit, excite emulation, and commemorate glorious exploits, by bestowing medals and other honorary marks of public approbation and distinction for extraordinary instances of personal courage and fidelity in defence of the Province.' The preface to the *Report* mentions that 'the sister-colony of Nova Scotia, excited by the barbarous conflagration of the town of Newark [Niagara-on-the-Lake] and the devastation on that frontier, had, by a legislative act, contributed largely to the relief of this Province.'

In an appeal to the British public, signed by Chief Justice Scott, it is stated that 'the subscription of the town of York amounted in a few days to eight hundred and seventy-five pounds five shillings, Provincial currency, dollars at five shillings each,[4] to be paid annually during the war; and that at Kingston to upwards of four hundred pounds.'

Medals were struck in London by order of the Loyal and Patriotic Society of Upper Canada, but they were never distributed. The difficulty of deciding who were to receive them was found to be too great. They were defaced and broken up in York with such rigour that not a solitary specimen is known to exist. Rumours of one lurking somewhere continue to this day to tantalize local numismatists. What became of the bullion of which they were composed used to be one of the favourite vexed questions among the old people of York. Its value doubtless was added to the surplus that remained of the funds of the Society which, after the year 1817, were devoted to benevolent objects. To the building fund of the York General Hospital, we believe, a considerable donation was made. The medal, we are told, was two and one-half inches in diameter. On the obverse, within a wreath of laurel, were the words 'FOR MERIT'. On this side was also the legend: 'PRESENTED BY A GRATEFUL COUNTRY'. On the reverse was the following elaborate device: A strait between two lakes: on the north side a beaver (emblem of peaceful industry), the ancient cognizance of Canada; in the background an English Lion slumbering. On the south side of the Strait, the American eagle planing in the air, as if checked from seizing the Beaver by the presence of the Lion. Legend on this side: 'UPPER CANADA PRESERVED'.

Scott Street conducts to the site, on the north side of Hospital[5] Street, westward of the home of Mr James Baby, and eastward to that of Mr Peter Macdougall, two notable citizens of York.

Mr Macdougall was a gentleman of Scottish descent but, like his compatriots in the neighbourhood of Murray Bay, so thoroughly Lower-Canadianized as to be imperfectly acquainted with the English language to the last. He was a successful merchant of the town of York, and filled a place in the old

---

[4] Though there was no official local coinage, for accounting purposes five shillings local currency equalled four shillings English currency or one American dollar.

[5] Richmond Street.

local conversational talk in which he was sometimes spoken of as 'Wholesale, Retail, Pete McDoug'—an expression adopted by himself on some occasion. He is said once to have been perplexed by the item 'ditto' occurring in a bill of lading furnished of goods under way; he could not remember having given orders for any such article. He was a shrewd businessman. An impression prevailed in certain quarters that his profits were now and then extravagant. On hearing a brother dealer lament that by a certain speculation he should after all make only 5 per cent, he expressed his surprise, adding that he himself would be satisfied with 3 or even 2 (taking the figures 2, 3, &c., to mean 2 hundred, 3 hundred, &c.) .

Of Yonge Street itself, at which we now arrive, we propose to speak at large hereafter. Just westward from Yonge Street was the abode, surrounded by pleasant grounds and trees, of Mr Macaulay, at a later period Sir James Macaulay, Chief Justice of the Common Pleas, a man beloved and honoured for his sterling excellence in every relation. A full-length portrait of him is preserved in Osgoode Hall.

Advancing a little further, we came in front of one of the earliest examples in these parts of an English-looking rustic cottage, with verandah and sloping lawn. This was occupied for a time by Major Hillier of the 74th regiment, aide-de-camp and military secretary to Sir Peregrine Maitland. The well-developed native thorn-tree, to the north of the site of this cottage, on the property of Mr Andrew Mercer, is a relic of the woods that once ornamented this locality.

Next came the residence of Mr Justice [D'Arcy] Boulton [Sr], a spacious family domicile of wood painted white, situated in an extensive area and placed far back from the road. The Judge was an English gentleman of spare Wellington physique; like many of his descendants, a lover of horses and a spirited rider; a man of wit, too, and humour, fond of listening to and narrating anecdotes of the *ben trovato* class. The successor to this family home was Holland House [1831], a structure of a baronial cast round which one might expect to find the remains of a moat; a reproduction, in some points, as in name, of the building in the suburbs of London in which was born the

Judge's immediate heir, Mr H. J. Boulton, successively Solicitor-General for Upper Canada and Chief Justice of Newfoundland.[6]

When Holland House passed out of the hands of its original
possessor, it became the property of Mr Alexander Manning, an
alderman of Toronto.[7] It was at Holland House that the Earl
and Countess of Dufferin kept high festival during a brief
sojourn in the capital of Ontario in 1872.

We now passed the grounds and house of Chief Justice Powell. In this place we shall only record our recollection of the pro-
found sensation created far and wide by the loss of the Chief-
Justice's daughter in the packet-ship *Albion,* wrecked off the
Head of Kinsale, on the 22nd of April 1822.

After the house and grounds of Chief Justice Powell came
the property of Dr Strachan [on the west side of York Street],
of whom much hereafter. In view of the probable future requirements of his position in a growing town and growing
country, Dr Strachan built, in 1818, a residence here of capacious dimensions and good design, with extensive and very
complete appurtenances.[8] A brother of the Doctor's, Mr James
Strachan, an intelligent bookseller of Aberdeen, visited York
in 1819 soon after the first occupation of the new house by its
owners. The two brothers, John and James, had not seen each
other since 1799 when John, a young man just twenty-one, was
setting out for Canada to undertake a tutorship in a family at
Kingston—setting out with scant money outfit, but provided
with what was of more value, a sound constitution, a clear
head, and a good strong understanding trained in Scottish

---

6 Henry John Boulton, who built Holland House, was the second son of
D'Arcy Boulton Sr, so the description 'immediate heir' is misleading. The
eldest son, D'Arcy Jr, inherited the Grange which was the family home
after the frame structure Scadding mentions. Later it became the home of
Professor Goldwin Smith, who married the widow of the son of D'Arcy
Boulton Jr, and it is now part of the Art Gallery of Toronto.

7 Alexander Manning was mayor in 1873 the year in which *Toronto of Old*
was originally published, and again in 1885.

8 The house, or 'Palace' as it came to be known after Strachan became
bishop in 1839, was of the same Georgian design as the still-standing Grange
and the Sir William Campbell house at the head of Frederick Street.

schools and colleges, and by familiar intercourse with shrewd Scottish folk.

As James entered the gates leading into the new mansion and cast a comprehensive glance at the fine façade of the building before him and over its pleasant and handsome surroundings, he suddenly paused; and indulging in a stroke of sly humour, addressed his brother with the words, spoken in grave confidential undertone: 'I hope it's a' come by honestly, John'.

On his return to Scotland, Mr James Strachan published *A Visit to the Province of Upper Canada in 1819*, an interesting book, now scarce and desired by Canadian collectors. The bulk of the information contained in this volume was confessedly derived from Dr Strachan.

The bricks used in the construction of the house here in 1818 were manufactured on the spot. One or two earlier brick buildings at York were composed of materials brought from Kingston or Montreal, recalling the parallel fact that the first bricks used for building in New York were imported from Holland; just as in the present day (though now, of course, for a different reason), houses are occasionally constructed at Quebec with white brick manufactured in England.

We next arrived at a large open space [west of Simcoe Street], much broken up by a rivulet—'Russell's Creek'—that meandered most recklessly through it. This piece of ground was long known as Simcoe Place and was set apart in the later plan for the extension of York westward as a Public Square. Overlooking this area from the north-west, at the present day, is one of the elms of the original forest—an unnoticeable sapling at the period referred to, but now a tree of stately dimensions and of very graceful form resembling that of the Greek letter Psi. It will be a matter of regret when the necessities of the case shall render the removal of this relic indispensable.

At the corner to the south of this conspicuous tree was an inn long known as the Greenland Fishery. Its sign bore on one side, quite passably done, an Arctic or Greenland scene, and on the other vessels and boats engaged in the capture of the whale. A travelling sailor, familiar with whalers and additionally a man of some artistic taste and skill, paid his reckoning in labour by executing for the landlord, Mr Wright, these spirited paintings which proved an attraction to the house.

John Street, which passes north by the Greenland Fishery, bears one of the Christian names of the first Governor of Upper Canada. Graves Street, on the east side of the adjoining Square, bore his second Christian name, but Graves Street has in recent times been transformed into Simcoe Street.

When the Houses of Parliament, now to be seen stretching across Simcoe Place,[9] were first built, a part of the design was a central pediment supported by four stone columns. This would have relieved and given dignity to the long front. The stone platform before the principal entrance was constructed with a flight of steps leading thereto; but the rather graceful portico which it was intended to sustain was never added. The monoliths for the pillars were duly cut out at a quarry near Hamilton. They long remained lying there in an unfinished state. In the lithographic view of the Parliament Buildings published by J. Young,[10] their architect, in 1836, the pediment of the original design is given as though it existed.

Along the edge of the water, below the properties, spaces, and objects which we have been engaged in noticing, once ran a shingly beach of a width sufficient to admit of the passage of vehicles. A succession of dry seasons must then have kept the waters low. In 1815, however, the waters of the Lake appear to have been unusually high. An almanac of that year, published by John Cameron at York, offers, seriously as it would seem, the subjoined explanation of the phenomenon: 'The comet which passed to the northward three years since', the writer suggests, 'has sensibly affected our seasons: they have become colder; the snows fall deeper; and from lesser exhalation, and other causes, the Lakes rise much higher than usual.'

The Commissariat store-houses were situated here, just beyond the broken ground of Simcoe Place—long white struc-

---

[9] These buildings were demolished about 1904 and the site is now covered by railway yards.

[10] Thomas Young, not 'J' Young, was one of the leading architects in the city at the period. He was the engraver of the picture, but the actual architect of the Legislature was J. G. Chewett.

tures of wood, with the shutters of the windows always closed, built on a level with the bay yet having an entrance in the rear by a narrow gangway from the cliff above on which, close by, was the guard-house, a small building painted of a dun colour with a roof of one slope, inclining to the south, and an arched stoup or verandah open to the north. Here a sentry was ever to be seen, pacing up and down. A light bridge over a deep water-course led up to the guard-house.

Over other depressions or ravines close by here were long to be seen some platforms or floored areas of stout plank. These were said to be spaces occupied by different portions of the renowned canvas house of the first Governor, a structure manufactured in London and imported. The convenience of its plan, and the hospitality for which it afforded room, were favourite topics among the early people of the country. We have it in Bouchette's *British North America* a reference to this famous canvas house. 'In the spring (i.e. of 1793),' that writer says, 'the Lieutenant-Governor moved to the site of the new capital (York), attended by the regiment of the Queen's Rangers, and commenced at once the realization of his favourite project. His Excellency inhabited, during the summer, and through the winter, a canvas-house, which he imported expressly for the occasion; but, frail as was its substance, it was rendered exceedingly comfortable, and soon became as distinguished for the social and urbane hospitality of its venerable and gracious host, as for the peculiarity of its structure.'

The canvas house had been the property of Capt. Cook, the circumnavigator. On its being offered for sale in London, Gov. Simcoe, seeing its possible usefulness to himself as a moveable government house, purchased it.

Some way to the east of the Commissariat store-house was the site of the Naval Building Yard where an unfinished ship-of-war and the materials collected for the construction of others were destroyed when the United States forces took possession of York in 1813.

It appears that Col. Joseph Bouchette had just been pointing out to the Government the exposed condition of the public property here. In a note at p. 89 of his *British North America*, that officer remarks: 'The defenceless situation of York, the mode of its capture, and the destruction of the large ship then on the stocks, were but too prophetically demonstrated in my report to headquarters in Lower Canada, on my return from a responsible mission to the capital of the Upper Province, in the early part of April. Indeed the communications of the result of my reconnoitring operations and the intelligence of the successful invasion of York, and the firing of the new ship by the enemy, were received almost simultaneously.'

The Governor-in-Chief, Sir George Prevost, was blamed for having permitted a frigate to be laid down in an unprotected position. There was a 'striking impropriety', as the Third Letter of *Veritas*, a celebrated correspondent of the Montreal *Herald* in 1815, points out, 'in building at York, without providing the means of security there, as the works of defence, projected by General Brock, (when he contemplated, before the war, the removal of the naval depot from Kingston to York, by reason of the proximity of the former to the States in water by the ice), were discontinued by orders from below [from Sir George Prevost, that is], and never resumed. The position intended to have been fortified by General Brock, near York, was', *Veritas* continues, 'capable of being made very strong, had his plan been executed; but as it was not, nor any other plan of defence adopted, a ship-yard without protection became an allurement to the enemy, as was felt to the cost of the inhabitants of York.'

In the year 1832 the interior of the Commissariat-store, decorated with flags, was the scene of the first charitable bazaar held in these parts. It was for the relief of distress occasioned by a recent visitation of cholera. The enterprise appears to have been remarkably successful. We have a notice of it in Sibbald's *Canadian Magazine* of January 1833, in the following terms: 'All the fashionable and well-disposed attended; the band of the gallant 79th played, at each table stood a lady; and in a very short time all the articles were sold to gentlemen,—who will keep "as the apple in their eye" the things made and presented by such hands.' The sum collected on the occasion, it is added, was three hundred and eleven pounds.

Where Windsor Street now appears—with its grand iron

gates at either end, inviting or forbidding the entrance of the
stranger to the prim, quaint, self-contained little village of
villas inside—formerly stood the abode of Mr John Beikie
whose tall, upright, staidly-moving form, generally enveloped
in a long snuff-coloured overcoat, was one of the *dramatis
personæ* of York. He had been, at an early period, Sheriff of the
Home District [1810-15]; at a later time his signature was familiar to every eye attached in the *Gazette* to notices put forth by
the Executive Council of the day, of which rather aristocratic
body he was the Clerk [1832-9].

Passing westward, we had on the right the spacious home of
Mr Crookshank, a benevolent and excellent man, sometime
Receiver-General of the Province, of whom we shall again have
occasion to speak; and on the left, on a promontory suddenly
jutting out into the harbour, 'Captain Bonnycastle's cottage',
with garden and picturesque grove attached; all Ordnance
property in reality, and once occupied by Col. Coffin. The whole
has now been literally eaten away by the ruthless tooth of the
steam excavator. On the beach to the west of this promontory
was a much frequented bathing-place. Captain Bonnycastle, just
named, was afterwards Sir Richard, and the author of *Canada
as it was, is and may be* [1852] and *Canada and the Canadians
in 1846.* [1846]

The name 'Peter', attached to the street which flanks on the
west the ancient homestead and extensive outbuildings of Mr
Crookshank, is a memento of the president or administrator,
Peter Russell. It led directly up to Petersfield, Mr Russell's
park-lot on Queen Street.

We come here to the western boundary of the so-called New
Town—the limit of the first important extension of York westward [1798]. The limit, eastward, of the New Town was a
thoroughfare known in the former day as Toronto Street, which
was one street east of Yonge Street, represented now by Victoria
Street. At the period when the plan was designed for this grand
western and north-western suburb of York, Yonge Street was not
opened southward farther than Lot [Queen] Street. The roadway there suddenly veered to the eastward, and then, after a

short interval, passed down Toronto Street, a roadway a little
to the west of the existing Victoria Street.

After the laying-out in lots of the region comprehended in the
first great expansion of York, of which we have spoken, in-
quiries were instituted by the authorities as to the improvements made by the holders of each. In the chart accompanying
the report of Mr Stegman, the surveyor appointed to make the
examination, the lots are coloured according to the condition
of each, and appended are the following curious particulars
which smack somewhat of the ever-memorable town-plot of
Eden, to which Martin Chuzzlewit was induced to repair, and
which offered a lively picture of an infant metropolis in the
rough. (We must represent to ourselves a chequered diagram;
some of the squares white or blank; some tinted blue; some
shaded black; the whole entitled 'Sketch of the Part of the Town
of York west of Toronto Street'.) 'Explanation: The blank lots
are cleared, agreeable to the notice issued from His Excellency
the Lieutenant-Governor, bearing date September the fourth,
1800. The lots shaded blue are chiefly cut, but the brush not
burnt; and those marked with the letter A, the brush only cut.
The lots shaded black, no work done. The survey made by
order of the Surveyor-General's office, bearing date April the
23rd, 1801.' A more precise examination appears to have been
demanded. The explanations appended to the second plan,
which has squares shaded brown, in addition to those coloured
blue and black, are: '1st. The blank lots are cleared. 2nd. The
lots shaded black, *no work done*. 3rd. The lots shaded brown,
the brush cut and burnt. 4th. The lots shaded blue, *the brush
cut and not burnt*. N.B. The lots 1 and 2 on the north side of
Newgate [Adelaide] Street (the site subsequently of the dwelling-house of Jesse Ketchum, of whom hereafter), are mostly
clear of the large timber, and some *brush cut* also, but *not
burnt;* therefore omitted in the first report. This second examination done by order of the Honourable JOHN ELMSLEY,
ESQ.'

The second extension of York westward included the Government Common [1831]. The staking out of streets here was a
comparatively late event. Brock Street [south Spadina Avenue],

to which we have now approached, had its name, of course, from the General officer slain at Queenston, and its extra width from the example set in the Avenue [Spadina] to the north, into which it merges after crossing Queen Street.

A little to the west of Brock Street was the old military bury-ing-ground, a clearing in the thick brushwood of the locality: of an oblong shape, its four picketed sides directed exactly towards the four cardinal points. The setting off of the neigh-bouring streets and lots at a different angle caused the boundary lines of this plot to run askew to every other straight line in the vicinity. Over how many a now-forgotten and even obliterated grave have the customary farewell volleys here been fired!— those final honours to the soldier, always so touching; intended doubtless, in the old barbaric way, to be an incentive to en-durance in the sound and well and consolatory in anticipation to the sick and dying.

Among the remains deposited in this ancient burial-plot are those of a child of the first Governor of Upper Canada, a fact commemorated on the exterior of the mortuary chapel over his own grave in Devonshire, by a tablet on which are the words: 'Katharine, born in Upper Canada, 16th Jan., 1793; died and was buried at York Town, in that Province, in 1794.'

Returning now again to Brock Street [Spadina Avenue], and placing ourselves at the middle point of its great width, im-mediately before us to the north, on the ridge which bounds the view in the distance, we discern a white object. This is Spadina House, from which the avenue into which Brock Street passes takes its name. The word Spadina itself is an Indian term tastefully modified, descriptive of a sudden rise of land like that on which the house in the distance stands. Spadina was the residence of Dr W. W. Baldwin, to whom reference has already been made.[11] A liberal in his political views, he nevertheless was strongly influenced by the feudal feeling which was a second nature with most persons in the British Islands some years ago. His purpose was to establish in Canada a family whose head

---

11 Spadina stood on the same site as the large house to the north-east of Casa Loma. Dr Baldwin also had a town house on Bay Street.

was to be maintained in opulence by the proceeds of an entailed estate. There was to be forever a Baldwin of Spadina.

It is singular that the first inheritor of the newly-established patrimony [Robert Baldwin] should have been the statesman whose lot it was to carry through the Legislature of Canada the abolition of the rights of primogeniture [1851]. The son grasped more readily than the father what the genius of the North American continent will endure and what it will not.

Spadina Avenue was laid out by Dr Baldwin on a scale that would have satisfied the designers of St Petersburg or Washington. Its width is one hundred and thirty-two feet. Its length from the water's edge to the base of Spadina Hill would be nearly three miles. Garnished on both sides by a double row of full-grown chestnut trees, it would vie in magnificence, when seen from an eminence, with the Long Walk at Windsor.[12]

Westward of Spadina House, on the same elevation of land, was Davenport, the picturesque and château-like home of Col. Wells, formerly of the 43rd regiment, built at an early period [1820]. The view of the Lake and intervening forest, as seen from Davenport and Spadina, before the cultivation of the alluvial plain below, was always fine. (On his retirement from the army, the second Col. Wells took up his abode at Davenport.)

Returning again to the front. The portion of the Common that lies immediately west of the foot of Brock Street was enclosed for the first time and ornamentally planted by Mr Jameson. Before his removal to Canada, Mr Jameson had filled a judicial position in the West Indies. In Canada he was successively Attorney-General and Vice-Chancellor, the Chancellorship itself being vested in the Crown. The conversational powers of Mr Jameson were admirable; and no slight interest attached to the pleasant talk of one who, in his younger days, had been the familiar associate of Southey, Wordsworth, and Samuel Taylor Coleridge. Mr Jameson was a man of high culture and fine

---

12 Baldwin was also responsible for the extra width of the section of Queen Street stretching to the east of Spadina. The point where Queen narrows marks the end of his property.

literary tastes. He was, moreover, an amateur artist of no ordinary skill, as extant drawings of his in water-colours attest. His countenance, especially in his old age, was of the Jeremy Bentham stamp.

It was from the house on the west of Brock Street that Mrs Jameson dated the letters which constitute her well-known *Winter Studies and Summer Rambles.* That volume thus closes: 'At three o'clock in the morning, just as the moon was setting on Lake Ontario, I arrived at the door of my own house in Toronto, having been absent on this wild expedition [to the Sault] just two months.' York had then been two years Toronto. (For having ventured to pass down the rapids at the Sault, she had been formally named by the Otchipways of the locality, *Was-sa-je-wun-e-qua,* 'Woman of the Bright Stream.')

Mrs Jameson was unattractive in person at first sight, although, as could scarcely fail to be the case in one so highly endowed, her features, separately considered, were fine and boldly marked. Intellectually she was an enchantress. Besides an originality and independence of judgement on most subjects, and a facility in generalizing and reducing thought to the form of a neat aphorism, she had a strong and capacious memory, richly furnished with choice things. Her conversation was consequently of the most fascinating kind.

She sang, too, in sweet taste, with a quiet softness, without display. She sketched from nature with great elegance, and designed cleverly. The seven or eight illustrations which appear in the American edition of the *Characteristics* dated at Toronto are etched by herself, and bear her autograph 'Anna'. The same is to be observed of the illustrations in the English edition of her *Commonplace Book of Thoughts, Memories, and Fancies;* and in her larger volumes on various art subjects. She had supereminently beautiful hands, which she always scrupulously guarded from contact with the outer air.

Westward from the house and the grounds whose associations have detained us so long, the space that was known as the Government Common is now transversed from south to north by two streets. Their names possess some interest, the first of them being that of the Duke of Portland, Viceroy of Ireland, Colonial

Secretary, and three times Prime Minister in the reign of George the Third; the other that of Earl Bathurst, Secretary for the Colonies in George the Fourth's time.

Eastward of Bathurst Street, in the direction of the military burying-ground, there was long marked out by a furrow in the sward the ground-plan of a church. In 1830 the military chaplain, Mr Hudson, addressed to the commander of the forces a complaint 'of the very great inconvenience to which the troops are exposed in having to march so far to the place of worship, particularly when the weather and roads are so unfavourable during a greater part of the year in this country, the distance from the Barracks to the Church being two miles'; adding, 'In June last, the roads were in such a state as to prevent the Troops from attending Church for four successive Sundays.' He then suggested 'the propriety of erecting a chapel on the Government reserve for the accommodation of the Troops.' The Horse Guards refused to undertake the erection of a chapel here but made a donation of one thousand pounds towards the re-edification of St James' Church, 'on condition that accommodation should be permanently provided for His Majesty's Troops.' The outline in the turf was a relic of Mr Hudson's suggestion.

We now soon arrive at the ravine of the 'Garrison Creek'. In the rivulet below, for some distance up the valley, before the clearing away of the woods, salmon used to be taken at certain seasons of the year. Crossing the stream, and ascending to the arched gateway of the Fort (we are speaking of it as it used to be), we pass between the strong iron-studded portals, which are thrown back: we pass a sentry just within the gate, and the guard-house on the left. At present we do not tarry within the enclosure of the Fort. We simply glance at the loopholed blockhouse on the one side, and the quarters of the men, the officers, and the commandant on the other; and we hurry across the gravelled area, recalling rapidly a series of spirit-stirring ordinal numbers—40th, 41st, 68th, 79th, 42nd, 15th, 32nd, 1st—each suggestive of a gallant assemblage at some time here; of a vigorous, finely disciplined, ready-aye-ready group that, like the successive generations on the stage of human life, came and went just once, as it were—as the years rolled on and the eye saw them again no more.

We pass on through the western gate to the large open green space which lies on the farther side. This is the Garrison Reserve. It bears the same relation to the modern Toronto and the ancient York as the Plains of Abraham do to Quebec. It was here that the struggle took place, in the olden time, that led to the capture of the town. In both cases the leader of the aggressive expedition 'fell victorious'. But the analogy holds no further; as, in the case of the inferior conquest, the successful power did not retain permanent possession.

The Wolfe's Cove—the landing-place of the invader—on the occasion referred to, was just within the curve of the Humber Bay, far to the west, where Queen Street now skirts the beach for a short distance and then emerges on it. The intention had been to land more to the eastward, but the vessels containing the hostile force were driven westward by the winds.

The debarkation was opposed by a handful of Indians, under Major Givins. The Glengarry Fencibles had been dispatched to aid in this service, but, attempting to approach the spot by a back road, they lost their way. A tradition exists that the name of the Grenadier's Pond, a lagoon a little to the west, one of the ancient outlets of the waters of the Humber, is connected with the disastrous bewilderment of a party of the regular troops at this critical period. It is at the same time asserted that the name 'Grenadier's Pond' was familiar previously. At length companies of the Eighth Regiment, of the Royal Newfoundland Regiment, and of Incorporated Militia, made their appearance on the ground and disputed the progress inland of the enemy. After suffering severely, they retired towards the Fort. This was the existing Fort. The result is now matter of history and need not be detailed. As portions of the cliff have fallen away from time to time along the shore here, numerous skeletons have been exposed to view, relics of friend and foe slain on the adjacent common, where also military ornaments and fragments of fire-arms used frequently to be dug up. Some of the bones referred to, however, may have been remains of early French and Indian traders.

The site of the original French stockade [Fort Rouillé], established here in the middle of the last century, was nearly at the middle point between the landing-place of the United States force in 1813 and the existing Fort. West of the white cut-stone [Stanley] Barracks, several earth-works and grass-grown excavations still mark the spot. These ruins, which we often visited when they were much more extensive and conspicuous than they are now, were popularly designated 'The Old French Fort'.

We now enter again the modern Fort, passing back through the western gate. On our right we have the site of the magazine which so fatally exploded in 1813; we learn from Gen. Sheaffe's dispatch to Sir George Prevost that it was 'in the western battery'. In close proximity to the magazine was the Government House of the day, an extensive rambling cluster of one-storey buildings, all 'riddled' or shattered to pieces by the concussion when the explosion took place. The ruin that thus befell the Governor's residence led, on the restoration of peace, to the purchase of Chief Justice Elmsley's house on King Street and its conversion into 'Government House'.[13]

From the main battery, which (including a small semi-circular bastion for the venerable flag-staff of the Fort) extends along the brow of the palisaded bank, south of the parade, the royal salutes, resounding down and across the lake, used to be fired on the arrival and departure of the Lieutenant-Governor, and at the opening and closing of the Legislature.

From the south-eastern bastion, overlooking the ravine below, a twelve-pounder was discharged every day at noon. 'The twelve-o'clock gun', when discontinued, was long missed with regret.

At the time of the invasion of Canada in 1812, the garrison of York was manned by the 3rd regiment of York militia. We have before us a relic of the period in the form of the contemporary regimental order-book of the Fort. An entry of the 29th of July 1812, showing the approach of serious work, has an

---

13 This property (the house was rebuilt after a fire in 1863) remained the residence of the lieutenant-governors of Upper Canada and later Ontario until 1912.

especial local interest. 'In consequence of an order from Major-General Brock, commanding the forces, for a detachment of volunteers, under the command of Major Allan,[14] to hold themselves in readiness to proceed in batteaux from the Head of the Lake to-morrow at 2 o'clock, the following officers, non-commissioned officers and privates will hold themselves in readiness to proceed at 2 o'clock, for the purpose of being fitted with caps, blankets and haversacks, as well as to draw provisions. On their arrival at the Head of the Lake, regimental coats and canteens will be ready to be issued to them.'

In view of the test to which the citizen-soldiers were about to be subjected, the General, like a good officer, sought by judicious praise to inspire them with self-confidence. 'Major-General Brock', the order-book proceeds, 'has desired me (Captain Stephen Heward) to acquaint the detachment under my command, of his high approbation of their orderly conduct and good discipline while under arms: that their exercise and marching far exceeded any that he had seen in the Province. And in particular he directed me to acquaint the officers how much he is pleased with their appearance in uniform and their perfect knowledge of their duty.'

On the 13th of August, we learn from other sources, Brock was on the Western Frontier with 700 soldiers, including the volunteers from York, and 600 Indians; and on the 16th the old flag was waving from the fortress of Detroit; but on the 13th October, the brave General, though again a victor in the engagement, was himself a lifeless corpse on the slopes above Queenston; and in April of the following year York, as we have already seen, was in the hands of the enemy. Such are the ups and downs of war. It is mentioned that 'Push on the York Volunteers!' was the order issuing from the lips of the General at the moment of the fatal shot. From the order-book referred to, we learn that 'Toronto' was the parole or countersign of the garrison on the 23rd July 1812.

The knoll on the east side of the Garrison Creek was covered

---

14 This was the same William Allan who was also postmaster, collector of customs, and the financial genius of the Family Compact.

with a number of buildings for the accommodation of troops in addition to the barracks within the Fort. Here also stood a block-house. Eastward were the surgeon's quarters, overhanging the bay; and further eastward still were the commandant's quarters, a structure popularly known, by some freak of military language, as Lambeth Palace. Here for a time resided Major-General Æneas Shaw, afterwards the owner and occupant of Oak Hill.

On the beach below the knoll there continued to be, for a number of years, a row of cannon dismounted, duly spiked and otherwise disabled—memorials of the capture in 1813, when these guns were rendered useless by the regular troops before their retreat to Kingston. The pebbles on the shore about here were also plentifully mixed with loose canister shot, washed up by the waves, after their submersion in the bay on the same occasion.

From the little eminence just referred to, along the edge of the cliff, ran a gravel walk which led first to the Guard House over the Commissariat Stores, in a direct line, with the exception of a slight divergence occasioned by 'Capt. Bonnycastle's cottage', and then eastward into the town. Where ravines occurred, cut in the drift by water-courses into the bay, the gulf was spanned by a bridge of hewn logs. This walk, kept in order for many years by the military authorities, was the representative of the path first worn bare by the soft tread of the Indian. From its agreeableness, overlooking as it did through its whole length the harbour and Lake, this walk gave birth to the idea, which became a fixed one in the minds of the early people of the place, that there was to be in perpetuity, in front of the whole town, a pleasant promenade on which the burghers and their families should take the air and disport themselves generally.

The Royal Patent by which this sentimental walk is provided for and decreed, issued on the 14th day of July in the year 1818, designates it by the interesting old name of MALL, and nominates 'John Beverley Robinson, William Allan, George Crookshank, Duncan Cameron and Grant Powell, all of the town of York, Esqs., their heirs and assigns forever, as trustees to hold

the same for the use and benefit of the inhabitants.' Stretching
from Peter Street in the west to the Reserve for Government
Buildings in the east, of a breadth varying between four and
five chains, following the line of Front Street on the one side
and the several turnings and windings of the bank on the other,
the area of land contained in this Mall was 'thirty acres, more
or less, with allowance for the several cross streets leading from
the said town to the water'. The paucity of open squares in the
early plans of York may be partly accounted for by this provision made for a spacious Public Walk.

While the archæologist must regret the many old landmarks
which were ruthlessly shorn away in the construction of the
modern Esplanade, he must nevertheless contemplate with
never-ceasing admiration that great and laudable work. It has
done for Toronto what the Thames embankment has effected
for London. Besides vast sanitary advantages accruing, it has
created space for the erection of a new front to the town. It has
made room for a board promenade some two or three miles in
length—not, indeed, of the *far niente* type, but with double and
treble railway tracks abreast of itself, all open to the deep water
of the harbour on one side and flanked almost throughout the
whole length on the other by a series of warehouses, mills,
factories and depots destined to increase every year in importance. The sights and sounds every day along this combination
of roadways and its surroundings are unlike anything dreamt
of by the framers of the old Patent of 1818. But it cannot be
said that the idea contained in that document has been wholly
departed from: nay, it must be confessed that it has been
grandly realized in a manner and on a scale adapted to the requirements of these latter days.[15]

For some time Front Street above the Esplanade continued
to be a raised terrace from which pleasant views and fresh lake
air could be obtained; and attempts were made, at several

---

15 The Esplanade today is a lane running from Bay Street to Berkeley
immediately north of the railway tracks. The elevated modern tracks, and
the reclaiming of the land along Fleet Street, have completely cut it off
from the lake so that what was intended as the showplace of the city has
become one of its most unprepossessing byways.

points along its southern verge, to establish a double row of
shade trees, which should recall in future ages the primitive
oaks and elms which overlooked the margin of the harbour.
But soon the erection of tall buildings on the newly-made land
below began to shut out the view and the breezes and to dis-
courage attempts at ornamentation by the planting of trees.

The gravelled path from the Fort to the Commissariat Stores,
as described above, in conjunction with a parallel track for
wheels along the cliff all the way to the site of the Parliament
Buildings, suggested in 1822 the restoration of a carriage-drive
to the Island which had some years previously existed. This involved the erection, or rather re-erection, of bridges over the
lesser and greater Don to enable the inhabitants of York to
reach the long lines of lake beach extending eastward to
Scarborough Heights and westward to Gibraltar Point.

All the old accounts of York in the topographical diction-
aries of 'sixty years since' spoke of the salubriousness of the
peninsula which formed the harbour. Even the aborigines, it
was stated, had recourse to that spot for sanative purposes. All
this was derived from the article in D. W. Smith's *Gazetteer*
[1813], which sets forth that 'the long beach or peninsula, which
affords a most delightful ride, is considered so healthy by the
Indians, that they resort to it whenever indisposed.'

So early as 1806 a bridge or float had been built over the
mouth of the Don. In the *Gazette* of June 18 in that year we
have the notice: 'It is requested that no person will draw sand
or pass with loaded waggons or carts over the new Bridge or
Float at the opening of the Don River, as this source of communication was intended to accommodate the inhabitants of
the town in a walk or ride to the Island. *York, 13th June, 1806.*'

Health, however, was not the sole object of all these arrangements. A race-course had been laid out on the sandy neck of
land connecting the central portion of the peninsula with the
main shore. Here races were periodically held; and we have
been assured by an eye-witness that twelve fine horses at a time
had been seen by him engaged in the contest of speed. The
hippodrome in question was not a ring but a long straight level

stadium, extending from the southern end of the second bridge to the outer margin of the lake.

When invasion was threatened in 1812, all the bridges in the direction of the Island were taken down. An earthwork was thrown up across the narrow ridge separating the last long reach of the Don from the Bay; and in addition, a trench was cut across the same ridge. This cut, at first insignificant, became ultimately by a natural process the lesser Don, a deep and wide outlet, a convenient short-cut for skiffs and canoes from the Bay to the Don proper, and from the Don proper to the Bay.

On the return of peace, the absence of bridges and the existence in addition of a second formidable water-filled moat speedily began to be matters of serious regret to the inhabitants of York, who found themselves uncomfortably cut off from easy access to the peninsula. From the *Gazette* of April 15, 1822, we learn that 'a public subscription among the inhabitants had been entered into, to defray the expense of erecting two bridges on the River Don, leading from this town towards the south, to the Peninsula.' And subjoined are the leading names of the place, guaranteeing various sums, in all amounting to £108, 5s. The timber was presented by Peter Robinson, Esq., M.P.P. The estimated expense of the undertaking was £325.

On the strength of the sums thus promised, an engineer, Mr E. Angell, began the erection of the bridge over the Greater Don. The *Gazette* before us reports that it was being constructed 'with hewn timbers on the most approved *European* principle'. (There is point in the italicized word: it hints the impolicy of employing United States engineers for such works.) The paper adds that 'the one bridge over the Great Don, consisting of five arches, is in a forward state; and the other, of one arch, over the Little Don, will be completed in or before the month of July next, when this line of road will be opened.'

By the *Weekly Register* of June 19, in the following year, it appears that the engineer, in commencing the bridge before the amount of its cost was guaranteed, had calculated without his host; and, as is usually the case with those who draw in advance on the proceeds of a supposed public enthusiasm, had been brought into difficulties. We accordingly find that 'on

Friday evening last, pursuant to public notice given in the *Upper Canada Gazette*, a meeting of the subscribers, and other inhabitants of the town of York, was held at the house of Mr Phair, in the Market-place, for the purpose of taking into consideration the circumstances in which the engineer had been placed by constructing a bridge, the charge of which was to be defrayed by voluntary subscription, over the mouth of the river Don.'

Resolutions were passed on the occasion approving of Mr Angell's proceedings and calling for additional donations. A new committee was now appointed, consisting of H. J. Boulton, Esq., Dr Widmer, S. Heward, Esq., Charles Small, Esq., and Allan MacNab, Esq. The editor of the *Weekly Register* (Fothergill) thus notices the meeting: 'It is satisfactory to find that there is at length some probability of the bridge over the Don in this vicinity being completed. We are, ourselves,' the writer of the article proceeds to say, 'the more anxious on this account, from the hope there is reason to entertain that these and other improvements in the neighbourhood will eventually lead to a draining of the great marsh at the east end of this town; for until that is done, it is utterly impossible that the place can be healthy at all seasons of the year. The public are not sufficiently impressed with the alarming insalubrity of such situations.'

The desired additional subscriptions do not appear to have come in. The works at the mouth of the Don proper were brought to a standstill. The bridge over the Lesser Don was not commenced. Thus matters remained for the long interval of ten years. Every inhabitant of York able to indulge in the luxury of a carriage or a saddle horse, or given to extensive pedestrian excursions, continued to regret the inaccessibleness of the peninsula. Especially among the families of the military, accustomed to the surroundings of sea-coast towns at home, did the desire exist to be able at will to take a drive or a canter or a vigorous constitutional on the sands of the peninsula where on the one hand the bold escarpments in the distance to the eastward, on the other the ocean-like horizon, and immediately in front the long rollers of surf tumbling in, all helped to stir recollections of (we will suppose) Dawlish or Torquay.

In 1834, through the intervention of Sir John Colborne, and by means of a subsidy from the military chest, the works on both outlets of the Don were re-commenced. In 1835 the bridges were completed. On the 22nd of August in that year they were handed over by the military authorities to the town, now no longer York but Toronto.

Some old-world formalities were observed on the occasion. The civic authorities approached the new structure in procession; a barricade at the first bridge arrested their progress. A guard stationed there also forbade further advance. The officer in command, Capt. Bonnycastle, appears, and the Mayor and Corporation are informed that the two bridges before them are, by the command of the Lieutenant-Governor, presented to them as a free gift for the benefit of the inhabitants, that they may in all time to come be enabled to enjoy the salubrious air of the peninsula; the only stipulation being that the bridges should be free of toll forever to the troops, stores, and ordnance of the sovereign.

The mayor, who as eye-witnesses report was arrayed in an official robe of purple velvet lined with scarlet, read the following reply: 'Sir—On the part of His Majesty's faithful and loyal city of Toronto, I receive at your hands the investiture of these bridges, erected by command of His Excellency the Lieutenant-Governor, and now delivered to the Corporation for the benefit and accommodation of the citizens. In the name of the Common Council and the citizens of Toronto, I beg you to convey to His Excellency the grateful feelings with which this new instance of the bounty of our most gracious sovereign is received; and I take this occasion on behalf of the city to renew our assurances of loyalty and attachment to His Majesty's person and government, and to pray, through His Excellency, a continuance of royal favour towards this city. I have, on the part of the corporation and citizens, to request you to assure His Excellency the Lieutenant-Governor that His Excellency's desire and generous exertions for the health and welfare of the inhabitants of this city are duly and gratefully appreciated;

and I beg you to convey to His Excellency the best wishes of myself and my fellow-citizens for the health and happiness of His Excellency and family. Permit me, Sir, for myself and brethren, to thank you for the very handsome and compliment-ary manner in which you have carried His Excellency's com-mands into execution.'

'Immediately', the narrative of the ceremonial continues, 'the band, who were stationed on the bridge, struck up the heart-stirring air, "God save the King", during the performance of which the gentlemen of the Corporation followed by a large number of the inhabitants, passed uncovered over the bridge. Three cheers were then given respectively for the King, for His Excellency the Lieutenant-Governor, for the Mayor and Coun-cil of the City of Toronto, and for Capt. Bonnycastle. The gentlemanly and dignified manner in which both the addresses were read did credit to the gentlemen on whom these duties devolved; and the good order and good humour that prevailed among the spectators present were exceedingly gratifying.'

We take this account from the Toronto *Patriot* of August 28th, 1835, wherein it is copied from the *Christian Guardian*. Mr R. B. Sullivan, the official representative of the city on the occasion just described, was the second mayor of Toronto. He was afterwards one of the Judges of the Court of Common Pleas.

The bridges thus ceremoniously presented and received had a short-lived existence. They were a few years afterwards seriously damaged during the breaking up of the ice and then carried away bodily in one of the spring freshets to which the Don is subject.

The peninsula in front of York was once plentifully stocked with goats, the offspring of a small colony established by order of Governor Hunter at Gibraltar Point for the sake, for one thing, of the supposed salutary nature of the whey of goat's milk. These animals were dispersed during the war of 1812-13.

III

KING

STREET

FROM

JOHN

STREET

TO

CHURCH

STREET

After our long stroll westward, we had purposed returning to the place of beginning by the route which constitutes the principal thoroughfare of the modern Toronto; but the associations connected with the primitive pathway on the cliff overlooking the harbour led us insensibly back along the track by which we came. In order that we may execute our original design, we now transport ourselves at once to the point where we had intended to begin our descent of King Street. That point [John Street] was the site of a building now wholly taken out of the way—the old General Hospital [1820]. Farther west on this line of road there was no object possessing any archæological interest.

The old hospital was a spacious, unadorned, matter-of-fact, two-storey structure of red brick, one hundred and seven feet long and sixty-six feet wide. It had, by the direction of Dr Grant Powell, as we have heard, the peculiarity of standing with its sides precisely east and west, north and south. At a subsequent period it consequently had the appearance of having being jerked round bodily, the streets in the neighbourhood not being laid out with the same precise regard to the cardinal points. The building exhibited recessed galleries on the north and south sides and a flattish hipped roof. The interior was conveniently designed.

In the fever wards here, during the terrible season of 1847, frightful scenes of suffering and death were witnessed among the newly-arrived emigrants; here it was that, in ministering to them in their distress, so many were struck down, some all but fatally, others wholly so—amongst the latter several leading medical men, and the Roman Catholic Bishop, Power.

When the Houses of Parliament at the east end of the town were destroyed by fire in 1824, the Legislature assembled for several sessions in the General Hospital [until 1829].

The building on King Street [west of Simcoe Street] known as 'Government House' was originally the private residence of Chief Justice Elmsley. For many years after its purchase by the Government it was still styled 'Elmsley House'. As at Quebec, the correspondence of the Governor-in-Chief was dated from the 'Château St Louis, or the 'Castle of St Louis', so here that of the Lieutenant-Governor of the Western Province was long dated from 'Elmsley House'. Mr Elmsley was a brother of the celebrated classical critic and editor, Peter Elmsley of Oxford. We shall have occasion frequently to speak of him.

On the left, opposite Government House, was a very broken piece of ground denominated 'Russell Square', afterwards, through the instrumentality of Sir John Colborne, converted into a site for an educational institution. Sir John Colborne, on his arrival in Upper Canada, was fresh from the Governorship of Guernsey, one of the Channel Islands. During his administration there he had revived a decayed Public School, at present known as Elizabeth College. Being of opinion that the new country to which he had been transferred was not ripe for a University on the scale contemplated in a royal Charter which had been procured [1827], he addressed himself to the establishment of an institution which should meet the immediate educational wants of the community.

Those who desire to trace the career of Upper Canada College *ab ovo* will be thankful for the following advertisements.

The first is from the *Loyalist* of May 2, 1829. 'Minor College. Sealed tenders for erecting a School House and four dwelling-houses will be received on the first Monday of June next. Plans, elevations and specifications may be seen after the 12th instant, on application to the Hon. Geo. Markland, from whom further information will be received. Editors throughout the Province are requested to insert this notice until the first Monday in June, and forward their accounts for the same to the office of the *Loyalist*, York. *York, 1st May, 1829.'*

The second advertisement is from the *Upper Canada Gazette* of Dec. 17, 1829. 'Upper Canada College, established at York. Visitor, the Lieutenant-Governor for the time being. This College will open after the approaching Christmas Vacation, on Monday the 8th of January, 1830, under the conduct of the Masters appointed at Oxford by the Vice Chancellor and other electors, in July last. Principal, the Rev. J. H. Harris, D.D., late Fellow of Clare Hall, Cambridge. . . . *York, Upper Canada, Dec. 2, 1829.'*

After Russell Square on the left came an undulating green field; near the middle of it was a barn of rural aspect, cased-in with upright, unplaned boards. The field was at one time a kind of *Campus Martius* for a troop of amateur cavalry who were instructed in their evolutions and in the use of the broadsword by a veteran, Capt. Midford, the Goodwin of the day, at York.

Nothing of note presented itself until after we arrived at the roadway which is now known as Bay Street, with the exception, perhaps, of two small rectangular edifices of red brick with bright tin roofs—dropped, as it were, one at the south-west, the other at the north-west, angle of the intersection of King and York Streets. The former was the office of the Manager of the Clergy Reserve Lands; the latter, that of the Provincial Secretary and Registrar. They are noticeable simply as being specimens, in solid material, of a kind of minute cottage that for a certain period was in fashion in York and its neighbourhood—little square boxes, one storey in height and without basement, looking as if, by the aid of a ring at the apex of the four-sided roof, they might with no great difficulty be lifted up, like the hutch provided for Gulliver by his nurse Glumdalclitch, and carried bodily away.

As we pass eastward of Bay Street, the memory comes back of Franco Rossi, the earliest scientific confectioner of York, who had on the south side near here a depot ever fragrant and ambrosial. In his specialities he was a superior workman. From him were procured the fashionable bridecakes of the day; as also the *noyeau, parfait-armour* and other liqueurs set out for visitors on New Year's Day. Rossi was the first to import hither good objects of art: fine copies of the Laocoön, the Apollo Belvedere, the Perseus of Canova, with other classical groups and figures sculptured in Florentine alabaster, were disseminated by him in the community.

Rossi is the Italian referred to by the author of 'Cyril Thornton' in his *Men and Manners in America* where, speaking of York, visited by him in 1832, he says: 'In passing through the streets I was rather surprised to observe an *affiche* intimating that ice-creams were to be had within. The weather being hot, I entered, and found the master of the establishment to be an Italian. I never ate better ice at Grange's'—some fashionable resort in London, we suppose. The outward signs of civilization at York must have been meagre when a chance visitor recorded his surprise at finding ice-creams procurable in such a place.

Great enthusiasm, we remember, was created far and near by certain panes of plate glass with brass divisions between them which, at a period a little later than Cyril Thornton's (Captain Hamilton's) visit, suddenly ornamented the windows of Mr Beckett's Chemical Laboratory close by Rossi's. Even Mrs Jameson, in her book of *Winter Studies and Summer Rambles*, referring to the shop fronts of King Street, pronounces, in a naive English watering-place kind of tone, 'that of the apothecary' to be 'worthy of Regent Street in its appearance'.

A little farther on, still on the southern side, was the first place of public worship of the Wesleyan Methodists. It was a long, low, wooden building, running north and south and placed a little way back from the street. Its dimensions in the first instance, as we have been informed by Mr Petch who was engaged in its erection, were 40 by 40 feet. It was then enlarged to 40 by 60 feet. In the gable end towards the street were two doors, one for each sex. Within the custom obtained of dividing the men from the women, the former sitting on the right hand of one entering the building, the latter on the left.

The Wesleyan chapel in King Street ceased to be used in 1833. It was converted afterwards for a time into a 'Theatre Royal'.

Jordan Street preserves one of the names of Mr Jordan Post, owner of the whole frontage extending from Bay Street to Yonge Street. The name of his wife is preserved in 'Melinda Street', which traverses his lot, or rather block, from east to west south of King Street. Two of his daughters bore respectively the unusual names of Sophronia and Desdemona. Mr Post was a tall New Englander of grave address. He was, moreover, a clockmaker by trade, and always wore spectacles. From the formal cut of his apparel and hair he was, quite erroneously, sometimes supposed to be of the Mennonite or Quaker persuasion.

So early as 1802 Mr Post is advertising in the York paper. In the *Oracle* of Sept. 18, 1802, he announces a temporary absence from the town. 'Jordan Post, watchmaker, requests all those who left watches with him to be repaired, to call at Mr Beman's and receive them by paying for the repairs. He intends returning to York in a few months. Sept. 11, 1802.' In the close of the same year he puts forth the general notice: 'Jordan Post, Clock and Watchmaker, informs the public that he now carries on the above business in all its branches, at the upper end of Duke Street. He has a complete assortment of watch furniture. Clocks and watches repaired on the shortest notice, and most reasonable terms, together with every article in the gold and silver line. N.B.—He will purchase old brass. *Dec. 11, 1802.*'

Besides the block described above, Mr Post had acquired other valuable properties in York, as will appear by an advertisement in the *Weekly Register* of Jan. 19, 1826, from which also it will be seen that he at one time contemplated a gift to the town of one-hundred-feet frontage and two hundred feet of depth, for the purpose of a second Public Market. 'Town Lots for Sale. To be sold by Auction on the Premises, on Wed-

nesday the first day of February next, Four Town Lots on
King Street, west of George Street. Also, to be leased at the
same time to the highest bidder, for twenty-one years, subject
to such conditions as will then be produced. Six Lots on the
west side of Yonge Street, and Twenty on Market [Wellington]
Street. The Subscriber has reserved a Lot of Ground of One
Hundred Feet front, by Two Hundred Feet in the rear, on
George Street, for a Market Place, to be given for that purpose.
He will likewise lease Ten Lots in front of said intended Mar-
ket. A plan of the Lots may be seen and further particulars
known, by application to the Subscriber. JORDAN POST. *York,
Jan. 4, 1826.'*

Where Yonge Street crosses King Street, forming at the present
day an unusually noble *carrefour*, as the French would say, or
rectangular intersection of thoroughfares as we are obliged to
word it, there was for a considerable time but one solitary
house at the north-east angle—a longish, one-storey, respectable
wooden structure painted white with paling in front and large
willow trees: it was the home of Mr Dennis, formerly superintendant of the dock-yard at Kingston. He was one of the
United Empire Loyalist refugees and received a grant of land
on the Humber near the site of the modern village of Weston.
His son, Mr Joseph Dennis, owned and commanded a vessel on
Lake Ontario in 1812. When the war with the United States
broke out, he and his ship were attached to the Provincial
Marine. His vessel was captured, and himself made a prisoner
of war, in which condition he remained for fifteen months. He
afterwards commanded the *Princess Charlotte*, an early steamboat on Lake Ontario.

To the eastward of Mr Dennis' house on the same side at an
early period was an obscure frame building of the most ordinary kind whose existence is recorded simply for having been
temporarily the District Grammar [High] School before the
erection of the spacious building on the Grammar School lot.

On the opposite side, still passing on towards the east, was
the Jail. This was a squat unpainted wooden building with
hipped roof, concealed from persons passing in the street by a

tall cedar stockade such as those which we see surrounding a Hudson's Bay post or a military wood-yard. At the outer entrance hung a billet of wood suspended by a chain communicating with a bell within; and occasionally Mr Parker, the custodian of the place, was summoned through its instrumentality by persons not there on legitimate business. We have a recollection of a clever youth [Henry Blackstone], an immediate descendant of the great commentator on British Law and afterwards himself distinguished at the Upper Canadian Bar, who was severely handled by Mr Parker's son on being caught in the act of pulling at this billet with the secret intention of running away after the exploit.

The English Criminal Code, as it was at the beginning of the century, having been introduced with all its enormities, public hangings were frequent at an early period in the new Province. A shocking scene is described as taking place at an execution in front of the old Jail at York. The condemned refuses to mount the scaffold. On this the moral-suasion efforts of the sheriff amount to the ridiculous, were not the occasion so seriously tragic. In aid of the sheriff the officiating chaplain steps more than once up the plank set from the cart to the scaffold to show the facility of the act and to induce the man to mount in like manner; the condemned demurs and openly remarks on the obvious difference in the two cases. At last the noose is adjusted to the neck of the wretched culprit where he stands. The cart is withdrawn, and a deliberate strangling ensues.

In a certain existing account of steps taken in 1811 to remedy the dilapidated and comfortless condition of the Jail, we get a glimpse of York, commercially and otherwise, at that date. In April 1811 the sheriff, Beikie, reports to the magistrates at Quarter Sessions 'that the sills of the east cells of the Jail of the Home District are completely rotten; that the ceilings in the debtors' rooms are insufficient; and that he cannot think himself safe, should necessity oblige him to confine any persons in said cells or debtors' rooms'[1].

---

1 In the early days the jail was used to confine debtors and lunatics as well as criminals.

An order is given in May to make the necessary repairs; but certain spike-nails are wanted of a kind not to be had at the local dealers in hardware. The chairman is consequently directed to 'apply to His Excellency the Lieutenant-Governor [Gore], that he will be pleased to direct that the spike-nails be furnished from the King's stores, as there are not any of the description required to be purchased at York'. A memorandum follows to the effect that on the communication of this necessity to His Excellency, 'the Lieutenant-Governor ordered that the Clerk of the Peace do apply for the spike-nails officially in the name of the Court: which he did', the memorandum adds, 'on the 8th of May, 1811, and received an answer on the day following, that an order had been issued that day for 1500 spike-nails, for the repair of the Home District Jail; the nails', it is subjoined, 'were received by carpenter Leach in the month of July following.'

Again: in December 1811 Mr Sheriff Beikie sets forth to the magistrates in Session that 'the prisoners in the cells of the Jail of the Home District suffer much from cold and damp, there being no method of communicating heat from the chimneys, nor any bedsteads to raise the straw from the floors, which lie nearly, if not altogether, on the ground.' He accordingly suggests that 'a small stove in the lobby of each range of cells, together with some rugs or blankets, will add much to the comfort of the unhappy persons confined.' The magistrates authorize the supply of the required necessaries and the order is marked 'instant'. (The month, we are to notice, was December.)

At a late period there were placed about the town a set of posts having relation to the Jail. They were distinguished from the ordinary rough posts, customary then at regular intervals along the sidewalks, by being of turned wood with spherical tops, the lower part painted a pale blue, the upper white. These were the 'limits'—the *certi denique fines*—beyond which *détenus* for debt were not allowed to extend their walks.

Leaving the picketted enclosure of the Prison, we soon arrived at an open piece of ground on the opposite (north) side of the street [between Toronto and Church Streets] afterwards known as the 'Court House Square'. One of the many rivulets or water-courses that traversed the site of York passed through it, flowing in a deep serpentine ravine, a spot to be remembered by the youth of the day as affording in the winter facilities for skating and sliding, and audacious exploits on 'leather ice'. In this open space a Jail and Court House of a pretentious character but of poor architectural style were erected in 1824. The two buildings, which were of two storeys and exactly alike, were placed side by side, a few yards back from the road. Their gables were to the south, in which direction were also the chief entrances. The material was red brick. Pilasters of cut stone ran up the principal fronts and up the exposed or outer sides of each edifice. At these sides, as also on the inner and unornamented sides, were lesser gables, but marked by the portion of the wall that rose in front of them, not to a point but finishing square in two diminishing stages and sustaining chimneys.

It was intended originally that lanterns should have surmounted and given additional elevation to both buildings, but these were discarded, together with tin as the material of the roofing, with a view to cutting down the cost and thereby enabling the builder to make the pilasters of cut stone instead of 'Roman cement'. John Hayden was the contractor. The cost, as reduced, was to be £3,800 for the two edifices.[2]

We extract from the *Canadian Review* for July 1824, published by H. H. Cunningham, Montreal, an account of the commencement of the new buildings: 'On Saturday, the 24th instant [April 1824], his Excellency the Lieutenant-Governor [Maitland], attended by his staff, was met by the Honourable the Members of the Executive Council, the Judges of the Court of King's Bench, and the Gentlemen of the Bar, with the Magistrates and principal inhabitants of York, in procession, for the purpose of laying the foundation-stone of the new Jail and Court House about to be erected in this Town.—A sovereign and half-sovereign of gold, and several coins of silver

---

[2] Dr William Warren Baldwin was the architect. The jail, extensively altered, survived as an office building until 1957-8.

and copper, of the present reign, together with some newspapers and other memorials of the present day, were deposited
in a cavity of the stone, over which a plate of copper, bearing
an appropriate inscription, was placed; and after his Excellency
had given the first blow, with a hammer handed to him for the
purpose, the ceremony concluded with several hearty cheers
from all who were present.'

In one of the lithographic views published in 1836 by Mr T.
Young, the Jail and Court House, now spoken of, are shewn.
Among the objects inserted to give life to the scene, the artist
has placed in the foreground a country waggon with oxen
yoked to it in primitive fashion. Near the front entrance of the
Jail stood, to the terror of evil-doers down to modern times, a
ponderous specimen of the 'parish stocks' of the old country in
good condition.

After 1825 the open area in front of the Jail and Court House
became the 'Public Place' of the town.[3] Crowds filled it at
elections and other occasions of excitement. We have here witnessed several scenes characteristic of the times in which they
occurred. We here once saw a public orator run away with in
the midst of his harangue [March 23, 1832]. This was Mr Jesse
Ketchum who was making use of a farmer's waggon as his
rostrum or platform when the vehicle was suddenly laid hold of
and wheeled rapidly down King Street, the speaker maintaining
his equilibrium in the meanwhile with difficulty. Mr Ketchum
was one of the most benevolent and beneficent of men. We shall
have occasion to refer to him hereafter.

It was on the same occasion, we believe, that we saw Mr W.
L. Mackenzie assailed by the missiles which mobs usually
adopt. From this spot we had previously seen the same personage, after one of his re-elections, borne aloft in triumph on a
kind of pyramidal car and wearing round his neck and across
his breast a massive gold chain and medal (both made of
molten sovereigns), the gift of his admirers and constituents.
In the procession at the same time was a printing-press, working as it was conveyed along in a low sleigh and throwing off

---

[3] In 1837 the land was sold for commercial purposes and the money realized
was applied towards the construction of the 1840 jail.

handbills which were tossed, right and left, to the accompanying crowd in the street.

The existing generation of Canadians, with the lights which they now possess, see pretty clearly that the agitator just named, and his party, were not in the abstract by any means so bad as they seemed, that in fact the ideas which they sought to propagate are the only ones practicable in the successful government of modern men.

Is there a reader nowadays that sees anything very startling in the enunciation of the following principles? 'The control of the whole revenue to be in the people's representatives; the Legislative Council to be elective; the representation in the House of Assembly to be as equally proportioned to the population as possible; the Executive Government to incur a real responsibility; the law of primogeniture to be abolished; impartiality in the selection of juries to be secured; the Judiciary to be independent; the military to be in strict subordination to the civil authorities; equal rights to the several members of the community; every vestige of Church-and-State union to be done away; the lands and all the revenues of the country to be under the control of the country; and education to be widely, carefully and impartially diffused; to these may be added the choice of our own Governor.'

These were the political principles sought to be established in the Governments of Canada by the party referred to, as set forth in the terms just given (almost *verbatim*) in *Patrick Swift's Almanac* [1834], a well-known popular annual brochure of Mr Mackenzie's. It seems singular now, in the retrospect, that doctrines such as these should have created a ferment.

But there is this to be said: it does not appear that there were, at the time, in the ranks of the party in power any persons of very superior intellectual gifts or of a wide range of culture or historical knowledge: so that it was not likely that, on that side, there would be a ready relinquishment of political traditions, of inherited ideas, which their possessors had never dreamt of rationally analysing, and which they deemed it all but treason to call in question.

And moreover it is to be remembered that the chief propa-

gandist of the doctrines of reform, although very intelligent
and ready of speech, did not himself possess the dignity and
repose of character which give weight to the utterances of
public men. Hence, with the persons who really stood in need
of instruction and enlightenment, his words had an irritating
rather than a conciliatory and convincing effect. This was a
fault which it was not in his power to remedy. For his micro-
scopic vision and restless temperament, while they fitted him to
be a very clever local Reformer, a very clever local editor, unfitted him for the grand role of a national statesman or heroic
conductor of a revolution.

Accordingly, although the principles advocated by him
finally obtained the ascendancy, posterity only regards him as
the Wilkes, the Cobbett, or the Hunt of his day in the annals
of his adopted country. In the interval between the outbreak
or feint at outbreak in 1837 and 1850, the whole Canadian
community made a great advance in general intelligence, and
statesmen of a genuine quality began to appear in our Parliaments.

Prior to the period of which we have just been speaking, a
name much in the mouths of our early settlers was that of
Robert Gourlay. What we have to say in respect to him, in our
retrospect of the past, will perhaps be in place here.

Nothing could be more laudable than Mr Gourlay's intentions at the outset [1817-18]. He desired to publish a statistical
account of Canada with a view to the promotion of emigration.
To inform himself of the actual condition of the young colony,
he addressed a series of questions to persons of experience and
intelligence in every township of Upper Canada. These questions are now lying before us; they extend to the number of
thirty-one. There are none of them that a modern reader would
pronounce ill-judged or irrelevant.

But here again it is easy to see that personal character and
temperament marred the usefulness of a clever man. His in-
ordinate self-esteem and pugnaciousness, insufficiently controlled, speedily rendered him offensive, especially in a community constituted as that was in the midst of which he had
suddenly lighted; and drove, naturally and of necessity, his

opponents to extreme measures in self-defence and himself to extreme doctrines by way of retaliation: thus he became overwhelmed with troubles from which the tact of a wiser man would have saved him. But for Gourlay, as the event proved, a latent insanity was an excuse.

It is curious to observe that in 1818 Gourlay, in his heat against the official party, whose headquarters were at York, threatened that town with extinction; at all events, with the obliteration of its name, and the transmutation thereof into that of TORONTO. In a letter to the Niagara *Spectator*, he says:— 'The tumult excited stiffens every nerve and redoubles the proofs of necessity for action. If the higher classes are against me, I shall recruit among my brother farmers, seven in eight of whom will support the cause of truth. If one year does not make Little York surrender to us, then we'll batter it for two; and should it still hold out, we have ammunition for a much longer siege. We shall raise the wind against it from Amherstburgh and Quebec—from Edinburgh, Dublin and London. It must be levelled to the very earth, and even its name be forgotten in TORONTO.'

But to return for a moment to Mr Mackenzie. On the steps of the Court House, which we are to suppose ourselves now passing, we once saw him under circumstances that were deeply touching. Sentence of death had been pronounced on a young man once employed in his printing-office. He had been vigorously exerting himself to obtain from the Executive a mitigation of the extreme penalty. The day and even the hour for the execution had arrived and no message of reprieve had been transmitted from the Lieutenant-Governor. As he came out of the Sheriff's room, after receiving the final announcement that there could be no further delay, the white collars on each side of his face were wet through and through with the tears that were gushing from his eyes and pouring down his cheeks! He was just realizing the fact that nothing further could be done; and in a few moments afterwards the execution actually took place.[4]

---

[4] This was the execution on October 23, 1828, of Charles French, a former apprentice of Mackenzie's who had taken to drink and shot a man he believed was threatening his life.

We approach comparatively late times when we speak of the cavalcade which passed in grand state the spot now under review, when Messrs Dunn and Buchanan were returned as members for the town [1841]. In the pageant on that occasion there was conspicuous a train of railway carriages, drawn of course by horse power, with the inscription on the sides of the carriages 'Do you not wish you may get it?'—the allusion being to the Grand Trunk which was then only a thing *in posse*.

And still referring to processions associated in our memory with Court House Square, the recollection of another comes up which once or twice a year used formerly to pass down King Street on a Sunday. The townspeople were familiar enough with the march of the troops of the garrison to and from Church to the sound of military music on Sundays. But on the occasions now referred to the public eye was drawn to a spectacle professedly of an opposite character—to the procession of the 'Children of Peace' so called.

These were a local off-shoot of the Society of Friends, the followers of Mr David Willson, who had his headquarters at Sharon, in Whitchurch [Township,] just north of Newmarket where he had built a 'Temple', a large wooden structure, painted white and resembling a high-piled house of cards.

The following account of the Temple erected by Willson at Sharon is by a visitor to the village in 1835. 'The building', says Mr Patrick Shirreff in his *Tour through North America*, published in Edinburgh in 1835, 'is of wood painted white externally, seventy feet high; and consists of three storeys. The first is sixty feet square, with a door in the centre of each side and three large windows on each side of the door. On two sides there is a representation of the setting sun and the word "Armageddon" inscribed below. The second storey is twenty-seven feet square with three windows on each side; and the third storey nine feet square with one window on each side.

'The corners of each of the storeys are terminated by square lanterns, with gilded mountings; and the termination of the building is a gilded ball of considerable size. The interior was filled with wooden chairs placed round sixteen pillars, in the centre of which is a square cabinet of black walnut with a door and windows on each side. There was a table in the centre of the cabinet covered with black velvet, hung with crimson merino and fringe, in which was deposited a Bible. On the four central pillars were painted the words Faith, Hope, Charity, and Love; and on the twelve others, the names of the Apostles. The central pillars seemed to support the second storey; and at the foot of each was a table covered with green cloth. The house was without ornament, being painted fawn, green and white; and had not a pulpit or place for addressing an audience. It is occupied once a month for collecting charity; and contains 2,952 panes of glass, and is lighted once a year with 116 candles.'

The materials of the frame-work of the Temple were, as we have been told, prepared at a distance from the site, and run rapidly up as far as possible without noise, in imitation of the building of Solomon's Temple. By the side of the principal edifice stood a structure 100 feet by 50 feet, used for ordinary meetings on Sundays. On the first Friday in September [there] used to be an annual feast when the Temple was illuminated. In this was an organ built by Mr Coates of York.[5]

Periodically he [Willson] deemed it proper to make a demonstration in town. His disciples and friends, dressed in their best, mounted their waggons and solemnly passed down Yonge Street, and then on through some frequented thoroughfare of York to a place previously announced where the prophet would preach. His topic was usually 'Public Affairs: their Total Depravity'.

The text of all of Willson's homilies might in effect be the following mystic sentence, extracted from the popular periodical already quoted—*Patrick Swift's Almanac*: 'The backwoodsman, while he lays the axe to the root of the oak in the forests of Canada, should never forget that a base basswood is growing in this his native land, which, if not speedily girdled, will throw its dark shadows over the country, and blast his best exertions. Look up, reader, and you will see the branches—the

---

[5] In the original edition this description of the temple appeared in a chapter called 'Yonge St, Bond's Lake to Holland Landing', pp. 487-8.

Robinson branch, the Powell branch, the Jones branch, the Strachan branch, the Boulton twig, &c.[6] The farmer toils, the merchant toils, the labourer toils, and the Family Compact reap the fruit of their exertions.' (*Almanac* for 1834.)

Into all the points here suggested Mr Willson would enter with great zest. When waxing warm in his discourse, he would sometimes, without interrupting the flow of his words, suddenly throw off his coat and suspend it on a nail or pin in the wall, waving about with freedom, during the residue of his oration, a pair of sturdy arms arrayed not indeed in the dainty lawn of a bishop but in stout, well-bleached American Factory. His address was divided into sections between which 'hymns of his own composing' were sung by a company of females dressed in white, sitting on one side, accompanied by a band of musical instruments on the other.

Considerable crowds assembled on these occasions, and once a panic arose as preaching was going on in the public room of Lawrence's hotel: the joists of the floor were heard to crack, a rush was made to the door, and several leaped out of the windows. A small brick school-house on Berkeley Street was also a place where Willson sometimes sought to get the ear of the general public.

Captain Bonnycastle, in *Canada as it Was, Is, and May Be* [1852], i. 285, thus discourses of David Willson in a strain somewhat too severe and satirical, but his words serve to show opinions which widely prevailed at the time he wrote: 'At a short distance from Newmarket,' the Captain says, 'which is about three miles to the right of Yonge Street, near its termination at the Holland Landing, on a river of that name running into Lake Simcoe, is a settlement of religious enthusiasts, who have chosen the most fertile part of Upper Canada, the country near and for miles round Newmarket, for the seat of their earthly tabernacle. Here numbers of deluded people have placed themselves under the temporal and spiritual charge of a high priest, who calls himself David. His real name is David Willson. The Temple (as the building appropriated to the

---

6 The leading clans of the Family Compact.

celebration of their rites is called), is served by this man, who affects a primitive dress, and has a train of virgin-ministrants clothed in white. He travels about occasionally to preach at towns and villages, in a waggon, followed by others, covered with white tilt-cloths; but what his peculiar tenets are beyond that of dancing and singing, and imitating David the King, I really cannot tell, for it is altogether too farcical to last long: but Mr David seems to understand clearly, as far as the temporal concerns of his infatuated followers go, that the old-fashioned signification of *meum* and *tuum* are religiously centered in his own *sanctum*. It was natural that such a field should produce tares in abundance.'

The following notice of the 'Children of Peace' occurs in *Patrick Swift's Almanac* for 1834, penned, probably, with an eye to votes in the neighbourhood of Sharon, or Hope, as the place is here called. 'This society,' the *Almanac* reports, 'numbers about 280 members in Hope, east of Newmarket. They have also started places of preaching, at the Old Court House, York, on Yonge Street, and at Markham. Their principal speaker is David Willson, assisted by Murdoch McLeod, Samuel Hughes, and others. Their music, vocal and instrumental, is excellent, and their preachers seek no pay from the Governor out of the taxes.'

On week-days Willson was often to be seen, like any other industrious yeoman, driving into town his own waggon loaded with the produce of his farm; dressed in home-spun, as the 'borel folk' of Yonge Street generally were. In the axis of one eye there was a slight divergency.

The expression 'Family Compact', occurring above, borrowed from French and Spanish History, appears also in the *Seventh Report of Grievances* in 1835 where this sentence is to be read: 'The whole system [of conducting Government without a responsible Executive] has so long continued virtually in the same hands, that it is little better than a family compact.'

After the Court House Square came the large area attached to St James' Church, to the memories connected with which we shall presently devote some space; as also to those connected with the region to the north, formerly the playground of the District Grammar School and afterwards transformed into March [Lombard] Street and its purlieus.

At the corner on the south side of King Street, just opposite the Court House, was the clock-and-watch-repairing establishment of Mr. Charles Clinkenbroomer [correctly Klingenbrumer]. To our youthful fancy, the general click and tick usually to be heard in an old-fashioned watchmaker's place of business was in some sort expressed by the name Clinkenbroomer. But in old local lists we observe the orthography of this name to have been Klinkenbrunner, which conveys another idea. Mr Clinkenbroomer's father, we believe, was attached to the army of General Wolfe, at the taking of Quebec.

Across Church Street from Clinkenbroomer's were the wooden buildings already referred to as having remained long in a partially finished state, being the result of a premature speculation. From this point we are induced to turn aside from our direct route for a few moments, attracted by a street which we see a short distance to the south, namely Market Lane, or Colborne Street, as the modern phraseology is.

In this passage was in the olden time the Masonic Hall [c.1822], a wooden building of two storeys. To the young imagination this edifice seemed to possess considerable dignity from being surmounted by a cupola, the first structure in York that ever enjoyed such a distinction. This ornamental appendage supported above the western gable by slender props (intended in fact for the reception of a bell which, so far as our recollection extends, was never supplied) would appear insignificant enough now; but it was the first budding of the architectural ambition of a young town which leads at length to turrets, pinnacles, spires, and domes.

A staircase on the outside led to the upper storey of the Masonic Hall. In this place were held the first meetings of the first Mechanics' Institute [1831-2], organized under the auspices of Moses Fish, a builder of York, and other lovers of knowledge of the olden time. Here were attempted the first popular lectures. Here we remember hearing—certainly some forty years ago—Mr John Fenton read a paper on the manufacture of steel, using diagrams in illustration: one of them showed the magnified edge of a well-set razor, the serrations all sloping in one direction, by which it might be seen, the lecturer remarked, that unless a man, in shaving, imparted to the instrument in his hand a carefully-studied movement, he was likely 'to get into a scrape'. The lower part of the Masonic Hall was for a considerable while used as a school, kept successively by Mr Stewart and Mr Appleton and afterwards by Mr Caldicott.

At the corner of Market Lane, on the north side towards the Market, was Frank's Hotel, an ordinary white frame building. The first theatre of York was extemporized in the ballroom of this house. When fitted up for dramatic purposes, that apartment was approached by a stairway on the outside.

Here companies performed under the management at one time of Mr Archbold; at another of Mr Talbot; at another of Mr Vaughan. The last-named manager, while professionally at York, lost a son by drowning in the bay. We well remember the poignant distress of the father at the grave, and that his head was bound round on the occasion with a white bandage or napkin. Mrs Talbot was a great favourite. She performed the part of Cora in *Pizarro*, and that of Little Pickle in a comedy of that name, if our memory serves us.

Pizarro, Barbarossa or the Siege of Algiers, Ali Baba and the Forty Thieves, The Lady of the Lake, The Miller and his Men were among the pieces here represented. The bodyguard of the Dey of Algiers, we remember, consisted of two men who always came in with military precision just after the hero and placed themselves in a formal manner at fixed distances behind him like two sentries. They were in fact soldiers from the garrison, we think. All this appeared very effective.

The dramatic appliances and accessories at Frank's were of the humblest kind. The dimensions of the stage must have been very limited: the ceiling of the whole room, we know, was low. As for orchestra—in those days the principal instrumental artist of the town was Mr Maxwell who, well remembered for his quiet manner, for the shade over one eye in which was some defect, and for his homely skill on the violin, was generally to be seen and heard, often alone, but sometimes with an associate or two, here, as at all other entertainments of importance, public or private. Nevertheless at that period, to an unsophisticated yet active imagination, innocent of acquaintance with more respectable arrangements, everything seemed charming; each scene, as the bell rang and the baize drew up, was invested with a magical glamour, similar in kind, if not equal in degree, to that which, in the days of our grandfathers, ere yet the modern passion for real knowledge had been awakened, fascinated the young Londoner at Drury Lane.

And how curiously were the illusions of the mimic splendors sometimes in a moment broken, as if to admonish the inexperienced spectator of the facts of real life. In the performance of *Pizarro*, it will be remembered that an attempt is made to bribe a Spanish soldier at his post. He rejects and flings to the ground what is called 'a wedge of massive gold': we recollect the *sound* produced on the boards of the stage in Frank's by the fall of this wedge of massive gold: it instantly betrayed itself by this, as well as by its nimble rebound, to be of course a gilded bit of wood.

It was in the assembly-room at Frank's, dismantled of its theatrical furniture, that a celebrated fancy ball was given on the last day of the year 1827 conjointly by Mr Galt, Commissioner of the Canada Company, and Lady Mary Willis, wife of Mr Justice Willis. On that occasion the general interests of the Company were to some extent studied in the ornamentation of the room, its floor being decorated with an immense representation, in chalks or water-colour, of the arms of the association. The supporters of the shield were of colossal dimensions: two lions rampant bearing flags turning opposite ways: below, on the riband, in characters proportionably large, was the motto of the Company, *Non mutat genus solum*. The sides and ceiling of the room, with the passages leading from the front door to it, were covered throughout with branchlets of the hemlock-spruce; nestling in the greenery of this perfect bower were innumerable little coloured lamps, each containing a floating light.

Here, for once, the potent, grave, and reverend Signors of

York, along with their sons and daughters, indulged in a little insanity. Lady Mary Willis appeared as Mary, Queen of Scots; the Judge himself, during a part of the evening, was in the costume of a gay old lady, the Countess of Desmond, aged one hundred years; Miss Willis, the clever amateur equestrienne, was Folly, with cap and bells; Dr W. W. Baldwin was a Roman senator; his two sons, William and St George, were the Dioscuri, *Fratres Helenæ, lucida Sidera*; his nephew, Augustus Sullivan, was Puss in Boots.

Mr Galt was only about three years in Canada, but this short space of time sufficed to enable him to lay the foundation of the Canada Company wisely and well, as is shewn by its duration and prosperity. The feat was not accomplished without some antagonism springing up between himself and the local governmental authorities, whom he was inclined to treat rather haughtily.

The first Church of St James at York [1807] was a plain structure of wood, placed some yards back from the road. Its gables faced east and west, and its solitary door was at its western end and was approached from Church Street. Its dimensions were 50 feet by 40 feet. The sides of the building were pierced by two rows of ordinary windows, four above and four below. Altogether it was, in its outward appearance, simply, as a contemporary American *Geographical View of the Province of Upper Canada* [1813] now before us describes it, a 'meeting-house for Episcopalians'.

The work just referred to, which was written by a Mr M. Smith before the war of 1812, thus depicts York: 'This village', it says, 'is laid out after the form of Philadelphia, the streets crossing each other at right angles; though the ground on which it stands is not suitable for building. This at present', the notice subjoins, 'is the seat of Government, and the residence of a number of English gentlemen. It contains some fine buildings, though they stand scattering, among which are a Court-house, Council-house, a large brick building, in which the King's store for the place is kept, and a meeting-house for Episcopalians; one printing and other offices.'

The reservation of land in which the primitive St James' Church stood long remained plentifully covered with the original forest.[1] In a wood-cut from a sketch taken early in the present century, prefixed to the *Annals of the Diocese of Toronto*, the building is represented as being in the midst of a great grove, and stumps of various sizes are visible in the foreground.

Up to 1803 the Anglican congregation had assembled for Divine Worship in the Parliament Building; and prior to the appointment of the Rev. Mr Stuart, or in his absence, a layman, Mr Cooper, afterwards the well-known wharfinger, used to read the service. In March 1799 there was about to be a Day of General Thanksgiving. The mode proposed for its solemn observance at York was announced as follows in the *Gazette and Oracle* of March 9: 'Notice is hereby given that Prayers will be read in the North Government Building in this Town, on Tuesday, the 12th instant, being the day appointed for a General Thanksgiving throughout the Province to Almighty God for the late important victories over the enemies of Great Britain. Service to begin half after eleven o'clock.'

We give a contemporary account of the proceedings at an important meeting of the subscribers to the fund for the erection of the first St James' Church at York, in 1803. It is from the *Oracle and Gazette* of January 22 in that year.

'At a Meeting of the subscribers to a fund for erecting a Church in the Town of York, holden at the Government Buildings, on Saturday the 8th day of January instant, the Hon. Chief Justice [Allcock] in the Chair. Resolved unanimously: That each subscriber shall pay the amount of his subscription by three instalments: the first being one moiety in one month from this day; the second being a moiety of the residue in two months; and the remainders in three months: That Mr William Allan and Mr Duncan Cameron shall be Treasurers, and shall receive the amount of the said subscriptions; and that they be jointly and severally answerable for all moneys paid

---

1 The land grant for a church and churchyard was set aside by Peter Russell in 1797.

into their hands upon the receipt of either of them: That His Honour the Chief Justice, the Honourable P. Russell, the Honourable Captain McGill, the Reverend Mr Stuart, Dr Macaulay, Mr Chewett, and the two Treasurers, be a Committee of the subscribers, with full power and authority to apply the moneys arising from subscriptions, to the purpose contemplated: Provided, nevertheless, that if any material difference of opinion should arise among them, resort shall be had to a meeting of the subscribers to decide. That the Church be built of stone, brick, or framed timber, as the Committee may judge most expedient, due regard being had to the superior advantages of a stone or brick building, if not counterbalanced by the additional expense: That eight hundred pounds of lawful money, be the extent upon which the Committee shall calculate their plan; but in the first instance, they shall not expend beyond the sum of six hundred pounds (if the amount of the sums subscribed and paid into the hands of the Treasurers, together with the moneys which may be allowed by the British Government, amount to so much), leaving so much of the work as can most conveniently be dispensed with, to be completed by the remaining two hundred pounds: Provided, however, that the said six hundred pounds be laid out in such manner that Divine Worship can be performed with decency in the Church: That the Committee do request the opinion of Mr Berczy, respecting the probable expenses which will attend the undertaking, and respecting the materials to be preferred; due regard being had to the amount of the fund, as aforesaid; and that after obtaining his opinion, they do advertise their readiness to receive proposals conformable thereto. N.B. The propriety of receiving contributions in labour or materials is suggested to the Committee. A. MAC-DONELL, *Secretary to the Meeting*.'

In the *Gazette and Oracle* of June 4, 1803, D. Cameron and W. Allan are inviting tenders for the supply of certain materials required for 'building a Church in this Town'.

'Advertisement. Wanted. A quantity of Pine Boards and Scantling, Stones and Lime, for building a Church in this Town. Any person inclined to furnish any of these articles will please to give in their proposals at the lowest prices, to the subscribers, to be laid before the Committee. D. CAMERON, W. ALLAN. *York, 1st June, 1803.*'

It would seem that in July the determination was to build the Church of stone.

'On Wednesday last, the 6th instant,' says the *Oracle and Gazette,* July 9th, 1803, 'a meeting of the subscribers to the fund for erecting a Church in this Town was held at the Government Buildings, on which occasion it was unanimously resolved: That the said Church should be built of Stone. That one hundred toises of Stone should accordingly be contracted for without delay. That a quantity of two-inch pine plank, not exceeding 6,000 feet, should also be laid in; and a reasonable quantity of Oak studs, and Oak plank, for the window-frames and sashes.—A future meeting we understand,' the *Oracle* adds, 'will be held in the course of the season, at which, when the different Estimates and Proposals have been examined, and the extent which the fund will reach, has been ascertained, something decisive will be settled.'

The idea of building in stone appears to have been subsequently relinquished; and a Church edifice in wood was decided on. We are informed that the Commandant of the Garrison, Col. Sheaffe, ordered his men to assist in raising the frame.[2]

In 1810 a portion of the Church-plot was enclosed, at an expense of £1 5s. for rails, of which five hundred were required for the purpose. At the same time the ground in front of the west end, where was the entrance, was cleared of stumps at an expense of £3 15s. In that year the cost for heating the building, and charges connected with the Holy Communion, amounted to £1 7s. 6d., Halifax currency.

In 1812 Dr Strachan succeeded Dr Stuart as incumbent of the church; and in 1818 he induced the congregation to effect some alterations in the structure.

On the north and south sides of the old building additional space was enclosed, which brought the axis of the Church and

---

2 Although most of the details of construction provided here date from 1803, the construction of the church was not actually finished until 1807.

its roof into a north and south direction. An entrance was opened at the southern end, towards King Street, and over the gable in this direction was built a square tower bearing a circular bell-turret, surmounted by a small tin-covered spire. The whole edifice, as thus enlarged and improved, was painted of a light blue colour, with the exception of the frames round the windows and doors, and the casings at the angles, imitating blocks of stone, alternately long and short, which were all painted white.

The original western door was not closed up. Its use almost exclusively was now, on Sundays and other occasions of Divine Worship, to admit the Troops, whose benches extended along by the wall on that side the whole length of the Church. The upper windows on all the four sides were now made circular-headed. On the east side there was a difference. The altar-window of the original building remained, only transformed into a kind of triplet, the central compartment rising above the other two, and made circular-headed. On the north and south of this east window were two tiers of lights, as on the western side.

In the bell-turret was a bell of sufficient weight sensibly to jar the whole building at every one of its semi-revolutions.

In the interior a central aisle or open passage led from the door to the southern end of the Church where, on the floor, was situated a pew of state for the Lieutenant-Governor: small square pillars at its four corners sustained a flat canopy over it, immediately under the ceiling of the gallery; and below this distinctive tester or covering, suspended against the wall, were the royal arms emblazoned on a black tablet of board or canvas.

Half-way up the central aisle, on the right side, was an open space in which were planted the pulpit, reading-desk, and clerk's pew in the old orthodox fashion, rising by gradations one above the other, the whole overshadowed by a rather handsome sounding-board sustained partially by a rod from the roof. Behind this mountainous structure was the altar, lighted copiously by the original east window. Two narrow side-aisles, running parallel with the central one, gave access to corresponding rows of pews, each having a numeral painted on its door. Two passages for the same purpose ran westward from the space in front of the pulpit. To the right and left of the Lieuten-ant-Governor's seat, and filling up (with the exception of two square corner pews) the rest of the northern end of the church, were two oblong pews; the one on the west appropriated to the officers of the garrison; the other, on the east, to the members of the Legislature.

Round the north, west, and south sides of the interior ran a gallery divided, like the area below, into pews. This structure was sustained by a row of pillars of turned wood, and from it to the roof above rose another row of similar supports. The ceiling over the parts exterior to the gallery was divided into four shallow semi-circular vaults, which met at a central point. The pews everywhere were painted of a buff or yellowish hue, with the exception of the rims at the top which were black. The pulpit and its appurtenances were white. The rims just re-ferred to, at the tops of the pews, throughout the whole church, exhibited at regular intervals small gimlet-holes: in these were inserted annually at Christmas-tide small sprigs of hemlock-spruce. The interior, when thus dressed, wore a cheerful, re-freshing look in keeping with the festival commemorated.

Within the interior used to assemble, periodically, the little world of York—occasionally a goodly proportion of the little world of all Upper Canada.

To limit ourselves to our own recollections: here, with great regularity, every Sunday was to be seen, passing to and from the place of honour assigned him, Sir Peregrine Maitland—a tall, grave officer, always in military undress; his countenance ever wearing a mingled expression of sadness and benevolence, like that which one may observe on the face of the predecessor of Louis Philippe, Charles the Tenth [King of France, 1824-30], whose current portrait recalls, not badly, the whole head and figure of this early Governor of Upper Canada.

In an outline representation which we accidentally possessed of a panorama of the battle of Waterloo, on exhibition in London, the 1st Foot Guards were conspicuously to be seen led on by 'Major-General Sir Peregrine Maitland'. It was a matter of no small curiosity to the boyish mind, and something that helped to rouse an interest in history generally, to be assured that the living personage here, every week, before the eye, was the commander represented in the panorama; one who had actually passed through the tremendous excitement of the real scene.

With persons of wider knowledge, Sir Peregrine was invested with further associations. Besides being the royal representative in these parts, he was the son-in-law of Charles Gordon Lennox, fourth Duke of Richmond, a name that stirred chivalrous feelings in early Canadians of both Provinces; for the Duke had come to Canada as Governor-in-Chief [1818] with a grand reputation acquired as Lord-Lieutenant of Ireland; and great benefits were expected, and probably would have been realized from his administration, had it been of long continuance. But he had been suddenly removed by an excruciating death. Whilst on a tour of inspection in the Upper Province, he had been fatally attacked with hydrophobia, occasioned by the bite of a pet fox [1819]. The injury had been received at Sorel; its terrible effects were fatally experienced at a place near the Ottawa, since named Richmond.

Some of the prestige of the deceased Duke continued to adhere to Sir Peregrine Maitland, for he had married the Duke's daughter, a graceful and elegant woman who was always at his side, here and at Stamford Cottage across the Lake. She bore a name not unfamiliar in the domestic annals of George the Third who once, it is said, was enamoured of a beautiful Lady Sarah Lennox, grandmother, as we suppose, or some other near relative, of the Lady Sarah here before us at York.[3] Moreover, conversationalists whispered about (in confidence) something supposed to be unknown to the general public—that the match between Sir Peregrine and Lady Sarah had been effected in spite of the Duke. The report was that there had been an elopement; and it was naturally supposed that the party of the sterner sex had been the most active agent in the affair.

To say the truth, however, in this instance, it was the lady who precipitated matters. The affair occurred at Paris [1815], soon after the Waterloo campaign. The Duke's final determination

---

[3] The original Lady Sarah was a great aunt of Lady Sarah Maitland.

against Sir Peregrine's proposals having been announced, the daughter suddenly withdrew from the father's roof and fled to the lodgings of Sir Peregrine, who instantly retired to other quarters. The upshot of the whole thing, at once romantic and unromantic, included a marriage and a reconciliation; and eventually a Lieutenant-Governorship for the son-in-law under the Governorship-in-Chief of the father, both dispatched together to undertake the discharge of vice-regal functions in a distant colony. At the time of his marriage with Lady Sarah Lennox, Sir Peregrine had been for some ten years a widower. On his staff here at York was a son by his first wife, also named Peregrine, a subaltern in the army.

The successor to Sir Peregrine Maitland in the Government of Upper Canada was another distinguished military officer, Sir John Colborne [1828-36]. With ourselves, the first impression of his form and figure is especially associated with the interior in which we are supposing the reader to be now standing. We remember his first passing up the central aisle of St James' Church. He had arrived early, in an unostentatious way; and on coming within the building, he quietly inquired of the first person whom he saw, sitting in a seat near the door: Which was the Governor's pew? The gentleman addressed happened to be Mr Bernard Turquand who, quickly recognizing the inquirer, stood up and extended his right arm and open hand in the direction of the canopied pew over which was suspended the tablet bearing the Royal Arms. Sir John, and some of his family after him, then passed on to the place indicated.

At school, in an edition of Goldsmith then in use, the name of 'Major Colborne' in connection with the account of Sir John Moore's death at Corunna [1809] had already been observed; and it was with us lads a matter of intense interest to learn that the new Governor was the same person.

The scene which was epitomized in the school-book is given at greater length in Gleig's *Lives of Military Commanders* [1831]. The following are some particulars from Colonel Anderson's narrative in that work: 'I met the General', Colonel Anderson says, 'on the evening of the 16th, bringing in, in a blanket and sashes. He knew me immediately, though it was almost dark, squeezed me by the hand and said "Anderson, don't leave me." At intervals he added "Anderson, you know that I have always wished to die in this way. I hope the people of England will be satisfied. I hope my country will do me justice. You will see my friends as soon as you can. Tell them everything. I have made my will, and have remembered my servants. Colborne has my will and all my papers." Major Colborne now came into the room. He spoke most kindly to him; and then said to me, "Anderson, remember you go to—, and tell him it is my request, and that I expect, he will give Major Colborne a lieutenant-colonelcy." He thanked the surgeons for their trouble. He pressed my hand close to his body, and in a few minutes died without a struggle.'

He had been struck by a cannon ball. The shot, we are told, had completely crushed his shoulder; the arm was hanging by a piece of skin, and the ribs over the heart, besides being broken, were literally stripped of flesh. Yet, the narrative adds, 'he sat upon the field collected and unrepining, as if no ball had struck him, and as if he were placed where he was for the mere purpose of reposing for a brief space from the fatigue of hard riding.'

Sir John Colborne himself afterwards at Ciudad Rodrigo [1812] came within a hair's-breadth of a similar fate. His right shoulder was shattered by a cannon shot. The escape of the right arm from amputation on the field at the hands of some prompt military surgeon on that occasion was a marvel. The limb was saved, though greatly disabled. The want of symmetry in Sir John Colborne's tall and graceful form, permanently occasioned by this injury, was conspicious to the eye. We happened to be present in the Council Chamber at Quebec in 1838 at the moment when this noble-looking soldier literally vacated the vice-regal chair and installed his successor Lord Durham in it, after administering to him the oaths.[4] The exchange was not for the better in a scenic point of view, although the features

---

4 Colborne was acting governor, in addition to his duties as commander-in-chief, both before and after Durham's brief governorship.

of Lord Durham, as his well-known portrait shews, were very fine, suggestive of the poet or artist.

Of late years a monument has been erected on Mount Wise at Plymouth in honour of the illustrious military chief and pre-eminently excellent man whose memory has just been recalled to us. It is a statue of bronze, by Adams, a little larger than life; and the likeness is admirably preserved. (When seen on horse-back at parades or reviews soldiers always averred that he greatly resembled 'the Duke'. Dr Henry, in *Trifles from my Portfolio*, thus wrote of him in 1833: 'When we first dined at Government House, we were struck by the strong resemblance he bore to the Duke of Wellington; and there is also', Dr Henry continues, 'a great similarity in mind and disposition, as well as in the lineaments of the face. In one particular they harmonize perfectly—namely, great simplicity of character, and an utter dislike to shew ostentation.')

On the four sides of the granite pedestal of the statue on Mount Wise are to be read the following inscriptions: in front JOHN COLBORNE, BARON SEATON. BORN MDCCLXXVIII. DIED MDCCCL-XIII. On the right side: CANADA. IONIAN ISLANDS. On the left side: PENINSULA. WATERLOO. On the remaining side: IN MEMORY OF THE DISTINGUISHED CAREER AND STAINLESS CHARACTER OF FIELD MARSHAL LORD SEATON, G.C.B., G.C.M.G., G.C.H. THIS MONU-MENT IS ERECTED BY HIS FRIENDS AND COMRADES.

Accompanying the family of Sir John Colborne to their place in the Church at York was to be seen every Sunday for some time a shy-mannered, black-eyed, Italian-featured Mr Jeune, tutor to the Governor's sons. This was afterwards the eminent Dr Jeune, Master of Pembroke College at Oxford, a great pro-moter of reform in that University, and Bishop of Peterborough. Sir John himself was a man of scholarly tastes, a great student of history, and a practical modern European linguist.

On Lord Seaton's [Colborne's] departure from Canada, he was successively Lord High Commissioner of the Ionian Islands and Commander-in-Chief in Ireland. He then retired to his own estate in the West of England where he had a beautiful seat in the midst of the calm, rural, inland scenery of Devonshire, not far from Plympton and on the slope descending southward from

the summits of Dartmoor. The name of the house is Beechwood
from the numerous clean, bold, magnificent beech trees that
adorn its grounds and give character to the neighbourhood
generally. In the adjoining village of Sparkwell he erected a
handsome schoolhouse and church.

On his decease at Torquay in 1863 his remains were deposited
in the Church at Newton Ferrers, the ancient family burying-
place of the Yonges.

Mrs Jameson's words in her *Winter Studies and Summer
Rambles* express briefly but truly the report which all that
remember him would give of this distinguished and ever memorable Governor of Canada. 'Sir John Colborne,' she says incidentally, in the Introduction to the work just named, 'whose
mind appeared to me cast in the antique mould of chivalrous
honour; and whom I never heard mentioned in either Province
but with respect and veneration.' Dr Henry in *Trifles from my
Portfolio*, once before referred to, uses similar language. 'I believe', he says, 'there never was a soldier of more perfect moral
character than Sir John Colborne.' The title 'Seaton', we may
add, was taken from the name of an ancient seaport town of
Devon, the Moridunum of the Roman period.

At the southern end of the Church, in which we are supposing
ourselves to be, opposite the Lieutenant-Governor's pew but
aloft in the gallery immediately over the central entrance underneath, was the pew of Chief Justice Powell, a long narrow enclosure with a high screen at its back to keep off the draughts
from the door into the gallery just behind. The whole of the
inside of the pew, together with the screen by which it was
backed, was lined with dark green baize or cloth. The Chief's
own particular place in the pew was its central point. There, as
in a focus, surrounded by the members of his family, he calmly
sat, with his face to the north, his white head and intelligent
features well brought out by the dark background of the screen
behind.

The spectator, on looking up and recognizing the presence
of the Chief Justice thus seated, involuntarily imagined himself,
for the moment, to be in court. In truth, in an absent moment

the Judge himself might experience some confusion as to his whereabouts. For below him, on his right and left, he would see many of the barristers, attorneys, jurors, and witnesses (to go no farther) who on weekdays were to be seen or heard before him in different compartments of the courtroom.

Chief Justice Powell was of Welsh descent. The name is, of course, Ap Howell, of which 'Caer Howell', 'Howell's Place', the title given by the Chief Justice to his park-lot at York, is a relic. His portrait exists in Toronto in possession of members of his family. He was a man of rather less than the ordinary stature. His features were round in outline, unmarked by the painful lines which usually furrow the modern judicial visage but wakefully intelligent. His hair was milky white. The head was inclined to be bald.

In the body of the Church below sat another Chief Justice, retired from public life [1816], and infirm—Mr Scott, the immediate predecessor of Chief Justice Powell, a white-haired, venerable form assisted to his place a little to the south of the Governor's pew every Sunday. We have already once before referred to Mr Scott.

And again, another judicial personage was here every week long to be seen, also crowned with the snowy honours of advanced age: Mr Justice Campbell, afterwards, in succession to Chief Justice Powell, Chief Justice Sir William Campbell. His place was on the west side of the central aisle. Sir William Campbell was born as far back as 1758. He came out from Scotland as a soldier in a Highland regiment and was taken prisoner at Yorktown when that place was surrendered by Cornwallis in 1781. In 1783 he settled in Nova Scotia and studied law. After practising as a barrister for nineteen years he was appointed Attorney-General for the Island of Cape Breton, from which post, after twelve years, he was promoted to a Judgeship in Upper Canada. This was in 1811. Fourteen years afterwards (in 1825) he became Chief Justice.

The funeral of Sir William Campbell in 1834 was one of unusual impressiveness. The Legislature was in session at the time and attended in a body, with the Bar and the Judges. At the same hour, within the walls of the same Church, St James', the obsequies of a member of the Lower House took place, namely, of Mr Roswell Mount, representative of the County of Middlesex, who had chanced to die at York during the session. A funeral oration on the two-fold occasion was pronounced by Archdeacon Strachan.

Dr Henry, author of *Trifles from my Portfolio*, attended Sir William Campbell in his last illness. In the work just named, his case is thus described: 'My worthy patient became very weak towards the end of the year,' the doctor says, 'his nights were restless—his appetite began to fail, and he could only relish tit bits. Medicine was tried fruitlessly, so his doctor prescribed snipes. At the point of the sandy peninsula opposite the barracks,' Dr Henry continues, 'are a number of little pools and marshes, frequented by these delectable little birds; and here I used to cross over in my skiff and pick up the Chief Justice's panacea. On this delicate food the poor old gentleman was supported for a couple of months; but the frost set in—the snipes flew away, and Sir William died.'

Appended to the account of the funeral ceremonies, in the York *Courier* of the day, we notice one of those familiar paragraphs which sensational itemists like to construct and which stimulate the self-complacency of small communities. It is headed LONGEVITY, and then thus proceeds: 'At the funeral of the late Sir W. Campbell, on Monday, there were twenty inhabitants of York, whose united ages exceed fourteen hundred and fifty years!'

It is certain that there were to be seen moving up the aisles of the old wooden St James' at York every Sunday a striking number of venerable and dignified forms. For one thing their costume helped to render them picturesque and interesting. The person of our immediate ancestors was well set off by their dress. Recall their easy partially cut-away black coats and upright collars; their so-called small-clothes and buckled shoes; the frilled shirt-bosoms and the white cravats—not apologies for cravats but real envelopes for the neck. (The comfortable, well-to-do Quaker of the old school still exhibits in use some of their homely peculiarities of garb.) And then remember the cut and arrangement of their hair, generally milky white, either from age or by the aid of powder; their smoothly-shaven cheek and chin, and the peculiar expression superinduced in the eye and the whole countenance by the governing ideas of the period, ideas which we are wont to style old-fashioned but which furnished, nevertheless, for the time being, very useful and definite rules of conduct.

From amongst the venerable heads and ancestral forms which recur to us as we gaze down in imagination from the galleries of the old wooden St James' of York, we will single out, in addition to those already spoken of, that of Mr Ridout, sometime Surveyor-General of the Province [1810-29], father of a numerous progeny, and tribal head, so to speak, of more than one family of connections settled here bearing the same name. He was a fine typical representative of the group to which our attention is directed. He was a perfect picture of a cheerful, benevolent-minded Englishman; of portly form, well advanced in years, his hair snowy-white naturally; his usual costume of the antique style above described.

Then there was Mr Small, Clerk of the Crown, an Englishman of similar stamp. We might sketch the rest separately as they rise before the mind's eye, but we should probably, after all, convey an idea of each that would be too incomplete to be interesting or of much value. We therefore simply name other members of the remarkable group of reverend seniors that assembled habitually in the church at York. Mr Justice [D'Arcy] Boulton [Sr], Colonel [Samuel] Smith, sometime President [Administrator] of the Province [1817-18]; Mr Allan, Mr Mc-Gill, Mr Crookshank, Colonel Givins, Major Heward, Colonel Wells, Colonel FitzGibbon, Mr Dunn, Dr Macaulay, Dr Baldwin, Dr Lee, Mr Samuel Ridout, Mr Chewett, Mr MacNab (Sir Allan's father); Mr Stephen Jarvis, who retained to the last the ancient fashion of tying the hair in a queue.

We might go on with several others, also founders of families that still largely people York and its vicinity; we might mention old Captain Playter, Captain Denison, Mr Scarlett, Captain Brooke senior, and others. Filial duty would urge us not to omit, in the enumeration, one [John Scadding] who, though at a very early period removed by a sudden casualty [1824], is vividly re-

membered not only as a good and watchful father but also as a
venerable form harmonizing perfectly in expression and costume with the rest of the group which used to gather in the
church at York.

Of course, mingled with the ancients of the congregation,
there was a due proportion of a younger generation. There was
for example Mr Simon Washburn, a bulky and prosperous barrister, afterwards Clerk of the Peace, who was the first, perhaps,
in these parts to carry a glass adroitly in the eye. There was Dr
Grant Powell, a handsome reproduction on a larger scale of
his father the Chief, as his portrait shews; there were the Messrs
Monro, George and John; the Messrs Stanton; Mr Billings; the
Messrs Gamble, John and William; Mr J. S. Baldwin, Mr Lyons,
Mr Beikie, and others—all men of note, distinguishable from
each other by individual traits and characteristics that might
readily be sketched.

And lastly in the interstices of the assemblage was to be seen
a plentiful representation of generation number three—young
men and lads of good looks, for the most part, well set-up limbs,
and quick faculties; in some instances, of course, of fractious
temperament and manners. As ecclesiastical associations are at
the moment uppermost, we note an ill habit that prevailed
among some of these younglings of the flock of loitering long
about the doors of the church for the purpose of watching the
arrivals, and then, when the service was well advanced, the
striplings would be seen sporadically coming in, each one
imagining, as he passed his fingers through his hair and marched
with a shew of manly spirit up the aisle, that he attracted a
degree of attention—attracted, perhaps, a glance of admiration
from some of the many pairs of eyes that rained influence from
a large pew in the eastern portion of the north gallery where
the numerous school of Miss Purcell and Miss Rose held a
commanding position.

It would have been a singular exception to a general law had
the interior into which we are now gazing, and whose habitués
we are now recalling, not been largely frequented by the feminine portion of society at York. Seated in their places in various
directions along the galleries and in the body of the old wooden

church were to be regularly seen specimens of the venerable great-grandmammas of the old English and Scottish type (in one or two instances to be thought of to this day with a degree of awe by reason of the vigour, almost masculine, of their character); specimens of kindly maiden aunts; specimens of matronly wives and mothers keeping watch and ward over bevies of comely daughters and nieces.

Lady Sarah Maitland herself cannot be called a fixed member of society here, but having been for so long a time a resident, it seems now, in the retrospect, as if she had been really a development of the place. Her distinguished style, native to herself, had its effect on her contemporaries of the gentler sex in these parts. Mrs Dunn, also, and Mrs Wells may likewise be named as special models of grace and elegance in person and manner. In this all-influential portion of the community, a tone and air that were good prevailed widely from the earliest period.

It soon became a practice with the military, and other temporary sojourners attached to the Government, to select partners for life from the families of York. Hence it has happened that, to this day, in England, Ireland and Scotland, and in the dependencies of the Empire on the other side of the globe, many are the households that rise up and call a daughter of Canada blessed as their maternal head.

Local aspirants to the holy estate were thus unhappily, now and then, to their great disgust, baulked of their first choice. But a residue was always left sufficient for the supply of the ordinary demand, and manifold were the interlacings of local connections; a fact in which there is nothing surprising and nothing to be condemned: it was from political considerations alone that such affinities came afterwards to be referred to, in some quarters, with bitterness.

Occasionally, indeed, a fastidious young man, or a disappointed widower, would make a selection in parts remote from the home circle quite unnecessarily. We recall especially to mind the sensible emotion in the congregation of the first advent amongst them of a fair bride from Montreal, the then Paris of Canada; and several lesser excitements of the same class on the appearance in their midst of aerial veils and orange blossoms from Lobo, from New York, from distant England. Once the selection of a 'helpmeet' from a rival religious communion, in the town of York itself, led to the defection from the flock of a prominent member [1833]; an occurrence that led also to the publication of two polemical pamphlets, which made a momentary stir—one of them a declamation by a French bishop, the other a review of the same by the pastor of the abandoned flock.[5]

The strictures on the intelligence and moral feeling of the feminine as well as the masculine portion of society at York, delivered by such world-experienced writers as Mrs Jameson and such enlightened critics as were two or three of the later Governors' wives, may have been just in the abstract, to a certain extent, as from the point of view of old communities in England and Germany; but they were unfair as from the point of view of persons calmly reviewing all the circumstances of the case. Here again the maxim applies: *Tout comprendre, c'est tout pardonner.*

We have said that the long pew on the west side of the Governor's seat was alloted to the military. In this compartment we remember often scanning with interest the countenance and form of a youthful and delicate-looking ensign simply because he bore, hereditarily, a name and title all complete, distinguished in the annals of science two centuries ago—the Hon. Robert Boyle: he was one of the aides-de-camp of Sir Peregrine Maitland. Here also was to be seen for a time a Major Browne, a brother of the formerly popular poetess, Mrs Hemans. Here too sat a Zachary Mudge, another hereditary name complete, distinguished in the scientific annals of Devonshire. He was an officer of Artillery and one of Sir John Colborne's aides-de-camp; for some unexplained reason he committed suicide at York and his remains were deposited in the old military burying-ground. In this pew familiar forms were also—Major Powell,

---

[5] The 'defector' was John Elmsley, son of the chief justice and one of the wealthiest men in the city. To explain his conversion to Catholicism he published some observations of the Bishop of Strasbourg, and Strachan replied with *The Poor Man's Preservative against Popery* (1834).

Capt. Grubbe, Major Hillier, Capt. Blois, Capt. Phillpott, brother of the Bishop [of Worcester].

The compartment on the east side of the Governor's pew was, as we have said, appointed for the use of the members of the Legislature when in session. Here at certain periods, generally in mid-winter, were to be observed all the political notabilities of the day; for at the period we are glancing at, non-conformists as well as conformists were to be seen assisting now and again at public worship in St James' Church.

In their places here the outward presentments of Col. Nichol (killed by driving over the precipice at Queenston), of Mr Horner (a Benjamin Franklin style of countenance), of Dr Lefferty, of Hamnet Pinhey, of Mahlon Burwell, of Absalom Shade, of other owners of old Canadian names, are well remembered. The spare, slender figure of Mr Speaker Sherwood, afterwards a judge of the King's Bench, was noticeable. Mr Chisholm of Oakville used facetiously to object to the clause in the Litany where 'heresy and schism' are deprecated, it so happening that the last term was usually, by a Scotticism, read 'Chisholm'. Up to the Parliamentary pew we have seen Mr William Lyon Mackenzie himself hurriedly make his way with an air of great animation and take his seat to the visible, but of course repressed, disconcertment of several honourable members and others.

Altogether it was a very complete little world, this assemblage within the walls of the old wooden church at York. There were present, so to speak, king, lords, and commons; gentle and simple in due proportion, with their wives and little ones; judges, magistrates, and gentry; representatives of governmental departments, with their employees; legislators, merchants, tradespeople, handicraftsmen; soldiers and sailors—a great variety of class and character.

All seemed to be in harmony, real or conventional, here; whatever feuds, family or political, actually subsisted, no very marked symptoms thereof could be discerned in this place. But the history of all was known, or supposed to be known, to each. The relationship of each to each was known, and how it was brought about. It was known to all how every little scar, every trivial mutilation or disfigurement, which chanced to be visible on the visage or limb of any one, was acquired, in the performance of what boyish freak, in the execution of what practical jest, in the excitement of what convivial or other occasion.

Here and there sat one who, in obedience to the social code of the day, had been 'out' for the satisfaction, as the term was, of himself or another, perhaps a quondam friend—satisfaction obtained (let the age be responsible for the terms we use), in more than one instance, at the cost of human life.

It is beginning, perhaps, to be thought preposterous that we have not as yet said anything of the occupants of the pulpit and desk in our account of this church interior. We are just about to supply the deficiency.

Here was to be seen and heard, at his periodical visits, Charles James Stewart, the second Bishop of Quebec, a man of saintly character and presence; long a missionary in the Eastern Townships of Lower Canada before his appointment to the Episcopate. The contour of his head and countenance, as well as something of his manner even, may be gathered from a remark of the late Dr Primrose of Toronto who, while a stranger, had happened to drop in at the old wooden church when Bishop Stewart was preaching: 'I just thought', the doctor said, 'it was the old King in the pulpit!' i.e., George III.

Here Dr Okill Stuart, formerly rector of this church [1801-11] but subsequently of St George's, Kingston, used occasionally, when visiting York, to officiate—a very tall, benevolent, and fine featured ecclesiastic with a curious delivery characterized by unexpected elevations and depressions of the voice irrespective of the matter, accompanied by long closings of the eyes, and then a sudden re-opening of the same. Whenever this preacher ascended the pulpit, one member of the congregation, Mr George Duggan, who had had, it was understood, some trivial disagreement with the doctor during his incumbency in former years, was always expected by on-lookers to rise and walk out. And this he accordingly always did. The movement seemed a regular part of the programme of the day, and never occasioned any sensation.

Here the Rev. Joseph Hudson officiated now and then, a military chaplain appointed at a comparatively late period to this post; a clergyman greatly beloved by the people of the town generally, both as a preacher and as a man. He was the first officiating minister we ever saw wearing the academical hood over the ordinary vestment.

Here, during the sittings of Parliament, of which he was chaplain, Mr [Robert] Addison of Niagara was sometimes to be heard. The Library of this scholarly divine of the old school was presented by him *en bloc* to St Mark's Church, Niagara [-on-the-Lake], of which he was incumbent [1792-1829]. It remained for some years at 'Lake View', the private residence of Mr Addison; but during the incumbency of Dr McMurray it has been removed to the rectory-house at Niagara where it is to continue, in accordance with the first rector's will, for the use of the incumbent for the time being.

It is a remarkable collection, as exhibiting the line of reading of a thoughtful and intelligent man of the last century: many treatises and tracts of contemporary but now defunct interest not elsewhere to be met with, probably, in Canada are therein preserved. The volumes for the most part retain their serviceable bindings of old pane-sided calf; but some of them, unfortunately, bear marks of the havoc made by damp and vermin before their transfer to their present secure place of shelter. Mr Addison used to walk to and from Church in his canonicals in the old-fashioned way, recalling the Johnsonian period when clergy very generally wore the cassock and gown in the streets.

Another chaplain to the Legislative Assembly was Mr William Macaulay, a preacher always listened to with a peculiar attention whenever he was to be heard in the pulpit here. Mr Macaulay was a member of the Macaulay family settled at Kingston. He had been sent to Oxford where he pursued his studies without troubling himself about a degree. While there he acquired the friendship of several men afterwards famous, especially of Whately, sometime Archbishop of Dublin, with whom a correspondence was maintained.

One more chaplain of the House may be named, frequently

heard and seen in this church—Dr Thomas Phillips, another divine, well read, of a type that has now disappeared. His personal appearance was very clerical in the old-fashioned sense. He was one of the last wearers of hair powder in these parts. In reading the Creed he always endeavoured to conform to the old English custom of turning towards the east; but to do this in the desk of the old church was difficult.

Dr Phillips was formerly of Whitchurch in Herefordshire. He died in 1849, age 68, at Weston on the Humber where he founded and organized the parish of St Philip. His body was borne to its last resting-place by old pupils. We once had in our possession a pamphlet entitled 'The Canadian Remembrancer, a Loyal Sermon, preached on St George's Day, April 23, 1826, at the Episcopal Church (York), by the Rev. T. Phillips, D.D., Head Master of the Grammar School. Printed at the *Gazette* Office.'

There remains to be noticed the 'pastor and master' of the whole assemblage customably gathered together in St James' Church—Dr John Strachan. On this spot, in successive edifices, each following the other in rapid succession and each surpassing the other in dignity and propriety of architectural style, he, for more than half a century, was the principal figure [1812-67].

The story of his career is well known, from his departure from Scotland, a poor but spirited youth in 1799 to his decease in 1867 as first Bishop of Toronto, with its several intermediate stages of activity and promotion. His outward aspect and form are also familiar from the numerous portraits of him that are everywhere to be seen. In stature slightly under the medium height, with countenance and head of the type of Milton's in middle age, without eloquence, without any extraordinary degree of originality of mind, he held together here a large congregation, consisting of heterogeneous elements, by the strength and moral force of his personal character. Qualities innate to himself—decisiveness of intellect, firmness, a quick insight into things and men, with a certain fertility of resource—conspired to win for him the position which he filled, and enabled him to retain it with ease; to sustain, with a graceful and unassuming dignity, all the augmentations which naturally accumulated round it, as the community, of which he was so vital a part, grew and widened and rose to a higher and higher level, on the swelling tide of the general civilization of the continent.

In all his public ministrations he was to be seen officiating without affectation in manner or style. A stickler in ritual would have declared him indifferent to minutiæ. He wore the white vesture of his office with an air of negligence, and his doctor's robe without any special attention to its artistic adjustment upon his person. A technical precisian in modern popular theology would pronounce him out now and then in his doctrine. What he seemed especially to drive at was not dogmatic accuracy so much as a well-regulated life, in childhood, youth, and manhood. The good sense of the matter delivered—and it was never destitute of that quality—was solely relied on for the results to be produced: the topics of modern controversy never came up in his discourse. At the period to which we refer they were in most quarters dormant, their re-awakening deferred until the close of a thirty years' peace, but then destined to set mankind by the ears when now relieved from the turmoil of physical and material war, but roused to great intellectual activity.

Many a man that dropped in during the time of public worship inclined from prejudice to be captious, inclined even to be merry over certain national peculiarities of utterance and diction which to a stranger for a time made the matter delivered not easy to be understood, went out with quite a different sentiment in regard to the preacher and his words.

In the early days of Canada, a man of capacity was called upon, as we have seen in other instances, to play many parts. It required tact to play them all satisfactorily. In the case of Dr Strachan—the voice that today would be heard in the pulpit, offering counsel and advice as to the application of sacred principles to life and conduct, in the presence of all the civil functionaries of the country, from Sir Peregrine Maitland to Mr Chief Constable Higgins; from Chief Justice Powell to the usher of his court, Mr Thomas Phipps; from Mr Speaker Sherwood or MacLean to Peter Shaver, Peter Perry, and the other popular representatives of the Commons in Parliament—the voice that today would be heard in the desk leading liturgically the devotions of the same mixed multitude, tomorrow was to be heard by portions, large or small, of the same audience, amidst very different surroundings, in other quarters; by some of them, for example, at the Executive Council Board, giving a lucid judgement on a point of governmental policy, or in the Chamber of the Legislative Assembly delivering a studied oration on a matter touching the interests and well-being of the whole population of the country, or reading an elaborate original report on the same or some cognate question, to be put forth as the judgement of a committee. Or elsewhere the same voice might be heard at a meeting for patriotic purposes—at the meeting of a Hospital, Educational, or other important secular Trust; at an emergency meeting when sudden action was needed on the part of the charitable and benevolent.

Without fail that voice would be heard by a large portion of the juniors of the flock on the following day amidst the busy commotion of School, apportioning tasks, correcting errors, deciding appeals, regulating discipline; at one time formally instructing, at another jocosely chaffing, the sons and nephews of nearly all the well-to-do people, gentle and simple, of York and Upper Canada.

To have done all this without awkwardness shews the possession of much prudence and tact. To have had all this go on for some decades without any blame that was intended to be taken in very serious earnest; nay, winning in the process applause and gratitude on the right hand and on the left—this argues the existence of something very sterling in the man.

Nor let us local moderns, whose lot it is to be part and parcel of a society no longer rudimentary, venture to condemn one who while especially appointed to be a conspicuous minister of religion, did not decline the functions, diverse and multiform, which an infant society, discerning the qualities inherent in him and lacking instruments for its uses, summoned him to undertake.[6] Let no modern caviller, we say, do this, unless he

---

[6] Scadding is here excusing the leading role Strachan played in all parts of the government and administration, particularly during the 1820s.

is prepared to avow the opinion that to be a minister of religion, a man must of necessity be only partially developed in mind and spirit, incapable, as a matter of course, of offering an opinion of value on subjects of general human interest.

The long possession of unchallenged authority within the immediate area of his ecclesiastical labours rendered Dr Strachan for some time opposed to the projects that began, as the years rolled on, to be mooted for additional churches in the town of York. He could not readily be induced to think otherwise than as the Duke of Wellington thought in regard to Reform in the representation, or as ex-Chancellor Eldon thought in regard to greater promptitude in Chancery decisions, that there was no positive need of change.

'Would you break up the congregation?' was the sharp rejoinder to the early propounders of schemes for Church-extension in York. But as years passed over, and the imperious pressure of events and circumstances was felt, this reluctance gave way.[7] The beautiful cathedral mother-church, into which, under his own eye and through his own individual energy the humble wooden edifice of 1807 at length, by various gradations, developed, forms now a fitting mausoleum for his mortal remains—a stately monument to one who was here in his day the human mainspring of so many vitally-important and far-reaching movements.[8]

Other memorials in his honour have been projected and thought of. One of them we record for its boldness and originality and fitness, although we have no expectation that the æsthetic feeling of the community will soon lead to the practical adoption of the idea thrown out. The suggestion has been this: that in honour of the deceased Bishop there should be erected in some public place in Toronto an exact copy of Michelangelo's 'Moses', to be executed at Rome for the purpose and shipped hither. The conception of such a form of monument is due to

---

[7] In the 1840s three Anglican churches were founded in the Toronto area: 'Little' Trinity, 1843; St George the Martyr, 1844; and Holy Trinity, 1847.

[8] Bishop Strachan, the Rev. H. J. Grasett, first Dean of Toronto, and Mrs Grasett are all buried in a vault under the high altar.

the Rev. W. Macaulay of Picton. We need not say what dignity would be given to the whole of Toronto by the possession of such a memorial object within its precincts as this, and how great in all future time would be the effect, morally and educationally, when the symbolism of the art-object was discovered and understood. Its huge bulk, its boldly-chiselled and only partially-finished limbs and drapery, raised aloft on a plain pedestal of some Laurentian rock, would represent, not ill, the man whom it would commemorate—the character, roughly-outlined and incomplete in parts but, when taken as a whole, very impressive and even grand, which looms up before us, whichever way we look, in our local Past.

One of the things that ennoble the old cities of continental Europe and give them their own peculiar charm is the existence of such objects in their streets and squares, at once works of art for the general eye and memorials of departed worth and greatness. With what interest, for example, does the visitor gaze on the statue of Gutenberg at Mainz; and at Marseilles on that of the good Bishop Belzunce!—of whom we read that he was at once 'the founder of a college, and a magistrate, almoner, physician and priest to his people.' The space in front of the west porch of the cathedral of St James' would be an appropriate site for such a noble memorial-object as that which Mr Macaulay suggests—just at the spot where was the entrance, the one sole humble portal, of the structure of wood out of which the existing pile has grown.[9]

Our notice of the assembly usually to be seen within the walls of the primitive St James' would not be complete were we to omit all mention of Mr John Fenton, who for some time officiated therein as parish clerk. During the palmy days of parish clerks in the British Islands, such functionaries, deemed at the time locally as indispensable as the parish minister himself, were a very peculiar class of men. He was a rarity amongst them who could repeat in a rational tone and manner the responses delegated to him by the congregation. This arose from the circumstance that he was usually an all but illiterate village

---

[9] A Gothic war memorial now occupies the suggested site.

rustic, or narrow-minded small-townsman, brought into a prominence felt on all sides to be awkward.

Mr Fenton's peculiarities, on the contrary, arose from his intelligence, his acquirements, and his independence of character. He was a rather small shrewd-featured person, at a glance not deficient in self-esteem. He was a proficient in modern popular science, a ready talker and lecturer. Being only a proxy, his rendering of the official responses in church was marked perhaps by a little too much individuality, but it could not be said that it was destitute of a certain rhetorical propriety of emphasis and intonation. Though not gifted in his own person with much melody of voice, his acquisitions included some knowledge of music. In those days congregational psalmody was at a low ebb, and the small choirs that offered themselves fluctuated, and now and then vanished wholly. Not unfrequently Mr Fenton, after giving out the portion of Brady and Tate which it pleased him to select, would execute the whole of it as a solo to some accustomed air with graceful variations of his own. All this would be done with great coolness and apparent self-satisfaction.

While the discourse was going on in the pulpit above him, it was his way, often, to lean himself resignedly back in a corner of his pew and throw a white cambric handkerchief over his head and face. It illustrates the spirit of the day to add that Mr Fenton's employment as official mouth-piece to the congregation of the English Church did not stand in the way of his making himself useful at the same time as a class-leader among the Wesleyan Methodists.

The temperament and general style of this gentleman did not fail of course to produce irritation of mind in some quarters. The *Colonial Advocate* [or its editor, William Lyon Mackenzie] one morning averred its belief that Mr Fenton had, on the preceding Sunday, glanced at itself and its patrons in giving out and singing (probably as a solo) the Twelfth Psalm: 'Help, Lord, for good and godly men do perish and decay; and faith and truth from worldly men are parted clean away; whoso doth with his neighbour talk, his talk is all but vain; for every man bethinketh now to flatter, lie and feign!' Mr Fenton after-

wards removed to the United States, where he obtained Holy
Orders in the Episcopal Church. His son was a clever and ingenious youth. We remember a capital model in wood of 'Cæsar's
Bridge over the Rhine' constructed by him from a copper-plate
engraving in an old edition of the *Commentaries* used by him in
the Grammar School at York.

The predecessor of Mr Fenton in the clerk's desk was Mr
Hetherington—a functionary of the old-country village stamp.
His habit was, after giving out a psalm, to play the air on a
bassoon; and then to accompany with fantasias on the same
instrument such vocalists as felt inclined to take part in the
singing. This was the day of small things in respect of ecclesiastical music at York. A choir from time to time had been
formed. Once, we have understood, two rival choirs were heard
on trial in the Church; one of them strong in instrumental resources, having the aid of a bass-viol, clarionet, and bassoon; the
other more dependent on its vocal excellencies. The instrumental choir triumphantly prevailed, as we are assured, and in
1819 an allowance of £20 was made to Mr Hetherington for
giving instruction in church music. One of the principal en-
couragers of the vocalist party was Dr Burnside. But all ex-
pedients for doing what was, in reality, the work of the congregation itself were unreliable, and the clerk or choir-master
too often found himself a solitary performer. Mr Hetherington's bassoon, however, may be regarded as the harbinger and
foreshadow of the magnificent organ presented in after-times
to the congregation of the 'Second Temple' of St James' by Mr
Dunn—a costly and fine-toned instrument (presided over for a
short time by the eminent Dr Hodges, subsequently of Trinity
Church, New York) but destined to be destroyed by fire, together
with the whole church after only two years of existence in 1839.

In the conflagration of 1839 another loss occurred, not so
much to be regretted; we refer to the destruction of a very large
triplet window of stained glass over the altar of the church containing three life-size figures by Mr Craig, a local 'historical and
ornamental painter', not well skilled in the ecclesiastical style.
As home-productions, however, these objects were tenderly
eyed; but Mrs Jameson in her work on Canada cruelly de-

nounced them as being 'in a vile tawdry taste'. Conceive, in the presence of these three Craigs, the critical authoress of the *History of Sacred and Legendary Art* accustomed, in the sublime cathedrals of Europe, to

> *See the great windows like the jewell'd gates*
> *Of Paradise, burning with harmless fire.*

Mr Dunn, named above as donor of an organ to the second St James', had provided the previous wooden church with Communion Plate. In the *Loyalist* of March 1, 1828, we read: 'The undersigned acknowledges the receipt of £112. 18. 5 from the Hon. John Henry Dunn, being the price of a superb set of Communion Plate presented by him to St James' Church at this place. J. B. MACAULAY, *Church Warden, York, 23rd Feb. 1828.*'

Before leaving St James' Church and its precincts, it may be well to give some account of the steps taken in 1818 for the enlargement of the original building. This we are enabled to do, having before us an all but contemporary narrative. It will be seen that great adroitness was employed in making the scheme acceptable, and that pains were shrewdly taken to prevent a burdensome sense of self-sacrifice on the part of the congregation. At the same time a pleasant instance of voluntary liberality is recorded. 'A very respectable church was built at York in the Home District, many years ago'—the narrative referred to, in the *Christian Recorder* for 1819, p. 214, proceeds to state— 'which at that time accommodated the inhabitants; but for some years past, it has been found too small, and several attempts were made to enlarge and repair it. At length, in April 1818, in a meeting of the whole congregation, it was resolved to enlarge the church, and a committee was appointed to suggest the most expeditious and economical method of doing it. The committe reported that a subscription in the way of loan, to be repaid when the seats were sold, was the most promising method. No subscription to be taken under twenty-five pounds, payable in four instalments.

'Two gentlemen', the narrative continues, 'were selected to carry the subscription paper round; and in three hours from twelve to thirteen hundred pounds were subscribed. Almost all the respectable gentlemen gave in loan Fifty Pounds; and the Hon. Justice Boulton, and George Crookshank, Esq., contributed £100 each, to accomplish so good an object. The church was enlarged, a steeple erected, and the whole building with its galleries, handsomely finished. In January last (1819),' our authority proceeds to say, 'when everything was completed, the pews were sold at a year's credit, and brought more money than the repairs and enlargement cost. Therefore', it is triumphantly added, 'the inhabitants at York erect a very handsome church at a very little expense to themselves, for every one may have his subscription money returned, or it may go towards payment of a pew; and, what is more, the persons who subscribed for the first church count the amount of their subscription as part of the price of their new pews. This fair arrangement has been eminently successful; and gave great satisfaction.'

The special instance of graceful voluntary liberality above referred to is then subjoined in these terms: 'George Crookshank, Esq., notwithstanding the greatness of his subscription, and the pains which he took in getting the church well finished, has presented the clergymen with cushions for the pulpit and reading desk, covered with the richest and finest damask; and likewise cloth for the communion-table. This pious liberality', the writer remarks, 'cannot be too much commended; it tells us that the benevolent zeal of ancient times is not entirely done away. The congregation were so much pleased', it is further recorded, 'that a vote of thanks was unanimously offered to Mr Crookshank for his munificent present.' (The pulpit, sounding-board, and desk had been a gift of Governor Gore to the original church, and had cost the sum of one hundred dollars.)

When the necessity arose in 1830 for replacing the church thus enlarged and improved by an entirely new edifice of more respectable dimensions, the same cool, secular ingenuity was again displayed in the scheme proposed; and it was resolved by the congregation (among other things) 'that the pew-holders of the present church, if they demanded the same, be credited one-third of the price of the pews that they purchased in the new church, not exceeding in number those which they possessed in the old church; that no person be entitled to the privilege granted by the last resolution who shall not have paid up the whole purchase money of his pew in the old church; that the present church remain as it is, till the new one is finished; that after the new church is completed, the materials of the present one be sold to the highest bidder, and the proceeds of the same be applied to the liquidation of any debt that may be contracted in erecting the new church, or furnishing the same; that the upset price of pews in the new church be twenty five pounds currency;' and so on.

The stone edifice then erected [1833] (measuring within about 100 by 75 feet), but never completed in so far as related to its tower, was destroyed by fire in 1839. Fire, in truth, may be said to be, sooner or later, the 'natural death' of public buildings in our climate where, for so many months in every year, the maintenance within them of a powerful artificial heat is indispensable.

Ten years after the re-edification of the St James' burnt in 1839, its fate was again to be totally destroyed. But now fire was communicated to it from an external source—from a general conflagration raging at the time in the part of the town lying to the eastward [the first Great Fire]. On this occasion was destroyed in the belfry of the tower a public clock, presented to the inhabitants of Toronto by Mr Draper on his ceasing to be one of their representatives in Parliament.

In the later annals of St James' Church, the year 1873 is memorable.

Several very important details in Mr Cumberland's noble design for the [1850-3] building had long remained unrealized. The tower and spire were absent, as also the fine porches on the east, west, and south sides, the turrets at the angles, and the pinnacles and finials of the buttresses. Meanwhile the several parts of the structure where these appendages were in due time to be added were left in a condition to shew to the public the mind and intention of the architect.

In 1872, by the voluntary munificence of several members of the congregation, a fund for the completion of the edifice in accordance with Mr Cumberland's plans was initiated, to which generous donations were immediately added; and in 1873 the edifice, of whose humble [inception] in 1803 we have sought, in a preceding section, to preserve the memory, was finally brought to a state of perfection.

By the completion of St James' Church, a noble aspect has been given to the general view of Toronto. Especially has King Street been enriched, the ranges of buildings on its northern side, as seen from east or west, culminating centrically now in an elevated architectural object of striking beauty and grandeur, worthy alike of the comely, cheerful, interesting thoroughfare which it overlooks, and of the era when the finial crowning its apex was at length set in its place.

Worthy of special commemorative record are those whose thoughtful liberality originated the fund by means of which St James' Church was completed. The Dean, the Very Rev. H. J. Grasett, gave the handsome sum of five thousand dollars. Mr John Worthington, four thousand dollars. Mr C. Gzowski, two thousand dollars. Mr J. Gillespie, one thousand dollars. Mr E. H. Rutherford, one thousand dollars. Mr W. Cawthra, one thousand dollars. Mr Gooderham and Mr Worts, conjointly, one thousand dollars. Miss Gordon, the daughter of a former ever-generous member of the congregation, the Hon. J. Gordon, one thousand dollars. Sums in endless variety, from eight hundred dollars downwards, were in a like good spirit offered on the occasion by other members of the congregation, according to their means. An association of young men connected with the congregation undertook and effected the erection of the southern porch.

Let it be added, likewise, that in 1866 the sum of fourteen thousand nine hundred and forty-five dollars was expended in the purchase of a peal of bells, and in providing a chamber for its reception in the tower—a free gift to the whole community greatly surpassing in money's worth the sum above named: for have not the chimes, with all old-countrymen at least, within the range of their sound, the effect of an instantaneous translation to the other side of the Atlantic? Close the eyes and at once the spirit is far, far away, harkening, now in the calm of a summer's evening, now between the fitful wind-gusts of a boisterous winter's morn, to music in exactly the same key, with exactly the same series of cadences, given out from tree-embosomed tower in some ancient market-town or village, familiar to the listener in every turn and nook in days bygone.

And further, let it be added that in 1870, to do honour to the memory of the then recently deceased Bishop Strachan, the congregation of St James' 'beautified' the chancel of their church at a cost of seven thousand five hundred dollars, surrounding the spacious apse with an arcade of finely carved oak, adding seats for the canons, a decanal stall, a bishop's throne, a pulpit and desk, all in the same style and material, elaborately carved, with a life-like bust in white marble of the departed prelate by Forsyth of Montreal in a niche constructed for its reception in the western wall of the chancel, with a slab of dark stone below bearing the following inscription in gilded letters:

NEAR THIS SPOT REST THE MORTAL REMAINS OF JOHN STRACHAN, FIRST BISHOP OF TORONTO, WHO DEPARTED THIS LIFE NOVEMBER THE 1ST, 1867, IN THE NINETIETH YEAR OF HIS AGE AND THE TWENTY-NINTH YEAR OF HIS EPISCOPATE. HIS CONSPICVOVS LABOVRS, FORESIGHT, AND CONSTANCY IN THE SERVICE OF THE CHVRCH AND COMMONWEALTH, AS AN EDVCATOR, AS A MINISTER OF RELIGION, AS A STATESMAN, FORM AN IMPORTANT PORTION OF THE EARLY HISTORY OF WESTERN CANADA. DVRING THIRTY-FIVE YEARS HE WAS RECTOR OF THIS CHURCH AND PARISH. IN REMEMBERANCE OF HIM, THE CONGREGATION HAVE BEAVTIFIED THE CHANCEL AND ERECTED THIS MEMORIAL. EASTER, 1870.

V

KING
STREET
FROM
CHURCH
STREET
TO
GEORGE
STREET
WITH
DIGRESSIONS
AT CHURCH
AND DUKE
STREETS

Immediately north of the church plot, and separated from it by an allowance for a street [Adelaide], was a large field, almost square, containing six acres. In a plan of the date 1819, and signed 'T. Ridout, Surveyor-General', this piece of ground is entitled 'College Square'. (In the same plan the church reservation is marked 'Church Square'; and the block to the west 'Square for Court House and Jail'. The fact that the Jail was to be erected there accounts for the name 'Newgate Street', formerly borne by what is now Adelaide Street.

In the early days when the destined future was but faintly realized 'College Square' was probably expected to become in time, and to continue forever, an ornamental piece of ground round an educational institution. The situation in the outskirts of York would be deemed convenient and airy.[1]

---

[1] Although east of the modern centre of the city, this area was actually located on the western outskirts of early York.

For many years this six-acre field was the playground of the District Grammar [High] School. Through the middle of it, from north to south, passed a shallow 'swale' where water collected after rains, and where in winter small frozen ponds afforded not bad sliding places. In this moist region numerous crayfish were to be found in summer. Their whereabouts was always indicated by small clay chimneys of a circular form, built by the curious little nipping creatures themselves over holes for the admission of air.

In different places in this large area were remains of huge pine-stumps, underneath the long roots of which it was an amusement to dig and form cellars or imaginary treasure-vaults and powder-magazines. About these relics of the forest still grew remains of the ordinary vegetation of such situations in the woods—especially an abundance of the sorrel-plant, the taste of which will be remembered as being quite relishable. In other places were wide depressions showing where large trees had once stood. Here were no bad places, when the whim so was, to lie flat on the back and note the clouds in the blue vault overhead; watch the swallows and house-martins when they came in spring; and listen to their quiet prattle with each other as they darted to and fro—sights and sounds still every year, at the proper season, to be seen and heard in the same neighbourhood, yielding to those who have an eye or ear for such matters a pleasure ever new; sights and sounds to this day annually resulting from the cheery movements and voices of the direct descendants, doubtless, of the identical specimens that flitted hither and thither over the playground of yore.

White clover, with other herbage that commonly appears spontaneously in clearings, carpeted the whole of the six acres, with the exception of the places worn bare where favourable spots had been found for the different games of ball in vogue—amongst which, however, cricket was not then in these parts included, except, perhaps, under a form most infantile and rudimentary. After falls of moist snow in winter, gigantic balls used here to be formed, gathering as they were rolled along, until by reason of their size and weight they could be urged forward no further, and snow castles on a large scale were laboriously built, destined to be defended or captured with immense displays of gallantry. Preparatory to such contest, piles of ammunition would be stored away within these structures. It was prohibited, indeed, in the articles to be observed in operations of attack and defence, to construct missiles of very wet snow; to dip a missile in melted snow-water prior to use; to subject a missile after a saturation of this kind to the action of a night's frost; to secrete within the substance of a missile any foreign matter. Yet, nevertheless, occasionally such acts were not refrained from; and wounds and bruises of an extra-serious character, inflicted by hands that could not always be identified, caused loud and just complaints. Portions of the solid and extensive walls of the extemporized snow-fortresses were often conspicious in the playground long after a thaw had removed the wintry look from the rest of the scene.

The building into which the usual denizens of the six-acre playground were constrained, during certain portions of each day, to withdraw themselves, was situated at a point 114 feet from its western, and 104 from its southern boundary. It was a large frame structure, about fifty-five feet long and forty wide; of two storeys, each of a respectable altitude. The gables faced east and west. On each side of the edifice were two rows of ordinary sash windows, five above, and five below. At the east end were four windows, two above, two below. At the west end were five windows and the entrance-door. The whole exterior of the building was painted of a bluish hue, with the exception of the window and door frames which were white. Within, on the first floor, after the lobby, was a large square apartment. About three yards from each of its angles, a plain timber prop or post helped to sustain the ceiling. At about four feet from the floor, each of these quasi-pillars began to be chamfered off at its four angles. Filling up the south-east corner of the room was a small platform approached on three sides by a couple of steps. This sustained a solitary desk about eight feet long, its lower part cased over in front with thin deal boards so as to shut off from view the nether extremities of whosoever might be sitting at it.

On the general level of the floor below, along the whole length of the southern and northern sides of the chamber, were narrow desks set close against the wall with benches arranged at their outer side. At right angles to these, and consequently running out on each side into the apartment, stood a series of shorter desks with double slopes, and benches placed on either side. Through the whole length of the room from west to east, between the ends of the two sets of cross benches, a wide space remained vacant. Every object and surface within this interior were of the tawny hue which unpainted pine gradually assumes. Many were the gashes that had furtively been made in the ledges of the desks and on the exterior angles of the benches; many the ducts cut in the slopes of the desks for spilt ink or other fluid; many the small cell with sliding lid for the incarceration of fly or spider; many the initials and dates carved here, and on other convenient surfaces, on the wainscot and the four posts.

On the benches and at the desks enumerated and described, on either side, were ordinarily to be seen the figures and groups which usually fill up a school interior, all busily engaged in one or other of the many matters customary in the training and informing the minds of boys. Here at one time was to be heard on every side the mingled but subdued sound of voices conning or repeating tasks, answering and putting questions; at another time the commotion arising out of a transposition of classes or the breaking up of the whole assembly into a fresh set of classes; at another time a hushed stillness preparatory to some expected allocution, or consequent on some rebuke or admonition. It was manifest at a glance that the whole scene was under the spell of a skilled disciplinarian.

Here again the presiding genius of the place was Dr Strachan. From a boy he had been in the successful discharge of the duties of a schoolmaster. At the early age of sixteen we find that he was in charge of a school at Carmyllie [Scotland] with the grown-up sons of the neighbouring farmers and of some of the neighbouring clergy well under control. At that period he was still keeping his terms and attending lectures, during the winter months, at King's College, Aberdeen. Two years afterwards he obtained a slightly better appointment of the same kind at Denino, still pursuing his academical studies, gathering, as is evident from his own memoranda, a considerable knowledge of men and things and forming friendships that proved life-long. Then for two years more, and up to the moment of his bold determination to make trial of his fortunes in the new world beyond the seas, he is in charge of the parish-school of Kettle.

In the history of Dr Strachan's educational labours in Canada, the school at York presents fewer points of interest than that at Cornwall, which is rendered illustrious by having had enrolled on its books so many names familiar in the annals of Upper Canada. Among the forty-two subscribers to an address accompanying a piece of Plate in 1833 there are Robinsons and Macaulays and McDonells and McLeans and Joneses and Stantons and Bethunes; a Jarvis, a Chewett, a Boulton, a Vankoughnet, a Smith of Kingston, an Anderson, with some others now less known. So illustrative is that address of the skill and earnest care of the instructor on the one hand, and of the value set upon his efforts by his scholars on the other, after the lapse of many years, that we are induced to give here a short extract from it.

'Our young minds,' the signers of the address in 1833 say, referring to their school-days in Cornwall—'our young minds received there an impression which has scarcely become fainter from time, of the deep and sincere interest which you took, not only in our advancement in learning and science, but in all that concerned our happiness or could affect our future prospects in life.' To which Dr Strachan replies by saying, among many other excellent things: 'It has ever been my conviction that our scholars should be considered for the time our children; and that as parents we should study their peculiar dispositions, if we really wish to improve them; for if we feel not something of the tender relation of parents toward them, we cannot expect to be successful in their education. It was on this principle I attempted to proceed: strict justice tempered with parental kindness; and the present joyful meeting evinces its triumph: it treats the sentiments and feelings of scholars with proper consideration; and while it gives the heart and affections full freedom to shew themselves in filial gratitude on the one side, and fatherly affection, on the other, it proves that unsparing labour accompanied with continual anxiety for the learner's progress never fails to ensure success and to produce a friendship between master and scholar which time can never dissolve.'

We have ourselves a good personal recollection of the system of the school at York, and of the interest which it succeeded in awakening in the subjects taught. The custom of mutual questioning in classes, under the eye of the master, was well adapted to induce real research, and to impress facts on the mind when discovered.

In the higher classes each lad in turn was required to furnish a set of questions to be put by himself to his class-fellows on a given subject with the understanding that he should be ready to set the answerer right should he prove wrong. And again: any lad who should be deemed competent was permitted to challenge another, or several others, to read or recite select rhetorical pieces; a memorandum of the challenge was recorded; and, at the time appointed, the contest came off, the class or the school deciding the superiority in each case, subject to the criticism or disallowance of the master.

Here is an account of [Strachan's] method of teaching arithmetic, taken from the introduction to a little work on the subject published by himself in 1809: 'I divide my pupils', he says, 'into separate classes, according to their progress. Each class has one or more sums to produce every day, neatly wrought upon their slates: the work is carefully examined; after which I command every figure to be blotted out, and the sums to be wrought under my eye. The one whom I happen to pitch upon first, gives, with an audible voice, the rules and reasons for every step; and as he proceeds the rest silently work along with him, figure for figure, but ready to correct him if he blunder, that they may get his place. As soon as this one is finished, the work is again blotted out, and another called upon to work the question aloud as before, while the rest again proceed along with him in silence, and so on round the whole class. By this method the principles are fixed in the mind; and he must be a very dull boy indeed who does not understand every question thoroughly before he leaves it. This method of teaching Arithmetic possesses this important advantage, that it may be pursued without interrupting the pupil's progress in any other useful study. The same method of teaching Algebra has been used with equal success. Such a plan is certainly very laborious, but it will be found successful; and he that is anxious to spare labour ought not to be a public Teacher. When boys remain long enough, it has been my custom to teach them the theory, and give them a number of curious questions in Geography, Natural Philosophy and Astronomy.'

The youths to be dealt with in early Canadian schools were not all of the meek, submissive species. With some of them occasionally a sharp regimen was necessary; and it was adopted without hesitation. On this point, the address just quoted thus speaks: 'One of the greatest advantages you have derived from your education here, arises from the strictness of our discipline. Those of you who have not already perceived how much your tranquillity depends upon the proper regulation of the temper, will soon be made sensible of it as you advance in years. You will find people who have never known what it is to be in habitual subjection to precept and just authority, breaking forth into violence and outrage on the most frivolous occasions. The passions of such persons, when once roused, soon become ungovernable; and that impatience of restraint, which they have been allowed to indulge, embitters the greatest portion of their lives. Accustomed to despise the barriers erected by reason, they rush forward to indulgence, without regarding the consequences. Hence arises much of that wretchedness and disorder to be met with in society. Now the discipline necessary to correct the impetuosity of the passions is often found nowhere but in well-regulated schools: for though it should be the first care of parents, they are too apt to be blinded by affection, and grant liberties to their children which reason disapproves. . . . . . That discipline therefore, which you have sometimes thought irksome, will henceforth present itself in a very different light. It will appear the teacher of a habit of the greatest consequence in the regulation of your future conduct; and you will value it as the promoter of that decent and steady command of temper so very essential to happiness, and so useful in our intercourse with mankind.'

These remarks on discipline will be the more appreciated when it is recollected that during the time of the early settlements in this country, the sons of even the most respectable families were brought into contact with semi-barbarous characters. A sporting ramble through the woods, a fishing excursion on the waters, could not be undertaken without communications with Indians and half-breeds and bad specimens of the French *voyageur*. It was from such sources that a certain idea was derived which, as we remember, was in great vogue among the more fractious of the lads at the school at York. The proposition circulated about, whenever anything went counter to their notions, always was 'to run away to the Nor'-west'. What that process really involved, or where the 'Nor'-west' precisely was, were things vaguely realized. A sort of savage 'land of Cockaigne', a region of perfect freedom among the Indians, was imagined; and to reach it, Lakes Huron and Superior were to be traversed.

At Cornwall the temptation was in another direction: there the idea was to escape to the eastward, to reach Montreal or Quebec and get on board of an ocean-going ship, either a man-of-war or merchantman. The flight of several lads with such intentions was on one occasion intercepted by the unlooked-for appearance of the headmaster by the side of the stagecoach as it was just about to start for Montreal in the dusk of the early morning with the young truants in or upon it.

As to the modes of discipline in the school at York, for minor indiscretions a variety of remedies prevailed. Now and then a lad would be seen standing at one of the posts above mentioned with his jacket turned inside out; or he might be seen there in a kneeling posture for a certain number of minutes; or standing with the arm extended holding a book. An 'ally' or apple brought out inopportunely into view during the hours of work might entail the exhibition, article by article, slowly and reluctantly, of all the contents of a pocket. Once we remember the furtive but too audible twang of a jewsharp was followed by its owner's being obliged to mount on the top of a desk and

perform there an air on the offending instrument for the benefit of the whole school.

Occasionally the censors (senior boys appointed to help in
keeping order) were sent to cut rods on Mr McGill's property
adjoining the playground on the north; but the dire implements were not often called into requisition: it would only be
when some case of unusual obstinacy presented itself, or when
some wanton cruelty or some act or word exhibiting an unmistakable taint of incipient immorality was proven.

Once a year, before the breaking-up at midsummer, a 'feast'
was allowed in the schoolroom at York—a kind of picnic to
which all that could contributed in kind—pastry and other
dainties, as well as more substantial viands, of which all partook. It was sometimes a rather riotous affair.

At the south-east corner of the six-acre playground, about
half-an-acre had been abstracted, as it were, and enclosed: here
a public school had been built and put in operation. It was
known as the Central School and was what would now be called
a Common [Public] School, conducted on the 'Bell and Lan-
caster' principle.[2] Large numbers frequented it.

Between the lads attending the Central School and the boys
of the Grammar School difficulties of course arose; and on
many occasions feats of arms, accompanied with considerable
risk to life and limb, were performed on both sides with sticks
and stones. Youngsters, ambitious of a character of extra daring,
had thus an opportunity of distinguishing themselves in the
eyes of their less courageous companions. The same would-be
heroes had many stories to tell of the perils to which they were
exposed in their way to and from school. Those of them who
came from the western part of the town had, according to their
own shewing, mortal enemies in the men of Ketchum's tannery
with whom it was necessary occasionally to have an encounter,
while those who lived to the east of the school narrated in re-
sponse the attacks experienced or delivered by themselves in
passing Shaw's or Hugill's brewery.

---

[2] This was a method of teaching, much favoured by Sir Peregrine Maitland,
under which the elder children taught the younger ones, thus reducing the
number of teachers required.

Mr Spragge, the master of the Central School, had enjoyed the superior advantage of a regular training in England as an instructor of the young. Though not in Holy Orders, his air and costume were those of the dignified clergyman. Of the Central School, the words of Shenstone, spoken of a kindred establishment, became, in one point at all events, true to the letter:

> *E'en now sagacious foresight points to shew*
> *A little bench of bishops here,—*
> *And there, a chancellor in embryo,*
> *Or bard sublime.*

A son of Mr Spragge's became in 1869 the Chancellor of Ontario or Western Canada, after rising with distinction through the several grades of the legal profession and filling previously also the post of Vice-Chancellor. Mr John Godfrey Spragge, who attained to this eminence, and his brothers Joseph and William, were likewise pupils in their maturer years in the adjoining more imposing Royal Grammar or Home District School.

Mr Spragge's predecessor at the Central School was Mr Appleton, mentioned in a preceding section; and Mr Appleton's assistant for a time was Mr John Fenton.

Across the road from the playground at York, on the south side [of Adelaide], eastward of the church-plot, there was a row of dilapidated wooden buildings inhabited for the most part by a thriftless and noisy set of people. This group of houses was known in the school as 'Irish-town'; and 'to raise Irish-town' meant to direct a snowball or other light missive over the playground fence in that direction. Such act was not unfrequently followed by an invasion of the field from the insulted quarter. Some wide chinks, established in one place here between the boards, which ran lengthwise, enabled anyone so inclined to get over the fence readily. We once saw two men, who had quarrelled in one of the buildings of Irish-town, adjourn from over the road to the playground accompanied by a few approving friends and there, after stripping to the skin, have a regular fight with fists; after some rounds, a number of men and women interfered and induced the combatants to return to the house whence they had issued forth for the settlement of their dispute.

The Parliamentary Debates, of which mention has more than once been made in connection with the District School, took place on ordinary occasions in the central part of the school-room where benches used to be set out opposite to each other for the temporary accommodation of the speakers. These exercises consisted simply of a memoriter repetition, with some action, of speeches, slightly abridged, which had actually been delivered in a real debate on the floor of the House of Commons. But they served to familiarize Canadian lads with the names and characters of the great statesmen of England and with what was to be said on both sides of several important public questions; they also probably awakened in many a young spirit an ambition, afterwards gratified, of being distinguished as a legislator in earnest.

On public days the Debates were held upstairs on a platform at the east end of a long room with a partially vaulted ceiling, on the south side of the building. On this platform the public recitations also took place; and here on some of the anniversaries a drama by Milman and Hannah More was enacted. Here we ourselves took part in one of the hymns or choruses of the 'Martyr of Antioch'.

(Other reminiscences of Dr Strachan, the District Grammar School, and Toronto generally, are embodied in *The First Bishop of Toronto, a Review and a Study*, a small work published by the writer in 1868.)

The immediate successor of Dr Strachan in the school was Mr Samuel Armour, a graduate of Glasgow, whose profile resembled that of Cicero as shewn in some engravings. Being fond of sporting, his excitement was great when the flocks of wild pigeons were passing over the town and the report of firearms in all directions was to be heard. During the hours of school his attention on these occasions would be much drawn off from the class-subjects.

In those days there was not a plentiful supply in the town of every book wanted in the school. The only copy that could be procured of a *Eutropius*, which we ourselves on a particular occasion required, was one with an English translation at the end. The book was bought, Mr Armour stipulating that the English portion of the volume should be sewn up; in fact he himself stitched the leaves together. In Mr Armour's time there was, for some reason now forgotten, a barring-out. A pile of heavy wood (sticks of cordwood whole used then to be thrust into the great schoolroom stove) was built against the door within; and the master had to effect, and did effect, an entrance into his school through a window on the north side. Mr Armour became afterwards a clergyman of the English Church, and officiated for many years in the township of Cavan.

The master who succeeded Mr Armour was Dr Phillips who came out from England [c. 1825] to take charge of the school. He had been previously master of a school at Whitchurch in Herefordshire. His degree was from Cambridge, where he graduated as a B.A. of Queen's in the year 1805. He was a venerable-looking man—the very ideal, outwardly, of an English country parson of an old type. The costume in which he always appeared (shovel-hat included) was that usually assumed by the senior clergy some years ago. He also wore powder in the hair except when in mourning. According to the standards of the day, Dr Phillips was an accomplished scholar, and a good reader and writer of English. He introduced into the school at York the English public-school traditions of the strictest type. His text-books were those published and used at Eton as Eton then was. The *Eton Latin Grammar*, without note or comment, displaced *Ruddiman's Rudiments*—the book to which we had previously been accustomed and which really did give hints of something rational underlying what we learnt out of it. Even the *Eton Greek Grammar*, in its purely mediæval untranslated state, made its appearance: it was through the medium of that very uninviting manual that we obtained our earliest acquaintance with the first elements of the Greek tongue. Our *Palæphatus* and other Extracts in the *Græca Minora* were translated by us not into English but into Latin, in which language all the notes and elucidations of difficulties in that book were given.

In the time of Dr Phillips there was put up by subscription across the whole of the western end of the schoolhouse, over the door, a rough lean-to of considerable dimensions. A large covered space was thus provided for purposes of recreation in bad weather. This room is memorable as being associated with our first acquaintance with the term 'Gymnasium': that was the title which we were directed to give it.

It was stated above that cricket was not known in the playground of the District Grammar School, except possibly under the mildest of forms. Nevertheless, one, afterwards greatly distinguished in the local annals of cricket, was long a master in the School.

Mr George Antony Barber accompanied Dr Phillips to York in 1825 as his principal assistant, and continued to be associated with him in that capacity. Nearly half a century later than 1826, when cricket had now become a social institution throughout Western Canada, Mr Barber, who had been among the first to give enthusiastic encouragement to the manly English game, was the highest living local authority on the subject, and still an occasional participator in the sport.

We here close our notice of the Old Blue School at York. In many a brain, from time to time, the mention of its name has exercised a spell like that of Wendell Holmes's *Mare Rubrum*, as potent as that was, to summon up memories and shapes from the Red Sea of the Past—

> *Where clad in burning robes are laid*
> *Life's blossomed joys untimely shed,*
> *And where those cherish'd forms are laid*
> *We miss awhile, and call them dead.*

The building itself has been shifted bodily from its original position to the south-east corner of Stanley [Lombard] and Jarvis Streets. It, the centre of so many associations, is degraded now into being a depot for 'General Stock'—in other words, a receptacle for Rags and Old Iron.

The six acres of playground are thickly built over. A thoroughfare of ill-repute traverses it from west to east. This street was at first called March [Lombard] Street and under that appellation acquired an evil report. It was hoped that a nobler designation would perhaps elevate the character of the place, as the name 'Milton Street' had helped to do for the ignoble Grub Street in London. But the purlieus of the neighbourhood continue, unhappily, to be the Alsatia of the town. The filling up of the old breezy field with dwellings, for the most part of a wretched class, has driven 'the schoolmaster' away from the region. His return to the locality, in some good missionary sense, is much to be wished, and after a time will probably be an accomplished fact.[3]

(Since these lines were written, the old District Grammar School building has wholly vanished. It will be consolatory to know that, escaping destruction by fire, it was deliberately dismantled and taken to pieces; and, at once, walls of substantial brick overspread the whole of the space which it had occupied.)

We were arrested in our progress on King Street by St James' Church. Its associations, and those of the District Grammar School and its playground to the north, have detained us long. We now return to the point reached when our recollections compelled us to digress.

Before proceeding, however, we must record the fact that the break in the line of building on the north side of the street here was the means of checking the tide of fire which was rolling irresistibly westward in the great conflagration of 1849. The energies of the local fire-brigade of the day had never been so taxed as they were on that memorable occasion. Aid from steam-power was then undreamt-of. Simultaneous outbursts of flame from numerous widely-separated spots had utterly disheartened everyone and had caused a general abandonment of effort to quell the conflagration. Then it was that the open space about St James' Church saved much of the town from destruction.[4]

To the west the whole sky was, as it were, a vast canopy of meteors streaming from the east. The church itself was consumed, but the flames advanced no further. A burning shingle was seen to become entangled in the luffer-boards of the belfry

---

[3] By the 1830s the area had become a centre of low-class taverns and brothels. The schoolmaster has not returned, but the city morgue is located there now.

[4] The First Great Fire in 1849 was stopped by a combination of the open space around St James', a sudden rainfall, and the arrival of the troops from the Garrison to reinforce the tired fire-fighters.

and slowly to ignite the woodwork there. From a very minute start at that point a stream of fire soon began to rise—soon began to twine itself about the upper stages of the tower and to climb nimbly up the steep slope of the spire, from the summit of which it then shot aloft into the air, speedily enveloping and overtopping the golden cross that was there.

At the same time the flames made their way downwards within the tower till the internal timbers of the roofing over the main body of the building were reached. There, in the natural order of things, the fire readily spread; and the whole interior of the church, in the course of an hour, was transformed, before the eyes of a bewildered multitude looking powerlessly on, first into a vast 'burning fiery furnace' and then, as the roof collapsed and fell, into a confused chaos of raging flame.

The heavy gilt cross at the apex of the spire came down with a crash and planted itself in the pavement of the principal entrance below, where the steps, as well as the inner-walls of the base of the tower, were bespattered far and wide with the molten metal of the great bell.

While the work of destruction was going fiercely and irrepressibly on, the Public Clock in the belfry, Mr Draper's gift to the town, was heard to strike the hour as usual, and the quarters thrice—exercising its functions and having its appointed say amidst the sympathies, not loud but deep, of those who watched its doom; bearing its testimony, like a martyr at the stake, in calm and unimpassioned strain up to the very moment of time when the deadly element touched its vitals.

Opposite the southern portal of St James' Church was to be seen, at a very early period, the conspicuous trade-sign of a well-known furrier of York, Mr Joseph Rogers. It was the figure of an Indian Trapper holding a gun and accompanied by a dog, all depicted in their proper colours on a high, upright tablet set over the doorway of the store below. Besides being an appropriate symbol of the business carried on, it was always an interesting reminder of the time, then not so very remote, when all of York, or Toronto, and its commerce that existed was the old French trading-post on the common to the west and a few native hunters of the woods congregating with their packs of 'beaver' once or twice a year about the entrance to its picketed enclosure. Other rather early dealers in furs in York were Mr Jared Stocking and Mr John Bastedo.

In the *Gazette* for April 25, 1822, we notice a somewhat pretentious advertisement headed 'Muskrats' which announces that the highest market price will be given in cash for 'good seasonable muskrat skins and other furs at the store of Robert Coleman, Esquire, Market Place, York'.

Mr Rogers' descendants continue to occupy the identical site on King Street indicated above, and the Indian Trapper, renovated, is still to be seen—a pleasant instance of Canadian persistence and stability.

In Great Britain and Europe generally, the thoroughfares of ancient towns had, as we know, character and variety given them by the trade-symbols displayed up and down their misty vistas. Charles the First gave, by letters patent, express permission to the citizens of London 'to expose and hang in and over the streets, and ways, and alleys of the said city and suburbs of the same, signs and posts of signs, affixed to their houses and shops, for the better finding out such citizens' dwellings, shops, arts, and occupations, without impediment, molestation or interruption of his heirs or successors.' And the practice was in vogue long before the time of Charles. It preceded the custom of distinguishing houses by numbers. At periods when the population generally were unable to read, such rude appeals to the eye had, of course, their use. But as education spread, and architecture of a modern style came to be preferred, this mode of indicating 'arts and occupations' grew out of fashion.

Of late, however, the pressure of competition in business has been driving men back again upon the customs of bygone illiterate generations. For the purpose of establishing a distinct individuality in the public mind, the most capricious freaks are played. The streets of the modern Toronto exhibit, we believe, two leonine specimens of auro-ligneous zoology, between which the sex is announced to constitute the difference. The lack of such clear distinction between a pair of glittering symbols of this genus and species in our Canadian London was the occasion of much grave consideration in 1867 on the part of the highest authority in our Court of Chancery. Although in that *cause célèbre*, after a careful physiognomical study by means of photographs transmitted, it was allowed that there *were* points of difference between the two specimens in question—as, for example, that 'one looked older than the other', that 'one, from the sorrowful expression of its countenance, seemed more resigned to its position than the other'—still the decree was issued for the removal of one of them from the scene —very properly the later-carved of the two.[5]

Of the ordinary trade-signs that were to be seen along the thoroughfare of King Street, no particular notice need be taken. The Pestle and Mortar, the Pole twined round with the black strap, the Crowned Boot, the Tea-chest, the Axe, the Broad-axe, the Saw (mill, cross-cut and circular), the colossal Fowling-piece, the Cooking-stove, the Plough, the Golden Fleece, the Anvil and Sledge-Hammer, the magnified Horse-shoe, each told its own story as indicating indispensable wares or occupations.

Passing eastward from the painted effigy of the Indian Trapper, we soon came in front of the Market Place which, so long as only a low wooden building occupied its centre, had an open, airy appearance. We have already dwelt upon some of the occurrences and associations connected with this spot.

On King Street, about here, the ordinary trade and traffic of the place came, after a few years, to be concentrated. Here business and bustle were every day, more or less, created by the usual wants of the inhabitants and by the wants of the country farmers whose waggons in summer and sleighs in winter thronged in from the north, east, and west. And hereabout at one moment or another every lawful day would be surely seen, coming and going, the oddities and street-characters of the town and neighbourhood. Having devoted some space to the leading and prominent personages of our drama, it will be only proper

---

[5] This was the case of Walker v. Alley. Walker operated a dry-goods store called the 'Golden Lion' which had a gilt lion over the door. Alley, his manager for many years, resigned and opened a store nearby with similar name and trade-mark. Chancellor Vankoughnet decided that this action was an infringement of the trade-mark and ordered the lion removed.

to bestow a few words on the subordinates—the Calibans and Gobbos, the Nyms and Touchstones—of the piece.

From the various nationalities and races of which the community was a mixture, these were drawn. There was James O'Hara, for example, a poor humorous Irishman, a perfect representative of his class in costume, style, and manner, employed as bellman at auctions and so on. When the town was visited by the Papyrotomia—travelling cutters-out of likenesses in black paper (some years ago such things created a sensation) —a full-length of O'Hara was suspended at the entrance to the rooms, recognized at once by every eye, even without the aid of the 'Shoot easy' inscribed on a label issuing from the mouth. (In the *Loyalist* of Nov. 24, 1827, we have O'Hara's death noted. 'Died on Friday the 16th instant, James O'Hara, long an inhabitant of this Town, and formerly a soldier in His Majesty's service.') There was Jock Murray, the Scotch carter; and after him, William Pettit, the English one; and the carter who drove the horse with the 'spring-halt' (every school-lad in the place was familiar with the peculiar twitch upwards of the near hind leg in the gait of this nag).

The Negro population was small. Every individual of colour was recognizable at sight. Black Joe and Whistling Jack were two notabilities, both of them Negroes of African birth. In military bands a Negro drummer or cymbal-player was formerly often to be seen. The two men just named, after obtaining discharge from a regiment here, gained an honest livelihood by chance employment about the town. Joe, a well-formed, well-trained figure, was to be seen, still arrayed in some old cast-off shell-jacket, acting as porter or engaged about horses; once already we have had a glimpse of him in the capacity of sheriff's assistant administering the lash to wretched culprits in the Market Place. The other, besides playing other parts, officiated occasionally as a sweep; but his most memorable accomplishment was a melodious and powerful style of whistling musical airs and a faculty for imitating the bagpipes to perfection. For the romantic sound of the name, the tall, comely Negress, Amy Pompadour, should also be mentioned in the record. But she was of servile descent: at the time at which we write slavery

was only just dying out in Upper Canada, as we shall have occasion to note hereafter more at large.

Then came the 'Jack of Clubs', a worthy trader in provisions
who had acquired among his fellow-townsmen a sobriquet from
a supposed likeness to that sturdy court-card figure. He was a
short, burly Englishman whose place of business was just opposite the entrance to the Market. So absolutely did the epithet
attach itself to him that late-comers to the place failed to learn
his real name, all which was good-humouredly borne for a time;
but at last the distinction became burdensome and irritating
and Mr Stafford removed in disgust to New York.

A well-known character often to be seen about here, too, was
an unfortunate English farmer of the name of Cowper, of dis-
ordered intellect, whose peculiarity was a desire to station himself in the middle of the roadway and from that vantage-ground
to harangue any crowd that might gather, incoherently but
always with a great show of sly drollery and mirthfulness.

On occasions of militia funeral processions, observant lads
and others were always on the look-out for a certain prosperous
cord-wainer of the town of York, Mr Wilson, who was sure then
to be seen marching in the ranks with musket reversed and
displaying with great precision and solemnity the extra-upright
carriage and genuine toe-pointed step of the soldier of the days
of George the Second. He had been for sixteen years in the 41st
regiment, and ten years and forty-four days in the 103rd; and
it was with pride and gusto that he exhibited the high pro-
ficiency to which he had in other days attained. The slow pace
required by the Dead March gave the on-looker time to study
the antique style of military movement thus exemplified.

It was at a comparatively late period that Sir John Smythe
and Spencer Lydstone, poets, were notabilities in the streets; the
latter, Mr Lydstone, recognizable from afar by a scarlet vest,
brought out, ever and anon, a printed broadside filled with
eulogiums or satires on the inhabitants of the town, regulated
by fees or refusals received. The former, Sir John Smythe, found
in the public papers a place for his productions which by their
syntactical irregularities and freedom from marks of punctuation proved their author (as a reviewer of the day once ob-

served) to be a man *supra grammaticam* and one possessed of a genius above commas. But his great hobby was a railway to the Pacific, in connection with which he brought out a lithographed map; its peculiarity was a straight black line conspicuously drawn across the continent from Fort William to the mouth of the Columbia river.

In a tract of his on the subject of this railway he provides, in the case of war with the United States, for steam communication between London in England and China and the East Indies by 'a branch to run on the north side of the township of Cavan and on the south side of Balsam Lake'. 'I propose this', he says, 'to run in the rear of Lake Huron and in the rear of Lake Superior, twenty miles in the interior of the country of the Lake aforesaid; to unite with the railroad from Lake Superior to Winnipeg, at the south-west main trading-post of the North West Company.' The document is signed 'SIR JOHN SMYTHE, *Baronet and Royal Engineer, Canadian Poet,* LL.D., *and Moral Philosopher*'.

The concourse of traffickers and idlers in the open space before the old Market Place were free of tongue; they sometimes talked, in no subdued tone, of their fellow-townsfolk of all ranks. In a small community everyone was more or less acquainted with everyone, with his dealings and appurtenances, with his man-servant and maid-servant, his horse, his dog, his waggon, cart or barrow.

Those of the primitive residentiaries to whom the commonalty had taken kindly were honoured in ordinary speech with their militia-titles of Colonel, Major, Captain, or the civilian prefix of Mister, Honourable Mister, Squire or Judge, as the case might be; whilst others, not held to have achieved any special claims to deference, were named, even in mature years, by their plain baptismal names—John, Andrew, Duncan, George, and so on.

And then there was a third marking-off of a few against whom, for some vague reason or another, there had grown up in the popular mind a certain degree of prejudice. These, by a curtailment or national corruption of their proper prenomen, would be ordinarily styled Sandy this, Jock that. In some instances the epithet 'old' would irreverently precede, and persons of considerable eminence might be heard spoken of as old Tom so-and-so, old Sam such-a-one.

And similarly in respect to the sons and nephews of these worthy gentlemen. Had the community never been replenished from outside sources, few of them would, to the latest moment of their lives, have ever been distinguished except by the plain John, Stephen, Allan, Christopher, and so on of their infancy, or by the Bill, Harry, Alec, Mac, Dolph, Dick, or Bob, acquired in the nursery or school.

But enough has been said, for the present at least, on the humours and ways of our secondary characters as exemplified in the crowd customarily gathered in front of the old Market at York. We shall now proceed on our prescribed route.

The lane leading northward from the north-west corner of Market Square used to be known as Stuart's Lane [Market Street] from the Rev. George Okill Stuart, once owner of property here. On its west side was a well-known inn, the Farmers' Arms, kept by Mr Bloor who, on retiring from business, took up his abode at Yorkville where it has curiously happened that his name has been attached to a fashionable street, the thoroughfare formerly known as the [second] Concession Line.

The street running north from the north-east angle of Market Square, now known as Nelson [Jarvis] Street, was originally New Street, a name which was commemorative of the growth of York westward. The terminal street of the town on the west, prior to the opening of this New Street, had been George Street. The name of 'New Street' should never have been changed, even for the heroic one of Nelson. As the years rolled on it would have become a quaint misnomer involving a tale, like the name of 'New College' at Oxford—a College about five hundred years old.

At a point about halfway between New Street and George Street, King Street was in 1841 the scene of an election *fracas* which in distant quarters damaged for a time the good name of the town. While passing in front of the Coleraine House, an inn on the north side of the street and a rendezvous of the unsuccessful [Tory] party, some persons walking in procession, in addition to indulging in the usual harmless groans, flung a missile into the house when a shot, fired from one of the windows, killed a man in the concourse below.

Owing to the happy settlement of numerous irritating public questions, elections are conducted now in our towns and throughout our Provinces in a calm and rational temper for the most part. Only two relics of evil and ignorant days remain amongst us, stirring bad blood twice a year, on anniversaries consecrated or otherwise, to the object.[6] A generous-hearted nation, transplanted as they have been almost *en masse* to a new continent, where prosperity, wealth, and honours have everywhere been their portion, would shew more wisdom in the repudiation than they do in the recognition and studied conservation of these hateful heirlooms of their race.

On passing George Street, as we intimated a moment ago, we enter the parallelogram which constituted the original townplot. Its boundaries were George Street, Duchess Street, Ontario Street (with the lane south of it), and Palace [Front] Street. From this, its old core, York spread westward and northward, extending at length in those directions respectively (under the name of TORONTO) to the Asylum and Yorkville; while eastward its developments—though here less solid and less shapely—were finally bounded by the windings of the Don. Were Toronto an old town on the European Continent, George Street, Duchess Street, Ontario Street, and Palace Street would probably now be boulevards, showing the space once occupied by stout stone walls. The parallelogram just defined represents 'the City' in modern London, or 'la Cité' in modern Paris—the original nucleus round which gradually clustered the dwellings of later generations.

Before, however, we enter upon what may be styled King Street proper, it will be convenient to make a momentary digression northwards into Duke Street, anciently a quiet, retired thoroughfare skirted on the right and left by the premises and grounds and houses of several most respectable inhabitants. At

---

6 St Patrick's Day and July 12.

the north-west angle of the intersection of this street with
George Street was the home of Mr Washburn, but this was comparatively a recent erection. Its site previously [to 1808] had
been the brickyard of Henry Hale, a builder and contractor
who put up the wooden structure, possessing some architectural
pretensions, on the south-east angle of the same intersection,
diagonally across; occupied in the second instance by Mr Moore
of the Commissariat; then by Dr Lee; and afterwards by Mr
J. Murchison.

(The last named was for a long time the Stultz[7] of York,
supplying all those of its citizens, young and old, who desired
to make an attractive or intensely respectable appearance with
vestments in fine broadcloth.)

A little to the north, on the left side of George Street, was the
famous Ladies' School of Mrs Goodman, presided over subsequently by Miss Purcell and Miss Rose. This had been previously the homestead of Mr Stephen Jarvis, of whom again immediately. Two or three of these familiar names appear in an
advertisement relating to land in this neighbourhood in the
Gazette of March 23rd, 1826: 'For Sale: Three lots or parcels of
land in the town of York, the property of Mrs Goodman, being
part of the premises on which Miss Purcell now resides, and
formerly owned by Col. Jarvis. The lots are each fifty feet in
width and one hundred and thirty in depth, and front on the
street running from King Street to Mr Jarvis's Park lot. If not
disposed of by private sale, they will be put up at auction on
the first day of May next. Application to be made to Miss Purcell, or at the Office of the *U. C. Gazette. York, March 10, 1826.*'

Advancing on Duke Street eastward a little way, we came, on
the left [at the head of Frederick Street], to the abode of Chief
Justice Sir William Campbell, of whom before. Sir William
erected here in 1822 a mansion of brick in good style. It was
subsequently for many years the hospitable home of the Hon.
James Gordon, formerly of Amherstburgh.

Then on the right, one square beyond, at the south-easterly

---

[7] George Stultz was a famous Regency tailor in London's West end. The
firm he founded was located on Clifford Street from 1809 to 1915.

corner where Caroline [Sherbourne] Street intersects, we reached the house of Mr Secretary [William] Jarvis, a man of great note in his day whose name is familiar to all who have occasion to examine the archives of Upper Canada in the administrations of Governors Simcoe, Hunter, and Gore. A fine portrait of him exists but, as we have been informed, it has been transmitted to relatives in England. Mr Stephen Jarvis, above named, was long the Registrar of Upper Canada. His handwriting is well known to all holders of early deeds. He and the Secretary were first cousins—of the same stock as the well-known Bishop Jarvis of Connecticut and the Church Historian Dr Samuel Farmer Jarvis. Both were officers in incorporated Colonial regiments before the independence of the United States; and both came to Canada as United Empire Loyalists. Mr Stephen Jarvis was the founder of the leading Canadian family to which the first Sheriff [William Botsford] Jarvis belonged. Mr Samuel Peters Jarvis, from whom 'Jarvis Street' has its name, was the son of Mr Secretary Jarvis.

On the left, one square beyond the abode of Mr Secretary Jarvis, came the premises and home of Mr Surveyor-General [Thomas] Ridout, the latter a structure still to be seen in its primitive outlines, a good specimen of the old type of early Upper Canadian family residence of a superior class; combining the qualities of solidity and durability with those of snugness and comfort in the rigours of winter and the heats of summer. In the rear of Mr Ridout's house was for some time a family burial-plot; but, like several similar private enclosures in the neighbourhood of the town, it became disused after the establishment of regular cemeteries.

Nearly opposite Mr Ridout's, in one of the usual long, low, Upper Canadian one-storey dwellings, shaded by lofty Lombardy poplars, was the home of the Macintoshes; and here, at a later period, lived for a long time Mr Andrew Warffe and his brother John. Mr Andrew Warffe was a well-known employee in the office of the Inspector-General, Mr Baby, and a lieutenant in the Incorporated Militia.

By one of the vicissitudes common in the history of family residences everywhere, Mr Secretary Jarvis's house, which we just now passed, became afterwards the place of business of a memorable cutler and gunsmith named Isaac Columbus. During the war of 1812 Mr Columbus was employed as armourer to the Militia and had a forge near the garrison. Many of the swords used by the Militia officers were actually manufactured by him. He was a native of France; a liberal-hearted man, ever ready to contribute to charitable objects; and a clever artisan. Whether required to 'jump' the worn and battered axe of a backwoodsman, to manufacture the skate-irons and rudder of an ice-boat, to put in order a surveyor's theodolite, or to replace for the young geometrician or draughtsman an instrument lost out of his case, he was equally *au fait*. On occasion he could even supply an elderly lady or gentleman with a set of false teeth and insert them.

In our boyhood we had occasion to get many little matters attended to at Mr Columbus's. Once on leaving word that a certain article must be ready by a particular hour, we remember being informed that 'must' was only for the King of France. His political absolutism would have satisfied Louis xiv himself. He positively refused to have anything to do with the 'liberals' of York, expressly on the ground that in his opinion the modern ideas of government 'hindered the King from acting as a good father to the people'.

An expression of his, 'First quality, blue!', used on a particular occasion in reference to an extra finish to be given to some steelwork for an extra price, passed into a proverb among us boys at school and was extensively applied by us to persons and things of which we desired to predicate a high degree of excellence.

Over Columbus's workshop, at the corner of Caroline Street, we are pretty sure his name appeared as here given; and so it was always called. But we observe in some lists of early names in York that it is given as 'Isaac Collumbes'. It is curious to note that the great discoverer's name is a latinization of Colon, Coulon, Colombe, descendant each of *columba*, dove, of which *columbus* is the masculine form.

VI

KING

STREET

FROM

GEORGE

STREET

TO THE

BRIDGE

AND

ACROSS IT

We now retrace our steps to King Street at its intersection with George Street, and here our eye immediately lights on an object connected with the early history of education in York.

Attached to the east side of the house at the south-east angle of the intersection is a low building, wholly of stone, resembling a small root-house. Its structure is concealed from view now by a coating of clapboards. This was the first school-house possessing a public character in York. It was where Dr Stuart taught, afterwards Archdeacon of Kingston. The building was on his property, which became afterwards that of Mr George Duggan [Sr], once before referred to. (In connection with St James' Church, it should have been recorded that Mr Duggan was the donor and planter of the row of Lombardy poplars which formerly stood in front of that edifice, and which figured conspicuously in the old engravings of King Street. He was an Irishman of strong opinions. He once stood for the town against Mr Attorney-General [John Beverley] Robinson, but without success. When the exigencies of later times required the up-rooting of the poplar trees [1845], now become overgrown, he warmly resented the removal and it was at the risk of grievous bodily harm that the church-warden of the day, Mr T. D. Harris, carried into effect the resolution of the Vestry.)

Dr Stuart's was the Home District School. From a contemporary record now before us, we learn that it opened on June the first, 1807.

From the same record it appears that female pupils were not excluded from the primitive Home District School. On the roll are names which surviving contemporaries would recognize as belonging to the *beau monde* of Upper Canada, distinguished and admired in later years.

A building-lot, eighty-six feet in front and one hundred and seventeen in depth, next to the site of the school is offered for sale in the *Gazette* of the 18th of March 1822; and in the advertisement it is stated to be 'one of the most eligible lots in the Town of York, and situated in King Street, in the centre of the Town'.

To the left, just across from this choice position, was, in 1833, Wragg & Co.'s establishment, where such matter-of-fact articles as the following could be procured 'Bending and unbending nails, as usual; wrought nails and spikes of all sizes (a change since 1810): ox-traces and cable chains; tin; double and single sheet iron; sheet brass and copper; bar, hoop, bolt and rod iron of all sizes; shear, blister and cast steel; with every other article in the heavy line, together with a very complete assortment of shelf goods, cordage, oakum, tar, pitch, and rosin: also a few patent machines for shelling corn.' A much earlier resort for such merchandise was Mr Peter Paterson's on the west side of the Market Square.

Of a date somewhat subsequent to that of Messrs Wragg's advertisement was the depot of Mr Harris for similar substantial wares. This was situated on the north side of King Street, westward of the point at which we are now pausing. It long resisted the great conflagration of 1849, towering up amidst the flames like a black, isolated crag in a tempestuous sea; but at length it succumbed. Having been rendered, as it was supposed, fireproof externally, no attempt was made to remove the contents of the building.

To the east of Messrs Wragg's place of business, on the same side, and dating back to an early period, was the dwelling house and mart of Mr Mosley the principal auctioneer and appraiser of York, a well-known and excellent man. He had suffered the severe calamity of a partial deprivation of the lower limbs by frostbite; but he contrived to move about with great activity in a room or on the sidewalk by means of two light chairs, shifting himself adroitly from the one to the other. When required to go to a distance or to church (where he was ever punctually to be seen in his place), he was lifted by his son or sons into and out of a wagonette, together with the chairs.

On the same (north) side was the place where the Messrs Lesslie, enterprising and successful merchants from Dundee, dealt at once in two remunerative articles—books and drugs. The left side of the store was devoted to the latter; the right to the former. Their first headquarters in York had been further up the street, but a move had been made to the eastward to be, as things were then, nearer the heart of the town.

This firm had houses carrying on the same combined businesses in Kingston and Dundas. There exists a bronze medal or token of good design, sought-after by collectors, bearing the legend, 'E. Lesslie and Sons, Toronto and Dundas, 1822'. The date has been perplexing, as the town was not named Toronto in 1822. The intention simply was to indicate the year of the founding of the firm in the two towns; the first of which assumed the name of Toronto at the period the medal was really struck, viz. 1834. On the obverse it bears a figure of Justice with scales and sword: on the reverse, a plough with the mottoes, 'Prosperity to Canada', 'La Prudence et la Candeur'. A smaller token of the same firm is extant on which 'Kingston' is inserted between 'Toronto' and 'Dundas'.[1]

Nearly opposite was the store of Mr [George] Monro. Regarding our King Street as the Broadway of York, Mr Monro was

---

[1] These are the famous Lesslie tokens. The smaller piece, a halfpenny, was probably issued in the mid-1820s and has the name 'York', not 'Toronto', in the legend. The larger piece, a twopence, was issued after 1834 as Scadding says. Kingston was dropped because the Kingston branch of the firm was closed in 1834.

for a long time its Stewart.[2] But the points about his premises that linger now in our recollection the most are a tasteful flower-garden on its west side and a trellised verandah in that direction with canaries in a cage, usually singing therein. Mr Monro was Mayor of Toronto in 1841. He also represented in Parliament the South Riding of York, in the Session of 1845-7.

At the north-west corner, a little further on [King and Frederick Streets], resided Mr Alexander Wood whose name appears often in the Report of the Loyal and Patriotic Society of 1812, to which reference before has been made and of which he was the Secretary. At first in co-partnership with Mr Allan [1797-1801], and at a later period independently, he had made money at York by business. He continued on the same spot until after the War of 1812 the commercial operation which had been so prosperously begun and then retired.

At the time to which our recollections are just now transporting us, the windows of the part of the house that had been the store were always seen with the shutters closed. Mr Wood was a bachelor, and it was no uncosy sight, towards the close of the shortening autumnal days, before the remaining front shutters of the house were drawn in for the evening, to catch a glimpse in passing of the interior of his comfortable quarters lighted up by the blazing logs on the hearth, the table standing duly spread close by, and the solitary himself ruminating in his chair before the fire, waiting for candles and dinner to be brought in.

On sunny mornings in winter he was often to be seen pacing the sidewalk in front of his premises for exercise, arrayed in a long blue overcoat, with his right hand thrust for warmth into the cuff of his left sleeve and his left hand into that of his right. He afterwards returned to Scotland where, at Stonehaven, not far from Aberdeen, he had family estates known as Woodcot and Woodburnden. He died without executing a will [1844], and it was some time before the rightful heir to his property in Scotland and here was determined. It had been his intention, we

---

[2] Alexander T. Stewart was the leading dry-goods merchant of New York and Monro held a similar position in Toronto.

believe, to return to Canada. The streets which run eastward from Yonge Street north of Carleton Street, named respectively 'Wood' and 'Alexander', pass across land that belonged to Mr Wood.

Many are the shadowy forms that rise before us as we proceed on our way—phantom-revisitings from the misty past, the shapes and faces of enterprising and painstaking men of whose fortunes King Street hereabout was the cradle. But it is not necessary in these reminiscences to enumerate all who, on the right hand and on the left, along the now comparatively deserted portions of the great thoroughfare, amassed wealth in the olden time by commerce and other honourable pursuits—laying the foundation, in several instances, of opulent families.

[Laurent] Quetton St George, however, must not be omitted, builder of the solid and enduring house [1807] on the corner opposite to Mr Wood's, a structure that—for its size and air of respectability; for its material, brick, when as yet all the surrounding habitations were of wood; for its tinned roof, its graceful porch, its careful and neat finish generally—was for a long time one of the York lions.

Mr Quetton St George was a French royalist officer and a chevalier of the order of St Louis. With many other French gentlemen, he emigrated to Canada at the era of the Revolution. He was of the class of the noblesse, as all officers were required to be; which class, just before the Revolution, included, it is said, 90,000 persons all exempt from the ordinary taxes of the country.

The surname of St George was assumed by M. Quetton to commemorate the fact that he had first set foot on English ground on St George's day. On proceeding to Canada, he, in conjunction with Jean Louis, Vicomte de Chalûs, and other distinguished *émigrés*, acquired a large estate in wild lands in the rough region north of York, known as the 'Oak Ridges'.[3] Finding it difficult, however, to turn such property speedily to

---

[3] This refers to the unsuccessful attempt of the Comte de Puisaye to settle French royalists on these lands, which were located in Markham and Vaughan townships, in 1799. The settlement failed because of poor land and the settlers' lack of knowledge of farming procedures.

account, he had recourse to trade with the Indians and remote
inhabitants. Numerous stations, with this object in view, were
established by him in different parts of the country before his
final settlement in York. One of these posts was at Orillia, on
Lake Couchiching; and in the Niagara *Herald* of August the
7th, 1802, we meet with the following advertisement: 'New
Store at the House of the French General, between Niagara and
Queenston. Messrs Quetton St George and Co., acquaint the
public that they have lately arrived from New York with a
general assortment of Dry Goods and Groceries, which will be
sold at the lowest price for ready money, for from the uncertainty of their residing any time in these parts they cannot
open accounts with any person. Will also be found at the same
store a general assortment of tools for all mechanics. They have
likewise well-made Trunks; also empty Barrels. *Niagara, July
23.*'

The co-partnership implied was with M. de Farcy. The
French General referred to was the Comte de Puisaye. The
house spoken of still exists, beautifully situated at a point on
the Niagara River, where the carriage-road between Queenston
and the town of Niagara [-on-the-Lake] approaches the very
brink of the lofty bank whose precipitous side is even yet richly
clothed with fine forest trees, and where the noble stream below,
closed in towards the south by the heights above Lewiston and
Queenston, possesses all the features of a picturesque inland
lake.[4]

Attached to the house in question is a curious old fire-proof
structure of brick, quaintly buttressed with stone: the walls are
of a thickness of three or four feet, and the interior is beautifully
vaulted and divided into two compartments, having no communication with each other; and above the whole is a long loft
of wood, approached by steps on the outside. The property here
belonged for a time in later years to Shickluna, the shipbuilder
of St Catharines, who happily did not disturb the interesting

---

[4] The home of the Count, who preferred the more comfortable area near
Niagara to his settlement at Oak Ridges, was taken over by the Ontario
government in 1965 to prevent its demolition and will be restored at a new
location.

relic just described. The house itself was in some respects modernized by him; but with its steep roof and three dormer windows it still retains much of its primitive character.

In 1805 we find Mr St George removed to York. The co-partnership with M. de Farcy is now dissolved. In successive numbers of the *Gazette and Oracle,* issued in that and the following year, he advertises at great length. But on the 20th of September 1806, he abruptly announces that he is not going to advertise any more: he now, once for all, begs the public to examine his former advertisements where they will find, he says, an account of the supply which he brings from New York every spring, a similar assortment to which he intends always to have on hand: and N. B., he adds: Nearly the same assortment may be found at Mr Boiton's at Kingston and at Mr Boucherville's at Amherstburgh 'who transact business for Mr St George'.

Rendered rich in money and lands by his extemporized mercantile operations, Mr St George returned to his native France soon after the restoration of Louis XVIII [1815], and passed the rest of his days partly in Paris and partly on estates in the neighbourhood of Montpellier. During his stay in Canada he formed a close friendship with the Baldwins of York; and on his departure, the house on King Street which has given rise to these reminiscences of him, together with the valuable commercial interests connected with it, passed into the hands of a junior member of that family, Mr John Spread Baldwin, who himself on the same spot subsequently laid the foundation of an ample fortune.

(It is a phenomen not uninteresting to the retrospective mind, to observe, in 1869, after the lapse of half a century, the name of Quetton St George reappearing in the field of Canadian Commerce.[5])

Advancing now on our way eastward we soon came in front of the abode of Dr Burnside, a New England medical man of

---

5 John Spread Baldwin and Jules Quesnel of Montreal acted as the Canadian partners of St George and carried on the business until 1832. The Baldwin family also acted as managers of St George's lands, and it was to take up possession of these properties that his son Henri Quetton St George returned at the time Scadding was writing.

tall figure, upright carriage, and bluff benevolent countenance, an early promoter of the Mechanics' Institute movement and an encourager of church music, vocal and instrumental. Dying without a family dependent on him, he bequeathed his property partly to charities in the town and partly to the University of Trinity College, where two scholarships perpetuate his memory.

Just opposite was the residence of the venerable Mrs Gamble, widow of Dr Gamble, formerly a surgeon attached to the Queen's Rangers. This lady died in 1859 in her 92nd year, leaving living descendants to the number of two hundred and four. To the west of this house was a well-remembered little *parterre*, always at the proper season gay with flowers.

At the next corner [Sherbourne], on the north side, a house now totally demolished was the original home of the millionaire Cawthra family, already once alluded to. In the *Gazette and Oracle* of June 21, 1806, Mr Cawthra senior thus advertises: 'J. Cawthra wishes to inform the inhabitants of York and the adjacent country that he has opened an Apothecary Store in the house of A. Cameron opposite Stoyell's Tavern in York, where the Public can be supplied with most articles in that line. He has on hand also, a quantity of Men's, Women's, and Children's shoes and Men's hats. Also for a few days will be sold the following articles, Table Knives and Forks, Scissors, Silver Watches, Maps and Prints, Profiles, some Linen, and a few Bed-Ticks, Teas, Tobacco, a few casks of fourth proof Cognac Brandy, and a small quantity of Lime Juice, and about twenty thousand Whitechapel Needles. *York, June 14, 1806.*'

A little way down the street which crosses here [Sherbourne] was Major Heward's house, long Clerk of the Peace for the Home District, of whom we had occasion to speak before. Several of his sons, while pursuing their legal and other studies, became also 'mighty hunters'—distinguished, we mean, as enthusiastic sportsmen. Many were the exploits reported of them in this line.

The younger Messrs Heward had a field for the exercise of their sportsman skill on the Island, just across the bay, where the black-heart plover were said always to arrive on a particular

day, the 23rd of May, every year, and the marshes about Ashbridge's Bay and York harbour itself all abounded with wild
fowl. Here loons of magnificent size used to be seen and heard;
and vast flocks of wild geese, passing and re-passing high in
air in their periodical migrations. The wild swan, too, was an
occasional frequenter of the ponds of the Island.

Returning again to King Street: at the corner of Caroline [Sher-
bourne] Street, diagonally across from the Cawthra homestead,
was the abode, when ashore, of Captain Oates, commander of
the *Duke of Richmond* sloop, the fashionable packet plying between Niagara and York.

Mr Oates was nearly connected with the family of President
Russell, but curiously obtained no share in the broad acres
which were, in the early day, so plentifully distributed to all
comers. By being unluckily out of the way, too, at a critical
moment subsequently, he missed a bequest at the hands of the
sole inheritor of the possessions of his relative [Elizabeth Rus-
sell].

Capt. Oates was a man of dignified bearing of more than the
ordinary height. He had seen service on the ocean as master
and owner of a merchantman. His portrait, which is still preserved in Toronto, somewhat resembles that of George IV.

A spot passed, a few moments since, on King Street is associated with a story in which the *Richmond* sloop comes up. It
happened that the nuptials of a neighbouring merchant [J. S.
Baldwin] had lately taken place [1822]. Some youths, employed
in an adjoining warehouse or law-office, took it into their heads
that a *feu de joie* should be fired on the occasion. To carry out
the idea they proceeded, under cover of the night, to the *Richmond* sloop, where she lay frozen in by the Frederick Street
wharf, and removed from her deck, without asking leave, a small
piece of ordnance with which she was provided. They conveyed
it with some difficulty, carriage and all, up into King Street, and
placed it in front of the bridegroom's house; ran it back, as we
have understood, even into the recess underneath the double
steps of the porch: when duly ensconced there, as within the
port of a man-of-war, they contrived to fire it off, decamping,

however, immediately after the exploit, and leaving behind them the source of the deafening explosion.

On the morrow the cannon is missed from the sloop (she was being prepared for the spring navigation): on instituting an inquiry, Capt. Oates is mysteriously informed the lost article is, by some means, up somewhere on the premises of Mr J. S. Baldwin, the gentleman who had been honoured with the salute, and that if he desired to recover his property he must dispatch some men thither to fetch it. (We shall have occasion to refer hereafter to the *Richmond* when we come to speak of the early Marine of York Harbour.)

Passing on our way eastward we came immediately, on the north side, to one of the principal hotels of York—a long, white, two-storey wooden building. It was called the Mansion House—an appropriate name for an inn when we understand 'Mansion' in its proper but somewhat forgotten sense as indicating a temporary abode, a place which a man occupies and then relinquishes to a successor. The landlord here for a considerable time was Mr De Forest, an American who in some way or other had been deprived of his ears. The defect, however, was hardly perceptible, so nicely managed was the hair. On the ridge of the Mansion House roof was to be seen for a number of years a large and beautiful model of a completely equipped sailing vessel.

We then arrived at the north-west angle of King and Princes Streets where a second public well (we have already commemorated the first) was sunk and provided with a pump in 1824—for all which the sum of £36 17s. 6d. was paid to John James on the 19th of August in that year. In the advertisements and contracts connected with this now-obliterated public convenience, Princes Street is correctly printed and written as it here meets the eye, and not 'Princess Street' as the recent corruption is.

Let not the record of our early water-works be disdained. Those of the metropolis of the Empire were once on a humble scale. Thus Master John Stow, in his *Survey of London, Anno 1598*, recordeth that 'at the meeting of the corners of the Old Jurie, Milke Street, Lad Lane, Aldermanburie, there was of old time a fair well with two buckets—of late years', he somewhat pathetically adds, 'converted to a pump.'

Just across, eastward from the pump, was one of the first buildings put up on King Street: it was erected by Mr Smith, who was the first to take up a building lot after the laying-out of the town-plot.

On the opposite side, a few steps further on was [John] Jordan's—the far-famed 'York Hotel'—at a certain period [c. 1805-20] the hotel *par excellence* of the place, than which no better could be found at the time in all Upper Canada. The whole edifice has now utterly disappeared. Its foundations giving way, it for a while seemed to be sinking into the earth, and then it partially threatened to topple over into the street. It was of antique style when compared with the Mansion House. It was only a storey-and-a-half high. Along its roof was a row of dormer windows. (Specimens of this style of hotel may still be seen in the country-towns of Lower Canada.)

When looking in later times at the doorways and windows of the older buildings intended for public and domestic purposes, as also at the dimensions of rooms and the proximity of the ceilings to the floors, we might be led for a moment to imagine that the generation of settlers passed away must have been of smaller bulk and stature than their descendants. But points especially studied in the construction of early Canadian houses in both provinces were warmth and comfort in the long winters. Sanitary principles were not much thought of and happily did not require to be much thought of when most persons passed more of their time in the pure outer air than they do now.

Jordan's York Hotel answered every purpose very well. Members of Parliament and other visitors considered themselves in luxurious quarters when housed there. Probably in no instance have the public dinners or fashionable assemblies of a later era gone off with more *éclat* or given more satisfaction to the persons concerned in them than did those which from time to time, in every season, took place in what would now be considered the very diminutive ballroom and dininghall of Jordan's.

In the ballroom here, before the completion of the brick building which replaced the Legislative Halls, destroyed by the

Americans in 1813, the Parliament of Upper Canada sat for one session.

In the rear of Jordan's, detached from the rest of the buildings, there long stood a solid circular structure of brick of considerable height and diameter, dome-shaped without and vaulted within. This was the public oven of Paul Marian, a native Frenchman who had a bakery here before the surrounding premises were converted into a hotel by Mr Jordan. In the *Gazette* of May 19, 1804, Paul Marian informs his friends and the public 'that he will supply them with bread at their dwellings, at the rate of nine loaves for a dollar, on paying ready money'.

About the same period another Frenchman, François Belcour, is exercising the same craft in York. In *Gazettes* of 1803 he announces that he is prepared 'to supply the ladies and gentlemen who may be pleased to favour him with their custom, with bread, cakes, buns, etc. And that for the convenience of small families, he will make his bread of different sizes, viz, loaves of two, three, and four pounds' weight, and will deliver the same at the houses, if required.' He adds that 'families who may wish to have beef, etc., baked, will please send it to the bake-house'. In 1804 he offers to bake 'at the rate of pound for pound; that is to say he will return one pound of Bread for every pound of Flour which may be sent to him for the purpose of being baked into bread.'

After the abandonment of Jordan's as a hotel, Paul Marian's oven, repaired and somewhat extended, again did good service. In it was baked a goodly proportion of the supplies of bread furnished in 1838-9 to the troops and incorporated militia at Toronto by Mr Jackes and Mr Reynolds.

As the sidewalks of King Street were apt to partake in bad weather of the impassableness of the streets generally at such a time, an early effort was made to have some of them paved. Some yards of foot-path, accordingly, about Jordan's, and here and there elsewhere, were covered with flat flagstones from the lake-beach of very irregular shapes and of no great size: the effect produced was that of a very coarse, and soon a very uneven, mosaic.

At Quebec, in the neighbourhood of the Court House, there is retained some pavement of the kind now described; and in the early lithograph of Court House Square at York, a long stretch of sidewalk is given in the foreground, seamed over curiously like the surface of an old Cyclopean or Pelasgic wall.

On April the 26th, 1823, it was ordered by the magistrates at Quarter Sessions that '£100 from the Town and Police Fund, together with one-fourth of the Statute Labour within the Town, be appropriated to flagging the sidewalks of King Street, commencing from the corner of Church Street and proceeding east to the limits of the Town, and that both sides of the street do proceed at the same time.' One hundred pounds would not go very far in such an undertaking. We do not think the sidewalks of the primitive King Street were ever paved throughout their whole length with stone.[6]

After Jordan's came Dr Widmer's surgery, associated with many a pain and ache in the minds of the early people of York, and scene of the performance upon their persons of many a delicate and daring and successful remedial experiment. Nearly opposite was property appertaining to Dr Stoyell, an immigrant non-practising medical man from the United States with Republican proclivities, as it used to be thought, who, previous to his purchasing here, conducted an inn at Mrs Lumsden's corner [Sherbourne Street]. (The house on the other side of Ontario Street, westward, was Hayes' Boarding House, noticeable simply as being in session-time, like Jordan's, the temporary abode of many Members of Parliament.)

After Dr Widmer's, towards the termination of King Street on the south side, was Mr Small's, originally one of the usual low-looking domiciles of the country, with central portion and two-gable wings somewhat after the fashion of many an old country manor-house in England. The material of Mr Small's dwelling was hewn timber. It was one of the earliest domestic erections in York [c. 1794]. When reconstructed at a subsequent

---

6 There was no real attempt to pave the city's sidewalks before 1836—the paving in the picture Scadding mentions is probably the fancy of the artist, Thomas Young (who adds a non-existent tower to St James'), rather than actual flagstones.

period, Mr Charles Small preserved, in the enlarged and elevated building now known as Berkeley House, the shape and even a portion of the inner substance of the original strcture.[7]

We have before us a curious plan (undated but old) of the piece of ground originally occupied and enclosed by Mr Small as a yard and garden round his primitive homestead—occupied and enclosed, as it would seem, before any building lots were set off by authority on the Government reserve or common here. The plan referred to is entitled 'A sketch showing the land occupied by John Small, Esq., upon the Reserve appropriated for the Government House at York by His Excellency Lt. Gov. Simcoe'. An irregular oblong, coloured red, is bounded on the north side by King Street and is lettered within: 'Mr Small's Improvements'. Round the irregular piece thus shewn, lines are drawn enclosing additional space and bringing the whole into the shape of a parallelogram: the parts outside the irregularly shaped red portion are coloured yellow, and on the yellow the memorandum appears: 'This added would make an Acre.' The block thus brought into shapely form is about one-half of the piece of ground that at present appertains to Berkeley House.

The plan before us also incidentally shows where the Town of York was supposed to terminate:—an inscription, 'Front Line of the Town', runs along the following route: up what is now the lane through Dr Widmer's property and then at a right angle eastward along what is now the north boundary of King Street opposite the block which it was necessary to get into shape round Mr Small's first 'Improvements'. King Street proper, in this plan, terminates at 'Ontario Street'; from the eastern limit of Ontario Street the continuation of the highway is marked 'Road to Quebec', with an arrow shewing the direction in which the traveller must keep his horse's head if he would reach that ancient city. The arrow at the end of the inscription just given points slightly upwards, indicating the fact that the said 'Road to Quebec' trends slightly to the north after leaving Mr Small's clearing.

---

[7] The house was demolished in 1925.

We now propose to pass rapidly down the 'Road to Quebec' as far as the Bridge. First we cross, in the hollow, Goodwin's creek, the stream which enters the bay by the cut-stone jail [1840]. Lieutenant Givins (afterwards Colonel Givins), on the occasion of his first visit to Toronto in 1793, forced his way in a canoe with a friend up several of the meanderings of this stream under the impression that he was exploring the Don. He had heard that a river leading to the North West entered the Bay of Toronto somewhere near its head, and he mistook the lesser for the greater stream, thus on a small scale performing the exploit accomplished by several of the explorers of the North American coast who, under the firm persuasion that a water highway to Japan and China existed somewhere across this continent, lighted upon Baffin's Bay, Davis Strait, the Hudson River, and the St Lawrence itself in the course of their investigations.

On the knoll to the right, after crossing Goodwin's creek, was Isaac Pilkington's lowly abode, a little group of white buildings in a grove of pines and acacias.

Parliament Street, which enters near here from the north, is a memorial of the olden time when, as we have seen, the Parliament Buildings of Upper Canada were situated in this neighbourhood. In an early section of these Recollections we observed that what is now called Berkeley Street was originally Parliament Street, a name which, like that borne by a well-known thoroughfare in Westminster for a similar reason, indicated the fact that it led down to the Houses of Parliament.

The road that at present bears the name of Parliament Street shows the direction of the track through the primitive woods opened by Governor Simcoe to his summer house on the Don, called Castle Frank, of which fully in its place hereafter.

Looking up Parliament Street, we are reminded that a few yards westward from where Duke Street enters it lived at an early period Mr Richard Coates, an estimable and ingenious man whose name is associated in our memory with the early dawn of the fine arts in York. Mr Coates, in a self-taught way, executed not unsuccessfully portraits in oil of some of our ancient worthies. Among things of a general or historical char-

acter, he painted also for David Willson, the founder of the
'Children of Peace', the symbolical decorations of the interior
of the Temple at Sharon. He cultivated music likewise, vocal
and instrumental; he built an organ of some pretensions, in his
own house, on which he performed; he built another for David
Willson at Sharon. Mr Coates constructed besides, in the yard
of his house, an elegantly finished little pleasure yacht of about
nine tons' burden.

This passing reference to infant Art in York recalls again the
name of Mr John Craig who has before been mentioned in our
account of the interior of one of the many successive St Jameses.
Although Mr Craig did not himself profess to go beyond his
sphere as a decorative and heraldic painter, the spirit that
animated him really tended to foster in the community a taste
for art in a wider sense.

Mr Charles Daly, also, as a skilful teacher of drawing in
water-colours and introducer of superior specimens, did much
to encourage art at an early date. In 1834 we find Mr Daly
promoting an exhibition of Paintings by the 'York Artists and
Amateur Association', and acting as 'Honorary Secretary' when
the Exhibition for the year took place. Mr James Hamilton, a
teller in the bank, produced too some noticeable landscapes in
oil.

As an auxiliary in the cause, and one regardful of the wants
of artists at an early period, we name likewise Mr Alexander
Hamilton who, in addition to supplying materials in the form
of pigments and prepared colours, contributed to the tasteful
setting off of the productions of pencil and brush by furnishing
them with frames artistically carved and gilt.

Out of the small beginnings and rudiments of Art at York,
one artist of a genuine stamp was in the lapse of a few years
developed—Mr Paul Kane who, after studying in the schools of
Europe, returned to Canada and made the illustration of Indian
character and life his specialty. By talent exhibited in this class
of pictorial delineation, he acquired a distinguished reputation
throughout the North American continent; and by his volume
of beautifully illustrated travels, published in London, and
entitled *Wanderings of an Artist among the Indians of North*

America [1859], he obtained for himself a recognized place in the literature of British Art.[8]

In the hollow, a short distance westward of Mr Coates's, was one of the first buildings of any size ever erected in these parts wholly of stone. It was put up by Mr Hutchinson. It was a large, square, family house of three storeys. It still exists, but its material is hidden under a coating of stucco. Another building, wholly of stone, was Mr Hunter's house on the west side of Church Street. A portion of Hugill's Brewery likewise exhibited walls of the same solid, English-looking substance. We now resume our route.

We immediately approach another road [Power Street] entering from the north, which again draws us aside. This opening led up to the only Roman Catholic church in York [St Paul's 1822], an edifice of red brick, substantially built. Mr Ewart was the contractor. The material of the north and south walls was worked into a kind of tesselated pattern, which was considered something very extraordinary. The spire was originally surmounted by a large and spirited effigy of the bird that admonished St Peter and not by a cross. It was not a flat, moveable weathercock, but a fixed, solid figure, covered with tin.

In this building officiated for some time an ecclesiastic named O'Grady. Mingling with a crowd, in the over-curious spirit of boyhood, we here, at funerals and on other occasions, first witnessed the ceremonial forms observed by Roman Catholics in their worship; and once we remember being startled at receiving, by design or accident, from an overcharged *aspergillum* in the hands of a zealous ministrant of some grade passing down the aisle, a copious splash of holy water in the eye.

Functionaries of this denomination are generally remarkable for their quiet discharge of duty and for their apparent submissiveness to authority. They sometimes pass or repass for years before the indifferent gaze of multitudes holding another creed without exciting any curiosity even as to their personal names. But Mr O'Grady was an exception to the general run

---

8 Many of Kane's Indian paintings may now be seen in the Royal Ontario Museum.

of his order. He acquired a distinctive reputation among outsiders. He was understood to be an unruly presbyter; and through his instrumentality letters of his bishop, evidently never intended to meet the public eye, got into general circulation. He was required to give an account of himself, subsequently, at the feet of the 'Supreme Pontiff'.[9]

Power Street, the name now applied to the road which led up to the Roman Catholic church, preserves the name of the Bishop [Michael Power] of this communion who sacrificed his life in attending to the sick emigrants in 1847.

The road to the south, a few steps further on, led to the windmill built by Mr Worts senior in 1832. In the possession of Messrs Gooderham & Worts are three interesting pictures in oil which from time to time have been exhibited. They are intended to illustrate the gradual progress in extent and importance of the mills and manufacturers at the site of the windmill. The first shows the original structure—a circular tower of red brick, with the usual sweeps attached to a hemispherical revolving top; in the distance town and harbour are seen. The second shows the windmill dismantled but surrounded by extensive buildings of brick and wood, sheltering now elaborate machinery driven by steam power. The third represents a third stage in the march of enterprise and prosperity. In this picture, gigantic structures of massive, dark-coloured stone tower up before the eye, vying in colossal proportions and ponderous strength with the works of the castle-builders of the feudal times. Accompanying these interesting landscape views, all of them by Forbes, a local artist of note, a group of life-size portraits in oil has occasionally been seen at art exhibitions in Toronto—Mr Gooderham senior and his seven sons, all of them well-developed, sensible-looking, substantial men, manifestly capable of undertaking and executing whatever practical work the exigencies of a young and vigorous community may require to be done.

---

[9] The priest involved, William O'Grady, was a Reformer, whereas Bishop Macdonell was a Tory. The result was a quarrel which led to the unfrocking of O'Grady who then became editor of a new Reform paper, the *Canadian Correspondent* (1832).

When the families of Mr Gooderham and Mr Worts crossed the Atlantic, on the occasion of their emigration from England [1832], the party, all in one vessel, comprised, as we are informed, so many as fifty-four persons more or less connected by blood or marriage.

We have been told by Mr James Beaty that when out duck shooting, now nearly forty years since, he was surprised by falling in with Mr Worts senior rambling apparently without purpose in the bush at the mouth of the Little Don—all the surrounding locality was then in a state of nature and frequented only by the sportsman or trapper. On entering into conversation with Mr Worts, Mr Beaty found that he was there prospecting for an object; that, in fact, somewhere near the spot where they were standing, he thought of putting up a windmill! The project at the time seemed sufficiently Quixotic. But posterity beholds the large practical outcome of the idea then brooding in Mr Worts' brain. In their day of small things the pioneers of new settlements may take courage from this instance of progress in one generation, from the rough to the most advanced condition. For a century to come there will be bits of this continent as unpromising, at the first glance, as the mouth of the Little Don forty years ago, yet as capable of being reclaimed by the energy and ingenuity of man and being put to divinely intended and legitimate uses. Returning now from the windmill, once more to the 'Road to Quebec', in common language the Kingston Road, we passed at the corner the abode of one of the many early settlers in these parts who bore German names—the tenement of Peter Ernst, or Ernest as the appellation afterwards became.

From these Collections and Recollections, matters of comparatively so recent a date as 1849 have for the most part been excluded. We make an exception in passing the Church ['Little' Trinity] which gives name to Trinity Street, for the sake of recording an inscription on one of its interior walls. It reads as follows: 'To the Memory of the Reverend William Honywood Ripley, B.A., of University College, Oxford, First Incumbent of this Church, son of the Rev. Thomas Hyde Ripley, Rector of Tockenham, and Vicar of Wootton Bassett in the County of

Wilts, England. After devoting himself during the six years of his ministry, freely, without money and without price, to the advancement of the spiritual and temporal welfare of this congregation and neighbourhood, and to the great increase amongst them of the knowledge of Christ and His Church, he fell asleep in Jesus on Monday the 22nd of October, 1849, aged 34 years. He filled at the same time the office of Honorary Secretary to the Church Society of the Diocese of Toronto, and was Second Classical Master of Upper Canada College. This Tablet is erected by the Parishoners of this Church as a tribute of heartfelt respect and affection. Remember them that have the rule over you, who have spoken unto you the Word of God: whose faith follow, considering the end of their conversation.'

Canadian society in all its strata has been more or less leavened from England. One of the modes by which the process has been carried on is revealed in the inscription just given. In 1849, while this quarter of Toronto was being taken up and built over, the influence of the clergyman commemorated was singularly marked within it. Mr Ripley in his boyhood had been trained under Dr Arnold at Rugby; and his father had been at an early period a private tutor to the Earl of Durham who came out to Canada in 1838 as High Commissioner. As to the material fabric of Trinity Church—its erection was chiefly due to the exertions of Mr Alexander Dixon, an alderman of Toronto.

The brick schoolhouse attached to Trinity Church bears the inscription: 'ERECTED BY ENOCH TURNER, 1848.' Mr Turner was a benelovent Englishman who prospered in this immediate locality as a brewer and died in 1866. Besides handsome bequests to near relations, Mr Turner left by will to Trinity College, Toronto, £2,000; to Trinity Church £500; to St Paul's £250; to St Peter's £250.

Just opposite on the left was where Angell lived, the arcitect of the abortive bridges over the mouths of the Don. We obtain from the York *Observer* of December 11, 1820, some earlier information in regard to Mr Angell. It is in the form of a 'Card' thus headed: 'York Land Price Current Office, King Street.' It then proceeds: 'In consequence of the Increase of the population of the Town of York, and many applications for family accommodation upon the arrival of strangers desirous of becoming settlers, the Subscriber intends to add to the practice of his Office the business of a *House Surveyor* and *Architect*, to lay out Building Estate, draw Ground plans, *Sections* and *Elevations*, to *order*, and upon the most approved *European* and *English* customs. Also to make *estimates* and provide contracts with *proper securities* to prevent impostures for the performance of the same. E. ANGELL. N.B. — Land proprietors having estate to dispose of, and persons requiring any branch of the above profession to be done, will meet with the most respectful attention on application by letter, or at this office. *York, Oct. 2, (1820).*'

The expression 'York Price Current Office' above used is explained by the fact that Mr Angell commenced at this early date the publication of a monthly, 'Land Price Current List of Estates on Sale in Upper Canada, to be circulated in England, Ireland, Scotland and Wales'.

Near Mr Angell on the same side lived also Mr Cummins, the manager of the *Upper Canada Gazette* printing office; and at a later period Mr Watson, another well-known master-printer of York, who lost his life during the great fire of 1849 in endeavouring to save a favourite press from destruction in the third storey of a building at the corner of King and Nelson streets, a position occupied subsequently by the Caxton Press of Mr Hill.

On some of the fences along here we remember seeing in 1827-8 an inscription written up in chalk or white paint, memorable to ourselves personally as being the occasion of our first taking serious notice of one of the political questions that were locally stirring the people of Upper Canada. The words inscribed were —NO ALIENS! Like the LIBERTY, EQUALITY, FRATERNITY, which we ourselves also subsequently saw painted on the walls of Paris, these words were intended at once to express and to rouse public feeling; only in the present instance, as we suppose now, the inscription emanated from the oligarchical rather than the popular side. The spirit of it probably was 'Down with Aliens' and not 'Away with the odious distinction of Aliens!'

A dispute had arisen between the Upper and the Lower House as to the legal terms in which full civil rights should be conferred on a considerable portion of the inhabitants of the country. After the acknowledgement of independence in 1783, emigrants from the United States to the British Provinces came in no longer as British subjects but as foreigners. Many such emigrants had acquired property and exercised the franchise without taking upon themselves, formally, the obligations of British subjects. After the War of 1812, the law in regard to this matter began to be distinctly remembered. The desire then was to check an undue immigration from the southern side of the Great Lakes; but the effect of the revival of the law was to throw doubt on the land titles of many inhabitants of long standing, doubt on their claim to vote and to fill any civil office.

The consent of the Crown was freely given to legislate on the subject, and in 1825-6 the Parliament resolved to settle the question. But a dispute arose between the Lower and Upper House. The Legislative Council sent down a Bill which was so amended in terms by the House of Assembly that the former body declared it then to be 'at variance with the laws and established policy of Great Britain, as well as of the United States; and therefore if passed into a law by this Legislature, would afford no relief to many of those persons who were born in the United States, and who have come into and settled in this Province.' The Upper House party set down as disloyal all that expressed themselves satisfied with the Lower House amendments. It was from the Upper House party, we think, that the cry of 'No Aliens!' had proceeded.

The Alien measure had been precipitated by the cases of Barnabas Bidwell and of his son Marshall [Spring Bidwell], of whom the former, after being elected, and taking his seat as member for Lennox and Addington [1821], had been expelled the House on the ground of his being an alien; and the latter had met with difficulties at the outset of his political career from the same objection against him. In the case of the former, however, his alien character was not the only thing to his disadvantage.[10]

It was in connection with the expulsion of Barnabas Bidwell that Dr Strachan gave to a member of the Lower House, when hesitating as to the legality of such a step, the remarkable piece of advice, 'Turn him out, turn him out! Never mind the law!'— a *dictum* that passed into an adage locally, quoted usually in the Aberdeen dialect.

Barnabas Bidwell is thus commemorated in Mackenzie's *Almanac* for 1834: 'July 27, 1833: Barnabas Bidwell, Esq., Kingston, died, aged 69 years and 11 months. He was a sincere friend of the rights of the people; possessed of extraordinary powers of mind and memory, and spent many years of his life in doing all the good he could to his fellow-creatures, and promoting the interests of society.'

Irritating political questions have now, for the most part, been disposed of in Canada. We have entered into the rest, in this respect, secured for us by our predecessors. The very fences which, some forty years ago, were muttering 'No Aliens!' we saw, during the time of a late general election, exhibiting in conspicuous painted characters the following exhortation: 'To the Electors of the Dominion—Put in Powell's Pump'— a humorous advertisement, of course, of a particular contrivance for raising water from the depths. We think it a sign of general peace and content when the populace are expected to enjoy a little jest of this sort.[11]

A small compact house with a pleasant flower garden in front, on the left a little way on, was occupied for a while by Mr Joshua Beard, at the time Deputy Sheriff but afterwards well known as owner of extensive iron works in the town.

We then came opposite to the abode, on the same side, of Mr Charles Fothergill, sometime King's Printer for Upper Canada. He was a man of wide views and great intelligence, fond of

---

10 Barnabas Bidwell had been a county treasurer in Connecticut and had fled to Canada when accused of malversation of funds.

11 Scadding's general peace and content were shortly to be shattered by the Pacific Scandal, which cast Sir John A. Macdonald out of office before the end of 1873.

science and an experienced naturalist. Several folio volumes of closely written manuscript on the birds and animals generally of this continent by him must exist somewhere at this moment. They were transmitted to friends in England, as we have understood.[12]

We remember seeing in a work by Bewick a horned owl of this country, beautifully figured, which, as stated in the context, had been drawn from a stuffed specimen supplied by Mr Fothergill. He himself was a skilful delineator of the living creatures that so much interested him.

In 1832 Mr Fothergill sat in Parliament as member for Northumberland, and for expressing some independent opinions in that capacity he was deprived of the office of King's Printer. He originated the law which established Agricultural Societies in Upper Canada.

In 1836 he appears to have been visited in Pickering by Dr Thomas Rolph when making notes for his *Statistical Account of Upper Canada*. 'The Township of Pickering', Dr Rolph says, 'is well settled and contains some fine land, and well watered. Mr Fothergill', he continues, 'has an extensive and most valuable museum of natural curiosities at his residence in this township, which he has collected with great industry and the most refined taste. He is a person of superior acquirements, and ardently devoted to the pursuit of natural philosophy.'

It was Mr Fothergill's misfortune to have lived too early in Upper Canada. Many plans of his in the interests of literature and science came to nothing for the want of a sufficient body of seconders. In conjunction with Dr Dunlop and Dr Rees, it was the intention of Mr Fothergill to establish at York a Museum of Natural and Civil History, with a Botanical and Zoological Garden attached; and a grant of land on the Government Reserve between the Garrison and Farr's Brewery was actually secured as a site for the buildings and grounds of the proposed institution [1836].

A prospectus now before us sets forth in detail a very comprehensive scheme for this Museum or Lyceum, which embraced

---

[12] Some of Fothergill's notebooks are now in the Royal Ontario Museum.

also a picture gallery 'for subjects connected with Science and Portraits of individuals' and did not omit 'Indian antiquities, arms, dresses, utensils, and whatever might illustrate and make permanent all that we can know of the Aborigines of this great Continent, a people who are rapidly passing away and becoming as though they had never been' [1835].

For several years Mr Fothergill published *The York Almanac and Royal Calendar* which gradually became a volume of between four and five hundred duodecimo pages filled with practical and official information on the subject of Canada and the other British American Colonies. This work is still often resorted to for information.

Hanging in his study we remember noticing a large engraved map of 'CABOTIA'. It was a delineation of the British Possessions in North America—the present Dominion of Canada, in fact. It had been his purpose in 1823 to publish a *Canadian Annual Register*, but this he never accomplished. While printing the *Upper Canada Gazette*, he edited in conjunction with that periodical and on the same sheet the *Weekly Register*, bearing the motto, 'Our endeavour will be to stamp the very body of the time—its form and pressure: we shall extenuate nothing, nor shall we set down aught in malice.' From this publication may be gathered much of the current history of the period. In it are given many curious scientific excerpts from his Common Place Book. At a later period [1837-9] he published at Toronto a weekly paper in quarto shape named the *Palladium* [*of British North America*].

Among the non-official advertisements in the *Upper Canada Gazette* in the year 1823 we observe one signed 'Charles Fothergill' offering a reward 'even to the full value of the volumes' for the recovery of missing portions of several English standard works which had belonged formerly, the advertisement stated, to the 'Toronto Library', broken up 'by the Americans at the taking of York.' It was suggested that probably the missing books were still scattered about, up and down, in the town. It is odd to see the name of 'Toronto' cropping out in 1823 in connection with a library. (In a much earlier York paper we notice the 'Toronto Coffee House' advertised.)

Eastward from the house where we have been pausing, the road took a slight sweep to the south and then came back to its former course towards the Don bridge, descending in the meantime into the valley of a creek or watercourse and ascending again from it on the other side. Hereabout, to the left, standing on a picturesque knoll and surrounded by the natural woods of the region, was a good-sized two-storey dwelling; this was the abode of Mr David MacNab, sergeant-at-arms to the House of Assembly, as his father had been before him. With him resided several accomplished, kind-hearted sisters, all of handsome and even stately presence, one of them the belle of the day in society at York.

Here were the quarters of the Chief MacNab whenever he came up to York from his Canadian home on the Ottawa. It was not alone when present at church that this remarkable gentleman attracted the public gaze; but also when surrounded or followed by a group of his fair kinsfolk of York he marched with dignified steps along through the whole length of King Street and down or up the Kingston Road to and from the Mac-Nab homestead here in the woods near the Don.

In his visits to the capital the Chief always wore a modified Highland costume which well set off his stalwart, upright form: the blue bonnet and feather and richly embossed dirk always rendered him conspicuous, as well as the tartan of brilliant hues depending from his shoulder after obliquely swathing his capacious chest; a bright scarlet vest with massive silver buttons and dress coat, always jauntily thrown back, added to the picturesqueness of the figure.

It was always evident at a glance that the Chief set a high value on himself. 'May the MacNab of MacNabs have the pleasure of taking wine with Lady Sarah Maitland?' suddenly heard above the buzz of conversation, pronounced in a very deep and measured tone by his manly voice, made mute for a time, on one occasion, the dinner-table at Government House. So the gossip ran. Another story of the same class, but less likely, we should think, to be true, was that seating himself, without uncovering, in the Court-room one day, a messenger was sent to him by the Chief Justice, Sir William Campbell, on the Bench, requiring the removal of his cap, when the answer returned as he instantly rose and left the building was that 'the MacNab of MacNabs doffs his bonnet to no man!'

We now arrived at the Don bridge. The valley of the Don, at the place where the Kingston Road crosses it, was spanned in 1824 by a long wooden viaduct raised about twenty-five feet above the marsh below. This structure consisted of a series of ten trestles or frames of hewn timber supporting a roadway of plank which had lasted since 1809. A similar structure spanned the Humber and its marshes on the west side of York. Both of these bridges about the year 1824 had become very much decayed; and occasionally both were rendered impassible at the same time by the falling in of worn-out and broken planks. The York papers would then make themselves merry on the well-defended condition of the town in a military point of view, approach to it from the east and west being effectually barred.

Prior to the erection of the bridge on the Kingston Road, the Don was crossed near the same spot by means of a scow, worked by the assistance of a rope stretched across the stream. In 1810 we observe that the Humber was also crossed by means of a ferry. In that year the inhabitants of Etobicoke complained to the magistrates in session at York of the excessive toll demanded there; and it was agreed that for the future the following should be the charges: For each foot passenger, 2½d.; for every hog, 1d.; for every sheep, the same; for horned cattle, 2½d. each; for every horse and rider, 5d.; for every carriage drawn by two horses, 1s. 3d. (which included the driver); for every carriage with one horse, 1s. It is presumed that the same tolls were exacted at the ferry over the Don while in operation.

In 1824 not only was the Don bridge in bad repair but, as we learn from a petition addressed by the magistrates to Sir Peregrine Maitland in that year, the bridge over the Rouge in Pickering also is said to be 'from its decayed state, almost impassible, and if not remedied', the document goes on to state, 'the communication between this town (York) and the eastern parts of the Province, as well as with Lower Canada by land, will be entirely obstructed.'

At length the present earthwork across the marsh at the Don

was thrown up and the river itself spanned by a long wooden tube put together on a suspension principle, roofed over and closed in on the sides, with the exception of oblong apertures for light. It resembled in some degree the bridges to be seen over the Reuss at Lucerne and elsewhere in Switzerland, though not decorated with paintings in the interior as they are. Stone piers built on piles sustained it at either end. All was done under the superintendence of a United States contractor named Lewis. It was at him that the *italics* in Mr Angell's advertisement glanced [see page 145]. The innuendo was that for engineering purposes there was no necessity for calling in the aid of outsiders.

From a kind of small Friar-Bacon's study, occupied in former years by ourselves, situated on a bold point some distance northwards up the valley, we remember watching the pile-driver at work in preparing the foundation of the two stone piers of the Don bridge: from where we sat at our books we could see the heavy mallet descend; and then, after a considerable interval, we would hear the sharp stroke on the end of the piece of timber which was being driven down. From the same elevated position also, previously, we used to see the teams crossing the high frame-work over the marsh on their way to and from town, and hear the distant clatter of the horses' feet on the loosely-laid planks.

The tubular structure which succeeded the trestle-work bridge did not retain its position very long. The pier at its western extremity was undermined by the water during a spring freshet and gave way. The bridge, of course, fell down into the swirling tide below and was carried bodily away, looking like a second Ark as it floated along towards the mouth of the river where at length it stranded and became a wreck.

On the breaking up of the ice every spring the Don, as is well known, becomes a mighty rushing river, stretching across from hill to hill. Ordinarily it occupies but a small portion of its proper valley, meandering along like an English tide-stream when the tide is out. The bridge carried away on this occasion was notable so long as it stood for retaining visible marks of an attempt to set fire to it during the troubles of 1837.

The next appliance for crossing the river was another tubular frame of timber, longer than the former one; but it was never provided with a roof and never closed in at the sides. Up to the time that it began to show signs of decay, and to require cribs to be built underneath it in the middle of the stream, it had an unfinished, disreputable look. It acquired a tragic interest in 1859 from being the scene of the murder by drowning of a young Irishman named Hogan, a barrister, and at the same time a member of the Parliament of Canada.

When crossing the high trestlework which preceded the present earth-bank, the traveller, on looking down into the marsh below on the south side, could see the remains of a still earlier structure, a causeway formed of unhewn logs laid side by side in the usual manner but decayed and for the most part submerged in water, resembling, as seen from above, some of the lately discovered substruction in the lakes of Switzerland. This was probably the first road by which wheeled vehicles ever crossed the valley of the Don here. On the protruding ends of some of the logs of this causeway would be always seen basking, on a warm summer's day, many fresh-water turtles; amongst which, as also amongst the black snakes, which were likewise always to be seen coiled up in numbers here, and among the shoals of sunfish in the surrounding pools, a great commotion would take place when the jar was felt of a waggon passing over on the framework above.

The rest of the marsh, with the exception of the space occupied by the ancient corduroy causeway, was one thicket of wild willow, alder, and other aquatic shrubbery, among which was conspicuous the *spiræa*, known amongst boys as 'seven-bark' or 'nine-bark' and prized by them for the beautiful hue of its rind which when rubbed becomes a bright scarlet.

Here also the blue iris grew plentifully, and reeds, frequented by the marsh hen; and the bulrush, with its long cat-tails sheathed in chestnut-coloured felt and pointed upwards like toy sky-rockets ready to be shot off. (These cat-tails, when dry and stripped, expand into large, white, downy spheres of fluff and actually are as inflammable as gunpowder, going off with a mighty flash at the least touch of fire.)

The view from the old trestlework bridge, both up and down the stream, was very picturesque, especially when the forest, which clothed the banks of the ravine on the right and left, wore the tints of autumn. Northward, while many fine elms would be seen towering up from the land on a level with the river, the bold hills above them and beyond were covered with lofty pines. Southward, in the distance, was a great stretch of marsh, with the blue lake along the horizon. In the summer this marsh was one vast jungle of tall flags and reeds where would be found the conical huts of the muskrat and where would be heard at certain seasons the peculiar *gulp* of the bittern; in winter, when crisp and dry, here was material for a magnificent pyrotechnical display which usually once a year came off, affording at night to the people of the town a spectacle not to be contemned.

Through a portion of this marsh on the eastern side of the river, Mr Justice [D'Arcy] Boulton [Sr] at a very early period cut, at a great expense, an open channel in front of some property of his: it was expected, we believe, that the matted vegetation on the outer side of this cutting would float away and leave clear water when thus disengaged; but no such result ensued. The channel, however, has continued open and is known as the 'Boulton ditch'. It forms a communication for skiffs between the Don and Ashbridge's Bay.

At the west end of the bridge, just across what is now the gore between Queen Street and King Street, there used to be the remains of a military breastwork thrown up in the War of 1812. At the east end of the bridge, on the south side of the road, there still stands a lowly edifice of hewn logs, erected before the close of the last century by the writer's father [John Scadding], who was the first owner and occupant of the land on both sides of the Kingston Road at this point.[13] The roadway down to the original crossing-place over the river in the days of the Ferry and the time of the first corduroy bridge, swerving as it did considerably to the south from the direct line of the

---

[13] The Scadding cabin has been moved to the Exhibition Grounds and is open to the public at the time of the Canadian National Exhibition.

Kingston Road, must have been in fact a trespass on his lot on the south side of the road; and we find that so noteworthy an object was the solitary house, just above the bridge, in 1799, that the bridge itself, in popular parlance, was designated by its owner's name. Thus in the *Upper Canada Gazette* for March 9, 1799, we read that at a Town Meeting Benjamin Morley was appointed overseer of highways and fence-viewer for the section of road 'from Scadding's bridge to Scarborough'. In 1800 Mr Ashbridge is appointed to the same office, and the section of highway placed under his charge is on this occasion named 'the Bay Road from Scadding's bridge to Scarborough'.

This Mr Ashbridge is the early settler from whom Ashbridge's Bay was so called. His farm lay along the lower portion of that sheet of water. Next to him, westward, was the property of Mr Hastings whose Christian name was Warren. Years ago, when first beginning to read Burke, we remember wondering why the name of 'the great proconsul' of Hindostan looked so familiar to the eye, when we recollected that in our childhood we used frequently to see here along the old Kingston road the name WARREN HASTINGS appended in conspicuous character to placards posted up advertising a 'Lost Cow' or some other homely animal, gone astray. Adjoining Mr Hastings' farm, still moving west, was that of Mr Mills, with whose name in our mind is associated the name of 'Hannah Mills', an unmarried member of his household who was the Sister of Charity of the neighbourhood, ever ready in times of sickness and bereavement to render, for days and nights together, kindly, sympathetic, and consolatory aid.

When in 1799 staid inhabitants were found seriously dignifying the group of buildings then to be seen on the borders of the bay with the magnificent appellation of the 'City of York', it is no wonder that at a later period indignation is frequently expressed at the ignominious epithet of 'Little' which persons in the United States were fond of prefixing to the name of the place. Thus, for example, in the *Weekly Register* so late as June 1822, we have the editor speaking thus in a notice to a correspondent: 'Our friends on the banks of the Ohio, 45 miles below Pittsburg, will perceive', the editor remarks, 'that notwithstanding he has made us pay postage (and postage in those days was heavy), we have not been unmindful of his request. We shall always be ready at the call of charity when not mis-applied: and we hope the family in question will be successful in their object.—There is one hint, however,' the editor goes on to say, 'we wish to give Mr W. Patton, P.M.; which is, although there may be many '*Little*' Yorks in the United States, we know of no place called '*Little York*' in Canada; and beg that he will bear this *little* circumstance in his recollection when he again addresses us.'[14]

Gourlay also, as we have seen, when he wished to speak cuttingly of the authorities at York, used the same epithet. In gubernatorial proclamations, the phrase modestly employed is 'OUR TOWN OF YORK'.

A short distance east from the bridge a road turned north-ward, known as the 'Mill Road'. This communication was open in 1799. It led originally to the Mills of Parshall Terry, of whose accidental drowning in the Don there is a notice in the *Gazette* of July 23, 1808. In 1800 Parshall Terry is 'Overseer of Ways from the Bay Road to the Mills'. In 1802 the language is 'from the Bay Road to the Don Mills', and in that year Mr John Playter is elected to the office held in the preceding year by Parshall Terry. (In regard to Mr John Playter, the solitary house which overlooked the original Don Bridge and Ferry was occupied by him during the absence of its builder and owner in England; and here Mr Emanuel Playter, his eldest son, was born.)

In 1821 and down to 1849 the Mill Road was regarded chiefly as an approach to the multifarious works—flour-mills, saw-mills, fulling-mills, carding-mills, paper-mills and breweries—founded near the site of Parshall Terry's Mills by the Helliwells, a vig-orous and substantial Yorkshire family whose heads first settled and commenced operations on the brink of Niagara Falls, on the Canadian side, in 1818, but then in 1821 transferred them-selves to the upper valley of the Don where that river becomes a

---

[14] Dislike of the name 'Little York' or 'Muddy Little York' was one of the reasons for the return to the name Toronto in 1834.

shallow, rapid stream and where the surroundings are, on a small scale, quite Alpine in character—a secluded spot at the time, in the rudest state of nature, a favourite haunt of wolves, bears, and deer; a spot presenting difficulties peculiarly formidable for the new settler to grapple with, from the loftiness and steepness of the hills and the kind of timber growing thereabout, massive pines for the most part. Associated with the Helliwells in their various enterprises, and allied to them by co-partnerships and intermarriage, were the Skinners and Eastwoods, all shrewd and persevering folk of the Midland and North-country English stock. It was Mr Eastwood who gave the name of Todmorden to the village overlooking the mills. Todmorden, partly in Yorkshire and partly in Lancashire, was the old home of the Helliwells.

Farther up the river, on the hills to the right, were the Sinclairs, very early settlers from New England; and beyond, descending again into the vale, the Taylors and Leas, substantial and enterprising emigrants from England.

Hereabout were the 'Forks of the Don' where the west branch of that stream, seen at York Mills, enters. The hills in this neighbourhood are lofty and precipitous, and the pines that clothed them were of a remarkably fine growth. The tedious circuit which teams were obliged to make in order to get into the town from these regions by the Don bridge has since been, to some extent, obviated by the erection of two additional bridges at points higher up the stream north of the Kingston Road.

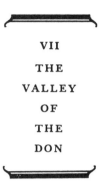

VII

THE

VALLEY

OF

THE

DON

I. FROM THE BRIDGE ON THE KINGSTON ROAD TO TYLER'S

Retracing our steps. Placing ourselves again on the bridge [at
Queen Street] and turning northwards, we see on the right,
nearby, a field or rough space which has undergone excavation,
looking as though the brick-maker or potter had been at work
on it; and we may observe that a large quantity of the displaced
material has been spread out over a portion of the marshy tract
enclosed here by a bend of the river westward. What we see is a
relic of an effort made long ago by Mr Washburn, a barrister of
York, to whom reference has been made before, to bring this
piece of land into cultivation. In its natural state the property
was all but useless, from the steepness of the hillside on the
one hand and from the ever wet condition of the central portion
of the flat below on the other. By grading down the hill and
filling in the marsh, and establishing a gentle slope from the
margin of the stream to the level of the top of the bank on the
right, it was easy to see that a large piece of solid land in an
eligible position might be secured. The undertaking, however,
was abandoned before the work was finished, the expense probably being found heavy and the prospect of a return for the
outlay remote.

At a later period Mr O'Neill, with greater success and completeness, cut down the steep ridges of the bank at Don Mount,
a short distance up, and filled in the marsh below. These ex-

I.   Henry Scadding, 1813-1901. (courtesy *Metropolitan Toronto Library*.)

II. Jail and Courthouse, York, Upper Canada, 1829.James Pattison Cockburn. (courtesy *Royal Ontario Museum.*)

III. View of Upper Canada College, Toronto1835 Thomas Young. (courtesy *Royal Ontario Museum.*)

IV. Fish Market, Toronto, 1838. W.H. Bartlett. Published in Canadian Scenery (1842). (courtesy *Metropolitan Toronto Library.*)

V. King Street, Toronto, c. 1840. John Gillespie. (courtesy *Royal Ontario Museum.*)

VI. Holy Trinity Church on Trinity Square, Toronto, c. 1870-5. From the T.A. Reed Collection. (courtesy *Metropolitan Toronto Library*)

VII. A View of Henry Scadding's Study, 6 Trinity Square, Toronto. (courtesy *Metropolitan Toronto Library*)

VIII. Another View of Henry Scadding's Study, 6 Trinity Square, Toronto. (courtesy *Metropolitan Toronto Library*)

periments show how the valley of the Don, along the eastern outskirts of the town, will ultimately be turned to account when the necessities of the population demand the outlay. At present such improvements are discouraged by the length of time required to cover large surfaces of new clay with vegetable mould. But in future years it will be for mills and factories, and not for suburban and villa purposes, that the parts referred to will be held valuable.

These marshes along the sides of the Don, from the point where its current ceases to be perceptible, appear to be remains of the river as it was at an epoch long ago. The rim or levee that now, on the right and left, confines and defines the meanderings of the stream in the midst of the marshes has been formed by the alluvial matter deposited in the annual overflowings. The bed of the stream has probably in the same manner been by degrees slightly raised. The solid tow-path, as it were, thus created on each side of the river-channel affords at present a great convenience to the angler and fowler. It forms, moreover, as shown by the experiments above alluded to, a capital breastwork towards which the engineer may advance when cutting down the adjoining hills and disposing of their material on the drowned land below.

Once more imagining ourselves on the bridge and looking obliquely to the north-west, we may still discern close by some remains of the short, shallow, winding ravine by which in winter the sleighs used to ascend from the level of the river and regain, through a grove of pines and hemlocks, the high road into the town. As soon as the steady cold set in every year the long reaches and grand sweeps of the river Don became peculiarly interesting. Firmly frozen over everywhere and coated with a good depth of snow, bordered on each side by a high shrubbery of wild willow, alder, wych-hazel, dog-wood, tree-cranberry, and other specimens of the lesser brushwood of the forest, plentifully overspread and interwoven in numerous places with the vine of wild grape, the whole had the appearance of a fine, clear, level English coach-road or highway, bounded throughout its winding course by a luxuriant hedge, seen as such English roads and their surroundings were wont to 'be, all snow-clad at Christmas-tide from the top of the fast mail to Exeter, for example, in the old coaching days.

Down the river, thus conveniently paved over, every day came a cavalcade of strong sleighs, heavily laden, some with cordwood, some with sawn lumber, some with hay, a whole stack of which at once, sometimes, would seem to be on the move.

After a light fall of snow in the night, the surface of the frozen stream would be marked all over with footprints innumerable of animals, small and great, that had been early out a-foraging: tracks of field-mice, minks and martens, of land-rats, water-rats, and muskrats; of the wild-cat sometimes, and of the fox; and sometimes of the wolf. Up this valley we have heard at night the howling of the wolf; and in the snow of the meadows that skirt the stream we have seen the bloodstained spots where sheep had been worried and killed by that ravenous animal.

In one or two places where the bends of the river touched the inner high bank, and where diggings had abortively been made with a view to the erection of a factory of some kind, beautiful frozen gushes of water from springs in the hillside were every winter to be seen, looking at a distance like small motionless Niagaras. At one sheltered spot, we remember, where a tannery was begun but never finished, solid ice was sometimes to be found far on in the summer.

In the spring and summer, a pull up the Don while yet its banks were in their primeval state was something to be enjoyed. After passing certain potasheries and distilleries that at an early period were erected a short distance northward of the bridge, the meadow land at the base of the hills began to widen out; and numerous elm trees, very lofty, with gracefully-drooping branches, made their appearance with other very handsome trees as the lime or basswood and the sycamore or button-wood.

At a very early period, we have been assured that brigades of North West Company boats en route to Lake Huron used to make their way up the Don as far as the Forks, by one of which they then passed westward towards the track now known as Yonge Street: they there were taken ashore and carried on trucks to the Holland River. The help gained by utilizing this piece of waterway must have been slight when the difficulties to be overcome high up the stream were taken into account. We have conversed with an early inhabitant who, at a more recent period, had seen the North West Company's boats drawn on trucks by oxen up the line of modern Yonge Street, but in his day starting, mounted in this manner, from the edge of the bay. In both cases they were shifted across from the Lake into the harbour at the 'Carrying-place'—the narrow neck or isthmus a little to the west of the mouth of the Don proper where the lake has now made a passage [the Eastern Gap].

We add one more of the spectacles which in the olden time gave animation to the scene before us. Along the winding stream, where in winter the sleighs were to be seen coming down, every summer at night would be observed a succession of moving lights, each repeated in the dark water below. These were the iron cressets, filled with unctuous pine knots all ablaze, suspended from short poles at the bows of the fishermen's skiffs out in the quest of salmon and such other large fish as might be deemed worth a thrust of the long-handled, sharply-barbed trident used in such operations. Before the establishment of mills and factories, many hundreds of salmon were annually taken in the Don, as in all the other streams emptying into Lake Ontario. We have ourselves been out on a night-fishing excursion on the Don when in the course of an hour some twenty heavy salmon were speared; and we have a distinct recollection of the conspicuous appearance of the great fish as seen by the aid of the blazing 'jack' at the bow, nozzling about at the bottom of the stream.

II. FROM TYLER'S TO THE BIG BEND

Not far from the spot where at present the Don Street bridge crosses the river [at Queen Street], on the west side and to the north, lived for a long time a hermit-squatter named Joseph Tyler, an old New Jersey man of picturesque aspect. With his rather fine, sharp, shrewd features set off by an abundance of white hair and beard, he was the counterpart of an Italian artist's stock-model. The mystery attendant on his choice of a life of complete solitude, his careful reserve, his perfect self-reliance in regard to domestic matters, and at the same time the evident wisdom of his contrivances and ways, and the propriety and sagacity of his few words, all helped to render him a good specimen in actual life of a secular anchorite. He had been in fact a soldier in the United States army in the War of Independence, and was in the receipt of a pension from the other side of the lakes. He was familiar, he alleged, with the personal appearance of Washington.

His abode on the Don was an excavation in the side of the steep hill a little way above the level of the river bank. The flue of his winter fire-place was a tubular channel bored up through the clay of the hillside. His sleeping-place or berth was exactly like one of the receptacles for human remains in the Roman catacombs, an oblong recess likewise carved in the dry material of the hill. To the south of his cave he cultivated a large garden and raised among other things the white sweet edible Indian corn, a novelty here at the time, and very excellent tobacco. He moreover manufactured pitch and tar in a little kiln or pit dug for the purpose close by his house.

He built for himself a magnificent canoe, locally famous. It consisted of two large pine logs each about forty feet long, well shaped and deftly hollowed out, fastened together by cross dovetail pieces let in at regular distances along the interior of its bottom. While in process of construction in the pine woods through which the 'Mill Road' passes [leading to the Helliwell mills], on the high bank eastward of the river, it was a wonderment to all the inquisitive youth of the neighbourhood and was accordingly often visited and inspected by them.

In this craft he used to pole himself down the windings of the stream all the way round into the bay and on to the landing-place at the foot of Caroline Street, bringing with him the produce of his garden and neat stacks of pine knots, ready split for the fishermen's lightjacks. He would also on occasion undertake the office of ferryman. On being hailed for the purpose, he would put across the river persons anxious to make a short-cut into the town from the eastward. Just opposite his den there was for a time a rude causeway over the marsh.

At the season of the year when the roads through the woods were impracticable, Tyler's famous canoe was employed by the Messrs Helliwell for conveying into town from a point high up the stream the beer manufactured at their breweries on the Don. We are informed by Mr William Helliwell of the Highland Creek that twenty-two barrels at a time could be placed in it, in two rows of eleven each laid lengthwise side by side, still leaving room for Tyler and an assistant to navigate the boat.

The large piece of meadowland on the east side of the river above Tyler's abode, enclosed by a curve which the stream makes towards the west, has a certain interest attached to it from the fact that therein was reproduced, for the first time in these parts, that peculiarly pleasant English scene, a hop-garden. Under the care of Mr James Case, familiar with the hop in Sussex, this graceful and useful plant was here for several seasons to be seen passing through the successive stages of its scientific cultivation—in early spring sprouting from the surface of the rich black vegetable mould, then trained gradually over, and at length clothing richly the poles or groups of poles set at regular distances throughout the enclosure; overtopping these supports; by and by loading them heavily with a plentiful crop of swaying clusters; and then finally, when in a sufficiently mature state, prostrated, props and all, upon the ground, and stripped of their fragrant burden, the real object of all the pains taken. From this field many valuable pockets of hops were gathered, and the quality of the plant was pronounced to be good. Mr Case afterwards engaged extensively in the same occupation in the neighbourhood of Newmarket.

About the dry, sandy table-land that overlooked the river on each side in this neighbourhood, the burrows of the fox, often with little families within, were plentifully to be met with. The marmot, too, popularly known as the woodchuck, was to be seen on sunny days sitting up upon its haunches at holes in the hillside. We could at this moment point out the ancient home of a particular animal of this species whose ways we used to note with some curiosity. Here were to be found racoons also; but these, like the numerous squirrels—black, red, flying, and striped—were visible only towards the decline of summer when the maize and th enuts began to ripen. At that period also bears, he-bears and she-bears accompanied by their cubs, were not unfamiliar objects wherever the blackberry and raspberry grew. In the forest, moreover, hereabout a rustle in the underbrush and something white seen dancing up and down in the distance like the plume of a mounted knight might at any moment indicate that a group of deer had caught sight of one of the dreaded human race and, with tails uplifted, had bounded incontinently away.

Pines of a great height and thickness crowded the tops of these hills. The paths of hurricanes could be traced over extensive tracts by the fallen trunks of trees of this species, their huge bulks lying one over the other in a titanic confusion worthy of a sketch by Doré in illustration of Dante; their heads all in one direction, their upturned roots, vast mats of woody ramifications and earth, presented sometimes a perpendicular wall of a great height. Occasionally one of these upright masses, originating in the habit of the pine to send out a widespread but shallow rootage, would unexpectedly fall back into its original place when, in the clearing of the land, the bole of the tree to which it appertained came to be gashed through. In this case it would sometimes happen that a considerable portion of the trunk would appear again in a perpendicular position. As its top would of course show that human hands had been at work there, the question would be propounded to the newcomer as to how the axe could have reached to such a height. The suppositions usually encouraged in him were either that the snow must have been wonderfully deep when that particular tree was felled or else that some one of the very early settlers must have been a man of exceptional stature.

Among the lofty pines here and there one more exposed than the rest would be seen with a piece of the thickness of a strong fence-rail stripped out of its side, from its extreme apex to its very root, spirally, like the groove of a rifle-bore. It in this manner showed that at some moment it had been the swift conductor down into the earth of the contents of a passing electric cloud. One tree of the pine species we remember that had been severed in the midst by lightning so suddenly that the upper half had descended with perfect perpendicularity and such force that it planted itself upright in the earth by the side of the trunk from which it had been smitten.

Nor may we omit from our remembered phenomena of the pine forests hereabout the bee-trees. Now and then a huge pine would fall, or be intentionally cut down, which would exhibit in cavernous recesses at a great distance from what had been its root end the accumulated combs of it might be a half century, those of them that were of recent construction filled with honey.

A short distance above the hop ground of which we have spoken, the Don passed immediately underneath a high sandy bluff. Where after a long reach in its downward course it first impinged against the steep cliff, it was very deep. Here was the only point in its route, so far as we recall, where the epithet was applicable which Milton gives to its English namesake when he speaks of

Utmost Tweed, or Ouse, or gulphy *Don.*

This very noticeable portion of the river was known as the 'Big Bend'.

Towards the summit of the high bluff just mentioned, the holes made by the sand-martins were numerous. Hereabout we have met with the snapping turtle. This creature has not the power of withdrawing itself wholly within a shell. A part of its protection consists in the loud threatening snap of its strong horny jaws, armed in front with a beak-like hook bent downwards. What the creature lays hold of, it will not let go. Let it grasp the end of a stout stick and the sportsman may sling it over his shoulder and so carry it home with him. When allowed to reach its natural term of life, it probably attains a very great age. We remember a specimen captured near the spot at which we are pausing which, from its vast size and the rough, lichen-covered condition of its shell, must have been extremely old. We also once found near here a numerous deposit of this animal's eggs—all white and spherical, of the diameter of about an inch, and covered with a tough parchment-like skin.

The ordinary lesser tortoises of the marsh were of course plentiful along the Don: their young frequently to be met with creeping about were curious and ever-interesting little objects. Snakes too there were about here, of several kinds: one, often very large and dangerous-looking, the copper-head, of a greenish brown colour and covered with oblong and rather loose scales. The striped garter-snake of all sizes was very common. Though reported to be harmless, it always indulged, when interfered with, in the menacing action and savage attempts to strike of the most venomous of its genus. Then there was the beautiful grass-green snake; and in large numbers the black water-snake. In the rank herbage along the river's edge the terrified piping of a pursued frog was often heard.

It recurs to us as we write that once on the banks of the Humber we saw a bird actually in the grasp of a large garter-snake—just held by the foot. As the little creature fluttered violently in the air, the head of the reptile was swayed rapidly to and fro. All the small birds in the vicinity had gathered together in a state of noisy excitement and many spirited dashes were made by several of them at the common foe. No great injury having been as yet inflicted, we were enabled to effect a happy rescue.

From the high sandy cliff, to which our attention has been drawn, it was possible to look down into the waters of the river; and on a sunny day it afforded no small amusement to watch the habits, not only of the creatures just named, but of the fish also, visible below in the stream—the simple sunfish, for example, swimming about in shoals (or *schools*, as the term used to be) ; and the pike, crafty as a fox, lurking in solitude, ready to dart on his unwary prey with the swiftness and precision of an arrow shot from the bow.

III. FROM THE BIG BEND TO CASTLE FRANK BROOK

Above the 'Big Bend', on the west side, was 'Rock Point'. At the water's edge hereabout was a slight outcrop of shaly rock where crayfish were numerous, and black bass. The adjoining marshy land was covered with a dense thicket in which wild gooseberry bushes and wild black-currant bushes were noticeable. The flats along here were a favourite haunt of woodcock at the proper season of the year: the peculiar succession of little twitters uttered by them when descending from their flight, and the very different deep-toned note, the signal of their having alighted, were both very familiar sounds in the dusk of the evening.

A little further on was 'the Island'. The channel between it and the 'mainland' on the north side was completely choked up with logs and large branches brought down by the freshets. It was itself surrounded by a high fringe or hedge of the usual brush that lined the riverside all along, matted together and clambered over almost everywhere by the wild grape-vine. In the waters at its northern end wild rice grew plentifully, and the beautiful sweet-scented white water-lily or lotus.

This minute bit of insulated land possessed, to the boyish fancy, great capabilities. Within its convenient circuit, what phantasies and dreams might not be realized? A Juan Fernandez, a Barataria, a New Atlantis. At the present moment we find that what was once our charmed isle has now become *terra firma*, wholly amalgamated with the mainland. Silt has hidden from view the tangled lodgments of the floods. A carpet of pleasant herbage has overspread the silt. The border-strip of shrubbery and grape-vine, which so delightfully walled it round, has been improved, root and branch, out of being.

Near the Island, on the left side, a rivulet (of which more immediately) pouring down through a deep, narrow ravine, entered the Don. On the right, just at this point, the objectionable marshes began to disappear and the whole bottom of the vale was early converted into handsome meadows. Scattered about were grand elm and butternut, fine basswood and buttonwood trees, with small groves of the Canadian willow which pleasantly resembles, in habit, the olive tree of the south of Europe. Along the flats, remains of Indian encampments were often met with, tusks of bears and other animals, with fragments of coarse pottery, streaked or furrowed rudely over, for ornament. And all along the valley, calcareous masses, richly impregnated with iron, were found, detached from time to time, as was supposed, from certain places in the hillsides.

At the long-ago epoch when the land went up, the waters came down with a concentrated rush from several directions into the valley just here from some accidental cause, carving out in their course, in the enormous deposit of the drift, a number of deep and rapidly descending channels, converging all upon this point. The drainage of a large extent of acreage to the eastward, also at that period, found here for a time its way into the Don, as may be seen by a neighbouring gorge, and the deep and wide but now *dry* water-course leading to it, known where the 'Mill Road' crosses it as the 'Big Hollow'.

Bare and desolate, at that remote era, must have been the appearance of these earth-banks and ridges and flats, as also those in the vicinity of all our rivers: for many a long year they must have resembled the surroundings of some great tidal river, to which the sea, after ebbing, had failed to return.

One result of the ancient down-rush of waters just about here was that on both sides of the river there were to be observed several striking specimens of that long, thin, narrow kind of hill which is popularly known as a 'hog's back'. One on the east side afforded along its ridge a convenient ascent from the meadows to the table-land above, where fine views up and down the vale were obtainable, somewhat Swiss in character, including in the distance the lake to the south. Overhanging the pathway, about half-way up, a group of white-birch trees is remembered by the token that, on their stems, a number of young men and maidens of the neighbourhood had, in sentimental mood, after the manner of the Corydons and Amaryllises of classic times, incised their names.

The west side of the river, as well as the east, of which we have been more especially speaking, presented here also a collection of convergent 'hog's backs' and deeply channelled watercourses. One of the latter still conducted down a living stream to the Don. This was the rivulet already noticed as entering just above the Island. It bore the graceful name of 'Castle Frank Brook'.

IV. CASTLE FRANK

Castle Frank was a rustic château or summer-house built by Governor Simcoe in the midst of the woods [1796] on the brow of a steep and lofty bank which overlooks the vale of the Don a short distance to the north of where we have been lingering [near Parliament and Bloor Streets]. The construction of this edifice was a mere *divertissement* while engaged in the grand work of planting in a field literally and entirely new the institutions of civilization.

All the way from the site of the town of York to the front of this building, a narrow carriage-road and convenient bridle-path had been cut out by the soldiers and carefully graded. Remains of this ancient engineering achievement are still to be traced along the base of the hill below the Necropolis and elsewhere. The brook—Castle Frank Brook—a little way from where it enters the Don was spanned by a wooden bridge. Advantage being taken of a narrow ridge that opportunely had its commencing point close by on the north side, the roadway here began the ascent of the adjoining height. It then ran slantingly up the hillside, along a cutting which is still to be seen. The table-land at the summit was finally gained by utilizing another narrow ridge. It then proceeded along the level at the top for some distance through a forest of lofty pines until the château itself was reached.

The cleared space where the building stood was not many yards across. On each side of it the ground precipitously descended, on the one hand to the Don, on the other to the bottom of the ravine where flowed the brook. Notwithstanding the elevation of the position, the view was circumscribed, hillside and table-land being alike covered with trees of the finest growth.

Castle Frank itself was an edifice of considerable dimensions, of an oblong shape; its walls were composed of a number of rather small, carefully hewn logs of short lengths. The whole wore the hue which unpainted timber, exposed to the weather, speedily assumes. At the gable end, in the direction of the road-way from the nascent capital, was the principal entrance over which a rather imposing portico was formed by the projection of the whole roof, supported by four upright columns reaching the whole height of the building and consisting of the stems of four good-sized, well-matched pines with their deeply-chapped corrugated bark unremoved. The doors and shutters to the windows were all of double thickness made of stout plank running up and down on one side and crosswise on the other and thickly studded over with the heads of stout nails. From the middle of the building rose a solitary, massive chimney-stack.

We can picture to ourselves the cavalcade that was wont, from time to time, to be seen in the summers and autumns of 1794-'5-'6, wending its way leisurely to the romantically situated château of Castle Frank[1] along the reaches and windings, the descents and ascents of the forest road, expressly cut out through the primitive woods as a means of access to it.

First, mounted on a willing and well-favoured horse, as we will suppose, there would be General Simcoe himself—a soldierly personage in the full vigour of life, advanced but little beyond his fortieth year, of thoughtful and stern yet benevolent aspect, as shewn by the medallion in marble on his monument in the cathedral at Exeter—revolving ever in his mind schemes for the development and defence of the new Society which he was engaged in founding; a man 'just, active, enlightened, brave, frank', as the French Duke de Liancourt described him in 1795; 'possessing the confidence of the country, of the troops, and of all those who were joined with him in the administration of public affairs.' 'No hillock catches his eye', the same observant writer remarks, 'without exciting in his mind the idea of a fort which might be constructed on the spot, associating with the construction of this fort the plan of operations for a campaign; especially of that which should lead him to Philadelphia', i.e., to recover by force of arms to the allegiance of England the Colonies recently revolted.

By the side of the soldier and statesman Governor, also on

---

[1]Castle Frank was not built until the winter of 1795-6, but the site was a favourite picnic spot of the Simcoes.

horseback, would be his gifted consort, small in person, 'handsome and amiable', as the French Duke again speaks, 'fulfilling', as he continues to say, 'all the duties of the mother and wife with the most scrupulous exactness; carrying the latter so far', de Liancourt observes, 'as to be of great assistance to her husband by her talent for drawing, the practice of which, in relation to maps and plans, enabled her to be extremely useful to the Governor,' while her skill and facility and taste in a wider application of that talent were attested, the French traveller might have added, by numerous sketch-books and portfolios of views of Canadian scenery in its primitive condition taken by her hand, to be treasured up carefully and reverently by her immediate descendants but unfortunately not accessible generally to Canadian students.

This memorable lady—memorable for her eminent Christian goodness as well as for her artistic skill and taste and superior intellectual endowments—survived to the late period of 1850. Her maiden name is preserved among us by the designation borne by two of our townships, East and West 'Gwillim'-bury. Her father, at the time one of the aides-de-camp to General Wolfe, was killed at the taking of Quebec [1759].

Conspicuous in the group would likewise be a young daughter and son, the latter about five years of age and bearing the name of Francis. The château of which we have just given an account was theoretically the private property of this child and took its name from him, although the appellation, by accident as we suppose, is identical, in sound at all events, with that of a certain 'Castel-franc' near Rochelle, which figures in the history of the Huguenots.

The Iroquois at Niagara had given the Governor a title expressive of hospitality—Deyonynhokrawen, 'One whose door is always open.' They had, moreover, in Council declared his son a chief and had named him Tioga or Deyoken—'Between the Two Objects'; and to humour them in return, as Liancourt informs us, the child was occasionally attired in Indian costume. For most men it is well that the future is veiled from them. It happened eventually that a warrior's fate befell the young chieftain Tioga. The little spirited lad who had been seen at one time moving about before the assembled Iroquois at Niagara, under a certain restraint probably, from the unwonted garb of embroidered deerskin in which on such occasions he would be arrayed, and at another time clambering up and down the steep hillsides at Castle Frank with the restless energy of a free English boy, was at last, after the lapse of some seventeen years, seen a mangled corpse, one in that ghastly pile of 'English dead' which in 1812 closed up the breach at Badajoz.

Riding with the Governor out to his rustic lodge would be seen also his attached secretary, Major Littlehales, and one or other of his faithful aides-de-camp, Lieutenant Talbot or Lieutenant Givins; with men in attendance in the dark green undress of the famous Queen's Rangers, with a sumpter pony or two, bearing packages and baskets filled with a day's provender for the whole party. A few dogs also—a black Newfoundland, a pointer, a setter, white and tan, hying buoyantly about on the right and left, would give animation to the cavalcade as it passed sedately on its way—

Through the green-glooming twilight of the grove.

It will be of interest to add here the inscription on General Simcoe's monument in Exeter Cathedral: 'Sacred to the memory of John Graves Simcoe, Lieutenant-General in the army, and Colonel of the 22nd Regiment of Foot, who died on the 25th day of October, 1806, aged 54. In whose life and character the virtues of the hero, the patriot and the Christian were so eminently conspicuous, that it may justly be said, he served his king and his country with a zeal exceeded only by his piety towards God.' Above this inscription is a medallion portrait. On the right and left are figures of an Indian and a soldier of the Queen's Rangers. The remains of the General are not deposited in Exeter Cathedral but under a mortuary chapel on the estate of his family elsewhere.[2]

Our cavalcade to Castle Frank, as sketched above, was once challenged on the supposed ground that in 1794 there were no horses in Western Canada. Horses were no doubt at that date

---

[2] The province of Ontario has recently taken over the care and maintenance of the chapel, which is situated at Wolford in Devonshire.

scarce in the region named, but some were procurable for the use of the Governor and his suite. In a 'Journal to Detroit from Niagara, in 1793, by Major Littlehales', printed for the first time in the *Canadian Literary Magazine* for May 1833, we have it mentioned that, on the return of an exploring party, they were met at the end of the plains, near the Salt Lake Creek, by Indians, 'bringing horses for the Governor and his suite'. The French *habitants* about Sandwich and Detroit were in possession of horses in 1793, as well as their fellow countrymen in Lower Canada.

After the departure of General Simcoe from Canada [1796], Castle Frank was occasionally made the scene of an excursion or picnic by President Russell and his family; and a ball was now and then given there for which the appliances as well as the guests were conveyed in boats up the Don. At one time it was temporarily occupied by Captain John Denison, of whom hereafter. About the year 1829 the building, shut up and tenantless at the time, was destroyed by fire, the mischievous handiwork of persons engaged in salmon-fishing in the Don. A depression in the dry sand just beyond the fence which bounds the Cemetery of St James' northward, shews to this day the exact site of Castle Frank. The quantity of iron that was gathered out from this depression after the fire was, as we remember, something extraordinary, all the window shutters and doors having been, as we have said, made of double planks fastened together with an immense number of stout nails whose heads thickly studded the surface of each in regular order.

The immediate surroundings of the spot where Castle Frank stood fortunately continue almost in their original natural state. Although the site of the building itself is outside the bounds of the Cemetery of St James, a large portion of the lot which at first formed the domain of the château now forms a part of that spacious and picturesque enclosure. The deep glen on the west, immediately below where the house was built, and through which flows (and by the listener may be pleasantly *heard* to flow) the brook that bears its name, is to this day a scene of rare sylvan beauty. The pedestrian from the town, by a half-hour's easy walk, can here place himself in the midst of a forest solitude; and from what he sees he can form an idea of the whole surrounding region as it was when York was first laid out. Here he can find in abundance to this day specimens, gigantic and minute, of the vegetation of the ancient woods. Here at the proper seasons he can still hear the blue jay; the flute notes of the solitary wood-thrush; and at night, especially when the moon is shining bright, the whip-poor-will, hurriedly and in a high key, syllabling forth its own name.

V. ON TO THE FORD AND THE MILLS

We now resume our ramble up the valley of the Don. Northward of the gorge, where Castle Frank Brook entered and where so many other deep-cut ravines converge upon the present channel of the stream, the scenery becomes really good.

We pass along through natural meadows, bordered on both sides by fine hills which recede by a succession of slight plateaux, the uppermost of them clothed with lofty pines and oaks: on the slope nearest to 'the flats' on the east grew, along with the chokecherry and mayflower, numbers of the wild apple or crab, beautiful objects when in full bloom. Hereabout also was to be found the prickly ash, a rather uncommon and graceful shrub. (The long-continued precipitous bank on the west side of the Don, completely covered with forest with at last the roof of the rustic château appearing above, must have recalled in some slight degree the Sharpham woods and Sharpham to the mind of anyone who had ever chanced to sail up the Dart so far as that most beautiful spot.)

Immediately beyond the Castle Frank woods where now is the property known as Drumsnab came the estate of Captain George Playter, and directly across on the opposite side of the river that of his son Captain John Playter, both immigrants from Pennsylvania. When the town of York was in the occupancy of the Americans in 1813, many of the archives of the young province of Upper Canada were conveyed for safe keeping to the houses of these gentlemen. But boats, with men and officers from the invading force, found their way up the windings of the Don, and such papers and documents as could be found were carried away.

Just below Drumsnab, on the west side of the stream, and set down, as it were, in the midst of the valley, was and is a singular isolated mound of the shape of a glass shade over a French clock known in the neighbourhood as the 'Sugar Loaf'. It was completely clothed over with moderate-sized trees. When the whole valley of the Don was filled with a brimming river reaching to the summit of its now secondary banks, the top of the 'Sugar Loaf', which is nearly on a level with the summit of the adjacent hills, must have appeared above the face of the water as an island speck.

This picturesque and curious mound is noticed by Sir James Alexander, in the account which he gives of the neighbourhood of Toronto in his *L'Acadie, or Seven Years' Explorations in British America* [1849]: 'The most picturesque spot near Toronto,' says Sir James, 'and within four miles of it, is Drumsnab, the residence of Mr Cayley. The mansion is roomy and of one storey, with a broad verandah.[3] It is seated among fields and woods, on the edge of a slope; at the bottom winds a river; opposite is a most singular conical hill, like an immense Indian tumulus for the dead; in the distance, through a vista cut judiciously through the forest, are seen the dark blue waters of Lake Ontario. The walls of the principal room are covered with scenes from Faust, drawn in fresco, with a bold and masterly hand, by the proprietor.'

In the shadow thrown eastward by the 'Sugar Loaf' there was a 'ford' in the Don, a favourite bathing-place for boys, with a clean gravelly bottom and a current somewhat swift. That ford was just in the line of an allowance for a concession road which, from the precipitous character of the hills on both sides, has been of late years closed by Act of Parliament on the ground of its supposed impracticability forever, a proceeding to be regretted as the highway which would traverse the Don valley at the ford would be a continuation of Bloor Street in a right line

---

[3] A second storey was added to the house about 1860, and the structure still stands as 5 Castle Frank Place.

and would form a convenient means of communication between Chester and Yorkville.[4]

In the meadow on the left, just above the ford, a little meandering brook abounding in trout entered the Don. Hereabouts also was for a long while a rustic bridge over the main river, formed by trees felled across the stream.

Proceeding on our way, we now in a short time approached the great colony of the Helliwells which has already been described. The mills and manufactories established here by that enterprising family constituted quite a conspicuous village. A visit to this cluster of buildings in 1827 is described by Mr W. L. Mackenzie, in his *Sketches of Canada*, published in London by Effingham Wilson in 1833. At page 270 of that work, the writer says: 'About three miles out of town, in the bottom of a deep ravine, watered by the river Don, and bounded also by beautiful and verdant flats, are situated the York Paper Mills, distillery and gristmill of Messrs Eastwood & Co.; also Mr Shepard's axe-grinding machinery; and Messrs Helliwell's large and extensive Brewery. I went out to view these improvements a few days ago, and returned much gratified with witnessing the paper-manufacture in active operation—as also the bold and pleasant scenery on the banks of the Don. The river might be made navigable with small expense up to the brewery; and if the surrounding lands were laid out in five-acre lots all the way to town, they would sell to great advantage.'

---

[4] The site of the ford is now the location of the Prince Edward Viaduct connecting Bloor Street and the Danforth.

VIII

QUEEN

STREET

FROM THE

DON BRIDGE

TO

CAROLINE

STREET;

HISTORY

OF THE

EARLY PRESS

We return once more to the Don Bridge and from that point commence a journey westward along the thoroughfare now known as Queen Street but which at the period at present occupying our attention was non-existent. The region through which we at first pass was long known as the Park. It was a portion of government property, not divided into lots and sold until recent times [the mid-1830s].

Originally a great space extending from the first Parliament houses, bounded southward and eastward by the water of the Bay and Don and northward by the Castle Frank lot, was set apart as a 'Reserve for Government Buildings', to be, it may be, according to the idea of the day, a small domain of woods and forests in connection with them; or else to be converted in the course of time into a source of ways and means for their erection and maintenance.

The Park, as we remember it, was a tract of land in a state of nature, densely covered towards the north with massive pines and towards the south with a thick secondary growth of the same forest tree. Through these woods ran a devious and rather obscure track originating in the bridle-road cut out, before the close of the preceding century, to Castle Frank; one branch led off from it to the Playter estate, passing down and up two very steep and difficult precipices; and another, trending to the west and north, conducted the wayfarer to a point on Yonge Street about where Yorkville is now to be seen.

To the youthful imagination, the Park, thus clothed with veritable forest,

> *The nodding horror of whose shady brows*
> *Awed the forlorn and wandering passenger*

and traversed by irregular, ill-defined and very solitary paths leading to widely-separated localities, seemed a vast and rather mysterious region, the place which immediately flashed on the mind whenever in poem or fairy tale a wild or wold or wilderness was named. As time rolled on, too, it actually became the haunt and hiding-place of lawless characters.

After passing on our left the burial-plot attached to the first Roman Catholic Church of York [St Paul's, Power Street], and arriving where Parliament Street at the present day intersects, we reached the limit in that direction of the 'Reserve for Government Buildings'. Stretching from the point indicated there was on the right side of the way a range of 'park-lots' extending some two miles to the west, all bounded on the south by what at the present time is Queen Street but which, from being the great thoroughfare along the front of this very range, was long known as 'Lot Street'.

In the early plan of this part of York the names of the first locatees of the range of park-lots are given. On the first or easternmost lot we read that of John Small. On the next that of J. White.

In this collocation of names there is something touching when we recall an event in which the first owners of these two contiguous lots were tragically concerned. Friends, and associates in the Public Service—the one as Clerk of the Crown, the other as Attorney-General for Upper Canada, from 1792-1800—

their dream, doubtless, was to pass the evening of their days in pleasant suburban villas placed here side by side in the outskirts of the young capital. But there arose between them a difficulty, trivial enough probably at the beginning but which, according to the barbaric conventionality of the hour, could only be finally settled by a 'meeting', as the phrase was, in the field, where chance was to decide between them, for life or death, as between two armies—two armies reduced to the absurdity of each consisting of one man. The encounter took place in a pleasant grove at the back of the Parliament Building immediately to the east of it, between what is now King Street and the water's edge. Mr White was mortally wounded and soon expired. At his own request his remains were deposited in his garden on the park-lot beneath a summer-house to which he had been accustomed to retire for purposes of study.

The *Oracle* of Saturday, January 4, 1800, records the duel in the following words: 'Yesterday morning a duel was fought back of the Government Buildings by John White, Esq., his Majesty's Attorney-General, and John Small, Esq., Clerk of the Executive Council, wherein the former received a wound above the right hip, which it is feared will prove mortal.' In the issue of the following Saturday, January 11th, the announcement appears:—'It is with much regret that we express to the public, the death of John White, Esq.' It is added: 'His remains were on Tuesday evening interred in a small octagon building, erected on the rear of his Park lot.' 'The procession', the *Oracle* observes, 'was solemn and pensive; and shewed that though death, "all eloquent," had seized upon him as his victim, yet it could not take from the public mind the lively sense of his virtues. *Vivit post funera virtus.*'

The *Constellation* at Niagara, of the date January 11th, 1800, also records the event, and enjoying a greater liberty of expression than the Government organ at York, indulges in some just and sensible remarks on the irrational practice of duelling in general, and on the sadness of the special case which had just occurred. We give the *Constellation* article:

'Died at York, on the 3rd instant, John White, Esq., Attorney-General of this Province. His death was occasioned by a wound he received in a duel fought the day before with John Small, Esq., Clerk of the Executive Council, by whom he was challenged. We have not been able to obtain the particulars of the cause of the dispute; but be the origin what it may, we have to lament the toleration and prevalency of a custom falsely deemed honourable, or the criterion of true courage, innocency or guilt, a custom to gratify the passion of revenge in a single person, to the privation of the country and a family, of an ornament of society, and support: an outrage on humanity that is too often procured by the meanly malicious, who have preferment in office or friendship in view, without merit to gain it, and stupidly lacquey from family to family, or from person to person, some wonderful suspicion, the suggestions of a soft head and evil heart; and it is truly unfortunate for Society that the evil they bring on others should pass by their heads to light on those the world could illy spare. We are unwilling to attribute to either the Attorney-General or Mr Small any improprieties of their own, or to say on whom the blame lies; but of this we feel assured, that an explanation might easily have been brought about by persons near to them, and a valuable life preserved to us. The loss is great; as a professional gentleman, the Attorney-General was eminent, as a friend, sincere; and in whatever relation he stood was highly esteemed; an honest and upright man, a friend to the poor; and dies universally lamented and we here cannot refuse to mention, at the particular request of some who have experienced his goodness, that he has refused taking fees, and discharged suits at law, by recommending to the parties, and assisting them with friendly advice, to an amicable adjustment of their differences: and this is the man whom we have lost!'

For his share in the duel Mr Small was, on the 20th January 1800, indicted and tried before Judge Allcock and a jury, of which Mr Wm. Jarvis was the foreman. The verdict rendered was 'Not Guilty'. The seconds were Mr Sheriff Macdonell for Mr Small and the Baron de Hoen for Mr White.

(In 1871, as some labourers were digging out sand for building purposes, they came upon the grave of Attorney-General White. The remains were carefully removed under the inspection of Mr Clarke Gamble, and deposited in St James' Cemetery.)

Mr White's park-lot became afterwards the property of Mr Samuel Ridout, sometime Sheriff of the County, of whom we have had occasion to speak already. A portion of it was subsequently owned and built on by Mr Edward McMahon, an Irish gentleman, long well known and greatly respected as Chief Clerk in the Attorney-General's office. Mr McMahon's name was for a time preserved in that of a street which here enters Queen Street from the north [Seaton].

Sherbourne Street, which at present divides the White park-lot from Moss Park, commemorates happily the name of the old Dorsetshire home of the main stem of the Canadian Ridouts. The original stock of this family still flourishes in the very ancient and most interesting town of Sherbourne, famous as having been in the Saxon days the see of a bishop, and possessing still a spacious and beautiful minster, familiarly known to architects as a fine study.

Like some other English names, transplanted to the American continent, that of this Dorsetshire family has assumed here a pronunciation slightly different from that given to it by its ancient owners. What in Canada is Ri-dout, at Sherbourne and its neighbourhood is Rid-out.

On the park-lot which constituted the Moss-Park Estate, the name of D. W. Smith appears in the original plan. Mr D. W. Smith was acting Surveyor-General in 1794. He was the author of *A Short Topographical Description of His Majesty's Province of Upper Canada in North America, to which is annexed a Provincial Gazetteer* [1799]—a work of considerable antiquarian interest now, preserving as it does the early names, native, French, and English, of many places now known by different appellations. A second edition was published in London in 1813 and was designed to accompany the new map published in that year by W. Faden, Geographer to the King and Prince Regent. The original work was compiled at the desire of Governor Simcoe to illustrate an earlier map of Upper Canada.

We have spoken already in our progress through Front Street

of the subsequent possessor of Mr Smith's lot, Col. [William] Allan. The residence at Moss Park was built by him in comparatively recent times. The homestead previously had been, as we have already seen, at the foot of Frederick Street, on the south-east corner. To the articles of capitulation on the 27th April 1813, surrendering the town of York to Dearborn and Chauncey, the commanders of the United States force, the name of Col. Allan, at the time Major Allan, is appended following that of Lieut.-Col. Chewett.

Besides the many capacities in which Col. Allan did good service to the community, as detailed during our survey of Front Street, he was also in 1801 Returning Officer on the occasion of a public election. In the *Oracle* of the 20th of June, 1801, we have an advertisement signed by him as Returning Officer for the 'County of Durham, the East Riding of the County of York, and the County of Simcoe'—which territories conjointly are to elect one member. Mr Allan announces that he will be in attendance 'on Thursday, the 2nd day of July next, at 10 o'clock in the forenoon, at the Hustings under the Colonnade of the Government Buildings in the Town of York —and proceed to the election of one Knight to represent the said county, riding and county in the House of Assembly, whereof all freeholders of the said county, riding and county, are to take notice and attend accordingly.'

The writ, issuing from 'His Excellency, Peter Hunter, Esq.', directs the returning officer 'to cause one Knight, girt with a sword, the most fit and discreet, to be freely and indifferently chosen to represent the aforesaid county, riding and county, in Assembly, by those who shall be present on the day of election.'

Two candidates presented themselves, Mr A. Macdonell and Mr J. Small. Mr Macdonell was duly elected, 'there appearing for him', we are briefly informed in a subsequent number of the *Oracle*, '112 unquestionable votes; and for J. Small, Esq. 32: majority, 80.'

In 1804 there was another election, when the candidates were Mr A. Macdonell again, Mr D. W. Smith, of whom above, and Mr Weekes. The result of the election at York in 1804 is announced in the *Oracle* of June 16. As was probably to be expected, Mr Macdonell was the man returned.

The Mr Weekes who was an unsuccessful candidate for a seat in parliament in 1804 was nevertheless a member of the House in 1806, representing the constituencies to which he had previously offered himself. In 1806 he was killed in a duel with Mr Dickson at Niagara, another victim to the peculiar social code of the day which obliged gentlemen on certain occasions of difference to fire pistols at each other. In the *Oracle* of the 11th of October 1806, we read the announcement: 'Died on Friday, the 10th instant, at night, in consequence of a wound received that morning in a duel, William Weekes, Esq., Barrister-at-law, and a Member of the House of Assembly for the counties of York, Durham and Simcoe.' In the next issue of the paper, dated October 25, 1806, we have a second record of the event in the following terms, with a eulogy on Mr Weekes' character: 'It is with sentiments of the deepest regret that we announce to the public the death of William Weekes, Esq., Barrister-at-law in this Province; not only from the melancholy circumstances attendant on his untimely death, but also from a view of the many virtues this Province is deprived of by that death. In him the orphan has lost a father, the widow a friend, the injured a protector, society a pleasing and safe companion, and the Bar one of its ablest advocates. Mr Weekes was honest without the show of ostentation. Wealth and splendour held no lure for him; nor could any pecuniary motives induce him to swerve in the smallest degree from that which he conceived to be strictly honourable. His last moments were marked with that fortitude which was the characteristic of his life, convinced of the purity of which, he met death with pleasure.'

This duel, as we have been informed, was fought on the United States side of the river, near the French Fort.

Mr Weekes, we believe, was an unmarried man. He was fond of solitary rambles in the woods in search of game. Once he was so long missing that foul play was suspected; and some human remains having been found under a heap of logs on the property of Peter Ernest, Peter Ernest was arrested; and just as the

evidence was all going strongly against him, Mr Weekes appeared on the scene alive and well.

One more of these inhuman and unchristian encounters,
with fatal result, memorable in the early annals of York, we
shall have occasion to speak of hereafter when, in our intended
progress up Yonge Street, we pass the spot where the tragedy
was enacted.[1]

Mr Weekes was greatly regretted by his constituents. 'Overwhelmed with grief', they say in their address dated the 20th
September 1806, to the gentleman whom they desire to suc-
ceed him, 'at the unexpected death of our late able and upright
Representative; we, freeholders of these Counties of York,
Durham and Simcoe, feel that we have neglected our interests
in the season of sorrow. Now awake, it is to you we turn; notwithstanding the great portion of consolation which we draw
from the dawning of our impartial and energetic administration. (The allusion is to Gov. Gore.)

'Fully persuaded that the great object of your heart is the
advancement of public prosperity, the observance of the laws,
and the practice of religion and morality, we hasten with assurances of our warmest support, to invite you from your retreat
to represent us in Parliament. Permit us, however, to impress
upon you, that as subjects of a generous and beloved King; as
a part of that great nation which has for so long a time stood
the bulwark of Europe, and is now the solitary and inaccessible
asylum of liberty; as the children of Englishmen, guarded, protected and restrained by English laws; in fine, as members of
their community, as fathers and sons, we are induced to place
this confidence in your virtue, from the firm hope that, equally
insensible to the impulse of popular feeling and the impulse of
power, you will pursue what is right. This has been the body
of your decisions; may it be the spirit of your counsels! (Signed
by fifty-two persons, residing in the Town and Township of
York.)' The names not given.

These words were addressed to Mr Justice Thorpe. His reply

---

1 Scadding here refers to the Jarvis-Ridout duel in 1817; it is described on
page 292.

was couched in the following terms: 'Gentlemen: With pleasure I accede to your desire. If you make me your representative I will faithfully discharge my duty. Your confidence is not misplaced. May the first moment of dereliction be the last of my existence. Your late worthy representative I lament from my heart. Jn private he was a warm friend; at the Bar an able advocate, and in Parliament a firm patriot. It is but just to draw consolation from our Governor, when the first act of his administration granted to those in the U[nited] E[mpire Loyalist] list and their children, what your late most valuable member so strenuously laboured to obtain. Surely from this we have every reason to expect that the liberal interests of our beloved sovereign, whose chief glory is to reign triumphantly enthroned on the hearts of a free people, will be fulfilled, honouring those who give and those who receive, enriching the Province and strengthening the Empire. Let us cherish this hope in the blossom; may it not be blasted in the ripening.' A postscript is subjoined: 'P.S. If influence, threat, coercion or oppression should be attempted to be exercised over any individual, for the purpose of controlling the freedom of election, let me be informed.—R.T.'

In 1806 Judges were not ineligible to the Upper Canadian Parliament. Mr Justice Thorpe and Governor Gore did not agree. He was consequently removed from office. Some years later [1820], when both gentlemen were living in England as private persons, Mr Thorpe brought an action for libel against Mr Gore [for charges made at the time of his dismissal] and obtained a favourable verdict.

We now proceed on our prescribed course. So late as 1833, Walton, in his *York Commercial Directory, Street Guide, and Register,* when naming the residents on Lot Street, as he still designates Queen Street, makes a note on arriving at two parklots to the westward of the spot where we have been pausing to the effect that 'here this street is intercepted by the grounds of Capt. McGill, S. P. Jarvis, Esq., and Hon. W. Allan; past here [to the east] it is open to the Roman Catholic Church, and intended to be carried through to the Don Bridge.'

The process of levelling up, now become so common in

Toronto, has effectually disposed of the difficulty temporarily presented by the ravine or ancient water-course, yet partially to be seen either in front of or upon the park-lots occupied by the old inhabitants just named; and Queen Street at the present hour is an uninterrupted thoroughfare in a right line, and almost on a level the whole way, from the Don in the east to the Lunatic Asylum in the west, and beyond, on to the gracefully curving margin of Humber Bay. (The unfrequented and rather tortuous Britain Street is a relic of the deviation occasioned by the ravine, although the actual route followed in making the detour of old was Duchess Street.)

A little to the south of Britain Street, between it and Duchess Street, near the spot where Caroline [Sherbourne] Street, slightly diverging from the right line, passes northward to Queen Street, there stood in the early day a long, low wooden structure memorable to ourselves as being in our school-boy days the Government Printing Office. Here the *Upper Canada Gazette* was issued by 'R. C. Horne, Printer to the King's Most Excellent Majesty'.

We shall have occasion hereafter to notice among our early inhabitants some curious instances of change of profession. In the present case His Majesty's Printer was in reality an Army Surgeon once attached to the Glengarry Light Infantry. And again, afterwards the same gentleman was for many years the Chief Teller in the Bank of Upper Canada. An incident in the troubles of 1837 was 'the burning of Dr Horne's house' by a party of the malcontents who were making a show of assault upon the town.[2] The site of this building, a conspicuous, square two-storey frame family residence, was close to the toll-bar on Yonge Street in what is now Yorkville. On that occasion, we are informed, Dr Horne 'berated the Lieutenant-Governor for treating with avowed rebels, and insisted that they were not in sufficient force to give any ground of alarm.'

The *Upper Canada Gazette* was the first newspaper pub-

---

[2] Mackenzie, who was leading the force, burned the house personally—much to the horror of many of his followers who made comments to the effect that 'little Mac was completely off his head, and unfit to be at large'.

lished in Upper Canada. Its first number appeared at Newark or Niagara [-on-the-Lake], on Thursday, the 18th of April 1793. As it was apparently expected to combine with a record of the acts of the new government some account of events happening on the continent at large, it was made to bear the double title of *Upper Canada Gazette, or American Oracle*. Louis Roy was its first printer [1793-5], a skilled artisan engaged probably from Lower Canada where printing had been introduced about thirty years previously, soon after the English occupation of the country.

In 1801 J. Bennett becomes the printer and publisher of the *Gazette or Oracle*. In that year the printing-office is removed to 'the house of Mr A. Cameron, King Street', and, it is added, 'subscriptions will be received there and at the Toronto Coffee House, York.' From March 21st in this year, and onward for six weeks, the paper appears printed on blue sheets of the kind of material that used formerly to be seen on the outsides of pamphlets and magazines and Government 'Blue-books'. The stock of white paper has plainly run out and no fresh supply can be had before the opening of the navigation.

On Saturday, December 20th, 1801, is this statement, the whole of the editorial matter: 'It is much to be lamented that communication between Niagara and this town is so irregular and unfrequent: opportunities now do not often occur of receiving the American papers from our correspondents; and thereby prevents us for the present from laying before our readers the state of politics in Europe.' In the number for June 13th, the editorial 'leader' reads as follows: 'The *Oracle*, York, Saturday, June 13th. Last Monday was a day of universal rejoicing in this town, occasioned by the arrival of the news of the splendid victory gained by Lord Nelson over the Danes in Copenhagen Roads on the 2nd of April last: in the morning the great guns at the Garrison were fired: at night there was a general illumination, and bonfires blazed in almost every direction.' The writer indulges in no further comments.

It would have been gratifying to posterity had the printers of the *Gazette and Oracle* endeavoured to furnish a connected record of 'the short and simple annals' of their own immediate neighbourhood. But these unfortunately were deemed un-deserving of much notice. We have announcements of meetings and projects and subscriptions for particular purposes, unfol-lowed by any account of what was subsequently said, done, and effected; and when a local incident is mentioned, the detail is generally very meagre.

An advertisement in the number for the 27th August 1801 re-minds us that in the early history of Canada it was imagined that a great source of wealth to the inhabitants of the country in all future time would be the ginseng that was found growing naturally in the swamps. The market for ginseng was princi-pally China, where it was worth its weight in silver. The word is said to be Chinese for 'all-heal'. In 1801 we find that Mr Jacob Herchmer of York was speculating in ginseng. In his advertise-ment in the *Gazette and Oracle* he 'begs leave to inform the inhabitants of York and its vicinity that he will purchase any quantity of ginseng between this and the first of November next, and that he will give two shillings New York currency, per pound well dried, and one shilling for green.'

At one period, it will be remembered, the cultivation of hemp was expected to be the mainstay of the country's pros-perity. In the *Upper Canada Almanac* for 1804, among the public officers we have set down as 'Commissioners appointed for the distribution of Hemp Seed (gratis) to the Farmers of the Provinces, the Hon. John McGill, the Hon. David W. Smith, and Thomas Scott, Esquires.

The whole of the editorial matter of the *Gazette and Oracle* on the 2nd of January 1802 is the following: 'The *Oracle*, York, Saturday, January 2, 1802. The Printer presents his con-gratulary compliments to his customers on the New Year.' Note that the dignified title of Editor was yet but sparingly assumed. After the death of Governor Hunter, in September 1805, J. Bennett writes himself down 'Printer to the King's Most Ex-cellent Majesty'. Previously the colophon of the publication had been: 'York, printed by John Bennett, by the authority of His Excellency Peter Hunter, Esq., Lieut.-Governor.'

Happening to have at hand a bill of Bennett's against the Government, we give it here. The modern reader will be able to form from this specimen an idea of the extent of the government requirements in 1805 in regard to printing and the cost thereof. We give also the various attestations appended to the account:

York, Upper Canada, 24th June, 1805

The Government of Upper Canada,
To JOHN BENNETT, Government Printer.

Jan. 11. 300 copies Still Licenses, ½ sheet foolscap, pica type	0 16 6	
March 30. Printing 20 copies of an Act for altering the time of issuing Licenses for keeping of a House of Public Entertainment, ¼ sheet demy, pica type.	0 3 4	
April 5. Inserting a Notice to persons taking out Shop, Still or Tavern Licenses, 6 weeks in the *Gazette*, equal to 4½ advertisements.	1 16 0	
April 16. 1,000 copies of Proclamation, warning persons that possess and occupy Lands in this Province, without due titles having been obtained for such Lands, forthwith to quit and remove from the same, ½ sheet demy, double pica type.	4 18 4	
April 22. 100 copies of an Act to afford relief to persons entitled to claim Land in this Province as heirs or devises of the nominees of the Crown, one sheet demy, pica type....	3 6 3	
Printing Marginal notes to do.	0 5 0	
May 14. Printing 1,500 copies of the Acts of the First Session of the Fourth Parliament, three sheets demy, pica type.	45 0 0	
Marginal Notes to do., at 5s. per sheet.	0 15 0	
Folding, Stitching and Covering in Blue Paper, at 1d.	6 5 0	
Halifax currency.	£63 5 9	
	[*sic*]	

Amounting to sixty-three pounds five shillings and nine-pence Halifax currency. Errors excepted.

(*Signed*)   JOHN BENNETT

John Bennett of the Town of York, in the Home District, maketh oath and saith, that the foregoing account amounting to sixty-three pounds five shillings and ninepence Halifax currency, is just and true in all its particulars to the best of his knowledge and belief.

(*Signed*)   JOHN BENNETT

Sworn before me at York, this 20th day of July, 1805.

(*Signed*)   WM. DUMMER POWELL, J.

Audited and approved in Council 6th August 1805.

(*Signed*)   PETER RUSSELL
Presiding Councillor.

(*Examined*)

(*Signed*)   JOHN McGILL
Inspector Gen. P. P. Accts.
[A true copy.]

JOHN McGILL,
Inspector Gen. P. P. Accts.

Bennett published *The Upper Canada Almanac* [1804] containing, with the matter usually found in such productions, the Civil and Military Lists and the Duties, Imperial and Provincial. This work was admirably printed in fine Elzevir type, and in aspect as well as arrangement was an exact copy of the almanacs of the day published in London.

In 1813, during the war with the United States, Cameron is the printer of the official paper, which now for a time assumed the title of the *York Gazette* [1807-16].

In Bennett's time the government press was, as we have seen [page 187], set up in Mr Cameron's house on King Street. But at the period of the war in 1812, Mr Cameron's printing office was in a building which still exists—viz., the house on Bay Street associated with the name of Mr Andrew Mercer. During the occupation of York by the United States force, the press was broken up and the type dispersed. Mr Mercer once exhibited to ourselves a portion of the press which on that occasion was made useless. For a short period Mr Mercer himself had charge of the publication of the *York Gazette*.

In 1817 Dr Horne became the editor and publisher. On coming into his hands the paper resumed the name of *Upper Canada Gazette*, but the old secondary title of *American Oracle* was dropped. To the official portion of the paper there was nevertheless still appended abstracts of news from the United States and Europe, summaries of the proceedings in the Parliaments of Upper and Lower Canada, and much well-selected miscellaneous matter. The shape continued to be that of a small folio and the terms were four dollars per annum in advance, and if sent by mail, four dollars and a half.

In 1822 Mr Charles Fothergill (of whom we have already spoken) became the editor and publisher of the *Gazette*. Mr Fothergill revived the practice of having a secondary title, which was now the *Weekly Register* [1822-6]—a singular choice, by the way, that being very nearly the name of Cobbett's celebrated democratic publication in London. After Mr Fothergill came Mr Robert Stanton, who changed the name of the private [unofficial] portion of the *Gazette* sheet, styling it the *U. E. Loyalist* [1826-8].

In 1820 Mr John Carey had established the *Observer*[3] at York. The *Gazette* of May 11, 1820, contains the announcement of his design; and he therein speaks of himself as 'the person who gave the Debates' recently in another paper. To have the debates in Parliament reported with any fullness was then a novelty. The *Observer* was a folio of rustic, unkempt aspect, the paper and typography and matter being all somewhat inferior. It gave its adherence to the government of the day, generally: at a later period it wavered. Mr Carey was a tall, portly personage who from his bearing and costume might readily have been mistaken for a nonconformist minister of local importance. The *Observer* existed down to about the year 1830. Between the *Weekly Register* and the *Observer* the usual journalistic feud sprung up, which so often renders rival village newspapers ridiculous. With the *Register* a favourite sobriquet for the *Observer* is 'Mother C——y'. Once a correspondent is permitted to style it 'The Political Weathercock and Slang Gazetteer'. Mr Carey ended his days in Springfield on the River Credit where he possessed property.

The *Canadian Freeman*, established in 1825 by Mr Francis Collins, was a sheet remarkable for the neatness of its arrangement and execution and also for the talent exhibited in its editorials. The type was evidently new and carefully handled. Mr Collins was his own principal compositor. He is said to have transferred to type many of his editorials without the intervention of pen and paper, composing directly from copy mentally furnished. Mr Collins was a man of pronounced Celtic features, roughish in outline and plentifully garnished with hair of a sandy or reddish hue.

Notwithstanding the colourless character of the motto at the head of its columns—*Est natura hominum novitatis avida*: 'Human nature is fond of news'—the *Freeman* was a strong party paper. The hard measure dealt out to him in 1828 at the hands of the legal authorities, according to the prevailing spirit of the day, with the revenge that he was moved to take—and to take successsfully—we shall not here detail. Mr Collins died

---

[3] The first paper without any government connections.

of cholera in the year 1834.[4] We have understood that he was once employed in the office of the *Gazette*; and that when Dr Horne resigned, he was an applicant for the position of Government Printer.

The *Canadian Freeman* joined for a time in the general opposition clamour against Dr Strachan—against the influence, real or supposed, exercised by him over successive lieutenant-governors. But on discovering the good-humoured way in which its fulminations were received by their object, the *Freeman* dropped its strictures. It happened that Mr Collins had a brother in business in the town with whom Dr Strachan had dealings. This brother on some occasion thought it becoming to make some faint apology for the *Freeman's* diatribes. 'O don't let them trouble you,' the Doctor replied, 'they do not trouble me; but by the way, tell your brother,' he laughingly continued, 'I shall claim a share in the proceeds.' This, when reported to the Editor, was considered a good joke, and the diatribes ceased—a proceeding that was tantamount to Peter Pindar's confession when someone charged him with being too hard on the King: 'I confess there exists a difference between the King and me,' said Peter. 'The King has been a good subject to me; and I have been a bad subject to his Majesty.' During Mr Collins' imprisonment in 1828 for the application of the afterwards famous expression 'native malignancy' to the Attorney-General of the day, the *Freeman* still continued to appear weekly, the editorials, set up in type in the manner spoken of above, being supplied to the office from his room in the jail.

The newspaper which occupies the largest space in the early annals of the press at York is [William Lyon Mackenzie's] *Colonial Advocate*. Issuing first at Queenston in May 1824, it was removed in the following November to York. Its shape varied from time to time: now it was a folio, now a quarto. On all its pages the matter was densely packed, but printed in a very mixed manner: it abounded with sentences in italics, in small

---

4 Collins was sued, fined, and jailed by John Beverley Robinson for printing that Robinson suffered from a 'native malignancy'. He continued to publish the paper in jail and was eventually released by British action. Publication of the *Canadian Freeman* ceased at his death.

capitals, in large capitals; with names distinguished in like decided manner; with paragraphs made conspicuous by rows of
index hands and other typographical symbols at top, bottom,
and sides. It was editorial not in any one particular column but
throughout; and the opinions delivered were expressed for the
most part in the first person.

The *Weekly Register* fell foul of the *Advocate* at once. It
appears that the new audacious nondescript periodical, though
at the time it bore on its face the name of Queenston, was nevertheless for convenience' sake printed at Lewiston on the New
York side of the river. Hence it was denounced by the *Weekly
Register* in language that now astonishes us as a United States
production and as in the United States interest. 'This paper
of motley, unconnected, shake-bag periods,' cried the Editor of
the *Weekly Register*, 'this unblushing, brazen-faced *Advocate*,
affects to be a Queenston and Upper Canadian paper; whereas
it is to all intents and purposes, and radically, a Lewiston and
genu-wine Yankee paper. How can this man of truth, this pure
and holy Reformer and regenerator of the unhappy and pros-
trate Canada reconcile such barefaced and impudent decep-
tion?'

Nothing could more promote the success of the *Colonial
Advocate* than a welcome like this. To account for the *Register's* extraordinary warmth, it is to be said that the *Advocate*
in its first number had happened to quote a passage from an
address of its Editor to the electors of the County of Durham,
which seemed in some degree to compromise him as a servant
of the Government. Mr Fothergill had ventured to say: 'I know
some of the deep and latent causes why this fine country has so
long languished in a state of comparative stupor and inactivity,
while our more enterprising neighbours are laughing at us to
scorn. All I desire is an opportunity of attempting the cure of
some of the evils we labour under.' This was interpreted in the
Advocate to mean a censure upon the Executive. But the
Register replied that these words simply expressed the belief
that the evils complained of were remediable only by the action
of the House of Assembly on the well-known axiom 'that all
law is for the people, and from the people; and when inefficient,

must be remedied or rectified by the people; and that therefore Mr Fothergill was desirous of assisting in the great work.'

The end in fact was that the Editor of the *Register*, after his
return to parliament for the County of Durham, did not long
retain the post of King's Printer. After several independent
[anti-government] votes in the House, he was dismissed by Sir
Peregrine Maitland in 1826, after which date the awkwardness
of uniting with a Government Gazette a general newspaper
whose editor, as a member of the House of Assembly, might
claim the privilege of acting with His Majesty's opposition,
came to an end. In 1826 we have Mr Fothergill in his place in
the House supporting a motion for remuneration to the publisher of the *Advocate* on the ground that the wide and even
gratuitous circulation of that paper throughout Canada and
among members of the British House of Commons 'would help
to draw attention in the proper quarter to the country'.

Here is an account of Mackenzie's method in the collection
of matter for his various publications, the curious multifarious-
ness of which matter used to astonish while it amused. The
description is by Mr Kent, editor of a religious journal entitled the *Church*, published at Cobourg in 1838. Lord Clarendon's style has been exactly caught, it will be observed: 'Possessed of a taste for general and discursive reading', says Mr
Kent, 'he (Mackenzie) made even his very pleasures contribute
to the serious business of his life, and, year after year, accumulated a mass of materials, which he pressed into his service at
some fitting opportunity. Whenever anything transpired that
at all reflected on a political opponent, or whenever, in his
reading, he met with a passage that favoured his views, he not
only turned it to a present purpose, but laid it by, to bring it
forward at some future period, long after it might have been
supposed to be buried in oblivion.'

Some popular Almanacs of a remarkable character also emanated from Mackenzie's press. Whilst in the United States he
put forth the *Caroline Almanac*, a designation intended to keep
alive the memory of the cutting out of the *Caroline* steamer
from Fort Schlosser in 1837 and her precipitation over the Falls
of Niagara, an act sought to be held up as a great outrage on

the part of the Canadian authorities.[5] In the Canadian Almanacs, published by him, intended for circulation especially among the country population, the object kept in view was the same as that so industriously aimed at by the *Advocate* itself —viz., the exposure of the shortcomings and vices of the government of the day. At the same time a large amount of practically useful matter and information was supplied.

The earlier almanac was entitled *Poor Richard, or the Yorkshire Almanac* [1831], and the compiler professed to be one 'Patrick Swift, late of Belfast, in the Kingdom of Ireland, Esq., F.R.I., Grand-nephew of the celebrated Doctor Jonathan Swift, Dean of St Patrick's Dublin, etc. etc. etc.' This same personage was a contributor also of many pungent and humorous things in prose and verse in the columns of the *Advocate* itself. In 1834 the Almanac assumed the following title: *A new Almanac for the Canadian True Blues; with which is incorporated The Constitutional Reformer's Text Book, for the Millenial and Prophetic Year of the Grand General Election for Upper Canada, and total and everlasting Downfall of Toryism in the British Empire, 1834.* It was still supposed to be edited by Patrick Swift, Esq., who is now dubbed M.P.P. and Professor of Astrology, York.

As was to be expected, Dr Strachan was a standing subject of invective in all the publications of Mackenzie. Collins, editor of the *Freeman*, became, as we have seen, reticent in relation to him; but more or less a fusilade was maintained upon him in Mackenzie's periodicals as long as they issued.

In Mackenzie's opposition to Dr Strachan there was possibly a certain degree of national animus springing from the contemplation of a Scottish compatriot who, after rising to position in the young colony, was disposed from temperament to bear himself cavalierly towards all who did not agree with him in opinion. In addition, we have been told that at an early period in an interview between the two parties, Dr Strachan once

---

[5] Seizing the boat in American waters was a blunder on the part of the Canadian authorities and very nearly brought on a war with the United States.

chanced to express himself with considerable heat to Mackenzie, and proceeded to the length of showing him the door. The latter had called, as our information runs, to deprecate prejudice in regard to a brother-in-law of his, Mr Baxter, who was a candidate for some post under the Educational Board of which Dr S. was chairman, when great offence was taken at the idea being for a moment entertained that a personal motive would in the slightest degree bias him when in the execution of public duty.

At a late period in the history of both the now memorable Scoto-Canadians, we happened ourselves to be present at a scene in the course of which the two were brought curiously face to face with each other once more for a few moments. It will be remembered that after the subsidence of the political troubles and the union of Upper and Lower Canada, Mackenzie came back and was returned member of Parliament for Haldi-mand [1851]. While he was in the occupancy of this post, it came to pass that Dr Strachan, now Bishop of Toronto, had occasion to present a petition to the united House on the subject of the Clergy Reserves. To give greater weight and solemnity to the act, he decided to attend in person at the bar of the House, at the head of his clergy, all in canonicals. Mackenzie, seeing the procession approaching, hurried into the House and took his seat; and contrived at the moment the Bishop and his retinue reached the bar to have possession of the floor. Affecting to put a question to the Speaker before the Order of the Day was proceeded with, he launched out with great volubility and in excited strain on the interruptions to which the House was exposed in its deliberations; he then quickly came round to an attack in particular on prelates and clergy for their meddling and turbulence, infesting, as he averred, the lobbies of the Legislature when they should be employed on higher matters, filling with tumultuous mobs the halls and passages of the House, thronging (with an indignant glance in that direction) the very space below the bar set apart for the accommodation of peaceably disposed spectators.

The House had only just assembled and had not had time to settle down into perfect quiet: members were still dropping in, and it was a mystery to many, for a time, what could, at such an early stage of the day's proceedings, have excited the ire of the member for Haldimand. The courteous speaker, Mr Sicotte, was plainly taken aback at the sudden outburst of patriotic fervour; and, not being as familiar with the Upper Canadian past as many old Upper Canadians present were, he could not enter into the pleasantry of the thing; for after all it was humorously and not maliciously intended; the orator in possession of the floor had his old antagonist at a momentary disadvantage, and he chose to compel him while standing there conspicuously at the bar to listen for a while to a stream of *Colonial Advocate* in the purest vein.

After speaking against time, with an immense show of heat for a considerable while—a thing at which he was an adept— the scene was brought to a close by a general hubbub of impatience at the outrageous irrelevancy of the harangue, arising throughout the House, and obliging the orator to take his seat. The petition of the Bishop was then in due form received, and he, with his numerous retinue of robed clergy, withdrew.

We now proceed with our memorandum of the early press. When Fothergill was deprived of his office of King's Printer in 1826, he published for a time a quarto paper of his own, entitled the *Palladium* [*of British America,* 1837-9] composed of scientific, literary and general matter. Mr Robert Stanton King's Printer after Fothergill, issued on his own account for a few years a newspaper called the *U. E. Loyalist* [1828-9], the name, as we have seen, borne by the portion of the *Gazette* devoted to general intelligence while Mr Stanton was King's Printer. The *U. E. Loyalist* was a quarto sheet, well printed, with an engraved ornamental heading resembling that which surmounted the New York *Albion.* The *Loyalist* was conservative, as also was a local contemporary after 1829, the *Courier* [*of Upper Canada*], edited and printed by Mr George Gurnett, subsequently clerk of the Peace and Police Magistrate for the City of Toronto. The *Christian Guardian,* a local religious paper which still survives, began in 1829.[6] The *Patriot* appeared

---

[6] It ceased publication in 1925.

at York in 1832: it had previously been issued at Kingston. Its whole title was *The Patriot and Farmer's Monitor*, with the motto 'Common Sense' below. It was of the folio form, and its Editor, Mr Thos Dalton, was a writer of much force, liveliness, and originality.[7] The *Loyalist, Courier,* and *Patriot* were antagonists politically of the *Advocate* while the latter flourished, but all three laboured under the disadvantage of fighting on the side whose star was everywhere on the decline.

Notwithstanding its conservatism, however, it was in the *Courier* that the memorable revolutionary sentiments appeared, so frequently quoted afterwards in the *Advocate* publications: 'the minds of the well-affected begin to be unhinged; they already begin to cast about in their mind's eye for some new state of political existence, which shall effectually put the colony without the pale of British connection'—words written under the irritation occasioned by the dismissal of the Attorney- and Solicitor-General for Upper Canada in 1833.[8]

For a short time prior to 1837, Mackenzie's paper assumed the name of the *Constitution*.[9] A faithful portrait of Mackenzie will be seen at the beginning of the first volume of his *Life and Times* [1862] by Mr Charles Lindsay [his son-in-law], a work which will be carefully and profitably studied by future investigators in the field of Upper Canadian history. Excellent portraits of Mr Gurnett and of Mr Dalton are likewise extant in Toronto. [10]

Soon after 1838 the *Examiner* newspaper acquired great influence at York. It was established and edited by Mr Hincks. Mr Hincks had emigrated to Canada with the intention of en-

---

[7] Dalton was one of the few editors who could equal Mackenzie in invective —an ability possibly engendered by an advancing case of alcoholism.

[8] Attorney-General Henry John Boulton and Solicitor-General Christopher A. Hagerman were dismissed by the Colonial Office as a result of Mackenzie's complaints about their part in his expulsions from the Legislative Assembly. Tory irritation at the event was soon soothed when Hagerman was reappointed and Boulton became Chief Justice of Newfoundland.

[9] The *Constitution* was actually a new paper which Mackenzie began in 1836. The *Advocate* had been turned over to another Reform paper, the *Canadian Correspondent*, in 1834.

[10] The portrait of Gurnett hangs in the City Hall with those of the other mayors; that of Dalton is in the Ontario Archives.

gaging in commerce; and in Walton's *York Directory*, 1833-4, we read for No 21, west side of Yonge Street, 'Hincks, Francis, Wholesale Warehouse'. But Mr Hincks' attention was drawn to the political condition of Canada, especially to its finance. The accident of living in immediate proximity to a family that had already for a number of years been taking a warm and active interest in public affairs may have contributed to this. In the *Directory* just named, the Number after 21 on the west side of Yonge Street is 23, and the occupants are 'Baldwin, Doctor W. Warren; Baldwin, Robert, Esq., Attorney &c., Baldwin and Sullivan's Attorney's Office, and Dr Baldwin's Surrogate Office round the corner, in King Street, 195½'. It was not unnatural that the next-door neighbour of Dr Baldwin's family —their tenant, moreover, and attached friend—should catch a degree of inspiration from them. The subsequent remarkable career of Mr Hincks, afterwards so widely known as Sir Francis Hincks, has become a part of the general history of the country.

In glancing back at the supply of intelligence and literature provided at an early day for the Canadian community, it repeatedly occurs to us to name, as we have done, the *Albion* newspaper of New York. From this journal it was that almost everyone in our Upper Canadian York who had the least taste for reading derived the principal portion of his or her acquaintance with the outside world of letters as well as the minuter details of prominent political events. As its name implies, the *Albion* was intended to meet the requirements of a large number of persons of English birth and of English descent whose lot is cast on this continent but who nevertheless cannot discharge from their hearts their natural love for England, their natural pride in her unequalled civilization. *Cælum non animum mutant qui trans mare currunt,* was its gracefully-chosen and appropriate motto.

Half a century ago the boon of a judicious literary journal like the *Albion* was to dwellers in Canada a very precious one. The quarterlies were not then reprinted as now; nor were periodicals like the New York *Eclectic* or the Boston *Living Age* readily procurable. Without the weekly visit of the *Albion*, months upon months would have passed without any adequate knowledge being enjoyed of the current products of the literary world. For the sake of its extracted reviews, tales, and poetry, the New York *Albion* was in some cases, as we well remember, loaned about to friends and read like a much sought-after book in a modern circulating library. And happily its contents were always sterling and worth the perusal. It was a part of our own boyish experience to become acquainted for the first time with a portion of Keble's *Christian Year* [1827] in the columns of that paper.

The *Albion* was founded in 1822 by Dr John Charlton Fisher who afterwards became a distinguished editor at Quebec. The New York *Albion* still flourishes, retaining its high character for the superior excellence of its matter, retaining also many traits of its ancient outward aspect in the style of its type, in the distribution of its matter. It has also retained its old motto. Its familiar vignette heading of oak branches round the English rose, the thistle of Scotland, and the shamrock, has been thinned out and otherwise slightly modified; but it remains a fine artistic composition, well executed.

There was another journal from New York much esteemed at York for the real respectability of its character, the *New York Spectator*. It was read for the sake of its commercial and general information rather than for its literary news. To the minds of the young the Greek revolution had a singular fascination. We remember once entertaining the audacious idea of constructing a history of the struggle of Greece of which the authorities would, in great measure, have been copious cuttings from the *New York Spectator* columns. One advantage of the embryo design certainly was a familiarity acquired with the map of Hellas within and without the Peloponnesus.[11]

Partly in consequence of the eagerness with which the columns of the *New York Spectator* used to be ransacked with a view to the composition of the proposed historical work, we remember the peculiar interest with which we regarded the editor of that periodical at a later period on falling in with him

---

11 The Greek revolution against Turkish sovereignty raged during most of the 1820s and naturally captured a boy's fancy.

casually at the Falls of Niagara. Mr Hall was then well advanced in years; and from a very brief interview the impression received was that he was the beau ideal of a veteran editor of the highest type; for a man, almost omniscient, unslumberingly observant; sympathetic, in some way, with every passing occurrence and every remark; tenacious of the past, grasping the present on all sides with readiness, genial interest, and completeness. In aspect, and even to some extent in costume, Mr Hall might have been taken for an English bishop of the early part of the Victorian era.

IX

QUEEN
STREET
FROM
GEORGE
STREET
TO
YONGE
STREET

When we pass George Street we are in front of the park-lot originally selected by Mr Secretary [William] Jarvis. It is now divided from south to north by Jarvis Street, a thoroughfare opened up through the property in the time of Mr Samuel Peters Jarvis, the Secretary's son. Among the pleasant villas that now line this street on both sides there is one which still is the home of a Jarvis, the Sheriff of the County.[1]

Besides filling the conspicuous post indicated by his title, Mr Secretary Jarvis was also the first Grand Master of the Masons in Upper Canada. The archives of the first Masonic Lodges of York possess much interest. Through the permission of Mr Alfio de Grassi who has now the custody of them, we are enabled to give the following extracts from a letter of Mr Secretary Jarvis, bearing the early date of March 28th, 1792: 'I am in possession of my sign manual from his Majesty,' Mr Jarvis writes on the day just named, from Pimlico, to his relative Munson Jarvis at St John, New Brunswick, 'constituting me Secretary and Registrar of the Province of Upper Canada, with power of appointing my Deputies, and in every other re-spect a very full warrant. I am also', he continues, 'very much

---

[1] This was Frederick William Jarvis who succeeded his uncle, William Botsford Jarvis, as sheriff in 1864, and held the office until his death in 1887.

flattered to be enabled to inform you that the Grand Lodge of England have within these very few days appointed Prince Edward, who is now in Canada, Grand Master of Ancient Masons in Lower Canada; and William Jarvis, Secretary and Registrar of Upper Canada, Grand Master of Ancient Masons in that Province. However trivial it may appear to you who are not a Mason, yet I assure you that it is one of the most honourable appointments that they could have conferred. The Duke of Athol is the Grand Master of Ancient Masons in England. Lord Dorchester with his private Secretary, and the Secretary of the Province, called on us yesterday,' Mr Jarvis proceeds to say, 'and found us in the utmost confusion, with half a dozen porters in the house packing up. However his Lordship would come in, and sat down in a small room which was reserved from the general bustle. He then took Mr [Samuel] Peters home with him to dine: hence we conclude a favourable omen in regard to his consecration, which we hope is not far distant. Mrs Jarvis,' the Secretary informs his relative, 'leaves England in great spirits. I am ordered my passage on board the transport with the Regiment, and to do duty without pay for the passage only. This letter', he adds, 'gets to Halifax by favour of an intimate friend of Mr Peters, Governor Wentworth,[2] who goes out to take possession of his Government. The ship that I am alloted to is the *Henneker*, Captain Winter, a transport with the Queen's Rangers on board.'

The Prince Edward spoken of was afterwards Duke of Kent and father of the present Queen. Lord Dorchester was the Governor-General of the Province of Quebec before its division into Upper and Lower Canada. Mr Peters was *in posse* the Bishop of the new Province about to be organized. It was a part of the original scheme, as shewn by the papers of the first Governor of Upper Canada, that there should be an episcopal see in Upper Canada, as there already was at Quebec in the lower province [from 1793]. But this was not carried into effect until 1839, nearly half a century later.

---

[2] Sir John Wentworth, last royal governor of New Hampshire, and lieutenant-governor of Nova Scotia from 1792 to 1808.

When Jarvis Street was opened up through the Secretary's park-lot, the family residence of his son, Mr Samuel Peters Jarvis, a handsome structure of the early brick era of York, in the line of the proposed thoroughfare, was taken down. Its interior fittings of solid black walnut were bought by Captain Carthew and transferred by him without much alteration to a house which he put up on part of the Deer-park property on Yonge Street.

A large fragment of the offices attached to Mr Jarvis's house was utilized and absorbed in a private residence on the west side of Jarvis Street, and the gravel drive to the door is yet to be traced in the less luxuriant vegetation of certain portions of the adjoining flower gardens. Mr Secretary Jarvis died in 1817. He is described by those who remember him as possessing a handsome portly presence. Col. Jarvis, the first military commandant in Manitoba, is a grandson of the Secretary.

Of Mr [John] McGill, first owner of the next park-lot, and of his personal aspect, we have had occasion to speak in connection with the interior of St James' Church. Situated in fields at the southern extremity of a stretch of forest, the comfortable and pleasantly-situated residence erected by him for many years seemed a place of abode quite remote from the town. It was still to be seen in 1870 in the heart of McGill Square, and was long occupied by Mr McCutcheon, a brother of the inheritor of the bulk of Mr McGill's property, who in accordance with his uncle's will and by authority of an Act of Parliament, assumed the name of McGill and became subsequently well known throughout Canada as the Hon. Peter McGill.

(The founder of McGill College in Montreal [James McGill, 1744-1813] was of a different family. The late Capt. James McGill Strachan derived his name from the marriage-connection of his father with the latter.[3])

In the *Gazette and Oracle* of Nov 13th, 1803, we observe Mr McGill of York advertising as 'agent for purchases' for pork and beef to be supplied to the troops stationed 'at Kingston,

---

[3] Bishop Strachan married Anne Wood, the widow of Andrew McGill (1756-1805), the younger brother of the founder of the College.

York, Fort George, Fort Chippawa, Fort Erie, and Amherstburg'. In 1818 he is Receiver-General and Auditor-General of
land patents. He had formerly been an officer in the Queen's
Rangers, and his name repeatedly occurs in 'Simcoe's History'
of the operations of that corps during the war of the American
Revolution.

From that work we learn that in 1779 he, with the commander
himself of the corps, then Lieut.-Col. Simcoe, fell into the hands
of the revolutionary authorities and was treated with great
harshness in the common jail of Burlington, New Jersey; and
when a plan was devised for the Colonel's escape, Mr McGill
volunteered, in order to further its success, to personate his
commanding officer in bed and to take the consequences while
the latter was to make his way out. The whole project was
frustrated by the breaking of a false key in the lock of a door
which would have admitted the confined soldiers to a room
where 'carbines and ammunition' were stored away. Lieut.-Col.
Simcoe, it is added in the history just named, afterwards offered
Mr McGill an annuity or to make him Quarter-master of Cavalry; the latter, we are told, he accepted of, as his grandfather
had been an officer in King William's army; and 'no man', Col.
Simcoe notes, 'ever executed the office with greater integrity,
courage and conduct'.

The southern portion of Mr McGill's park-lot has, in the
course of modern events, come to be assigned to religious uses.
McGill Square, which contained the old homestead and its surroundings, and which was at one period intended, as its name
indicates, to be an open public square, was secured in 1870 by
the Wesleyan Methodist body and made the site of its principal
place of worship and of various establishments connected there-
with [the Metropolitan Church].

Immediately north, on the same property, the Roman Catholics had previously built their principal place of worship and
numerous appurtenances [St Michael's Cathedral, 1845], attracted possibly to the spot by the expectation that McGill
Square would continue forever an open ornamental piece of
ground.

A little farther to the north a cross-street, leading from Yonge

Street eastward, bears the name of McGill. An intervening cross-street preserves the name of Mr Crookshank who was Mr McGill's brother-in-law.

The name that appears on the original survey of York and its suburbs as first occupant of the park-lot westward of Mr Mc-Gill's is that of Mr George Playter. This is the Captain Playter senior of whom we have already spoken in our excursion up the valley of the Don. We have named him also among the forms of a past age whom we ourselves remember often seeing in the congregation assembled of old in the wooden St James'.

Mr Playter was an Englishman by birth but had passed many of his early years in Philadelphia where for a time he attached himself to the Society of Friends, having selected as a wife a member of that body. But on the breaking out of the troubles that led to the independence of the United States, his patriotic attachment to old far-off England compelled him, in spite of the peaceful theories of the denomination to which he had united himself, promptly to join the Royalist forces.

He used to give a somewhat humorous account of his sudden return to the military creed of ordinary mundane men. 'Lie there, Quaker!' cried he to his cutaway, buttonless, formal coat as he stripped it off and flung it down for the purpose of donning the soldier's habiliments. But some of the Quaker observances were never relinquished in his family. We well remember, in the old homestead on the Don and afterwards at his residence on Caroline Street, a silent mental thanksgiving before meals that always took place after everyone had taken his seat at the table; a brief pause was made and all bent for a moment slightly forwards. The act was solemn and impressive.

Old Mr Playter was a man of sprightly and humorous temperament, and his society was accordingly much enjoyed by those who knew him. A precise attention to his dress and person rendered him an excellent type in which to study the costume and style of the ordinary unofficial citizen of a past generation. Colonel M. F. Whitehead of Port Hope, in a letter kindly expressive of his interest in these reminiscences of York, incidentally furnished a little sketch that will not be out of place here. 'My visits to York, after I was articled to Mr Ward, in 1819',

Colonel Whitehead says, 'were frequent. I usually lodged at old Mr Playter's, Mrs Ward's father. (This was when he was still living at the homestead on the Don.) The old gentleman often walked into town with me, by Castle Frank; his three-cornered hat, silver knee-buckles, broad-toed shoes and large buckles, were always carefully arranged.' To the equipments, so well described by Colonel Whitehead, we add, from our own boyish recollection of Sunday sights, white stockings and a gold-headed cane of a length unusual now.

According to a common custom prevalent at an early time, Mr Playter set apart on his estate on the Don a family burial-plot where his own remains and those of several members of his family and their descendants were deposited. Mr George Playter, son of Captain George Playter, was sometime Deputy Sheriff of the Home District; and Mr Ely Playter, another son, represented for some sessions in the Provincial Parliament the North Riding of York. A daughter, who died unmarried in 1832, Miss Hannah Playter—'Aunt Hannah', as she was styled in the family—is pleasantly remembered as well for the genuine kindness of her character, as also for the persistency with which, like her father, she carried forward into a new and changed generation, and retained to the last the costume and manners of the reign of King George the Third.

Immediately in front of the extreme westerly portion of the park-lot which we are now passing, and on the south side of the present Queen Street in that direction, was situated an early Court House of York, associated in the memories of most of the early people with their first acquaintance with forensic pleadings and law proceedings.

This building was a notable object in its day. In an old plan of the town we observe it conspicuously delineated in the locality mentioned, the *other* public buildings of the place—viz., the Commissariat Stores, the Government House, the Council Chamber (at the present north-west corner of York and Wellington Streets), the District School, St James' Church, and the Parliament House (by the Little Don) —being marked in the same distinguished manner. It was a plain two-storey frame building, erected in the first instance as an ordinary place of

abode by Mr Montgomery, father of the Montgomerys, once of
the neighbourhood of Eglinton on Yonge Street. It stood in a
space defined by the present line of Yonge Street on the west,
by nearly the present line of Victoria Street on the east, by
Queen Street on the north and by Richmond Street on the
south. Though situated nearer Queen Street than Richmond
Street, it faced the latter and was approached from the latter.

It was Mr Montgomery who obtained by legal process the
opening of Queen Street in the rear of his property. In consequence of the ravine of which we have had occasion so often
to speak, the allowance for this street as laid down in the first
plans of York had been closed up by authority from Yonge
Street to Caroline Street.

It was seriously proposed in 1800 to close up Queen Street to
the westward also from Yonge Street 'so far as the Common'—
that is, the Garrison Reserve—on the ground that such street
was wholly unnecessary, there being in that direction already
one highway into the town, namely Richmond Street, situated
only ten rods to the south. In 1800 the southern termination of
Yonge Street was where we are now passing, at the corner of
Montgomery's lot. At this point the farmers' waggons from the
north turned off to the eastward, proceeding as far as Toronto
Street, down which they wended their way to Richmond Street
and so on to Church Street and King Street, finally reaching the
Market Place.

Of the opening of Yonge Street through a range of building
lots which in 1800 blocked the way from Queen Street south-
wards, we shall speak hereafter in the excursion which we propose to make through Yonge Street from south to north, the
moment we have finished recording our collections and recollections in relation to Queen Street.

MEMORIES OF THE OLD COURT HOUSE

In the old Court House, situated as we have described, we received our first boyish impressions of the solemnities and forms
observed in Courts of Law. In paying a visit of curiosity subsequently to the singular series of Law Courts which are to be

found ranged along one side of Westminster Hall in London—each one of them in succession entered through the heavy folds of lofty, mysterious-looking curtains, each one of them crowded with earnest pleaders and anxious suitors, each one of them provided with a judge elevated in solitary majesty on high, each one of them seeming to the passing stranger more like a scene in a drama than a prosaic reality—we could not but revert in memory to the old upper chamber at York where the remote shadows of such things were for the first time encountered.

It was startling to remember of a sudden that our early Upper Canadian judges, our early Upper Canadian barristers, came fresh from these Westminster Hall Courts! What a contrast must have been presented to these men in the rude wilds to which they found themselves transported. Riding the Circuit in the Home, Midland, Eastern and Western Districts at the beginning of the present century was no trivial undertaking.[4] Accommodation for man and horse was for the most part scant and comfortless. Locomotion by land and water was perilous and slow, and racking to the frame. The apartments procurable for the purposes of the Court were of the humblest kind.

Our pioneer jurisconsults in their several degrees, however, like our pioneers generally, unofficial as well as official, did their duty. They quietly initiated in the country customs of gravity and order which have now become traditional; and we see the result in the decent dignity which surrounds, at the present day, the administration of justice in Canada in the Courts of every grade.

Prior to the occupation of Mr Montgomery's house as the Court House of York, the Court of King's Bench held its sessions in a portion of the Government Buildings at the east end of the town, destroyed in the war in 1813. On June 25, 1812, the Sheriff, John Beikie, advertises in the *Gazette* that 'a Court of General Quarter Sessions of the Peace for the Home District will be holden at the Government Buildings in the town of York

---

4 These four districts covered all of what is now southern Ontario, and there were, of course, virtually no roads.

on Tuesday, the fourteenth day of July next ensuing, at the hour of ten o'clock in the forenoon of which all Justices of the Peace, Coroners, Gaolers, High Constables, Constables and Bailiffs are desired to take notice, and that they be then and there present with their Rolls, Records, and other Memoranda to do and perform those things which by reason of their respective offices shall be to be done.'

It is with the Court Room in the Government Buildings that the Judge, Sheriff, and Crown Counsel were familiar who were engulfed in Lake Ontario in 1804. The story of the total loss of the government schooner *Speedy*, Captain Thomas Paxton, is widely known. In that ill-fated vessel suddenly went down in a gale in the dead of night, along with its commander and crew, Judge Cochrane, Solicitor-General Gray, Mr Angus Macdonell, Sheriff of York [*sic*], Mr Fishe, the High Bailiff, an Indian prisoner about to be tried at Presqu'ile for murder, two interpreters, Cowan and Ruggles, several witnesses, and Mr Herchmer, a merchant of York; in all, thirty-nine persons, of whom no trace was ever afterwards discovered.

The weather was threatening, the season of the year stormy (7th October), and the schooner was suspected not to be seaworthy. But the orders of the Governor, General Peter Hunter, were peremptory. Mr Weekes, of whom we have heard before, escaped the fate that befell so many connected with his profession by deciding to make the journey to Presqu'ile on horseback. (For the seat[5] in the House rendered vacant by the sudden removal of Mr Macdonell, Mr Weekes was the successful candidate.)

The name of the Indian who was on his way to be tried was Ogetonicut. His brother, Whistling Duck, had been killed by a white man, and he took his revenge on John Sharp, another white man. The deed was done at Ball Point on Lake Scugog, where John Sharp was in charge of a trading-post for furs belonging to the Messrs Farewell. The Governor had promised, so it was alleged, that the slayer of Whistling Duck should be punished. But a twelvemonth had elapsed and nothing had

---

5 Glengarry and Prescott.

been done. The whole tribe—the Muskrat branch of the Chip-
pewas, with their Chief Wabbekisheco at their head—came up
in canoes to York on this occasion, starting from the mouth of
Annis's creek, near Port Oshawa, and encamping at Gibraltar
Point on the peninsula in front of York. A guard of soldiers
went over to assist in the arrest of Ogetonicut who, it appears,
had arrived with the rest. The Chief Wabbekisheco took the
culprit by the shoulder and delivered him up. He was lodged in
the jail at York.

During the summer it was proved by means of a survey that
the spot where Sharp had been killed was within the District
of Newcastle. It was held necessary, therefore, that the trial
should take place in that District. Sellick's, at the Carrying
Place [Prince Edward County], was to have been the scene of
the investigation, and thither the *Speedy* was bound when she
foundered. Mr Justice Cochrane was a most estimable character
personally, and a man of distinguished ability. He was only in
his 28th year, and had been Chief Justice of Prince Edward
Island before his arrival in Upper Canada. He was a native of
Halifax, in Nova Scotia, but had studied law in Lincoln's Inn,
and was called to the Bar in England.

In the old Court House, near which we are now passing, were
assigned to convicted culprits, with unflinching severity and in
a no inconsiderable number of instances, all the penalties en-
joined in the criminal code of the day—the lash, the pillory, the
stocks, the gallows. We have conversed with an old inhabitant
of Toronto who had not only here heard the penalty of branding ordered by the Judge but had actually seen it in open court
inflicted, the iron being heated in the great wood-stove that
warmed the room and the culprit made to stretch out his hand
and have burnt thereon the initial letter of the offence committed.

Here cases came up repeatedly arising out of the system of
slavery which at the beginning was received in Canada, apparently as an inevitable part and parcel of the social arrangements
of a colony on this continent.

On the first of March 1811 we have it on the record, 'William
Jarvis, of the Town of York, Esq. (this is the Secretary again),

informed the Court that a negro boy and girl, his slaves, had the evening before been committed to prison for having stolen gold and silver out of his desk in his dwelling-house, and escaped from their said master; and prayed that the Court would order that the said prisoners, with one Coachly, a free negro, also committed to prison on suspicion of having advised and aided the said boy and girl in eloping with their master's property.' Thereupon it was 'Ordered,—That the said negro boy, named Henry, commonly called Prince, be re-committed to prison, and there safely kept till delivered according to law, and that the girl do return to her said master; and Coachly be discharged.'

At the date just mentioned slavery was being gradually extinguished by an Act of the Provincial Legislature of Upper Canada passed at Newark in 1793, which forbade the further introduction of slaves, and ordered that all slave children born after the 9th of July in that year should be free on attaining the age of twenty-five.

Most gentlemen, from the Administrator of the Government downwards, possessed some slaves. Peter Russell, in 1806, was anxious to dispose of two of his, and thus advertised in the *Gazette and Oracle*, mentioning his prices: 'To be sold: a Black Woman named Peggy, aged forty years, and a Black Boy, her son, named Jupiter, aged about fifteen years, both of them the property of the subscriber. The woman is a tolerable cook and washerwoman, and perfectly understands making soap and candles. The boy is tall and strong for his age, and has been employed in the country business, but brought up principally as a house servant. They are each of them servants for life. The price of the woman is one hundred and fifty dollars. For the boy two hundred dollars, payable in three years, with interest from the day of sale, and to be secured by bond, &c. But one-fourth less will be taken for ready money. *York, Feb. 19th, 1806.* PETER RUSSELL.

According to our ideas at the present moment, such an advertisement as this is shocking enough. But we must judge the words and deeds of men by the spirit of the age in which they lived and moved.

Peter Russell's Peggy had been giving him uneasiness a few years previously to the advertisement copied above. She had been absenting herself without leave. Of this we are apprised in an advertisement dated York, September 2nd, 1803. It runs as follows: 'The subscriber's black servant Peggy, not having his permission to absent herself from his service, the public are hereby cautioned from employing or harbouring her without the owner's leave. Whoever will do so after this notice may expect to be treated as the law directs. PETER RUSSELL.'

Mr Sol.-General Gray, lost in the *Speedy*, manumitted by his will, dated August 27th, 1803, and discharged from the state of slavery in which, as that document speaks, 'she now is' his 'faithful black woman servant, Dorinda', and gave her and her children their freedom; and that they might not want, directed that £1200 should be invested and the interest applied to their maintenance. To his black servants, Simon and John Baker, he gave, besides their freedom, 200 acres of land each, and pecuniary legacies. The Simon here named went down with his master in the *Speedy*; but John long survived. He used to state that his mother Dorinda was a native of Guinea and to describe Governor Hunter as a rough old warrier who carried snuff in an outside pocket, whence he took it in handfuls, to the great disfigurement of his ruffled shirt-bosoms. His death was announced in the public papers by telegram from Cornwall, Ontario, bearing date January 17, 1871. 'A coloured man,' it said, 'named John Baker, who attained his 105th year on the 25th ult., died here to-day. He came here as a chattel of the late Colonel Gray, in 1792, having seen service in the Revolutionary war. Subsequently he served throughout the war of 1812. He was wounded at Lundy's Lane, and has drawn a pension for fifty-seven years.' Mr Gray, it may be added, was a native of our Canadian town of Cornwall. His place of abode in York was in what is now Wellington Street, on the lot immediately to the west of the old 'Council Chamber' (subsequently the residence of Chief Justice Draper).

We ourselves, we remember, used to gaze in former days with some curiosity at the pure negress, Amy Pompadour, here in

York, knowing that she had once been legally made a present of by Miss Elizabeth Russell to Mrs Captain Denison.

But enough of the subject of Canadian slavery to which we have been inadvertently led.

The old Court House, when abandoned by the law authorities for the new buildings on King Street, was afterwards occasionally employed for religious purposes. By an advertisement in the *Advocate*, in March 1834, we learn that the adherents of David Willson of Whitchurch sometimes made use of it. It is there announced that 'the Children of Peace will hold Worship in the Old Court House of York, on Sunday, the 16th instant, at Eleven and Three.' Subsequently it became for a time the House of Industry or Poor House of the town [1837].

Besides the legal cases tried and the judgements pronounced within the homely walls of the Old Court House, interest would attach to the curious scenes—could they be recovered and described—which there occurred, arising sometimes from the primitive rusticity of juries and sometimes from their imperfect mastery of the English language, many of them being, as the German settlers of Markham and Vaughan were indiscriminately called, Dutchmen. Peter Ernest, appearing in court with the verdict of a jury of which he was foreman, began to preface the same with a number of peculiar German-English expressions which moved Chief Justice Powell to cut him short by the remark that he would have to commit him if he swore: when Ernest observed that the perplexities through which he and the jury had been endeavouring to find their way were enough to make better men than they were express themselves in an unusual way. The verdict, pure and simple, was demanded. Ernest then announced that the verdict which he had to deliver was that half of the jury were for 'guilty' and half for 'not guilty'. That is, the Judge observed, you would have the prisoner half-hanged, or the half of him hanged. To which Peter replied, that would be as his Lordship pleased. It was a case of homicide. Being sent back, they agreed to acquit.

Odd passages, too, between pertinacious counsel and nettled judges sometimes occurred, as when Mr H. J. Boulton, fresh from the Inner Temple [c. 1815], sat down at the peremptory order of the Chief Justice, but added, 'I will sit down, my Lord, but I shall instantly stand up again.'

Chief Justice Powell, when on the Bench, had a humorous way occasionally of indicating by a kind of quiet by-play, by a gentle shake of the head, a series of little nods, or movements of the eye or eyebrow, his estimate of an outré hypothesis or an *ad captandum* argument. This was now and then disconcerting to advocates anxious to figure, for the moment, in the eyes of a simple-minded jury as oracles of extra authority.

Nights, likewise, there would be to be described, passed by juries in the diminutive jury-room, either through perplexity fairly arising out of the evidence or through the dogged obstinacy of an individual.

Once, as we have heard from a sufferer on the occasion, Colonel Duggan was the means of keeping a jury locked up for a night here, he being the sole dissentient on a particular point. That night, however, was converted into one of memorable festivity, our informant said, a tolerable supply of provisions and comforts having been conveyed in through the window, sent for from the homes of those of the jury who were residents of York. The recusant Colonel was refused a moment's rest throughout the livelong night. During twelve long hours, pranks and sounds were indulged in that would have puzzled a foreigner taking notes of Canadian Court House usages.

When 10 o'clock a.m. of the next day arrived, and the Court re-assembled, Colonel Duggan suddenly and obligingly effected the release of himself and his tormentors by consenting to make the necessary modification in his opinion.

Of one characteristic scene we have a record in the books of the Court itself. On the 12th of January, 1813, as a duly impanelled jury were retiring to their room to consider of their verdict, a remark was addressed to one of their number, namely Samuel Jackson, by a certain Simeon Morton who had been a witness for the defence: the remark, as the record notes, was in these words, to wit, 'Mind your eye!' to which the said Jackson replied 'Never fear!' The Crier of the Court, John Bazell, duly made affidavit of this illicit transaction. Accordingly, on the appearance in court of the jury, for the purpose of rendering

their verdict, Dr Baldwin, attorney for the prosecution, moved
that the said Jackson be taken into custody: and the Judge gave
order 'that Samuel Jackson do immediately enter into recogni-
zances, himself in £50, and two sureties in £25 each, for his
appearance on the Saturday following at the Office of the Clerk
of the Peace'—'which', as the record somewhat inelegantly adds,
'he done.' He duly appeared on the Saturday indicated, and,
pleading ignorance, was discharged.

In the Court House in 1822 was tried a curious case in respect of a horse claimed by two parties, Major Heward of York
and General Wadsworth, commandant of the United States
Garrison at Fort Niagara. Major Heward had reared a sorrel
colt on his farm east of the Don, and when it was three years
old it was stolen. Nothing came of the offer of reward for its
recovery until a twelve month after the theft, when a young
horse was brought by a stranger to Major Heward at York and
instantly recognized by him as his lost property. Some of the
major's neighbours likewise had no doubt of the identity of the
animal which, moreover, when taken to the farm, entered of his
own accord the stable and the stall the missing colt used to
occupy, and, when let out into the adjoining pasture, greeted in
a friendly way a former mate and ran to drink at the customary
watering place. Shortly after, two citizens of the United States,
Kelsey and Bond, make their appearance at York and claim the
horse which they find on Major Heward's farm as the property
of General Wadsworth, commandant at Fort Niagara. Kelsey
swore that he had reared the animal; that he had docked him
with his own hands when only a few hours old; and that he had
sold him about a year ago to General Wadsworth. Bond also
swore positively that this was the horse which Kelsey had reared
and that he himself had broken him in, prior to the sale to
General Wadsworth. It was alleged by these persons that a man
named Docksteader had stolen the horse from General Wadsworth at Fort Niagara and had conveyed him across to the
Canadian side.

In consequence of the positive evidence of these two men, the
jury gave their verdict in favour of General Wadsworth's claim,
with damages to the amount of £50. It was nevertheless general-

ly held that Kelsey and Bond's minute narrative of the colt's early history was a fiction; and that Docksteader, the man who transferred the animal from the United States side of the river to Canadian soil, had also had something to do with the transfer of the same animal from Canada to the United States a twelve-month previously.

The subject of this story survived to the year 1851, and was recognized and known among all old inhabitants as 'Major Heward's famous horse Toby'.

Within the Court House on Richmond Street took place in 1818 the celebrated trial of a number of prisoners brought down from the Red River Settlement on charges of 'high treason, murder, robbery, and conspiracy', as preferred against them by Lord Selkirk, the founder of the Settlement.[6] When our neighbourhood was itself in fact nothing more than a collection of small isolated clearings, rough-hewn out of the wild, 'the Selkirk Settlement' and the 'North West' were household terms among us for remote regions in a condition of infinite savagery, in comparison with which we, as we prided ourselves, were denizens of a paradise of high refinement and civilization. Now that the Red River district has attained the dignity of a province and become a member of our Canadian Confederation [1870], the trial referred to, arising out of the very birth-throes of Manitoba, has acquired a fresh interest.

---

[6] The Red River Settlement was founded in 1812 near the present site of Winnipeg. Clashes between the settlers and the Nor' Westers led to the Seven Oaks massacre in 1816 in which the governor and nineteen settlers were killed. As the Upper Canadian courts had jurisdiction over the region, the trial took place at York. The Nor' Westers were quite influential in Upper Canada and the juries handed down verdicts of not guilty.

X

QUEEN
STREET
FROM
YONGE
STREET
TO
COLLEGE
[UNIVERSITY]
AVENUE

Leaving now the site of our ancient Court House, the spot at which we arrive in our tour is one of very peculiar interest. It is the intersection at right angles of the two great military ways carved out through the primitive forest of Western Canada by order of its first Governor. Dundas Street and Yonge Street were laid down in the first MS. maps of the country as highways destined to traverse the land in all future time, as nearly as practicable in right lines, the one from east to west, the other from south to north. They were denominated 'streets' because their idea was taken from the famous ancient ways, still in several instances called 'streets', which the Romans, when masters of primitive Britain, constructed for military purposes.

Dundas Street has its name from the Right Hon. Henry Dundas, Secretary of State for the Colonies in 1794. In that year Governor Simcoe wrote as follows to Mr Dundas: 'Dundas Street, the road proposed from Burlington Bay to the River Thames, half of which is completed, will connect by an internal communication the Detroit and settlements at Niagara. It is intended', he says, 'to be extended northerly to York by the troops, and in process of time by the respective settlers to Kingston and Montreal.' In another dispatch to the same statesman, he says: 'I have directed the surveyor, early in the next spring to ascertain the precise distance of the several routes which I have done myself the honour of detailing to you, and hope to complete the Military Street or Road the ensuing autumn.' In a MS. map of about the same date, Dundas Street is laid down from Detroit to the Pointe au Bodêt, the terminus on the St Lawrence of the old boundary line between Upper and Lower Canada. From the Rouge River it is sketched as running somewhat further back than the line of the present Kingston Road; and after leaving Kingston it is drawn as though it was expected to follow the water-shed between the Ottawa and the St Lawrence. A road is sketched, running from the Pointe au Bodêt to the Ottawa, and this road is struck at an acute angle by Dundas Street.

A manuscript note appears on the map, 'The Dundas Street is laid out from Oxford to the Bay of Quinté; it is nearly finished from Oxford to Burlington Bay.'

In 1799 the *Constellation*, a paper published at Niagara, informs its readers, under the date of Friday, August 2nd in that year, that 'the wilderness from York to the Bay of Quinté is 120 miles; a road of this distance through it', it then says, 'is contracted out by Government to Mr Danforth, to be cut and completed by the first of July next; and which, when completed, will open a communication round the Lake by land from this town (Niagara) with the Bay, Kingston, &c. Hitherto,' the *Constellation* continues, 'in the season of winter our intercourse with that part of the province has been almost totally interrupted. Mr Danforth has already made forty miles of excellent road,' the editor encourages his patrons by observing, 'and procured men to the number sufficient for doing the whole extent by the setting in of winter. It would be desirable also,' Mr Tiffany [the editor] suggests, 'were a little labour expended in bridging the streams between Burlington Bay and York; indeed the whole country', it is sweepingly declared, 'affords room for amendment in this respect.'

It is plain from this extract that if the men of the present generation would have a just conception of what was the condition of the region round Lake Ontario seventy years ago, they must pay a visit to the head of Lake Superior and perform the journey by the Dawson Road and the rest of the newly opened route from Fort William to Winnipeg.

The *Gazette* of December 14, 1799, was able to speak approvingly of the road to the eastward. 'The road from this town (York) to the Midland District [i.e. Kingston] is', it says, 'completed as far as the Township of Hope, about sixty miles, so that sleighs, waggons, &c. may travel it with safety. The report which has been made to the Government by the gentleman appointed to inspect the work is', the *Gazette* then proceeds to say, 'highly favourable to Mr Danforth, the undertaker; and less imperfections could not be pointed out in so extensive a work. The remaining part', it is added, 'will be accomplished by the first of July next.' The road to which these various extracts refer is still known as the Danforth Road. It runs somewhat to the north of the present Kingston Road, entering it by the town line at the 'Four Mile Tree'.

Yonge Street, which we purpose duly to perambulate hereafter, has its name from Sir George Yonge, a member of the Imperial Government in the reign of George III. He was of a distinguished Devonshire family and a personal friend of Governor Simcoe's.

The first grantee of the park-lot which we next pass in our progress westward was Dr Macaulay, an army surgeon attached successively to the 33rd Regiment and the famous Queen's Rangers. His sons, Sir James Macaulay, first Chief Justice of the Common Pleas, and Colonel John Simcoe Macaulay, a distinguished officer of Engineers, are well remembered. Those who have personal recollections of Dr Macaulay speak of him in terms of great respect. The southern portion of this property was at an early period laid out in streets and small lots. The collection of houses that here began to spring up was known as Macaulay Town, and was long considered as bearing the relation to York that Yorkville does to Toronto now. So late as 1833 Walton, in his street guide and register, speaks of Macaulay Town as extending from Yonge Street to Osgoode Hall.

James Street retains the Christian name of Dr Macaulay. Teraulay [Bay] Street led up to the site of his residence, Teraulay Cottage, which, after having been moved from its original position in connection with the laying out of Trinity Square off Yonge Street, was destroyed by fire in 1848. The northern portion of Macaulay Town was bounded by Macaulay Lane, described by Walton as 'fronting the fields'. This is Albert Street.

Of the memorable possessor of the property on the south side of Queen Street opposite Macaulay Town, Mr Jesse Ketchum, we shall have occasion to speak hereafter when we pass his place of abode in our proposed journey through Yonge Street. The existing Free Kirk place of worship, known as Knox Church, stands on land given by Mr Ketchum and on a site previously occupied by a long oblong red brick chapel which looked towards what is now Richmond Street and in which a son-in-law of his, Mr Harris, officiated to a congregation of United Synod Presbyterians. The donor was probably unconscious of the remarkable excellence of this particular position as a site for a conspicuous architectural object. The spire that towers up from this now-central spot is seen with peculiarly good effect as one approaches Toronto by the thoroughfare of Queen Street whether from the east or from the west.[1]

DIGRESSION SOUTHWARD AT BAY STREET

Old inhabitants say that Bay Street, where we are now arrived, was at the first in fact 'Bear Street', and that it was popularly so called from a noted chase given to a bear out of the adjoining wood on the north which, to escape from its pursuers, made for the water along this route. Mr Justice [D'Arcy] Boulton's [Sr] two horses, Bonaparte and Jefferson, were once seen, we are told, to attack a monster of this species that intruded on their pasture on the Grange property a little to the west. They are described as plunging at the animal with their forefeet. In 1809 a straggler from the forest of the same species was killed in George Street by Lieut. Fawcett of the 100th regiment who cleft the creature's head open with his sword. This Lieut. Fawcett

---

[1] The spire was burned in the fire that destroyed Simpson's store in 1895 and was not rebuilt. Shortly afterwards the church sold the property to Simpson's and moved to Spadina Avenue.

was afterwards Lieut.-Col. of the 100th and was severely wounded in the War of 1812.

Bay street, as we pass it, recalls one of the early breweries of York. We have already in another place briefly spoken of Shaw's and Hugill's. At the second north-west corner southward [Adelaide], beer of good repute in the town and neighbourhood was manufactured by Mr John Doel up to 1847, when his brewery was accidentally burnt. Mr Doel's name is associated with the early post-office tradition of York. For a number of years he undertook and faithfully accomplished the delivery with his own hands of all the correspondence of the place that was in those days thus distributed. His presence at a door in the olden time was often a matter of considerable interest.

In the local commotions of 1837, Mr Doel ventured in an humble way to give aid and comfort to the promoters of what proved to be a small revolution. We cannot at this hour affirm that there was anything to his discredit in this. He acted, no doubt, in accordance with certain honest instincts. Men of his class and stamp, shrewd in their ideas and sturdy against encroachments, civil and religious, abound in old Somersetshire where he first drew breath. His supposed presumption in having opinions on public questions induced the satirists of the non-progressive side to mention him occasionally in their philippics and pasquinades. His name has thus become associated in the narrative of Upper Canadian affairs with those of the actual chiefs of the party of reform. In 1827 Robert Randall, M.P.P., was dispatched to London as a delegate on the part of the so-called 'Aliens' or unnaturalized British subjects of United States origin. A series of burlesque nominations, supposed to be suggested by Randall to the Colonial Secretary, appeared at this time, emanating of course from the friends of the officials of the day. We give the document. It will be seen that Mr Doel is set down in it for the Postmaster-Generalship. The other persons mentioned will be all readily recalled.

'Nominations to be dictated by the Constitutional Meeting, on Saturday next, in the petition for the redress of grievances to be forwarded to London by Ambassador Randall. BARNABAS BIDWELL—President of Upper Canada—with an extra annual allowance for a jaunt, for the benefit of his health, to his native State of Massachusetts. W. W. BALDWIN—Chief Justice and Surgeon-General to the Militia Forces—with 1,000,000 acres of land for past services, he and his family having been most shamefully treated in having grants of land withheld from them heretofore. JOHN ROLPH—Attorney-General, and Paymaster-General to the Militia—with 500,000 acres of land for his former accounts as District Paymaster, faithfully rendered. MARSHALL S. BIDWELL—Solicitor-General—with an annual allowance of as much as he may be pleased to ask for, rendering no account—for the purpose of "encouraging emigration from the United States," and a contingent account if he shall find it convenient to accompany the President to Massachusetts. The PUISNE JUDGES—to be chosen by ballot in the Market Square, on the 4th of July in each and every year, subject to the approval of W. W. B., the Chief Justice. Their salaries to be settled when going out of office. JESSE KETCHUM, JOS. SHEPARD, DR STOYELL, and A. BURNSIDE—Executive and Legislative Councillors. Joint Secretaries—WILLIAM LYON MACKENZIE and FRANCIS COLLINS, with all the printing. JOHN CAREY—Assistant Secretary, with as much of the printing as the Joint Secretaries may be pleased to allow him. MOSES FISH—Inspector of Public Buildings and Fortifications. J. S. BALDWIN—Contractor-General to the Province, with a monopoly of the trade. T. D. MORRISON—Surveyor-General and Inspector of Hospitals. LITTLE DOEL—Postmaster-General. PETER PERRY—Chancellor of the Exchequer and Receiver-General. The above persons being thus amply provided for, their friends, alias their stepping stones', the document just quoted proceeds to state, 'may shift for themselves; an opportunity, however, will be offered them for "doing a little business" by disposing of all other public offices to the lowest bidder, from whom neither talent nor security will be required for the performance of their duties. Tenders received at [The Legislature] Russell Square, Front Street, York. The Magistracy, being of no consequence, is to be left for after consideration. The Militia, at the particular request of Paul Peterson (M.P. for Prince Edward), to be done away altogether; and the roads to take care of themselves. The Welland Canal to be stopped immediately, and Colonel By to be recalled from the Rideau Canal. N.B. Any suggestions for further *improvements* will be thankfully received at Russell Square, as above.' (The humour of all this can of course be only locally understood.)[2]

Mr Doel arrived in York in 1818, occupying a month in the journey from Philadelphia to Oswego, and a week in that from Oswego to Niagara, being obliged from stress of weather to put in at Sodus Bay. At Niagara he waited three days for a passage to York. He and his venerable helpmeet were surviving in 1870, at the ages respectively of 80 and 82. Not without reason, as the event proved, they lived for many years in a state of apprehension in regard to the stability of the lofty spire of a place of worship close to their residence. In 1862 that spire [of the Zion Congregationalist Church] actually fell, eastward, as it happened, and not westward, doing considerable damage. Mr Doel died in 1871.

By the name of the short street passing from Adelaide Street to Richmond Street, a few chains to the west of Mr Doel's corner, we are reminded of Harvey Sheppard, a famous worker in iron of the former time whose imprint on axe, broad axe, or adze was a guarantee to the practical backwoodsman of its temper and serviceable quality. Harvey Sheppard's axe factory

---

2 This long quotation pokes fun at both the Reform leaders and their policies. A detailed analysis would occupy far too much space, but some typical points may be noted. Barnabas Bidwell, the suggested candidate for President of Upper Canada, had fled Massachusetts because of malversation of funds and a return to his native state would have been decidedly unhealthy. Dr W. W. Baldwin, who was both a lawyer and a medical doctor, was, in spite of his Reform leanings, one of the largest landholders in the province, for his wife had inherited the Peter Russell holdings. Ketchum, Shepard, Stoyell, and Burnside were all American emigrants, and the Reform leaders wanted to bring in the American system of election to judgeships. Mackenzie, Collins, and Carey were Reform editors who would naturally have the patronage of the government printing in such a Reform-dominated Upper Canada. John Spread Baldwin is a rather surprising addition to the list of office-holders, for, though he was a brother of William Warren Baldwin, he was closely connected with the Bank of Upper Canada and was generally regarded as a Tory. The Reformers were naturally against the magistracy who were Tories. They also opposed the Tory-dominated militia; and canal building and the costs involved were counter to their ideas of what the province could afford to spend on developmental projects.

was on the west side of this short street. Before his establishment here he worked in a smithy of the customary village type on King Street, on the property of Jordan Post. Like Jordan Post himself, Harvey Shepard was of the old-fashioned New England mould, elongated and wiry. After a brief suspension of business a placard hung up in the country inns characteristically announced to his friends and the public that he had resumed his former occupation and that he would, 'by the aid of Divine Providence', undertake to turn out as good axes as any that he had ever made; which acknowledgement of the source of his skill is commendable, surely, if unusual. So also there is no one who will refuse to applaud an epigrammatic observation of his when responding to an appeal of charity. 'Though dealing usually in iron only, I keep', he said, 'a little stock of silver and gold for such a call as this.' The factory on Sheppard Street was afterwards [c. 1834] worked by Mr J. Armstrong and subsequently by Mr Thomas Champion, formerly of Sheffield, who in 1838 advertised that he had 'a large stock of Champion's warranted cast steel axes, made at the factory originally built by the late Harvey Sheppard, and afterwards occupied by John Armstrong. As Sheppard's and Armstrong's axes have been decidedly preferred before any others in the Province,' the advertisement continues, 'it is only necessary to state that Champion's are made by the same workmen, and from the very best material, to ensure for them the same continued preference.' We now return from our digression southward at Bay Street.

Chief Justice Elmsley was the first possessor of the hundred acres westward of the Macaulay lot. He effected, however, a certain exchange with Dr Macaulay. Preferring land that lay higher, he gave the southern half of his lot for the northern half of his neighbour's, the latter at the same time discerning, as is probable, the prospective greater value of a long frontage on one of the highways into the town. Of Mr Elmsley we have had occasion to speak in our perambulation of King Street in connection with Government House, which in its primitive state was his family residence; and in our progress through Yonge Street hereafter we shall again have to refer to him. In

1802 he was promoted from [the Chief Justiceship of] Upper
Canada to the Chief Justiceship of Lower Canada.

The park-lot which follows was originally secured by one
who has singularly vanished out of the early traditions of York—
the Rev. T. Raddish. His name is inscribed on this property in
the first plan, and also on part of what is now the south-east
portion of the Government-house grounds. He emigrated to
these parts under the express auspices of the first Lieutenant-
Governor and was expected by him to take a position of influence in the young colony of Upper Canada. But, habituated
to the amenities and conveniencies of an old community, he
speedily discovered either that an entirely new society was not
suited to him or that he himself did not dovetail well into it.
He appears to have remained in the country only just long
enough to acquire for himself and heirs the fee simple of a
good many acres of its virgin soil. In 1826 the southern portion
of Mr Raddish's park-lot became the property of Sir John
Robinson, at the time Attorney-General. The site of Osgoode
Hall, six acres, was, as we have been assured, the generous gift
of Sir John Robinson to the Law Society, and the name which
the building bears was his suggestion.[3]

OSGOODE HALL

The east wing of the existing edifice was the original Osgoode
Hall, erected [1829-32] under the eye of Dr W. W. Baldwin,
at the time Treasurer of the Society. It was a plain, square,
matter-of-fact brick building two storeys and a half in height. In
1844-6 a corresponding structure was erected to the west, and
the two were united by a building between, surmounted by a
low dome. In 1857-60 the whole edifice underwent a renova-
tion; the dome was removed; a very handsome façade of cut
stone was put up; the inner area, all constructed of Caen stone,
reminding one of the interior of a Genoese or Roman Palace,
was added, with the Court Rooms, Library, and other appurtenances, on a scale of dignity and in a style of architectural
beauty surpassed only by the new Law Courts in London. The

---

[3] The land was not given but purchased for £1000.

pediment of each wing, sustained aloft on fluted Ionic columns, seen on a fine day against the pure azure of a northern sky, is something enjoyable.

Great expense has been lavished by the Benchers on this Canadian *Palais de Justice;* but the effect of such a pile, kept in its every nook and corner and in all its surroundings in scrupulous order, is invaluable, tending to refine and elevate each successive generation of our young candidates for the legal profession and helping to inspire amongst them a salutary esprit de corps.

The Library, too, here to be seen, noble in its dimensions and aspect, must, even independently of its contents, tend to create a love of legal study and research.

The Law Society of Osgoode Hall was incorporated in 1822. The Seal bears a Pillar on which is a beaver holding a Scroll inscribed MAGNA CHARTA. To the right and left are figures of Justice and Strength (Hercules).

An incident associated in modern times with Osgoode Hall is the Entertainment given there to the Prince of Wales during his visit to Canada in 1860, on which occasion, at night, all the architectural lines of the exterior of the building were brilliantly marked out by rows of minute gas-jets.

Here too were held the impressive funeral obsequies of Sir John Robinson, the distinguished Chief Justice of Upper Canada, in 1863. In the Library is a large painting of him in oil in which his finely cut Reginald Heber features are well delineated.[4] Sayer Street, passing northward on the east side of Osgoode Hall, was so named by Chief Justice Robinson in honour of his mother. In 1870 the name was changed [to Chestnut Street], probably without reflection and certainly without any sufficient cause.

The series of paintings begun in Osgoode Hall, conservative to future ages of the outward presentment of our Chief Justices, Chancellors, and Judges, is very interesting. All of them, we

---

4 The portrait still hangs in the library. Reginald Heber was bishop of Calcutta "and author of many hymns including 'Holy, Holy, Holy, Lord God Almighty'" from 1822 to 1826

believe, are by Berthon of Toronto. No portrait of Chief Justice Osgoode, however, is at present here to be seen.

We pause for a moment at York Street, opposite the east wing of Osgoode Hall.

It rather puzzles one to conceive why York Street received its name. If a commemoration of the Duke of York of sixty years since was designed, the name of the whole town was that sufficiently already. Frederick Street, besides, recorded his specific Christian name, and Duke Street his rank and title. Although interesting now as a memento of a name borne of old by Toronto, York Street, when Toronto was York, might well have been otherwise designated, it seeming somewhat irrational for any particular thoroughfare in a town to be distinguished by the name of that town. A certain poverty of invention in regard to street names has in other instances been evinced amongst us. Victoria Street, for example, was for a time called Upper George Street, to distinguish it from George Street proper, so named from George, Prince of Wales, the notable Prince Regent [1811-20]. It is curious that no other name but George should have been suggested for the second street; especially, too, as that street might have been so fittingly named Toronto Street, as being situated within a few feet of the line of the original thoroughfare of that name which figures so largely in the early descriptions of York. If in 'York Street' a compliment had been intended to Charles Yorke, Secretary at War in 1802, the orthography would have been 'Yorke Street'.

After all, however, the name 'York Street' may have arisen from the circumstance that, at an early period, this was for teams on their way to York, the beaten track suddenly turning off here to the south out of Dundas or Lot Street, the line of road which, if followed, would have taken the traveller to Kingston.

The street on the west of the grounds of Osgoode Hall is now known as University Street [Avenue]. By the donor to the public of the land occupied by the street, it was designated Park Lane—not without due consideration, as is likely. In London there is a famous and very distinguished Park Lane. It leads from Oxford Street to Piccadilly, and skirts the whole of the east side of Hyde Park. The position of what was our Park Lane is somewhat analogous, it being open along its whole length on the left to the plantations of an ornamental piece of ground. Unmeddled with, our Park Lane would have suggested from time to time in the mind of the ruminating wayfarer pleasant thoughts of a noble and interesting part of the great home metropolis. The change to University Street was altogether un-called for. It ignored the adjoining 'College Avenue', the name of which showed that a generally recognized 'University Street' existed already: it gave, moreover, a name which is pretentious, the roadway indicated being comparatively narrow.[5]

Of the street on the east side of the grounds of Osgoode Hall we have already spoken. But in connection with the ques-tion of changes in street names, we must here again refer to it. In this case the name 'Sayer' has been made to give place to 'Chestnut'. 'Elm Street', which intersects this street to the north, probably in some vague way suggested a tree name. 'Elm Street', however, had a reason for its existence. Many persons still remember a solitary elm, a relic of the forest, which was long conspicuous just where Elm Street enters Yonge Street. And there is a fitness likewise in the names of Pine Street and Sumach Street in the east, these streets passing through a region where pines and sumachs once abounded. But the modern Chestnut Street has nothing about it in the past or present asso-ciated with chestnut trees of any kind. The name 'Sayer' should have been respected.

It is unfortunate when persons, apparently without serious retrospective thought, have a momentary chance to make changes in local names. Chancery might well be invoked to undo in some instances what has been done, and to prohibit like inconsiderate proceedings in the future. Equity would surely say that a citizen's private right should be sustained, so long as it worked no harm to the community, and that perplex-ity in the registration and description of property should not needlessly be created.

Although we shall forestall ourselves a little, we may here

---

[5] The two parts of University Avenue originally had different names.

notice one more alteration in a street-name near Osgoode Hall. William Street, immediately west of the Avenue leading to the University, has in recent times been changed to Simcoe Street. It is true, William Street was nearly in a line with the street previously known as Simcoe Street; nevertheless, starting as it conspicuously did somewhat to the west of that line, it was a street sufficiently distinct to be entitled to retain an independent name. Here again, an item of local history has been obliterated. William Street was a record on the soil of the first name of an early Chief Justice of Upper Canada who projected the street and gave the land. Dummer [St Patrick] Street, the next street westward, bears his second name.

Of 'Powell', his third name, we have already spoken elsewhere and shall again almost immediately have to speak.

When it shall be proposed to alter the name of Dummer Street—with the hope, perhaps, of improving the fame of the locality along with its name—let the case of March [Lombard] Street be recalled. In the case of March Street, the rose, notwithstanding a change of name, retained its perfume, and the Colonial Minister of the day, Lord Stanley, received but a sorry compliment when his name was made to displace that of the Earl of March. (It was from this second title of the Duke of Richmond [who was also the Earl of March] that March Street had its name.) It is probable that the Dummer Street of today, like the March Street of yesterday, would under another name continue much what it is. In all such quarters, it is not a change of name that is of any avail, but the presence of the schoolmaster and home-missionary, backed up by landlords and builders, studious of the public health and morals as well as of private interests.[6]

DIGRESSION NORTHWARD AT THE COLLEGE AVENUE

The fine vista of the College [University] Avenue, opposite to which we have now arrived, always recalls to our recollection a

---

[6] March Street became first Stanley Street and then Lombard. In recent years there have been suggestions that the name of Jarvis Street should be changed for similar reasons.

certain bright spring morning when, on reaching school, a whole holiday was unexpectedly announced; and when, as a mode of filling up a portion of the unlooked-for vacant time, it was agreed between two or three young lads to pay a visit to the place on Lot Street where, as the report had spread amongst us, they were beginning to make visible preparations for the commencement of the University of King's College. The minds of growing lads in the neighbourhood of York at that period had very vague ideas of what a university really was. It was a place where studies were carried on, but how or under what conditions there was of necessity little conception. Curiosity, however, was naturally excited by the talk on the lips of every one that a university was one day to be established at York; and now suddenly we learned that actual beginnings were to be seen of the much-talked-of institution. On the morning of the fine spring day referred to, we accordingly undertook an exploration.

On arriving at the spot to which we had been directed, we found that a long strip of land running in a straight line northwards had been marked out, after the manner of a newly opened side-line or concession road in the woods [1830]. We found a number of men actually at work with axes and mattocks; yokes of oxen, too, were straining at strong ploughs, which forced a way in amongst the roots and small stumps of the natural brushwood, and here and there underneath a rough mat of tangled grass, bringing to light now black vegetable mould, now dry clay, now loose red sand. Longitudinally, up the middle of the space marked off, several bold furrows were cut, those on the right inclining to the left and those on the left inclining to the right, as is the wont in primitive turnpiking.

One novelty we discovered—viz., that on each side along a portion of the newly cleared ground, young saplings had been planted at regular intervals; these, we were told, were horse-chestnuts procured from the United States expressly for the purpose of forming a double row of trees here. In the neighbourhood of York the horse-chestnut was then a rarity.

Everywhere throughout the North American continent, as in

the numerous newly opened areas of the British Empire elsewhere on the globe's surface, instances of course abound of
wonderful progress made in a brief interval of time. For ourselves, we seem sometimes as if we were moving among the un-
realities of a dream when we deliberately review the steps in
the march of physical and social improvement which, within a
fractional portion only of a retrospect not very extended, can
be recalled in the region where our own lot has been cast and
in particular in the neighbourhood where we are at this moment pausing.

The grand mediæval-looking structure of University College
[built 1856-9] in the grounds at the head of the Avenue continues to this day to be a surprise somewhat bewildering to the
eye and mind whenever it breaks upon our view. It looks so
completely a thing of the old world and of an age long passed
away. To think that one has walked over its site before one
stone was laid upon another thereon seems almost like a mental
hallucination.

A certain quietness of aspect and absence of overstrain after
architectural effect give the massive pile an air of great genuine-
ness. The irregular grouping of its many parts appears the un-
designed result of accretion growing out of the necessities of
successive years. The whole looks in its place and as if it had
long occupied it. The material of its walls, left for the most
part superficially in the rough, has the appearance of being
weather-worn. An impression of age, too, is given by the smooth
finish of the surrounding grounds and spacious drives by which
on several sides the building is approached, as also by the
goodly size of the well-grown oaks and other trees through
whose outstretched branches it is usually first caught sight of
from across the picturesque ravine.

There used to be preserved in the Old Hospital a model in
cork and cardboard of the great educational establishment to
which, in the first instance, the Avenue was expected to form
an approach. It was very curious. Had it been really followed,
a large portion of the park provided for the reception of the
university would have been covered with buildings. A multitude of edifices, isolated and varying in magnitude, were

scattered about, with gardens and ornamental grounds inter-
spersed. These were halls of science, lecture-rooms, laborator-
ies, residences for president, vice-president, professors, officials,
and servants of every grade. On the widely extended premises
occupied by the proposed institution, a population was apparently expected to be found that would of itself have almost
sufficed to justify representation in Parliament—a privilege the
college was actually by its charter to enjoy [1827].[7] We should
have had in fact realized before our eyes, on a considerable
scale, a part of the dreams of Plato and More, a fragment of
Atlantis and Utopia.

When the moment arrived, however, for calling into visible
being the long-contemplated seat of learning, it was found expedient to abandon the elaborate model which had been constructed. Mr Young, a local architect, was directed to devise
new plans. His ideas appear to have been wholly modern. Notwithstanding the tenor of the Royal Charter, which suggested
the precedents of the old universities of 'our United Kingdom
of Great Britain and Ireland', wherever it should be practicable
to follow them, the architecture and arrangements customary
in those places were ignored. Girard College, Philadelphia,
seems to have inspired the new designs. However, only a minute
fragment of one of the buildings of the new plan was destined
ever to exist.[8]

The formal commencement of the abortive [never-com-
pleted] work took place on the 23rd of April 1842—a day indelibly impressed on the memory of those who participated in
the proceedings. It was one of the sunniest and brightest of
days. In the year just named it happened that so early as St
George's day the leaves of the horse-chestnut were bursting
their glossy sheaths and vegetation generally was in a very

---

[7] This was under the original charter. By the time the university began
operations in 1843, Upper and Lower Canada had been united and there
was no provision for university representation in the new legislature.

[8] This fragment, only a small part of the King's College that was designed
by Young, was begun in 1842, opened in 1843, and expropriated by the
government in 1853. After some years of serving as a lunatic asylum, it
was demolished in the mid-1880s to make way for the present provincial
Parliament Buildings.

advanced stage. A procession such as had never before been seen in these parts slowly defiled up the Avenue to the spot where the cornerstone of the proposed university was to be laid.

A highly wrought contemporary description of the scene is given in a note in *Curiæ Canadenses:* 'The vast procession opened its ranks, and his Excellency the Chancellor [Bagot], with the President, the Lord Bishop of Toronto [Strachan], on his right, and the Senior Visitor, the Chief Justice [Robinson], on his left, proceeded on foot through the College Avenue to the University grounds. The countless array moved forward to the sound of military music. The sun shone out with cloudless meridian splendour; one blaze of banners flushed upon the admiring eye. The Governor's rich Lord-Lieutenant's dress, the Bishop's sacerdotal robes, the Judicial Ermine of the Chief Justice, the splendid Convocation robes of Dr McCaul, the gorgeous uniforms of the suite, the accoutrements of the numerous Firemen, the national badges worn by the Office-bearers of the different Societies, and what on such a day (St George's) must not be omitted, the Red Crosses on the breasts of England's congregated sons, the grave habiliments of the Clergy and Lawyers, and the glancing lances and waving plumes of the First Incorporated Dragoons, all formed one moving picture of civic pomp, one glorious spectacle which can never be remembered but with satisfaction by those who had the good fortune to witness it.'

Another contemporary account adds: 'As the procession drew nearer to the site where the stone was to be laid, the 43rd Regiment lined the way, with soldiers bearing arms, and placed on either side, at equal intervals. The 93rd Regiment was not on duty here, but in every direction the gallant Highlanders were scattered through the crowd, and added by their national garb and nodding plumes to the varied beauty of the animated scene. When the site was reached,' this account says, 'a new feature was added to the interest of the ceremony. Close to the spot, the north-east corner, where the foundation was to be deposited, a temporary building had been erected for the Chancellor, and there, accompanied by the officers of the University and his

suite, he took his stand. Fronting this was a kind of amphitheatre of seats, constructed for the occasion, tier rising above
tier densely filled with ladies, who thus commanded a view of
the whole ceremony. Between this amphitheatre and the place
where the Chancellor stood, the procession ranged itself.'

The Chancellor above spoken of was the Governor General
of the day, Sir Charles Bagot, a man of noble bearing and
genial, pleasant aspect. He entered with all the more spirit into
the ceremonies described from being himself a graduate of one
of the old universities. Memories of far-off Oxford and Christ
Church [College] would be sure to be roused amidst the proceedings that rendered the 23rd of April 1842 so memorable
amongst us. A brother of Sir Charles' was at the time Bishop
of Oxford. In his suite, as one of his Secretaries, was Captain
Henry Bagot of the Royal Navy, his own son. Preceding him
in the procession, bearing a large gilded mace, was an 'Esquire
Bedell', like the Chancellor himself, a Christ Church man, Mr
William Cayley, subsequently a member of the Canadian government.

Although breaking ground for the university building had
been long delayed, the commencement now made proved to be
premature. The edifice begun was never completed, as we have
already intimated; and even in its imperfect, fragmentary condition, it was not fated to be for any great length of time a scene
of learned labours. In 1856 its fortune was to be converted into
a Female Department for the over-crowded Provincial Lunatic
Asylum.

The educational system inaugurated in the new building in
1843 was, as the plate enclosed in the foundation-stone finely
expressed it, *præstantissimum ad exemplar Britannicarum
Universitatum.* But the 'exemplar' was not, in practice, found
to be, as a whole, adapted to the genius of the Western Canadian people.

The revision of the university scheme with a view to the
necessities of Western Canada was signalized by the erection in
1856-9 of a new building [now University College] on an entirely different site, and a migration to it bodily of president,
professors, and students, without departing however from the

bounds of the spacious park originally provided for the institution; and it is remarkable that, while deviating educationally and otherwise in some points from the pattern of the ancient universities as they were in 1842, a nearer approach architecturally was made to the mediæval English College than any that had been thought of before. Mr Cumberland, the designer of the really fine and most appropriate building in which the university at length found a resting place, was, as is evident, a man after the heart of Wykeham and Waynflete.[9]

The story of our university is a part of the history of Upper Canada. From the first foundation of the colony the idea of some such seat of learning entered into the scheme of its organization. In 1791, before he had yet left England for the unbroken wilderness in which his government was to be set up, we have General Simcoe speaking to Sir Joseph Banks, the President of the Royal Society, of 'a college of a higher class' as desirable in the community which he was about to create. 'A college of a higher class', he says, 'would be eminently useful, and would give a tone of principles and of manners that would be of infinite support to Government.' In the same letter he remarks to Sir Joseph, 'My friend the Marquis of Buckingham has suggested that Government might allow me a sum of money to be laid out for a Public Library, to be composed of such books as might be useful in the colony. He instanced the Encyclopædia, extracts from which might occasionally be published in the newspapers. It is possible', he adds, 'private donations might be obtained, and that it would become an object of Royal munificence.'

It was naturally long before the community of Upper Canada was ripe for a college of the character contemplated; but provision for its ultimate existence and sustenance was made almost from the beginning in the assignment to that object of a fixed and liberal portion of the public lands of the country.

In the original planting of the Avenue, up whose fine vista

---

[9] Both William Wykeham (1324-1404) and William Waynflete (1395-1486) were bishops of Winchester and Chancellors of England. The first founded Winchester College, Winchester, and New College, Oxford; the second Magdalen College, Oxford.

we have been gazing, the mistake was committed of imitating nature too closely. Numerous trees and shrubs of different kinds and habits were mingled together as they are usually to be seen in a wild primitive wood, and thus the growth and fair development of all were hindered. The horse-chestnuts alone should have been relied on to give character to the Avenue; and of these there should have been on each side a double row, with a promenade for pedestrians underneath, after the manner of the great walks in the public parks of the old towns of Europe.

XI

QUEEN
STREET
FROM
COLLEGE
[UNIVERSITY]
AVENUE
TO THE
HUMBER

Pursuing our way now westward from the Avenue leading to the university, we pass the Powell park-lot, on which was, up to recent times, the family vault of the Powells, descendants of the Chief Justice. The whole property was named by the fancy of the first possessor, Caer-Howell—Castle Howell, in allusion to the mythic Hoel, to whom all ap-Hoels trace their origin. Dummer Street, which opens northward a little further on, retains, as we have said, the second baptismal name of Chief Justice Powell.

Beverley House and its surroundings, on the side opposite Caer Howell estate, recall one whose name and memory must repeatedly recur in every narrative of our later Canadian history, Sir John [Beverley] Robinson. This was the residence temporarily of Poulett Thomson, afterwards Lord Sydenham, while present in Toronto as Governor-General of the Canadas in 1839-40. A kitchen on a large scale which he caused to be built on the premises of Beverley House is supposed to have been an auxiliary, indirectly, in getting the Union measure through the Upper Canada Parliament.[1] In a letter to a friend, written at Montreal in 1840, he gives a sketch of his everyday

---

[1] Sydenham had great difficulties in gaining the consent of the Upper Canadian Legislature to the union of Upper and Lower Canada—a measure he accomplished only by the promise of a large loan and considerable wining and dining.

life: it describes equally well the daily distribution of his time here in Toronto. 'Work in my room', he says, 'till three o'clock; a ride with my aide-de-camp till five; work again till dinner; at dinner till nine; and work again till early next morning. This is my daily routine. My dinners last till ten, when I have company, which is about three times a week; except one night in the week, when I receive about 150 people.'

His policy was, as we know, very successful. Of the state of things at Toronto, and in Upper Canada generally, after the Union measure had been pushed through, he writes to a friend thus: 'I have prorogued my Parliament,' he says, 'and I send you my Speech. Never was such unanimity! When the Speaker read it in the Commons, after the prorogation, they gave me three cheers, in which even the ultras united. In fact, as the matter stands now, the Province is in a state of peace and harmony which, three months ago, I thought was utterly hopeless.'

Through Poulett Thomson, Toronto for a few months and to the extent of one half was the seat of a modern feudal barony. On being elevated to the peerage, the Governor-General, who had carried the Union, was created Baron Sydenham of Sydenham in Kent and Toronto in Canada.

At one time it was expected that Toronto would be the capital of the United Province, but its liege lord pronounced it to be 'too far and out of the way'; though at the same time he gives it as his opinion that 'Kingston or Bytown would do.' Thus in 1840, and in July 1841, he writes: 'I have every reason to be satisfied with having selected this place (Kingston) as the new Capital. There is no situation in the Province so well adapted for the seat of Government from its central position; and certainly we are as near England as we should be anywhere else in the whole of Canada. My last letters reached me', he says, 'in fifteen days from London! So much for steam and railways.' Being in very delicate health, it had been Lord Sydenham's intention to return to England in September 1841. On the 5th of June, he writes at Kingston to a friend: 'I long for September, beyond which I will not stay if they were to make me Duke of Canada and Prince of Regiopolis, as this place is called [in Latin].' But he was never more to see England. On the 4th of the September in which he had hoped to leave Canada, he suffered a fracture of the right leg and other injury by a fall from his horse. He never rallied from the shock. His age was only 42.[2]

The park-lot which follows that occupied by Chief Justice Powell was selected by Solicitor-General Gray, of whom fully already. It afterwards became the property of Mr D'Arcy Boulton [Jr], eldest son of Mr Justice Boulton, and was known as the Grange estate. The house which bears the name of the 'Grange' was built at the beginning of the brick era of York [c. 1818], and is a favourable specimen of the edifices of that period. (Beverley House, just noted, was, it may be added, also built by Mr D'Arcy Boulton.)

The Grange gate, now thrust far back by the progress of improvement, was long a familiar landmark on the line of Lot Street. It was just within this gate that the fight already recorded took [place] between Mr Justice Boulton's horses, Bonaparte and Jefferson, and the bear. A memorandum of Mr G. S. Jarvis, of Cornwall, in our possession affirms that Mr Justice Boulton drove a phaeton of some pretensions, and that his horses Bonaparte and Jefferson were the crack pair of the day at York. As to some other equipages, he says: 'The Lieut. Governor's carraige was considered a splendid affair, but some of the Toronto cabs would now throw it into the shade. The carriage of Chief Justice Powell, he adds, was a rough sort of omnibus, and would compare with the jail van used now.' (We remember Bishop Strachan's account of a carriage sent up for his own use from Albany or New York; it was constructed on the model of the ordinary oval stage coach, with a kind of hemispherical top.)

To our former notes of Mr Justice Boulton, we add that he was the author of a work in quarto published in London in 1805, entitled a *Sketch of the Province of Upper Canada*.

John Street, passing south just here, is, as was noted previously, a memorial, so far as its name is concerned, of the first Lieutenant Governor of Upper Canada. On the plan of the

---

[2] His death, on September 19, was actually caused by tetanus.

'new town'—as the first expansion westward of York was termed
—while this street is marked 'John', the next parallel thoroughfare eastward is named 'Graves', and the open square included
between the two, southward on Front Street, is 'Simcoe-place'.
The three names of the founder of York were thus commemorated. The expression 'Simcoe-place' has fallen into disuse. It
indicated, of course, the site of the present [1873] Parliament
Buildings of the Province of Ontario. Graves Street has become
Simcoe Street—a name, as we have seen, recently extended to the
thoroughfare northward with which it is nearly in a right line:
viz., William Street, which previously recorded, as we have
said, the first Christian name of Chief Justice Powell. The name
'John Street' has escaped change. The name sounds trivial
enough, but it has an interest.

In the minds of the present generation, with John Street will
be specially associated the memorable landing of the Prince of
Wales [the future Edward VII] at Toronto in 1860. At the foot
of John Street for that occasion there was built a vast semi-
colosseum of wood, opening out upon the waters of the bay—
a pile whose capacious concavity was densely filled again and
again during the Prince's visit with the inhabitants of the town
and the population of the surrounding country. And on the
brow of the bank, immediately above the so-called amphitheatre and exactly in the line of John Street, was erected a
finely designed triumphal arch, recalling those of Septimus
Severus and Titus.

This architectural object while it stood gave a peculiarly fine
finish to the vista, looking southward along John Street. The
usually monotonous water-view presented by the bay and lake,
and even the commonplace straight line of the Island, seen
through the framework of the three lofty vaulted passages, acquired for the moment a genuine picturesqueness. An ephemeral monument, but as long as it stood its effect was delightfully classical and beautiful. The whole group—the arch and the
huge amphitheatre below, furnished around its upper rim at
equal intervals with tall masts, each bearing a graceful gonfalon
and each helping to sustain on high a luxuriant festoon of ever-
green which alternately drooped and rose again round the

whole structure and along the two sides of the grand roadway up to the arch—all seen under a sky of pure azure, and bathed in cheery sunlight, surrounded too and thronged with a pleased multitude—constituted a spectacle not likely to be forgotten.

Turning down John Street a few chains, the curious observer may see on his left a particle of the old area of York retaining several of its original natural features. In the portion of the Macdonell block not yet divided into building-slips we have a fragment of one of the many shallow ravines which meandered capriciously, every here and there, across the broad site of the intended town. To the passer-by it now presents a refreshing bit of bowery meadow out of which towers up one of the grand elm trees of the country, with stem of great height and girth and head of very graceful form, whose healthy and undecayed limbs and long trailing branchlets clearly show that the human regard which has led to the preservation hitherto of this solitary survivor of the forest has not been thrown away. This elm and the surrounding grove are still favourite stations or resting-places for our migratory birds. Here, for one place, in the spring are sure to be heard the first notes of the robin.

At the south-west angle of the Macdonell block still stands in a good state of preservation the mansion put up by the Hon. Alexander Macdonell. We have from time to time spoken of the brick era of York. Mr Macdonell's imposing old homestead may be described as belonging to an immediately preceding era—the age of framed timber and weather-board which followed the primitive or hewn-log period. It is a building of two full storeys, each of considerable elevation. A central portico with columns of the whole height of the house gives it an air of dignity.

Mr Macdonell was one more in that large group of military men who served in the American Revolutionary War, under Col. Simcoe, and who were attracted to Upper Canada by the prospects held out by that officer when appointed Governor of the new colony. Mr Macdonell was the first Sheriff of the Home District. He represented in successive parliaments the Highland constituency of Glengarry, and was chosen Speaker of the House. He was afterwards summoned to the Upper House. He was a friend and correspondent of the Earl of Selkirk, and was desired by that zealous emigrational theorist to undertake the superintendence of the settlement at Kildonan on the Red River. Though he declined this task, he undertook the management of one of the other Highland settlements included in the Earl of Selkirk's scheme, namely that of Baldoon on Lake St Clair, Mr Douglas undertaking the care of that established at Moulton at the mouth of the Grand River.

Mr Macdonell—in person rather tall and thin, of thoughtful aspect, and in manner quiet and reserved—is one of the company of our early worthies whom we personally well remember. An interesting portrait of him exists in the possession of his descendants: it presents him with his hair in powder and otherwise in the costume of 'sixty years since'. He died in 1842 'amid the regrets of a community who', to adopt the language of a contemporary obituary, 'loved him for the mild excellence of his domestic and private character, no less than they esteemed him as a public man.'

Mr Miles Macdonell, the first Governor of Assiniboia [1812], under the auspices of the Hudson's Bay Company, and Alexander Macdonell, the chief representative in 1816 of the rival and even hostile Company of the North-West Traders of Montreal, were both near relations of Mr Macdonell of York, as also was the barrister, lost in the *Speedy*, and the well-known R. C. Bishop Macdonell of Kingston. Col. Macdonell, slain at Queenston with General Brock and whose remains are deposited beneath the column there, was his brother. His son, Mr Allan Macdonell, has on several occasions stood forward as the friend and spirited advocate of the Indian tribes, especially of the Lake Superior region, on occasions when their interests, as native lords of the soil, seemed in danger of being overlooked by the government of the day.

On Richmond Street, a little to the west of the Macdonell block, was the town residence of Col. [Samuel] Smith, sometime President [Administrator] of the Province of Upper Canada [1817-18]. He was also allied to the family of Mr Macdonell. Col. Smith's original homestead was on the Lake Shore to the west, in the neighbourhood of the river Etobicoke. Gour-

lay in his *Statistical Account of Upper Canada* has chanced
to speak of it. 'I shall describe the residence and neighbourhood
of the President of Upper Canada from remembrance,' he says,
'journeying past it on my way to York from the westward, by
what is called the Lake Road through Etobicoke. For many
miles', he says, 'not a house had appeared, when I came to that
of Colonel Smith, lonely and desolate. It had once been genteel
and comfortable; but was now going to decay. A vista had been
opened through the woods towards Lake Ontario; but the
riotous and dangling undergrowth seemed threatening to re-
take possession from the Colonel of all that had once been
cleared, which was of narrow compass. How could a solitary
half-pay officer help himself,' candidly asks Gourlay, 'settled
down upon a block of land, whose very extent barred out the
assistance and convenience of neighbours? Not a living thing
was to be seen around. How different might it be, thought I,
were a hundred industrious families compactly settled here
out of the redundant population of England!'

The house which led us to this notice of President Smith is,
as we have said, situated on Richmond Street. On Adelaide
Street, immediately south of this house, and also a little west
of the Macdonell block, was a residence of mark erected at an
early period by Mr Hugh Heward, and memorable as having
been the abode for a time of the Naval Commissioner or Commodore [*sic*], Joseph Bouchette, who first took the soundings
and constructed a map of the harbour of York. His portrait is to
be seen prefixed to his well-known *British Dominions in North
America* [1831]. The same house was also once occupied by
Dr Stuart, afterwards Archdeacon of Kingston; and at a later
period by Mrs Caldwell, widow of Dr Caldwell, connected with
the Naval establishment at Penetanguishene. Her sons John and
Leslie, two tall, sociable youths, now both deceased, were our
classmates at school. We observe in the *Oracle* of Saturday, May
28, 1803, a notice of Mr Hugh Heward's death in the following
terms: 'Died lately at Niagara, on his way to Detroit, after a
lingering illness, Mr Hugh Heward, formerly clerk in the Lieutenant-Governor's office, and a respectable inhabitant of this
town (York).'

A few yards further on was the home of Mr John Ross whose almost prescriptive right it gradually became, whenever a death occurred in one of the old families, to undertake the funeral obsequies. Few were there of the ancient inhabitants who had not found themselves at one time or another wending their way on a sad errand to Mr Ross's doorstep. On his sombre and very unpretending premises were put together the perishable shells in which the mortal remains of a large proportion of the primitive householders of York and their families are now reverting to their original dust. Almost up to the moment of his own summons to depart hence, he continued to ply his customary business, being favoured with an old age unusually green and vigorous, like 'the ferryman austere and stern', Charon; to whom also the *inculta canities* of a plentiful supply of hair and beard, along with a certain staidness, taciturnity, and rural homeliness of manner and attire further suggested a resemblance. Many things thus combine to render Mr John Ross not the least notable of our local dramatis personæ. He was led, as we have understood, to the particular business which was his usual avocation by the accident of having been desired, whilst out on active service as a militiaman in 1812, to take charge of the body of Gen. Brock when that officer was killed on Queenston Heights.

While in this quarter we should pause too for a moment before the former abode of Mr Robert Stanton, sometime King's Printer for Upper Canada, as noted already; afterwards editor of the *Loyalist;* and subsequently Collector of Customs at York: a structure of the secondary brick period and situated on Peter Street but commanding the view eastward along the whole length of Richmond Street. Mr Stanton's father was an officer in the Navy who, between the years 1771 and 1786, saw much active service in the East and West Indies, in the Mediterranean, at the siege of Gibraltar under General Elliott, and on the American coast during the Revolutionary war. From 1786 to 1828 he was in the public service in several military and civil capacities in Lower and Upper Canada. In 1806 he was for one thing, we find, issuer of Marriage Licences at York.

In one or two instances we are enabled to give the formal announcement in the *Gazette and Oracle* of the marriage for which the licence issued by Mr Stanton was so curtly recorded. In the paper of Jan. 27, 1808, we have: 'Married, on the 13th instant, by the Rev. G. O. Stuart, D'Arcy Boulton, Jr, Esq., barrister, to Miss Sarah Robinson, second daughter of the late C. Robinson, Esq., of York.'

And in the number for August 13, in the same year we read: 'Married by the Rev. G. O. Stuart, on Monday the 8th instant, John Powell, Esq., to Miss Shaw, daughter of the Hon. Æneas Shaw, of this place (York).' To this announcement the editor, as we suppose, volunteers the observation: 'This matrimonial connexion of the amiable parties we think replete with, and we wish it productive of, the most perfect human happiness.'

A complimentary epithet to the bride is not unusual in early Canadian marriage notices. In the *Gazette and Oracle* of Dec. 29, 1798, we have a wedding in the Playter family recorded thus: 'Married last Monday, Mr James Playter to the agreeable Miss Hannah Miles, daughter of Mr Abner Miles of this town.' In the same paper for Feb. 24, 1798, is the announcement: 'Married in this town (Niagara), by the Rev. Mr Burke, Captain Miles Macdonell of the Royal Canadian Volunteers, to the amiable Miss Katey Macdonell. (This union was of brief duration. In the *Constellation* of Sept. 6, 1799, we observe: 'Died lately at Kingston, Mrs Macdonell, of this town (Niagara), the amiable consort of Captain Miles Macdonell of the Canadian Volunteers.')

Again in the *Gazette and Oracle* for Saturday Oct. 26, 1799: 'Married, last Monday, by the Rev. Mr Addison, Colonel Smith, of the Queen's Rangers, to the most agreeable and accomplished Miss Mary Clarke.' (This was the Col. Smith who subsequently was for a time President of Upper Canada.)

In the *Constellation* of Nov. 23, 1799, in addition to the complimentary epithet, a poetical stanza is subjoined. Thus: 'Married at the seat of the Hon. Mr Hamilton, at Queenston, on Sunday last, Mr Thomas Dickson, merchant, to the amiable Mrs Taylor, daughter of Captain Wilkinson, commanding, Fort Erie.

For thee, best treasure of a husband's heart;
Whose bliss it is that thou for life art so;
That thy fond bosom bears a faithful part
In every casual change his breast may know.

But occasionally the announcement is almost as terse as one of Mr Stanton's entries. Thus in the *Constellation* of Dec. 28, 1799, Mr Hatt's marriage to Miss Cooly appears with great brevity: 'Married at Ancaster, Mr Richard Hatt to Miss Polly Cooly.'

The family of Mr Stanton, senior, was large. It was augmented by twins on five separate occasions. Not far from Mr Stanton's house a lesser edifice of brick of comparatively late date on the north side of Richmond Street, immediately opposite the premises associated just now with the memory of President Smith, may be noted as having been built and occupied by the distinguished Admiral Vansittart, and the first example in this region of a cottage furnished with light, tasteful verandahs in the modern style.

We now return from our digression into Richmond and Adelaide Streets and again proceed on our way westward.

The grantee of the park-lot which followed Solicitor-General Gray's was the famous Hon. Peter Russell, of whom we have had occasion again and again to speak. A portion of the property was brought under cultivation at an early period, and a substantial farm-house put up thereon—a building which in 1872 was still in existence. The name attached to this house and clearing was Petersfield.

Survivors of the primitive era in Upper Canada have been heard sometimes to express (like Lord Clive, after his dealings with the rajahs) their surprise that they did not provide for themselves more largely than they did, when the broad acres of their adopted country were to be had to any extent, almost for the asking. But this reflection should console them: in few instances are the descendants of the early very large landholders much better off at the present hour than probably they would have been had their fathers continued landless.

Mr Russell died at York on the 30th of September 1808. His obituary appears in the *Gazette and Oracle* of the following

day. 'Departed this life on Friday, the 30th ultimo, the Hon.
Peter Russell, Esquire, formerly President of the Government
of the Province, late Receiver General, and Member of the Executive and Legislative Councils: a gentleman who whilst living
was honoured, and sincerely esteemed; and of whose regular
and amiable conduct, the Public will long retain a favoured
and grateful remembrance.'

Of the funeral, which took place on the 4th of October, we
have a brief account in the paper of Oct. 8, 1808. It says: 'The
remains of the late Hon. Peter Russell were interred on Wednesday the 4th instant with the greatest decorum and respect.
The obsequies of this accomplished gentleman were followed
to the grave by His Excellency the Lieut. Governor (Gore) as
Chief Mourner; with the principal gentlemen of the town and
neighbourhood; and they were feelingly accompanied by all
ranks, evincing a reverential awe for the Divine dispensation.
An appropriate funeral sermon was preached by the Rev. Okill
Stuart. The Garrison, commanded by Major Fuller, performed
with becoming dignity the military honours of this respected
veteran, who was a Captain in the Army on half-pay.' The
editor then adds: 'deeply impressed with an ardent esteem for
his manly character, and the irreparable loss occasioned by his
death, we were not among those who felt the least at this last
tribute of respect to his memory and remains.' (The Major
Fuller, above named, was the father of the Rev. Thomas Brock
Fuller, in 1873 Archdeacon of Niagara [Bishop of Niagara
1875-84].)

But Petersfield was also associated with the history of Mr
Denison, who was the progenitor of the now-numerous Canadian family of that name. Through an intimacy with Mr Russell, springing out of several years' campaigning together in the
American Revolutionary war, Mr Denison was induced by that
gentleman, when about to leave England in an official capacity
in company with General Simcoe, to emigrate with his family
to Upper Canada in 1792. He first settled at Kingston, but in
1796 removed to York where, by the authority of Mr Russell, he
temporarily occupied Castle Frank on the Don. He then, as
we have seen, occupied 'the excellent dwelling-house' put up

'on a front lot' in the town of York by Mr Russell himself; and afterwards he was again accommodated by his friend with quarters in the newly-erected homestead of Petersfield.

We have evidence that in 1805 a portion of Petersfield was under cultivation and that under Mr Denison's care it produced fine crops of a valuable vegetable. Under date of York, 20th December 1805, in a contemporary *Oracle*, we have the following advertisement: 'POTATOES: To be sold at Mr Russell's Farm at Petersfield, by Mr John Denison, in any quantities not less than ten bushels, at Four Shillings, York Currency, the bushel, if delivered at the purchaser's house, or Three Shillings the bushel, if taken by them from the Farm.'

Our own personal recollection of Mr Denison is associated with Petersfield, the homely cosiness of whose interior, often seen during its occupancy by him, lighted up by a rousing hospitable fire of great logs, piled high in one of the usual capacious and lofty fire-places of the time, made an indelible impression on the boyish fancy. The venerable Mrs Sophia Denison, too—Mr Denison's better half—was in like manner associated in our memory with the cheery interior of the ancient Petersfield farm-house—a fine old English matron and mother of the antique, strongly-marked, vigorous, sterling type. She was one of the Taylors of Essex among whom, at home and abroad, ability and talent, and traits of a higher and more sacred character, are curiously hereditary. We shall have occasion further on to speak of the immediate descendants of these early occupants of Petersfield.

On the south side of the expansion of Queen Street, in front of Petersfield and a little beyond Peter Street (which, as we have previously noticed, had its name from Peter Russell), was the abode of Mr [John Henry] Dunn, long Receiver-General of Upper Canada. It was (and is) a retired family house, almost hidden from the general view by a grove of ornamental trees. A quiet-looking gate led into a straight drive up to the house out of Queen Street. Of Mr Dunn we have already discoursed, and of Mrs Dunn, one of the graceful lady-chiefs in the high life of York in the olden time. In the house at which we now pause was born their famous son, Alexander Roberts Dunn, in

1833, who not only had the honour of sharing in the charge of the Light Brigade at Balaclava in 1856, now so renowned in history and song, but who, of all the six hundred there, won the highest meed of glory.

The occupant of Mr Dunn's house at a later period was Chief Justice McLean, who died here in 1865. He was born at St Andrews, near Cornwall, in 1791. At the battle of Queenston he served as Lieutenant in Capt. Cameron's No. 1 Flank Company of York Militia, and received a severe wound in the early part of the engagement. He was afterwards for some time Speaker of the House. An admirable full-length painting of Chief Justice McLean exists at Osgoode Hall.

Immediately after the grounds and property of Mr Dunn, on the same side and across the very broad Brock Street [Spadina Avenue] which is an opening of modern date, was to be seen until recently a modest dwelling-place of wood—somewhat peculiar in expression; square, and rather tall for its depth and width; of dingy hue; its roof four-sided; below, a number of lean-to's and irregular extensions clustering round; in front low shrubbery, a circular drive, and a wide, open-barred gate. This was the home of one who has acquired a distinguished place in our local annals, military and civil—Colonel James FitzGibbon.

A memorable exploit of his, in the war with the United States in 1813, was the capture of a force of 450 infantry, 50 cavalry and two guns, when in command himself, at the moment, of only forty-eight men. He had been put in charge of a depot of stores at the Beaver Dams, between Queenston and Thorold. Colonel Boerstler, of the invading army, was dispatched from Fort George at Niagara with orders to take this depot. FitzGibbon was apprised of his approach. Reconnoitring, and discovering that Boerstler had been somewhat disconcerted on his march by a straggling fire from the woods, kept up by a few militiamen and about thirty Indians under Captain Kerr, he conceived the bold idea of dashing out and demanding a surrender of the enemy! Accordingly, spreading his little force judiciously, he suddenly presented himself, waving a white pocket-handkerchief. He was an officer, he hurriedly announced, in command of a detachment: his superior officer, with a large force, was in the rear, and the Indians were unmanageable. (Some extemporized war-whoops were to be heard at the moment in the distance.)

The suggestion of a capitulation was listened to by Colonel Boerstler as a dictate of humanity. The truth was, Major DeHaren of the Canadian force, to whom, in the neighbourhood of what is now St Catharines, a message had been sent, was momentarily expected with 200 men. To gain time Fitz-Gibbon made it a matter of importance that the terms of the surrender should be reduced to writing. Scarcely was the document completed when DeHaren arrived. Had there been the least further delay on his part, how to dispose of the prisoners would have been a perplexing question.

Lieutenant FitzGibbon was now soon Captain FitzGibbon. He had previously been a private in the 19th and 61st Regiments, having enlisted in Ireland at the age of seventeen. On the day of his enrolment he was promoted to the rank of sergeant, and a very few years later he was a sergeant-major. He saw active service in Holland and Denmark. His title of Colonel was derived from his rank in our Canadian Militia.

His tall, muscular figure, ever in buoyant motion; his grey, good-humoured, vivacious eye beaming out from underneath a bushy, light-coloured eyebrow; the cheery ring of his voice and its animated utterances were familiar to everyone. In the midst of a gathering of the young, whether in the schoolroom or on the playground, his presence was always warmly hailed. They at once recognized in him a genuine sympathizer with themselves in their ways and wants, and he had ever ready for them words of hope and encouragement.

Our own last personal recollection of Colonel FitzGibbon is connected with a visit which we chanced to pay him at his quarters in Windsor Castle where, in his old age, through the interest of Lord Seaton [Sir John Colborne], he had been appointed one of the Military Knights [1856]. Though most romantically ensconced and very comfortably lodged within the walls of the noblest of all the royal residences of Europe, his

heart, we found, was far away, ever recurring to the scenes of
old activities. Where the light streamed in through what seemed
properly an embrasure for cannon, pierced through a wall several yards in thickness, we saw a pile of Canadian newspapers.
To pore over these was his favourite occupation.

After chatting with him in his room, we went with him to
attend Divine Service in the magnificent Chapel of St George
close by. We then strolled together round the ramparts of the
Castle, enjoying the incomparable views. Since the time of William iv the habit of the Military Knights is that of an officer of
high rank in full dress, cocked hat and feather included. As
our venerable friend passed the several sentries placed at intervals about the Castle, arms were duly presented, an attention
which each time elicited from the Colonel the words, rapidly
interposed in the midst of a stream of earnest talk, and accompanied by deprecatory gestures of the hand, 'Never mind *me*,
boy! Never mind *me*!'

Colonel FitzGibbon took the fancy of Mrs Jameson when in
Canada. She devotes several pages of her *Winter Studies* to
the story of his life. She gives some account of his marriage. The
moment he received his captaincy, she tells us, 'he surprised
General Sheaffe, his commanding officer, by asking for a leave
of absence, although the war was still at its height [1814]. In
explanation, he said he wished to have his nuptials celebrated,
so that if a fatal disaster happened to himself, his bride might
enjoy the pension of a captain's widow. The desired leave was
granted, and after riding some 150 miles and accomplishing his
purpose, he was back in an incredibly short space of time at
head-quarters again. No fatal disaster occurred, and he lived',
Mrs Jameson adds, 'to be the father of four brave sons and one
gentle daughter.'

The name of Colonel FitzGibbon recalls the recollection of
his sister, Mrs Washburn, remarkable of old in York for dash
and spirit on horseback, spite of extra *embonpoint*; for a distinguished dignity of bearing combined with a marked Hibern-
ian heartiness and gaiety of manner. As to the 'four brave sons
and one gentle daughter', all have now passed away: one of the
former met with a painful death from the giving way of a

crowded gallery at a political meeting in the Market Square [1834], as previously narrated. All four lads were favourites with their associates and partook of their father's temperament.

Of Spadina Avenue, which we crossed in our approach to Col. FitzGibbon's old home, and of Spadina house, visible in the far distance at the head of the Avenue, we have already spoken in our Collections and Recollections connected with Front Street.

In passing we make an addition to what was then narrated. The career of Dr W. W. Baldwin, the projector of the Avenue and the builder of Spadina, is now a part of Upper Canadian history. It presents a curious instance of that versatility which we have had occasion to notice in so many of the men who have been eminent in this country. A medical graduate of Edinburgh, and in that capacity commencing life in Ireland, on settling in Canada he began the study of Law and became a leading member of the Bar.

On his arrival at York, from the first Canadian home of his father on Baldwin's Creek in the township of Clarke, Dr Baldwin's purpose was to turn to account for a time his own educational acquirements by undertaking the office of a teacher of youth. In several successive numbers of the *Gazette and Oracle* of 1802-3 we read the following advertisement: 'Dr. Baldwin understanding that some of the gentlemen of this Town have expressed some anxiety for the establishment of a Classical School, begs leave to inform them and the public that he intends on Monday the first day of January next, to open a School in which he will instruct Twelve Boys in Writing, Reading, and Classics and Arithmetic. The terms are, for each boy, eight guineas per annum, to be paid quarterly or half-yearly; one guinea entrance and one cord of wood to be supplied by each of the boys on opening the School. N.B.—Mr Baldwin will meet his pupils at Mr Willcocks' house on Duke Street. *York, December 18th, 1802.*' Of the results of this enterprise we have not at hand any record.

The Russell bequest augmented in no slight degree the previous possessions of Dr Baldwin. In the magnificent dimensions assigned to the thoroughfare opened up by him in the neighbourhood of Petersfield, we have probably a visible expression of the large-handed generosity which a pleasant windfall is apt to inspire. Spadina Avenue is 132 feet wide throughout its mile-and-a-half length; and the part of Queen Street that bounds the front of the Petersfield park-lot is made suddenly to expand to the width of 90 feet. Maria [Soho] Street also, a short street here, is of extra width. The portion of York, now Toronto, laid out by Dr Baldwin on a fraction of the land opportunely inherited will, when solidy built over, rival Washington or St Petersburg in grandeur of ground-plan and design [!].

The career of Dr [John] Rolph, another of our early Upper Canadian notabilities, resembles in some respects that of Dr Baldwin. Before emigrating from Gloucestershire, he began life as a medical man. On arriving in Canada he transferred himself to the Bar. In this case, however, after the attainment of eminence in the newly adopted profession, there was a return to the original pursuit, with the acquisition in that also of a splendid reputation. Both acquired the local style of Honourable: Dr Rolph by having been a member of the Hincks ministry from 1851 to 1854;[3] Dr Baldwin being summoned [1834], six months before his decease, to the Legislative Council of United Canada while his son was Attorney-General.

Mr William Willcocks, allied by marriage to Dr Baldwin's family, selected the park-lot at which we arrive after crossing Spadina Avenue. A lake in the Oak Ridges (Lake Willcocks) has its name from the same early inhabitant. In 1802 he was Judge of the Home District Court. He is to be distinguished from the ultra-Reformer, Sheriff Willcocks, of Judge Thorpe's day, whose name was Joseph; and from Charles Willcocks who in 1818 was proposing, through the columns of the *Upper Canada Gazette*, to publish by subscription a history of his own life. The advertisement was as follows (what finally came of it, we are not able to state): 'The subscriber proposes to publish,

---

[3] He was also briefly a member of Sir Francis Bond Head's Executive Council in 1836, when the entire Council resigned over the governor's refusal to consult them.

by subscription, a History of his Life. The subscription to be One Dollar, to be paid by each subscriber; one-half in advance; the other half on the delivery of the Book. The money to be paid to his agent, Mr Thomas Deary, who will give receipts and deliver the Books. CHARLES WILLCOCKS, *late Lieutenant, City of Cork Militia. York, March 17th ,1818.'*

This Mr Charles Willcocks once fancied he had grounds for challenging his namesake Joseph to mortal combat, according to the barbaric notions of the time. But at the hour named for the meeting, Joseph did not appear on the ground. Charles waited a reasonable time. He then chipped off a square inch or so of the bark of a neighbouring tree and, stationing himself at duelling distance, discharged his pistol at the mark which he had made. As the ball buried itself in the spot at which aim had been taken, he loudly bewailed his old friend's reluctance to face him. 'Oh, Joe, Joe!' he passionately cried. 'If you had only been here!'

Although Joseph escaped this time, he was not so fortunate afterwards. He fell 'foremost fighting' in the ranks of the invaders of Upper Canada in 1814. The incident is briefly mentioned in the Montreal *Herald* of the 15th of October, in that year, in the following terms: 'It is officially announced by General Ripley (on the American side, that is), that the traitor Willcocks was killed in the sortie from Fort Erie on the 4th ult., greatly lamented by his general and the army.' Undertaking with impetuosity a crusade against the governmental ideas which were locally in the ascendant, and encountering the resistance customary in such cases, he cut the knot of his discontent by joining the Republican force when it made its appearance.

The Willcocks park-lot, or a portion of it, was afterwards possessed by Mr Billings, a well-remembered Commissariat officer long stationed at York. He built the house subsequently known as Englefield which later was the home of Colonel Loring who, at the time of the taking of York in 1813, had his horse killed under him; and here he died. Mr Billings and Colonel Loring both had sons, of whom we make brief mention as having been in the olden times among our own school-boy

associates but who now, like so many more personal contemporaries already noted, are after brief careers deceased. An announcement in the Montreal *Herald* of February 4th, 1815,
admits us to a domestic scene in the household of Colonel, at
the time Captain, Loring. (The Treaty of Peace with the United
States was signed at Ghent, on the 24th of December 1814. Its
effect was being pleasantly realized in Canada in January 1815.)
'At Prescott', the *Herald* reports, 'on Thursday, 26th January,
the lady of Capt. Loring, Aide-de-Camp and Private Secretary
to His Honor Lieut.-Gen. Drummond, was safely delivered of a
daughter.' The *Herald* then adds: 'The happy father had returned from a state of captivity with the enemy, but a few
hours previous to the joyful event.' Capt. Loring had been
taken prisoner in the battle of Lundy's Lane in the preceding
July.

The first occupant of the next lot (No. 16) westward, was Mr
[Jacques] Baby, of whom we have spoken in former sections.
Opposite was the house of Bernard Turquand, an Englishman
of note, for many years first clerk in the Receiver-General's
department. He was an early promoter of amateur boating
among us, a recreation with which possibly he had become
familiar at Malta where he was long a resident. Just beyond
on the same side was the dwelling-place of Major Winniett—a
long, low, one-storey bungalow of a neutral tint in colour, its
roof spreading out verandah-wise on both sides.

After the name of Mr Baby on the early plan of the park-
lots comes the name of Mr Grant—'the Hon. Alexander Grant'.
During the interregnum between the death of Governor Hunter
and the arrival of Governor Gore, Mr Grant, as senior member
of the Executive Council, was President of Upper Canada[4]
[1805-6]. The Parliament that sat during his brief administration appropriated £800 to the purchase of instruments for il-
lustrating the principles of Natural Philosophy, 'to be deposited
in the hands of a person employed in the Education of Youth',

---

4 Peter Russell was at least as senior, and had been administrator in 1796-9,
but he was not reappointed because of internal disagreements in the
Council.

from the débris of which collection, preserved in a mutilated condition in one of the rooms of the Home District School building, we ourselves, like others probably of our contemporaries, obtained our very earliest inkling of the existence and significance of scientific apparatus.

In his speech at the close of the session of 1806, President Grant alluded to this action of Parliament in the following terms: 'The encouragement which you have given for procuring the means necessary for communicating useful and ornamental knowledge to the rising generation, meets with my approbation, and, I have no doubt, will produce the most salutary effects.' Mr Grant was also known as Commodore Grant, having had at one time command of the Naval Force on the Lakes.

After Mr Grant's name appears that of 'E. B. Littlehales'. This is the Major Littlehales with whom those who familiarize themselves with the earliest records of Upper Canada become so well acquainted. He was the writer, for example, of the interesting journal of an Exploring Excursion from Niagara to Detroit in 1793, to be seen in print in the *Canadian Literary Magazine* of May 1834, an expedition undertaken, as the document itself sets forth, by the Lieut.-Governor, accompanied by Captain Fitzgerald, Lieutenant Smith of the 5th Regiment, and Lieutenants Talbot,[5] Grey, and Givins, and Major Littlehales, starting from Niagara on the 4th of February, arriving at Detroit on the 18th, by a route which was 270 miles in length. The return began on the 23rd, and was completed on the 10th of the following month.

It was in this expedition that the site of London on the Thames was first examined, and judged to be 'a situation eminently calculated for the metropolis of all Canada'. 'Among other essentials', says Major Littlehales, 'it possesses the following advantages: command of territory—internal situation—central position, facility of water communication up and down the Thames into Lakes St Clair, Erie, Huron, and Superior—navig-

---

[5] This is the future Colonel Thomas Talbot who was to play such a large part in the settling of western Ontario.

able for boats to near its source, and for small craft probably
to the Moravian settlement—to the southward by a small portage to the waters flowing into Lake Huron—to the south-east
by a carrying-place into Lake Ontario and the River St Lawrence; the soil luxuriantly fertile—the land rich and capable
of being easily cleared, and soon put into a state of agriculture
—a pinery upon an adjacent high knoll, and other timber on the
heights, well calculated for the erection of public buildings—
a climate not inferior to any part of Canada.'

The intention of the Governor at one time was that the
future capital should be named GEORGINA, in compliment to
George III. Had that intention been adhered to, posterity would
have been saved some confusion. To this hour the name of our
Canadian London gives trouble in the post-office and elsewhere.

An incident not recorded in Major Littlehale's *Journal* was
the order of a grand parade (of ten men), and a formal discharge of musketry, issued in jocose mood by the Governor to
Lieut. Givins, which was duly executed as a ceremony of inauguration for the new capital.

Major Littlehales' park-lot became subsequently the property
of Capt. John Denison, and from him descended to his heir,
Col. George Taylor Denison, from whom the street now passing
from south to north has its name, Denison Avenue. This
thoroughfare was in the first instance the drive up to the homestead of the estate, Bellevue, a large, white, cheery-looking abode
lying far back but pleasantly visible from Lot Street through
a long vista of over-hanging trees. From the old Bellevue have
spread populous colonies at Dovercourt, Rusholme, and elsewhere, marked like their progenitor with vigour of character
and evincing in a succession of instances strong aptitude for
military affairs. Col. Denison's grandson, G. T. Denison *tertius,*
is the author of a work on *Modern Cavalry, its Organization,
Armament and Employment in War*, which has taken a recognized place in English strategical literature.

In accordance with an early Canadian practice, Capt. John
Denison set apart on his property a plot of ground as a re-
ceptacle for the mortal remains of himself and his decendants.
He selected for this purpose a picturesque spot on land pos-

sessed by him on the Humber River, entailing at the same time the surrounding estate. In 1853—although at that date an Act of Parliament had cancelled entails—his heir, Col. G. T. Denison *primus*, perpetually connected the land referred to, together with the burial plot, with his family and decendants, by converting it into an endowment for an ecclesiastical living, to be always in the gift of the legal representative of his name. This is the projected rectory of St John's on the Humber. In 1857 a son of Col. Denison's, Robert Brittain Denison, erected at his own cost, in immediate proximity to the old Bellevue homestead, the church of St Stephen [-in-the-Fields, College Street], and took steps to make it in perpetuity a recognized ecclesiastical benefice.

The boundary of Major Littlehales' lot westward was near what is now Bathurst Street. In front of this lot, on the south side of Lot Street and stretching far to the west, was the Government Common of which we have previously spoken, on which was traced out, at first ideally and at length in reality, the arc of the circle of 1,000 yards radius having the Garrison as its centre. Southward of the concave side of this arc no buildings were for a long time permitted to be erected. This gave rise to a curiously shaped enclosure northward of St Andrew's Market-house, wide towards the east but vanishing off to nothing on the west at the point where Lot Street formed a tangent with the military circle.

Of Portland Street and Bathhurst Street we have already spoken in our survey of Front Street. Immediately opposite Portland Street was the abode, at the latter period of his life, of Dr Lee, to whom we have referred in our accounts of Front and George Streets. Glancing northward as we pass Bathurst Street—which, by the way, north of Lot Street was long known as Crookshank's Lane—we are reminded again of Mr Murchison, whom we have likewise briefly commemorated elsewhere. The substantial abode to which he retired after acquiring a good competency, and where in 1870 he died, is to be seen on the east side of Bathurst Street.

The names which appear in the early plans of York and its suburbs as the first possessors of the park-lots westward of

Major Littlehales' are, in order of succession, respectively, Col. David Shank, Capt. Macdonell, Capt. S. Smith, Capt. Æ. Shaw, Capt. Bouchette. We then arrive at the line of the present Dundas Road where it passes at right angles north from the line of Queen Street. This thoroughfare is not laid down in the plans. Then follow the names of David Burns, William Chewett, and Alexander MacNab (conjointly), Thomas Ridout and William Allan (conjointly), and Angus Macdonell. We then reach a road duly marked, leading straight down to the French Fort, Fort Rouillé, commonly known as Fort Toronto. Across this road westward only one lot is laid off, and on it is the name of Benjamin Hallowell.

Most of the names first enumerated are very familiar to those whose recollections embrace the period to which our attention is now being directed. Many of them have occurred again and again in these papers.

In addition to the lot immediately after Major Littlehales', Col. Shank also possessed another in this range just beyond, viz., No. 21.

The Capt. Macdonell whose name appears on the lot that follows Col. Shank's first lot was the aide-de-camp of Gen. Brock who fell with that General at Queenston Heights. Capt. Macdonell's lot was afterwards the property of Mr Crookshank from whom what is now Bathurst Street North had, as we have remarked, for a time the name of Crookshank's Lane.

Capt. S. Smith, whose name follows those of Capt. Macdonell and Col. Shank, was afterwards President Smith, of whom already. The park-lot selected by him was subsequently the property of Mr Duncan Cameron, a member of the Legislative Council, freshly remembered. At an early period the whole was known by the graceful appellation of Gore Vale. Gore was in honour of the Governor of that name. Vale denoted the ravine which indented a portion of the lot through whose meadowland meandered a pleasant little stream. The southern half of this lot now forms the site and grounds of the University of Trinity College.[6] Its brooklet will hereafter be famous in

---

[6] The college has now been demolished, but the entrance gates still stand at the head of Strachan Avenue, and the grounds are still a park.

scholastic song. It will be regarded as the Cephissus of a Canadian Academus, the Cherwell of an infant Christ Church. The elmy dale which gives such agreeable variety to the park of Trinity College, and which renders so charming the views from the Provost's Lodge, is irrigated by it. (The cupola and tower of the principal entrance to Trinity College will pleasantly, in however humble a degree, recall to the minds of Oxford men the Tom Gate of Christ Church.) After the decease of Mr Cameron, Gore Vale was long occupied by his excellent and benevolent sister, Miss Janet Cameron.

On the steep mound which overhangs the Gore Vale brook, on its eastern side, just where it is crossed by Queen Street, was at an early period a Blockhouse commanding the western approach to York. On the old plans this military work is shown, as also a path leading to it across the Common from the Garrison, trodden often probably by the relief party of the guard that would be stationed there in anxious times.

In the valley of this stream a little farther to the west, on the opposite side of Queen Street, was a Brewery of local repute [established in 1819]: it was a long, low-lying, dingy-looking building of hewn logs; on the side towards the street a railed gangway led from the road to a door in its upper storey. Conspicuous on the hill above the valley on the western side was the house, also of hewn logs but cased over with clapboards, of Mr Farr, the proprietor of the brewery, a north-of-England man in aspect as well as in staidness and shrewdness of character. His spare form and slightly crippled gait were everywhere familiarly recognized. Greatly respected, he was still surviving in 1872. His chief assistant in the old brewery bore the name of Bowbeer.

The stream which is here crossed by Queen Street is the same that afterwards flows below the easternmost bastion of the Fort. A portion of the broken ground between Farr's and the Garrison was once designated by the local Government—so far as an Order-in-Council has force—and permanently set apart as a site for a Museum and Institute of Natural History and Philosophy, with Botanical and Zoological Garden attached [1836]. The project, originated by Dr Dunlop, Dr Rees, and Mr

Fothergill and patronized by successive Lieutenant-Governors, was probably too bold in its conception and too advanced to be justly appreciated and earnestly taken up by a sufficient number of the contemporary public forty years ago. It consequently fell to the ground. It is to be regretted that at all events the land, for which an Order-in-Council stands recorded, was not secured in perpetuity as a source of revenue for the promotion of science. In the Canadian Institute we have the kind of Association which was designed by Drs Dunlop and Rees and Mr Fothergill but minus the revenue which the ground-rent of two or three building lots in a flourishing city would conveniently supply.

Capt. Æneas Shaw, the original locatee of the park-lot next westward of Colonel Shank's second lot, was afterwards well known in Upper Canada as Major General Shaw. Like so many of our early men of note, he was a Scotchman: a Shaw of Tordorach in Strathnairn. Possessed of great vigour and decision, his adopted country availed itself of his services in a civil as well as a military capacity, making him a member of the legislative and executive councils. The name by which his house and estate at this point were known was Oakhill. The primitive domicile still exists and in 1871 was still occupied by one of his many descendants, Capt. Alex. Shaw. It was at Oakhill that the Duke of Kent was lodged during his visit to York in his second tour in Upper Canada. The Duke arrived at Halifax on the 12th of September 1799, after a passage from England of forty-three days, 'on board of the *Arethusa*'.

Of Col. Joseph Bouchette, whose name is read on the following allotment, we have had occasion already to speak. He was one of the many French Canadians of eminence who in the early days were distinguished for their chivalrous attachment to the cause and service of England. The successor of Col. Bouchette in the proprietorship of the park-lot at which we have arrived was Col. Givins. He, as we have already seen, was one of the companions of Gov. Simcoe in the first exploration of Upper Canada. Before obtaining a commission in the army, he had been as a youth employed in the North-West, and had acquired a familiar acquaintance with the Ojibway and Huron dialects. This acquisition rendered his services of especial value to the Government in its dealings with the native tribes, among whom also the mettle and ardour and energy of his own natural character gave him a powerful influence. At the express desire of Governor Simcoe he studied and mastered the dialects of the Six Nations, as well as those of the Ojibways and their Mississaga allies. We ourselves remember seeing a considerable body of Indian chiefs kept in order and good humour mainly through the tact excercised by Col. Givins. This was at a Council held in the garden at Government House some forty years since, and presided over by the then Lieutenant-Governor, Sir John Colborne [1828-36].

Col. Givins was Superintendent of Indian Affairs down to the year 1842. In 1828 his name was connected with an incident that locally made a noise for a time. A committee of the House of Assembly, desiring to have his evidence and that of Col. Coffin, Adjutant General of Militia, in relation to a trespass by one Forsyth on Government property at the Falls of Niagara, commanded their presence at a certain day and hour. On referring to Sir Peregrine Maitland, the Lieutenant-Governor at the time and also Commander-in-Chief of the Forces, permission to obey the mandate of the House was refused. Col. Givens and Col. Coffin were then arrested by the Sergeant-at-arms after forcible entry effected at their respective domiciles and were kept confined in the common gaol until the close of the session.[7]

The following is Col. Coffin's letter to Major Hillier, private secretary to the Governor, on the occasion: 'York, March 22nd, 1828. Sir,—I beg leave to request that you will state to the Lieutenant Governor that in obedience to the communication I received through you, that His Excellency could not give me

---

[7] William Forsyth was the owner of a property that overlooked Niagara Falls. In 1827 he built a fence around both his own land and the government reserve adjoining it so that people would have to pay him admission before they could see the Falls. Maitland had the fence torn down by the troops and Forsyth brought an action against the soldiers who had destroyed it. He also petitioned the Assembly which called Givins and Coffin as witnesses; this led to the incident described. The Colonial Office censured Maitland for his conduct, but Forsyth was certainly not a martyr to the cause of Reform as some members of the Assembly claimed.

permission to attend a Committee of the House of Assembly for the reason therein stated, that I did not attend the said Committee, and that in consequence thereof, I have been committed this evening to the common gaol of the Home District, by order of the House of Assembly. I have therefore to pray that His Excellency will be pleased to direct that I may have the advice and assistance of the Crown Officers, to enable me take such steps as I may be instructed on the occasion. I have the honour, &c., N. COFFIN, Adjt. Gen of Militia.'

No redress was to be had. The Executive Council reported in regard to this letter that upon mature consideration they could not advise that the Government should interfere to give any direction to the Crown Officers, as therein solicited. Sir Peregrine Maitland was removed from the Government in the same year. Sir George Murray, who in that year succeeded Mr Huskisson as Colonial Secretary, severely censured him for the line of action adopted in relation to the Forsyth grievance.

Colonels Givins and Coffin afterwards brought an action against the Speaker of the House for false imprisonment but they did not recover, for the legality of the imprisonment—that is, the right of the House to convict for what they had adjudged a contempt—was confirmed by the Court of King's Bench by a solemn judgement rendered in another cause then pending, which involved the same question.

Although its hundred-acre domain is being rapidly narrowed and circumscribed by the encroachments of modern improvement, the old family abode of Col. Givins still stands, wearing at this day a look of peculiar calm and tranquillity, screened from the outer world by a dark grove of second-growth pine and overshadowed by a number of acacias of unusual height and girth.

Governor Gore and his lady, Mrs Arabella Gore, were constant visitors at Pine Grove, as this house was named; and here to this day is preserved a very fine portrait in oil of that Governor. It will satisfy the ideal likely to be fashioned in the mind by the current traditions of this particular ruler of Upper Canada. In contour of countenance and in costume he is plainly of the type of the English country squire of a former day—

he looks good humoured and shrewd; sturdy and self-willed; and fond of good cheer.

The cavalier style adopted by Gov. Gore towards the local parliament was one of the seeds of trouble at a later date in the history of Upper Canada. 'He would dismiss the rascals at once.' Such was his determination on their coming to a vote adverse to his notions; and, scarcely like a Cromwell but rather like a Louis xiv, though still not, as in the case of that monarch, with a riding-whip in his hand, but nevertheless in the undress of the moment, he proceeded to carry out his hasty resolve.

The entry of the incident in the Journals of the House is as follows: 'On Monday, 7th April, at 11 o'clock a.m. [1817], before the minutes of the former day were read, and without any previous notice, the Commons, to the great surprise of all the members, were summoned to the bar of the Legislative Council, when his Excellency having assented, in his Majesty's name, to several bills, and reserved for his Majesty's pleasure the Bank bill, and another, to enable creditors to sue joint debtors separately, put an end to the session by the following speech:— "Honourable Gentlemen of the Legislative Council, and Gentlemen of the House of Assembly,—The session of the provincial legislature having been protracted by an unusual interruption of business at its commencement, your longer absence from your respective avocations must be too great a sacrifice for the objects which remain to occupy your attention. I have therefore come to close the session and permit you to return to your homes. In accepting, in the name of his Majesty, the supply for defraying the deficiency of the funds which have hitherto served to meet the charges of the administration of justice and support of the civil government of this province, I have great satisfaction in acknowledging the readiness manifested to meet this exigence." '

Upper Canadian society was, indeed, in an infant state; but the growing intelligence of many of its constituents, especially in the non-official ranks, rendered it unwise in rulers to push the feudal or paternal theory of government too far.

Six weeks after, Governor Gore was on his way to England— not recalled, as it would seem, but purposing to give an account

of himself in his own person. He never returned. He is understood to have had a powerful friend at Court in the person of
the Marquis of Camden.

One of the 'districts' of Upper Canada was called after Governor Gore. It was set off during his régime from the Home and
Niagara districts. But of late years county names have rendered
the old district names unfamiliar.[8] In 1837 'the men of Gore'
was a phrase invested with stirring associations.[9]

The town of Belleville received its name from Gov. Gore. In
early newspapers and other documents the word appears as
Bellville without the central *e*, which gives it now such a fine
French look. And this, it is said, is the true orthography. 'Bell',
we are told, was the Governor's familiar abbreviation of his
wife's name, Arabella: and the compound was suggested by the
Governor jocosely, as a name for the new village: but it was
set down in earnest and has continued, the sound at least, to
this day. This off-hand assignment of a local name may remind
some persons that Flos, Tay, and Tiny, which are names of
three now populous townships in the Penetanguishene region,
are a commemoration of three of Lady Sarah Maitland's lap-
dogs. Changes of names in such cases as these are not unjusti-
fiable.

In fact the Executive Council itself, at the period of which
we are speaking, had occasionally found it proper to change
local names which had been frivolously given. In the *Upper
Canada Gazette* of March 11th, 1822, we have several such
alterations. It would seem that someone having access to the
map or plan of a newly surveyed region had inscribed across the
parallelograms betokening townships a fragment of a well-
known Latin sentence, *jus et norma*, placing each separate
word in a separate compartment. In this way Upper Canada had
for a time a township of 'Jus' and, more wonderful still, a township of 'Et'. In the number of the *Gazette* of the date given

---

[8] The district rather than the county was the administrative unit for local
government prior to 1850 when all the old districts were abolished.

[9] The men of Gore, or the Gore District Militia, under the command of
Sir Allan MacNab, helped to defeat Mackenzie's attack on Toronto during
the Rebellion.

above these names are formally changed to Barrie and Palmerston respectively. In the same advertisement 'Norma', which might have passed, is made 'Clarendon'.

Other impertinent appellations are also at the same time changed. The township of 'Yea' is ordered to be hereafter the township of 'Burleigh', with a humorous allusion to the famous nod, probably. The township of 'No' is to be the township of Grimsthorpe; and the township of 'Aye' the township of Anglesea. The name 'Et' may recall the street known as 'Of' alley on the south side of the Strand in London, which 'Of' is a portion of the name and title 'George Villiers, Duke of Buckingham', distributed severally among a cluster of streets in that locality.

Gov. Gore was so fortunate as to be away from his Province during the whole of the war in 1812-14. He obtained leave of absence to visit England in 1811 and returned to his post in 1815, the Presidents, Isaac Brock, Roger Hale Sheaffe, [Baron Francis de Rottenburg,] and Gordon Drummond, Esquires, reigning in the interim.

Under date of York, U.C., Sept. 30, 1815, we read the following particulars in the *Gazette* of the day: 'Arrived on Monday last the 25th instant, His Excellency Francis Gore, Esq., Lieutenant-Governor of the Province of Upper Canada, to reassume the reins of government. His Excellency was received with a cordial welcome and the honours due to his rank; and was saluted by his M.S. *Montreal*, and Garrison.'

By one of the acts passed during the administration of Gov. Gore, the foundation was laid of a parliamentary library, to replace the one destroyed or dispersed during the occupation of York in 1813. In the session of 1816 the sum of £800 was voted for the purchase of books for the use of the Legislative Council and House of Assembly.

The sum of £800 for such a purpose contrasts poorly, however, with the £3,000 recommended in the same session, to be granted to Gov. Gore himself for the purchase of 'Plate'. The joint address of both Houses to the Prince Regent on this subject was couched in the following terms: 'To his Royal Highness, George, Prince of Wales, Prince Regent of the United Kingdom of Great Britain and Ireland, &c., &c., &c.: May it please your Royal Highness: We, his Majesty's most dutiful and loyal subjects, the Legislative Council and House of Assembly of the Province of Upper Canada, in Provincial Parliament assembled, impressed with a lively sense of the firm, upright, and liberal administration of Francis Gore, Esq., Lieutenant-Governor of this Province, as well as of his unceasing attention to the individual and general interests of the Colony during his absence, have unanimously passed a bill to appropriate the sum of three thousand pounds, to enable him to purchase a service of plate, commemorative of our gratitude. Apprized that this spontaneous gift cannot receive the sanction of our beloved Sovereign in the ordinary mode, by the acceptance of the Lieutenant-Governor in his name and behalf; we, the Legislative Council and Assembly of the Province of Upper Canada, humbly beg leave to approach your Royal Highness with an earnest prayer that you will approve this demonstration of our gratitude and graciously be pleased to sanction, in His Majesty's name, the grant of the Legislature, in behalf of the inhabitants of Upper Canada. WM. DUMMER POWELL, *Speaker, Legislative Council Chambers, 26th March, 1816*. ALLAN MACLEAN, *Speaker, Commons House of Assembly, 25th March, 1816.*'

To which, as we are next informed, his Excellency replied: 'Gentlemen: I shall transmit your address to His Majesty's Ministers, in order that their expression of your approbation of my past administration may be laid at the feet of His Royal Highness, the Prince Regent. Government House, York, 26th March, 1816.' The Bill which suggested this allowance was popularly spoken of as the 'Spoon-bill'. The House that passed the measure was the same that, a few weeks later, was so abruptly dismissed.

The name on the allotment following that occupied successively by Col. Bouchette and Col. Givins is 'David Burns'. Mr Burns, who had been a Navy surgeon, was the first Clerk of the Crown for Upper Canada and one of the 'Masters in Chancery'. He died in 1806.

Of Col. W. Chewett, whose name appears next, we have made mention more than once. His name, like that of his son, J. G. Chewett, is very familiar to those who have to examine the plans and charts connected with early Upper Canadian history. Both were long distinguished *attachés* of the Surveyor-General's department. In 1802 Col. W. Chewett was Registrar of the Home District.

Alexander Macnab, whose name occurs next in succession, was afterwards Capt. Macnab, who fell at Waterloo—the only instance, as is supposed, of a Canadian slain on that occasion. In 1868 his nephew, the Rev. Dr Macnab of Bowmanville, was presented by the Duke of Cambridge in person with the Waterloo medal due to the family of Capt. Macnab.

Alexander Macnab was also the first patentee of the plot of ground whereon stands the house on Bay Street noted in our account of the early press as being the place of publication of the *Upper Canada Gazette* at the time of the taking of York, and subsequently owned and occupied by Mr Andrew Mercer up to the time of his decease in 1871.

Of Messrs Ridout and Allan, whose names are inscribed conjointly on the following park-lot, we have already spoken; and Angus Macdonell, who took up the next lot, was the barrister who perished, along with the whole court, in the *Speedy*.

The name that appears on the westernmost lot of the range along which we have been passing is that of Benjamin Hallowell. He was a near connection of Chief Justice Elmsley's and father of the Admiral, Sir Benjamin Hallowell, K.C.B. We observe the notice of Mr Hallowell's death in the *Gazette and Oracle* of the day in the following terms: 'Died, on Thursday last (March 28th, 1799), Benjamin Hallowell, Esq, in the 75th year of his age. The funeral will be on Tuesday next, and will proceed from the house of the Chief Justice to the Garrison Burying Ground at one o'clock precisely. The attendance of his friends is requested.'

After passing the long range of suburban properties on which we have been annotating, the continuation in a right line westward of Lot [Queen] Street used to be known as the Lake Shore Road. This Lake Shore Road, after passing the dugway or steep descent to the sands that form the margin of the lake, first skirted the graceful curve of Humber Bay and then followed the irregular line of the shore all the way to the head of the lake. It was a mere track representing, doubtless, a trail trodden by the aborigines from time immemorial.

We now return to that point on Queen Street where, instead of continuing on westward by the Lake Shore Road, the traveller of a later era turned abruptly towards the north in order to pass into Dundas Street proper, the great highway projected, as we have observed, by the first organizer of Upper Canada and marked on the earliest manuscript maps of the Province but not made practicable for human traffic until comparatively recent times.

From an advertisement in the *Gazette and Oracle* of August 1806 we learn that Dundas Street was not, in that year, yet hewn out through the woods about the Credit. 'Notice is hereby given', thus runs the advertisement referred to, 'that the Commissioners of the Highways of the Home District will be ready on Saturday, the 23rd day of the present month of August, at eleven o'clock in the forenoon, at the Government Buildings in the town of York, to receive proposals and to treat with any person or persons who will contend to open and make the road called Dundas Street, leading through the Indian Reserve on the River Credit; and also to erect a Bridge over the said River at or near where the said Road passes. Also to bridge and causeway (in aid to the Statute Labour) such other parts of such Road passing through the Home District, when such works are necessary, and for the performance of which the said Statute Labour is not sufficient. THOMAS RIDOUT, *Clerk of the Peace, Home District. York, 6 August, 1806.*'

The early line of communication with the head of the Lake was by the Lake Shore Road. The cross thoroughfare between the park-lots of Mr Bouchette or Col. Givins and Mr David Burns was opened up by Col. G. T. Denison, senior, with the assistance of some of the embodied militia.

The work of opening the road here, as well as further on through the forest, was at first undertaken by a detachment of the regulars under the direction of an officer of the Royal Engineers. The plan adopted, we are told, was first to fell each tree by very laboriously severing it from its base close to the ground and then to smooth off the upper surface of the root or stump with an adze. As this process was necessarily slow, and after all not likely to result in a permanently good road, the proposal of Colonel, then Lieutenant, Denison, to set his militia-men to eradicate the trees bodily was accepted—an operation with which they were all more or less familiar on their farms and in their new clearings. A fine broad open track—ready, when the day for such further improvements should arrive, for the reception of plank or macadam—was soon constructed.

Immediately at the turn northwards, out of the line of Lot Street on the east side, was Sandford's Inn, a watering place for teams on their way into York, provided accordingly with a conspicuous pump and great trough, a long section of a huge pine-tree dug out like a canoe. Near by, a little to the east, was another notable inn—an early rival, as we suppose, of Sandford's: this was the Blue Bell. A sign to that effect at the top of a strong and lofty pole in front of its door swung to and fro within a frame.

Just opposite, on the Garrison Common, there were for a long while low log buildings belonging to the Indian department. One of them contained a forge in charge of Mr Higgins, armourer to the Department. Here the Indians could get, when necessary, their fishing-spears, axes, knives, and tomahawks, and other implements of iron, sharpened and put in order. One of these buildings was afterwards used as a school for the surrounding neighbourhood.

Immediately across from Sandford's, on the park-lot originally occupied by Mr Burns, was a house shaded with great willow trees and surrounded by a flower-garden and lawn, the abode for many years of [Sophia,] the venerable widow of Captain John Denison, who long survived her husband. Of her we have already once spoken in connection with Petersfield. She was, as we have intimated, a sterling old English gentlewoman of a type now vanishing, as we imagine. The house was afterwards long in the occupation of her son-in-law, Mr John Fennings Taylor, a gentleman well known to Canadian M.P.'s during a long series of years, having been attached as Chief Clerk and Master in Chancery first to the Legislative Council of United Canada and then to the Senate of the Dominion.

To the right and left, as we passed north, was a wet swamp, filled with cedars of all shapes and sizes and strewn plentifully with granitic boulders: a strip of land held in light esteem by the passers-by in the early days as seeming to be irreclaimable for agricultural purposes.

But how admirably reclaimable in reality the acres hereabout were for the choicest human purposes was afterwards seen when, for example, the house and grounds known as Foxley Grove came to be established. By the outlay of some money and the exercise of some discrimination, a portion of this same cedar swamp was rapidly converted into pleasure ground, with labyrinths of full-grown shrubbery ready-prepared by nature's hand. Mr Samuel Bealey Harrison, who thus transformed the wild into a garden and pleasance, will be long remembered for his skill and taste in the culture of flowers and esculents choice and rare, as well as for his eminence as a lawyer and jurist.

On turning westward into Dundas Street proper we were soon in the midst of a magnificent pine forest which remained long undisturbed. The whole width of the allowance for road was here for a number of miles completely cleared. The highway thus well defined was seen bordered on the right and left with a series of towering columns, the outermost ranges of an innumerable multitude of similar tall shafts set at various distances from each other and circumscribing the view in an irregular manner on both sides, all helping to bear up aloft a matted awning of deep green through which here and there glimpses of azure could be caught, looking bright and cheery. The yellow pine predominated, a tree remarkable for the straightness and tallness of its stems and for the height at which its branches begin.

No fence on either hand intervened between the road and the forest; the rider at his pleasure could rein his horse aside at any point and take a canter in amongst the columns, the underwood being very slight. Everywhere at the proper season the ground was sprinkled with wild flowers—with the wild lupin and the wild columbine—and everywhere at all times the air was more or less fragrant with resinous exhalations.

In the heart of the forest, midway between York and the

bridge over the Humber, was another famous resting place for teams—the Peacock Tavern, a perfect specimen of a respectable wayside hostelry of the olden time with very spacious driving-houses and other appropriate outbuildings on an extensive scale.

Not far from the Peacock a beaten track branched off westerly which soon led the equestrian into the midst of beautiful oak woods, the trees constituting it of no great magnitude, but as is often the case on sandy plains, of a gnarled, contorted aspect, each presenting a good study for the sketcher. This track also conducted to the Humber, descending to the valley of that stream where its waters, now become shallow but rapid, passed over sheets of shale. Here the surroundings of the bridle-road and foot-path were likewise picturesque, exhibiting rock plentifully amidst and beneath the foliage and herbage.

Here in the vale of the Humber stood a large Swiss-like structure of hewn logs, with two tiers of balcony on each of its sides. This was the house of Mr John Scarlett. It was subsequently destroyed by fire. Nearby were mills and factories also belonging to Mr Scarlett. He was well connected in England, a man of enlightened views and fine personal presence. He loved horses and was much at home in the saddle. A shrewd observer when out among his fellow men, at his own fireside he was a dignified student of books.

XII

YONGE

STREET

FROM

THE BAY

TO

YORKVILLE

The tourist of the present day who, on one of our great lake-steamers, enters the harbour of Toronto, observes, as he is borne swiftly along, an interesting succession of street vistas opening at intervals inland, each one of them somewhat resembling a scene on the stage. He obtains a glimpse for a moment of a thoroughfare gently ascending in a right line northward, with appropriate groups of men and vehicles reduced prettily to lilliputian size by distance.

Of all the openings thus transiently disclosed, the one towards which the boat at length shapes its course, with the clear intention of thereabout disburdening itself of its multifarious load, is quickly seen to be of preëminent importance. Thronged at the point where it descends to the water's edge with steamers and other craft, great and small, lined on the right and left up to the far vanishing-point with handsome buildings, its pavements and central roadway everywhere astir with life, its appearance is agreeably exciting and even impressive. It looks to be what in fact it is, the outlet of a great highway leading into the interior of a busy, populous country. The railway station seen on the right, heaving up its huge semi-circular metal back above the subjacent buildings and flanking the very sidewalk with its fine front and lofty ever-open portals, might be imagined a porter's lodge proportioned to the dignity of the avenue whose entrance it seems planted there to guard.[1]

We propose to pass, as rapidly as we may, up the remarkable street at the foot of which our tourist steps ashore. It will not be a part of our plan to enlarge on its condition as we see it at the present time, except here and there as in contrast with some circumstance of the past. We intend simply to take note, as we ramble on, of such recollections as may spring up at particular points, suggested by objects or localities encountered, and to recall at least the names, if not in every instance characteristic traits and words and acts, of some of the worthies of a bygone generation to whose toil and endurance the present occupants of the region which we shall traverse are so profoundly indebted.

Where Yonge Street opened on the harbour, the observer some forty years ago would only have seen on the east side the garden, orchard, and pleasure grounds of Chief Justice Scott, with his residence situated therein, afterwards the abode of Mr Justice Sherwood; and on the west side the garden, orchard, pleasure-grounds, and house of Mr Justice Macaulay, afterwards Chief Justice Sir James Macaulay, and the approaches to these premises were in both cases not from Yonge Street but from Front Street, or from Market [Wellington] Street in the rear.

The principal landing place for the town was for a series of years, as we have elsewhere stated, at the southern extremity of Church Street: and then previously, for another series of years, further to the east, at the southern extremity of Frederick Street. The country and local traffic found its way to these points not by Yonge Street, south of King Street, but by other routes which have been already specified and described.

Teams and solitary horses, led or ridden, seen passing into Yonge Street south of King Street, either out of King Street or out of Front Street, would most likely be on their way to the forge of old Mr Philip Klinger, a German, whose name we used to think had in it a kind of anvil ring. His smithy on the east

---

[1] This was the Great Western Railway Station which was a landmark for a century—approximately where the O'Keefe Centre is now located—until it burned in the early 1950s.

side, just south of Market Street, now Wellington Street, was almost the only attraction and occasion of resort to Yonge Street south of King Street. His successor here was Mr Calvin Davis, whose name became as familiar a sound to the ears of the early townsfolk of York as Mr Klinger's had been.

It seems in the retrospect but a very short time since Yonge Street south of King Street, now so solidly and even splendidly built up, was an obscure allowance for road, visited seldom by anyone and for a long while particularly difficult to traverse during and just after the rainy seasons.

Few persons in the olden time at which we are glancing ever dreamed that the intersection of Yonge Street and King Street was to be the heart of the town. Yet here in one generation we have the Carfax of Toronto, as some of our forefathers would have called it—the Quatrevoies or Grand Four-crossways where the golden milestone might be planted whence to measure distances in each direction.

What are the local mutations that are to follow? Will the needs of the population and the exigencies of business ever make of the intersection of Brock Street [Spadina Avenue] and Queen Street what the intersection of Yonge and King Street is now?

In the meantime those who recall the very commonplace look which this particular spot—viz., the intersection of King Street and Yonge Street—long wore when as yet only recently reclaimed from nature, cannot but experience a degree of mental amazement whenever now they pause for a moment on one of the crossings and look around.

A more perfect and well-proportioned rectangular meeting of four great streets is seldom to be seen. Take the view at this point, north, south, west or east, almost at any hour and at any season of the year, and it is striking.

It is striking in the freshness and coolness and comparative quiet of early morning when few are astir.

It is striking in the brightness and glow of noon when the sons and daughters of honest toil are trooping in haste to their mid-day meal.

A few hours later again it is striking when the phaetons, pony-carriages, and fancy equipages generally are out, and loungers of each sex are leisurely promenading, or here and there placidly engaged in the inspection and occasional selection of 'personal requisites'—of some one or other of the variegated tissues or artificial adjuncts demanded by the modes of the period—while the westering sun is now flooding the principal thoroughfare with a misty splendour and on the walls, along on either side, weird shadows slanting and enlongated are being cast.

Then later still the views here are by no means ordinary ones, when the vehicles have for the most part withdrawn and the passengers are once more few in number and the lamps are lighted and the gas is flaming in the windows.

Even in the closed-up sedate aspect of all places of business on a Sunday or public holiday, statutable or otherwise, these four streets by some happy charm are fair to see and cheery. But when dressed for a festive gala occasion, when gay with banners and festoons in honour of a royal birthday, a royal marriage, the visit of a prince, the announcement of a victory, they shew to special advantage.

So also they furnish no inharmonious framework or setting when processions and bands of music are going by, or bodies of military, horse or foot, or pageants such as those that in modern times accompany a great menagerie in its progress through the country—elephants in oriental trappings, teams of camels clad in similar guise, cavaliers in glittering mediæval armour, gorgeous cars and vans.

And again in winter peculiarly fine pictures characteristic of the season are presented here when, after a plentiful fall of snow, the sleighs are on the move without number and in infinite variety; or when on the contrary each long white vista, east, west, north, and south, glistening perhaps under a clear December moon, is a scene almost wholly of still life—scarcely a man or beast abroad, so keen is the motionless air, the mercury having shrunk down some way below the zero-line of Fahrenheit.

But we must proceed.

In the course of our perambulations we have already noticed some instances in the town of long persistency in one place of business or residence. Such evidences of staidness and substantiality are common enough in the old world but are of necessity somewhat rare amid the chances, changes, and exchanges of young communities on this continent. An additional instance we have to note here, at the intersection of King Street and Yonge Street. At its north-east angle where, as in a former section we have observed, stood the sole building in this quarter, the house of Mr John Dennis, for forty years at least has been seen with little alteration of external aspect the Birmingham, Sheffield, and Wolverhampton warehouse of the brothers Mr Joseph Ridout and Mr Percival Ridout. A little way to the north too, on the east side, the name of Piper has been for an equal length of time associated uninterruptedly with a particular business; but here, though outward appearances have remained to some extent the same, death has wrought changes.

Nearby also we see foundries still in operation where Messrs W. B. Sheldon, F. R. Dutcher, W. A. Dutcher, Samuel Andrus, J. Van Norman, and B. Van Norman, names familiar to all old inhabitants, were among the foremost in that kind of useful enterprise in York. Their advertisement, as shewing the condition of one branch of the iron manufacture in York in 1832, will be of interest. Some of the articles enumerated have become old-fashioned. 'They respectfully inform their friends and the public that they have lately made large additions to their establishments. They have enlarged their Furnace so as to enable them to make Castings of any size or weight used in this province, and erected Lathes for turning and finishing the same. They have also erected a Steam Engine of ten horse power, of their own manufacture, for propelling their machinery, which is now in complete operation, and they are prepared to build Steam Engines of any size, either high or low pressure. Having a number of experienced engineers employed, whose capability cannot be doubted, they hope to share the patronage of a generous public. They always keep constantly on hand and for sale, either by wholesale or retail, Bark Mills, Cooking, Franklin, Plate and Box Stoves, also, a general assortment of Hollow Ware, consisting of Kettles, from one to one hundred and twenty gallons; Bake-Ovens, Bake-Basins, Belly-Pots, High Pans, Tea Kettles, Wash-Kettles, Portable Furnaces, &c. Also are constantly manufacturing Mill-Gearing of all kinds; Sleigh Shoes,

50, 56, 30, 28, 15, 14, and 7 pound Weights, Clock and Sash Weights, Cranes, Andirons, Cart and Waggon Boxes, Clothiers' Plates, Plough Castings, and Ploughs of all kinds.'

We move on now towards Newgate Street, first noticing that nearly opposite to the Messrs Sheldon and Dutcher's foundry were the spirit vaults of Mr Michael Kane, father of Paul Kane, the artist of whom we have spoken previously. At the corner of Newgate Street or Adelaide Street, on the left and stretching along the southern side of that Street, the famous tannery yard of Mr Jesse Ketchum was to be seen [1812-39], with high stacks of hemlock-bark piled up on the Yonge Street side. On the north side of Newgate Street, at the angle opposite, was his residence, a large white building in the American style with a square turret bearing a railing, rising out of the ridge of the roof. Before pavements of any kind were introduced in York, the sidewalks hereabout were rendered clean and comfortable by a thick coating of tanbark.

Mr Ketchum emigrated hither from Buffalo at an early period. In the *Gazette* of June 11, 1803, we have the death of his uncle mentioned. 'On Wednesday last (8th June), departed this life, Mr Joseph Ketchum, aged 85. His remains', it is added, 'were interred the following day.' In 1806 we find Jesse Ketchum named at the annual 'town meeting' one of the overseers of high-ways and fence viewers. His section was from 'No. 1 to half the Big Creek Bridge (Hogg's Hollow) on Yonge Street'. Mr William Marsh, jun., then took up the oversight from half the Big Creek Bridge to No. 17. In the first instance Mr Ketchum came over to look after the affairs of an elder brother, deceased, who had settled here and founded the tannery works.[2] He then continued to be a householder of York until about 1845 when he returned to Buffalo, his original home, where he still retained valuable possessions. He was familiarly known in Buffalo in later years as 'Father Ketchum' and was distinguished for the lively practical interest which he took in schools for the young and for the largeness of his annual contributions to such in-

---

[2] Jesse Ketchum came to York in 1799 to join his brother Seneca, but he did not purchase the tannery until 1812 and Seneca lived until 1850.

stitutions. Two brothers, Henry and Zebulon, were also early inhabitants of Buffalo.

Mr Ketchum's York property extended to Lot Street. Hospital Street (Richmond Street) passed through it, and he himself projected and opened Temperance Street. To the facility with which he supplied building sites for moral and religious uses it is due that at this day the quadrilateral between Queen Street and Adelaide Street, Yonge Street and Bay Street, is a sort of miniature Mount Athos, a district curiously crowded with places of worship. He gave in Yorkville also sites for a school-house and Temperance Hall, and besides two acres for a Children's Park. The [Upper Canada] Bible and Tract Society like-wise obtained its house on Yonge Street on easy terms from Mr Ketchum on the condition that the Society should annually distribute in the public schools the amount of the ground rent in the form of books—a condition that continues to be punctually fulfilled. The ground rent of an adjoining tenement was also secured to the Society by Mr Ketchum, to be distributed in Sunday Schools in a similar way. Thus by his generous gifts and arrangements in Buffalo, and in our own town and neighbour-hood, his name has become permanently enrolled in the list of public benefactors in two cities.

Mr Ketchum died in Buffalo in 1867. He was a man of quiet, shrewd, homely appearance and manners and of the average stature. His brother Seneca was also a character well known in these parts for his natural benevolence and likewise for his desire to offer counsel to the young on every occasion. We have a distinct recollection of being, along with several young friends, the objects of a well-intended didactic lecture from Seneca Ketchum who, as we were amusing ourselves on the ice, ap-proached us on horseback.

It seems singular to us in the present day that those who laid out the region called the 'New Town'—that is, the land west-ward of the original town plot of York—did not apparently ex-pect the great northern road known as Yonge Street ever to ex-tend directly to the water's edge. In the plans of 1800, Yonge Street stops short at Lot Street, i. e., Queen Street. A range of lots block the way immediately to the south. The traffic from the

north was expected to pass down into the town by a thoroughfare called Toronto Street, three chains and seven links to the
east of the line of Yonge Street. Mr Ketchum's lot, and all the
similar lots southward, were bounded on the east by this street.

The advisability of pushing Yonge Street through to its
natural terminus must have early struck the owners of the
properties that formed the obstruction. We accordingly find
Yonge Street in due time 'produced' to the Bay. Toronto Street
was then shut up, and the proprietors of the land through which
the northern road now ran received in exchange for the space
usurped proportionate pieces of the old Toronto Street. In 1818
deeds for these fragments, executed in conformity with the
ninth section of an Act of the local Parliament, passed in the
fiftieth year of George III, were given to Jesse Ketchum, William
Bowkett, mariner, son of William Bowkett, and others by the
surveyors of highways, James Miles for the Home District and
William Richardson Caldwell for the County of York respectively.

The street which supplied the passage-way southward previously afforded by Toronto Street and which now formed the
easterly boundary of the easterly portions of the lots cut in two
by Yonge Street was, as we have had occasion already to state
in another place, called Upper George Street and afterwards
Victoria Street.

What the condition of some of the lots to which we have been
just referring was in 1801 we gather from a surveyor's report of
that date which we have already quoted in another connection.
We are now enabled to add the exact terms of the order issued
to the surveyor, Mr Stegman, on the occasion: 'Surveyor General's Office, 19th Dec., 1800. Mr John Stegman: Sir,—All persons
claiming to hold land in the town of York, having been required to cut and burn all the brush and underwood on the
said lots, and to fall all the trees which are standing thereon,
you will be pleased to report to me, without delay, the number
of the particular lots on which it has not been done. D.W.
SMITH, *Acting Surveyor General.*'

The continuation of the great northern highway in a continuous right line to the Bay, from its point of issue on Lot

Street, i. e., Queen Street, was the circumstance that eventually created for Yonge Street, regarded as a street in the usual sense, the peculiar renown which it popularly has for extraordinary length.[3] A story is told of a tourist, newly arrived at York, wishing to utilize a stroll before breakfast by making out as he went along the whereabouts of a gentleman to whom he had a letter. Passing down the hall of his hotel, he asks in a casual way of the book-keeper: 'Can you tell me where Mr So-and-so lives? (leisurely producing the note from his breast-pocket wallet). It is somewhere along Yonge Street here in your town.' 'Oh yes,' was the reply, when the address had been glanced at, 'Mr So-and-so lives on Yonge Street, about twenty-five miles up!' We have heard also of a serious demur on the part of a Quebec naval and military inspector at two agents for purchases being stationed on one street at York. However surprised, he was nevertheless satisfied when he learned that their posts were thirty miles apart.

Let us now direct your attention to Yonge Street north of Queen Street.

For some years previous to the opening of Yonge Street from Lot Street to the Bay, the portion of the great highway to the north between Lot Street and the road which is now the southern boundary of Yorkville [Bloor Street] was in an almost impracticable condition. The route was recognized, but no grading or causewaying had been done on it. In the popular mind, indeed practically, the point where Yonge Street began as a travelled road to the north was at Yorkville, as we should now speak.

The track followed by the farmers coming into town from the north veered off at Yorkville to the eastward and passed down in a haphazard kind of way over the sandy pineland in that direction and finally entered the town by the route later known as Parliament Street.

In 1800 the expediency was seen of making the direct northern approach to York more available. In the *Gazette* of Dec.

---

[3] The name Yonge Street was orginally applied to the whole route from Toronto to Penetanguishene.

20th, 1800, we have an account of a public meeting held on the subject. It will be observed that Yonge Street, between Queen Street and Yorkville, as moderns would phrase it, is spoken of therein for the moment not as Yonge Street, but as 'the road to Yonge Street'. 'On Thursday last, about noon,' the *Gazette* reports, 'a number of the principal inhabitants of this town met together in one of the Government Buildings, to consider the best means of opening the road to Yonge Street, and enabling the farmers there to bring their provisions to market with more ease than is practicable at present.' The account then proceeds: 'The Hon. Chief Justice Elmsley was called to the chair. He briefly stated the purpose of the meeting, and added that a subscription-list had been lately opened by which something more than two hundred dollars in money and labour had been promised, and that other sums were to be expected from several respectable inhabitants who were well-wishers to the undertaking, but had not as yet contributed towards it. These sums, he feared, however, would not be equal to the purpose, which hardly could be accomplished for less than between five and six hundred dollars. Many of the subscribers were desirous that what was already subscribed should be immediately applied as far as it would go, and that other resources should be looked for.'

A paper was produced and read containing a proposal from Mr Eliphalet Hale to open and make the road, or so much of it as might be required, at the rate of twelve dollars per acre for clearing it where no causeway was wanted, four rods wide, and cutting the stumps in the two middle rods close to the ground; and seven shillings and sixpence, provincial currency, per rod, for making a causeway eighteen feet wide where a causeway might be wanted. Mr Hale undertook to find security for the due performance of the work by the first of February following (1801). The subscribers present were unanimously of opinion that the subscription should be immediately applied as far as it would go. Mr Hale's proposition was accepted, and a committee consisting of Mr Secretary [William] Jarvis, Mr William Allan, and Mr James Playter, was appointed to superintend the carrying of it into execution. Additional subscriptions would be received by Messrs Allan and Wood.

At the same meeting a curious project was mooted, and a resolution in its favour adopted, for the permanent shutting up of a portion of Lot Street, and selling the land, the proceeds to be applied to the improvement of Yonge Street. There was no need of that portion of Lot Street, it was argued, there being already convenient access to the town in that direction by a way a few yards to the south. We gather from this that Hospital Street (Richmond Street) was the usual beaten track into the town from the west.

'It had been suggested', says the report of the meeting, 'that considerable aid might be obtained by shutting up the street which now forms the northern boundary of the town between Toronto Street and the Common, and disposing of the land occupied by it. This street, it was conceived, was altogether superfluous,' the report continues, 'as another street equally convenient in every respect runs parallel to it at the distance of about ten rods.'

In the *Gazette* of March 6, 1802, an editorial is devoted to the subject of the improvement of Yonge Street. It runs as follows: 'It affords us much pleasure to state to our readers that the necessary repair of Yonge Street is likely to be soon effected, as the work, we understand, has been undertaken with the assurance of entering upon and completing it without delay; and by every one who reflects upon the present sufferings of our industrious community on resorting to a market, it cannot but prove highly satisfactory to observe a work of such convenience and utility speedily accomplished. That the measure of its future benefits must be extreme indeed, we may reasonably expect; but whilst we look forward with flattering expectations of those benefits, we cannot but appreciate the immediate advantage which is afforded to us, in being relieved from the application of the statute labour to circuitous by-paths and occasional roads, and in being enabled to apply the same to the improvement of the streets, and the nearer and more direct approaches to the Town.'

The irregular track branching off eastward at Yorkville was an example of these 'circuitous by-paths and occasional roads'. Editorials were rare in the *Gazettes* of the period. Had there been more of them, subsequent investigators would have been better able than they are now to produce pictures of the olden time. Chief Justice Elmsley was probably the inspirer of the article just given.

The work appears to have been duly proceeded with. In the following June we have an advertisement calling a meeting of the committee entrusted with its superintendence. In the *Gazette* of June 12, 1802, we read: 'The committee for inspecting the repair of Yonge Street requests that the subscribers will meet on the repaired part of the said street at 5 o'clock on Monday evening, to take into consideration how far the moneys subscribed by them have been beneficially expended. S. MCNAB, *Secretary to Committee. York, 10th June, 1802.*'

In 1807, as we gather from the *Gazette* of Nov. 11 in that year, an effort was made to improve the road at the Blue Hill. A present of fifty dollars from the Lieutenant-Governor (Gore) to the object is acknowledged in the paper named. 'A number of public-spirited persons', the *Gazette* says, 'collected on last Saturday to cut down the Hill at Frank's Creek.' We shall see hereafter that the rivulet here was thus known as being the stream that flowed through the Castle Frank lot. 'The Lieutenant-Governor, when informed of it, dispatched a person with a present of Fifty Dollars to assist in improving the Yonge Street road.' It is then added by 'John Van Zante, pathmaster, for himself and the public,'—'To his Excellency for his liberal donation, and to the gentlemen who contributed, we return our warmest thanks.'

These early efforts of our predecessors to render practicable the great northern approach to the town are deserving of respectful remembrance.

The nature of the soil at many points between Lot Street and the modern Yorkville was such as to render the construction of a road that should be comfortably available at all seasons of the year no easy task. Down to the time when macadam was at length applied [after 1833], this approach to the town was notorious for its badness every spring and autumn. At one period an experiment was tried of a wooden tramway for a short distance at the worst part, on which the loaded waggons were expected to keep and so be saved from sinking hopelessly in the direful sloughs. Mr Sheriff Jarvis was the chief promoter of this improvement which answered its purpose for a time, and Mr Rowland Burr was its suggester. But we must not forestall ourselves.

We return to the point where Lot Street, or Queen Street, intersects the thoroughfare.

After passing Mr Jesse Ketchum's property, which had been divided into two parts by the pushing of Yonge Street southward to its natural termination, we arrived at another striking rectangular meeting of thoroughfares. Lot Street having happily escaped extinction westward and eastward, there was created at this spot a four-crossway possessed of an especial historic interest, being the conspicuous intersection of the two great military roads of Upper Canada, projected and explored in person by its first organizer. Four extensive reaches—two of Dundas Street (identical, of course, with Lot or Queen Street[4]) and two of Yonge Street—can here be contemplated from one and the same standpoint. In the course of time the views up and down the four long vistas here commanded will probably rival those to be seen at the present moment where King Street crosses Yonge Street. When lined along all its sides with handsome buildings, the superior elevation above the level of the Lake of the more northerly quadrivium will be in its favour.

Perhaps it will here not be out of order to state that Yonge Street was so named in honour of Sir George Yonge, Secretary of War in 1791, and M.P. for Honiton in the county of Devon from 1763 to 1796. The first exploration which led to the establishment of this communication with the north was made in 1793. On the early MS. map mentioned before in these papers, the route taken by Governor Simcoe on the memorable occasion in going and returning is shewn. Explanatory of the red dotted lines which indicate it, the following note is appended. It reveals the Governor's clear perception of the commercial and military importance of the projected road: 'Lieut.-Gov. Simcoe's route

---

4 Originally Dundas Street, when it reached the centre portion of the city, followed the present route of Queen Street.

on foot and in canoes to explore a way which might afford communication for the Fur-traders to the Great Portage, without passing Detroit in case that place were given up to the United States. The march was attended with some difficulties, but was quite satisfactory: an excellent harbour at Penetanguishene: returned to York, 1793.'

The objects that came to be familiar to the eye at the entrance to Yonge Street from Lot Street were, after the lapse of some years, on the west side, a large square white edifice known as the Sun Tavern, Elliott's; and on the east side, the buildings constituting Good's Foundry.

The open land to the north of Elliott's was the place generally occupied by the travelling menageries and circuses when such exhibitions began to visit the town.

The foundry, after supplying the country for a series of years with ploughs, stoves, and other necessary articles of heavy hardware, is memorable as having been the first in Upper Canada to turn out real railway locomotives. When novelties, these highly finished ponderous machines, seen slowly and very laboriously urged through the streets from the foundry to their destination, were startling phenomena. We have in the *Canadian Journal* [1853] an account of the first engine manufactured by Mr Good at the Toronto Locomotive Works, with a lithographic illustration. 'We have much pleasure', the editor of the *Canadian Journal* says, 'in presenting our readers with a drawing of the first locomotive engine constructed in Canada, and indeed, we believe, in any British Colony. The "Toronto" is certainly no beauty, nor is she distinguished for any peculiarity in the construction, but she affords a very striking illustration of our progress in the mechanical arts, and of the growing wants of the country. The "Toronto" was built at the Toronto Locomotive Works, which were established by Mr Good, in October, 1852. The order for the "Toronto" was received in February, 1853, for the Ontario, Simcoe and Huron Railroad.[5] The engine was completed on the 16th of April, and put on the track the 26th

---

[5] This became the **Northern Railway** in 1858, was taken over by the Grand Trunk Railway in 1886, and is now part of the Canadian National system.

of the same month. Her dimensions are as follows: cylinder 16 inches diameter, stroke 22 inches, driving wheel 5 feet 6 inches in diameter, length of internal fire box 4 feet 6 inches, weight of engine 25 tons, number of tubes 150, diameter of tubes 2 inches.'

With property a little to the north on the east side, the name of Macintosh was early associated and—Canadian persistency again—is still associated. It was opposite the residence of Captain John Macintosh that the small riot took place which signalized the return home of William Lyon Mackenzie, in 1849, after the civil tumults of 1837. Mr Mackenzie was at the time the guest of Captain Macintosh, who was related to him through a marriage connection.

Albert Street, which enters Yonge Street opposite the Macintosh property, was in 1833 still known as Macaulay Lane and was described by Walton [in his 1833 *Directory*] as 'fronting the Fields'. From this point a long stretch of fine forest-land extended to Yorkville. On the left side it was the property partly of Dr Macaulay and partly of Chief Justice Elmsley. The fields which Macaulay Lane fronted were the improvements around Dr Macaulay's abode. The white entrance gate to his house was near where now a street leads into Trinity Square. Wykham Lodge, the residence of Sir James Macaulay after the removal from Front Street, and Elmsley Villa, the residence of Captain J. S. Macaulay (Government House in Lord Elgin's day, and subsequently Knox College), were late erections on portions of these spacious suburban estates.

The first Dr Macaulay and Chief Justice Elmsley selected two adjoining park-lots, both of them fronting, of course, on Lot Street. They then effected an exchange of properties with each other. Dividing these two lots transversely into equal portions, the Chief Justice chose the upper or northern halves and Dr Macaulay the lower or southern. Dr Macaulay thus acquired a large frontage on Lot Street and the Chief Justice a like advantage on Yonge Street. Captain Macaulay acquired his interest in the southern portion of the Elmsley halves by marriage with a daughter of the Chief Justice. The northern portion of these halves descended to the heir of the Chief Justice, Capt.

John Elmsley, who, having become a convert to the Church of Rome, gave facilities for the establishment of St Basil's [church, St Michael's] college, and other Roman Catholic Institutions on his estate. Of Chief Justice Elmsley and his son we have previously spoken.

Dr Macaulay's clearing on the north side of Macaulay Lane was, in relation to the first town plot of York, long considered a locality particularly remote; a spot to be discovered by strangers not without difficulty. In attempting to reach it we have distinct accounts of persons bewildered and lost for long hours in the intervening marshes and woods. Mr Justice [D'Arcy] Boulton [Sr], travelling from Prescott in his own vehicle and bound for Dr Macaulay's domicile, was dissuaded, on reaching Mr Small's house at the eastern extremity of York, from attempting to push on to his destination, although it was by no means late, on account of the inconveniences and perils to be encountered; and half of the following day was taken up in accomplishing the residue of the journey.

Trinity Square is now completely surrounded with buildings; nevertheless an aspiring attic therein, in which many of these Collections and Recollections have been reduced to shape, has the advantage of commanding to this day a view still showing within its range some of the primitive features of the site of York.[6] To the north an extended portion of the rising land above Yorkville is pleasantly visible, looking in the distance as it anciently looked, albeit beheld now with spires intervening, and ornamental turrets of public buildings and lofty factory flues: while to the south, seen also between chimney stacks and steeples and long solid architectural ranges, a glimpse of Lake Ontario itself is procurable—a glimpse especially precious so long as it is to be had for not only recalling, as it does, the olden time when 'the Lake' was an element in so much of the talk of the early settlers—its sound, its aspect, its condition being matters of hourly observation to them—but also suggesting the thought of the far-off outer ocean stream—the silver moat that

---

[6] Dr Scadding's house, 6 Trinity Square, can still be seen in 1966, though it is threatened with demolition.

guards the fatherland and that forms the horizon in so many of its landscapes.

The Church with the twin turrets, now seen in the middle space of Trinity Square, was a gift of benevolence to Western Canada in 1846 from two ladies, sisters. The personal character of Bishop Strachan was the attraction that drew the boon to Toronto. Through the hands of Bishop Longley of Ripon, afterwards Archbishop of Canterbury, a sum of £5,000 sterling was transmitted by the donors to Bishop Strachan for the purpose of founding a church, two stipulations being that it should be forever, like the ancient churches of England, free to all for worship, and that it should bear the name of The Holy Trinity.[7] The sum sent built the Church and created a small endowment. Soon after the completion of the edifice, Scoresby, the celebrated Arctic navigator, author of *An Account of the Arctic Regions, with a History and Description of the Northern Whale Fishery* [1820], preached and otherwise officiated within its walls. Therein, too, at a later period was heard the voice of Selwyn, Bishop of Lichfield, but previously the eminent Missionary Bishop of New Zealand. Here also, while the Cathedral of St James was rebuilding after its second destruction by fire in 1849, Lord Elgin was a constant devout participant in Christian rites, an historical occasion connected with the building made worthy of preservation by the very remarkable public services of the Earl afterwards in China and India. We recall at this moment the *empressement* with which an obscure little chapel was pointed out to us in the small hamlet of Tregear in Cornwall, on account of the fact that John Wesley had once preached there. Well then: it may be that with some hereafter it will be a matter of curiosity and interest to know that several men of worldwide note did, in their day, while sojourning in this region, 'pay their vows' in the particular 'Lord's House' to which we now have occasion to refer.

In the grove which surrounded Sir James Macaulay's resi-

---

[7] The donor of the money was Mary Lambert Swale of Settle, Yorkshire, whose name was not made public until 1897. Colonel John Simcoe Macaulay donated the land on which the church is situated.

dence, Wykham Lodge, we had down to recent years a fragment of the fine forest which lined Yonge Street almost continuously from Lot Street to Yorkville some forty years since. The ruthless uprooting of the eastern border of this beautiful sylvan relic of the past for building purposes was painful to witness, however quickly the presence of rows of useful structures reconciled us to the change. The trees which cluster round the great school building[8] in the rear of these improvements will long, as we hope, survive to give an idea of what was the primeval aspect of the whole of the neighbourhood.

The land on the opposite side, a little to the north of the point at which we have arrived (Carleton Street), long remaining in an uncultivated condition, was a portion of the estate of Alexander Wood of whom we have already spoken. His family and baptismal names are preserved, as we have before noted, in 'Wood' Street and 'Alexander' Street.

The streets which we passed southward of Wood Street—Carleton, Gerrard, Shuter, with Gould Street in the immediate vicinity—had their names from personal friends of Mr [John] McGill, the first owner, as we have seen, of this tract. They are names mostly associated with the early annals of Montreal and seem rather inapposite here.

Northward, a little beyond where Grosvenor Street leads into what was Elmsley Villa and is now Knox College, was a solitary green field with a screen of lofty trees on three of its sides. In its midst was a Dutch barn or hay-barrack with movable top. The sward on the northern side of the building was ever eyed by the passer-by with a degree of awe. It was the exact spot where a fatal duel had been fought.

We have seen in repeated instances that the so-called code of honour was in force at York from the era of its foundation. 'Without it', Mandeville had said, 'there would be no living in a populous nation. It is the tie of society; and although we are beholden to our frailties for the chief ingredient of it, there has been no virtue, at least that I am acquainted with, which has proved half so instrumental to the civilizing of mankind, who,

---

8 This was the Bishop Strachan School.

in great societies, would soon degenerate into cruel villains and treacherous slaves, were honour to be removed from among them.' Mandeville's sophistical dictum was blindly accepted, and trifles light as air gave rise to the conventional hostile meeting. The merest accident at a dance—a look, a jest, a few words of unconsidered talk, of youthful chaff—were every now and then sufficient to force persons who previously, perhaps, had been bosom friends, companions from childhood, along with others sometimes in no wise concerned in the quarrel at first, to put on an unnatural show of thirst for each other's blood. The victim of the social usage of the day, in the case now referred to, was [John,] a youthful son of Surveyor-General Ridout.

Some years after the event, the public attention was drawn afresh to it. The surviving principal in the affair, Mr Samuel Jarvis, underwent a trial at the time and was acquitted. But the seconds were not arraigned. It happened in 1828, eleven years after the incident (the duel took place July 12, 1817), that Francis Collins, editor of the *Canadian Freeman*, a paper of which we have before spoken, was imprisoned and fined for libel. As an act of retaliation on at least some of those who had promoted the prosecution, which ended in his being thus sentenced, he set himself to work to bring the seconds into court. He succeeded. One of them, Mr Henry John Boulton, was now Solicitor-General, and the other, Mr James E. Small, an eminent member of the Bar. All the particulars of the fatal encounter were once more gone over in the evidence. But the jury did not convict.

Modern society, here and elsewhere, is to be congratulated on the change which has come over its ideas in regard to duelling. Apart from the considerations dictated by morals and religion, common sense, as we suppose, has had its effect in checking the practice. York in its infancy was no better and no worse in this respect than other places. It took its cue in this as in some other matters from very high quarters. The Duke of York, from whom York derived its name, had himself narrowly escaped a bullet from the pistol of Colonel Lennox: 'it passed so near to the ear as to discommode the side-curl,' the report said: but our Duke's action, or rather inaction, on the occasion helped perhaps to impress on the public mind the irrationality of duelling: he did not return the fire. 'He came out', he said, 'to give Colonel Lennox satisfaction, and did not mean to fire at him; if Colonel Lennox was not satisfied, he might fire again.'

Just to the north of the scene of the fatal duel which has led to this digression was the portion of Yonge Street where a wooden tramway was once laid down for a short distance; an experiment interesting to be remembered now as an early foreshadowing of the existing convenient street railway, if not of the great Northern Railway itself. Subterranean springs and quicksands hereabout rendered the primitive roadmaker's occupation no easy one; and previous to the application of macadam, the tramway, while it lasted, was a boon to the farmers after heavy rains.

Mr Charles Durand's modest cottage and bowery grounds near here recall at the present day an early praiseworthy effort of its owner to establish a local periodical devoted to Literature and Natural History, in conjunction with an advocacy of the cause of Temperance. A diligent attention to his profession as a lawyer did not hinder the editor of the *Literary Gem* from giving some of his leisure time to the observation and study of Nature. We accordingly have in the columns of that periodical numerous notes of the fauna and flora of the surrounding neighbourhood, which for their appreciativeness, simplicity, and minuteness, remind us of the pleasant pages of White's *Natural History of Selborne*. The *Gem* appeared in 1851-2 and had an extensive circulation. It was illustrated with good wood-cuts, and its motto was 'Humanity, Temperance, Progress'. The place of its publication was indicated by a square label suspended on one side of the front entrance of a small white office still to be seen adjoining the cottage which we are now passing.

Proceeding now onward a few yards, we arrived, in former times, at what was popularly called the Sandhill—a moderate rise showing where in bygone ages the lake began to shoal. Building requirements have at the present day occasioned the almost complete obliteration of the Sandhill. Innumerable loads of the loose silex of which it was composed have been removed.

Off to the eastward of the sandy rise which we are ascending was one of the early public nursery gardens of York, Mr Frank's. Kearsny House, Mr Proudfoot's, the grounds of which occupy the site of Frank's nursery garden, is a comparatively modern erection dating from about 1845, an architectural object regarded with no kindly glance by the final holders of shares in the Bank of Upper Canada—an institution which in the infancy of the country had a mission and fulfilled it, but which grievously betrayed those of the second generation who, relying on its traditionary sterling repute, continued to trust it. With Kearsny House, too, is associated the recollection not only of the president so long identified with the Bank of Upper Canada but of the financier, Mr Cassells, who, as a kind of *deus ex machina*, engaged at an annual salary of ten thousand dollars, was expected to retrieve the fortunes of the institution but in vain, although for a series of years after being pronounced moribund it continued to yield a handsome addition to the income of a number of persons.[9]

Mr Alexander Murray, subsequently of Yorkville and a merchant of the olden time at York, occupied the residence which preceded Kearsny House on the Frank property. One desires in passing to offer a tribute to the memory of a man of such genuine worth as was Mr Murray, although the singular unobtrusiveness which characterized him when living seems almost to forbid the act.

The residue of the Sandhill rise that is still to be discerned westward of Yonge Street has its winsome name, Clover Hill, from the designation borne by the home of Captain Elmsley, son of the Chief Justice, situated here. The house still stands, overshadowed by some fine oaks, relics of the natural woods. The rustic cottage lodge with diamond lattice windows, at the gate leading in to the original Clover Hill, was on the street a little further on. At the time of his decease [1863], Captain Elmsley had taken up his abode in a building apart from the principal residence of the Clover Hill estate—a building to

---

[9] The bank collapsed in 1866, basically because of speculation in land and the depression that began in 1857.

which he had pleasantly given the name of Barnstable as being in fact a portion of the outbuildings of the homestead turned into a modest dwelling.

Just before reaching the first concession road where Yorkville now begins, a family residence of an ornamental suburban character put up on the left by Mr Lardner Bostwick was the first of that class of building in the neighbourhood. His descendants still occupy it. Mr Botswick was an early property owner in York. The now-important square acre at the south-east angle of the intersection of King Street and Yonge Street, regarded probably when selected as a mere site for a house and garden in the outskirts of the town, was his. The price paid for it was £100. Its value in 1873 may be £100,000.

The house of comparatively modern date, seen next after Mr Bostwick, is associated with the memory of Mr de Blaquière, who occupied it before building for himself the tasteful residence—The Pines—not far off, where he died; now the abode of Mr John Heward.

Mr de Blaquière was the youngest son of the first Lord de Blaquière of Ardkill in Ireland. He emigrated in 1837, and was subsequently appointed to a seat in the Legislative Council of Upper Canada. In his youth he had seen active service as a midshipman. He was present at the battle of Camperdown in the *Bounty*, commanded by Captain Bligh. He was also in the Fleet at the Nore during the mutiny. He died suddenly here in his new house in 1860 aged 76. His fine character and prepossessing outward physique are freshly remembered.

The First Concession Road-line derived its modern name of Bloor Street from a former resident on its southern side eastward of Yonge Street. Mr Bloor, as we have previously narrated, was for many years the landlord of the Farmer's Arms near the market place of York, an inn conveniently situated for the accommodation of the agricultural public. On retiring from this occupation with a good competency, he established a brewery on an extensive scale in the ravine north of the first concession road. In conjunction with Mr Sheriff [W. B.] Jarvis, he entered successfully into a speculation on land, projecting and laying out the village of Yorkville which narrowly escaped being Bloor-ville. That name was proposed: as also was Rosedale after the Sheriff's homestead; and likewise 'Cumberland' from the county of some of the surrounding inhabitants. But Yorkville was at last decided on, an appellation preservative in part of the name just discarded in 1834 by Toronto.

Mr Bloor was an Englishman, respected by everyone. That his name should have become permanently attached to the northern boulevard of the City of Toronto, a favourite thoroughfare several miles in extent, is a curious fact which may be compared with the case of Pimlico, the famous west-end quarter of London. Pimlico has its name, it is said, from Mr Benjamin Pimlico, for many years the popular landlord of a hotel in the neighbourhood. Bloor Street was for a time known as St Paul's road; also as the Sydenham road.

While crossing the First Concession Line, now in our northward journey, the moment comes back to us when on glancing along the vista to the eastward formed by the road in that direction, we first noticed a church spire on the right-hand or southern side. We had passed that way a day or two before and we were sure no such object was to be seen there then; and yet, unmistakably now there rose up before the eye a rather graceful tower and spire of considerable altitude, complete from base to apex and coloured white.

The fact was: Mr J. G. Howard, a well-known local architect, had ingeniously constructed a tower of wood in a horizontal or nearly horizontal position on the ground close by, somewhat as a shipbuilder puts together 'the mast of some vast ammiral', and then, after attending to the external finish of at least the higher portion of it, even to a coating of lime wash, had in the space of a few hours, by means of convenient machinery, raised it on end and secured it permanently in a vertical position.

We gather some further particulars of the achievement from a contemporary account. The Yorkville spire was raised on the 4th of August 1841. It was 85 feet high, composed of four entire trees or pieces of timber, each of that length, bound together pyramidically, tapering from ten feet base to one foot at top and made to receive a turned ball and weather-cock. The base was sunk in the ground until the apex was raised ten feet from the ground; and about thirty feet of the upper part of the spire was completed, coloured, and painted before the raising. The operation of raising commenced about two o'clock p.m., and about eight in the evening the spire and vane were seen erect and appeared to those unacquainted with what was going on to have risen amongst the trees as if by magic. The work was performed by Mr John Richey, the framing by Mr Withrow, and the raising was superintended by Mr Joseph Hill.

The plan adopted was this: three gin-poles, as they are called, were erected in the form of a triangle; each of them was well braced, and tackles were rove at their tops: the tackles were hooked to strong straps about fifty feet up the spire, with nine men to each tackle and four men to steady the end with following poles. It was raised in about four hours from the commencement of the straining of the tackles and had a very beautiful appearance while rising. The whole operation, we have been told, was conducted as nearly as possible in silence, the architect himself regulating by signs the action of the groups at the gin-poles, being himself governed by the plumb-line suspended in a high frame before him.

> *No workman steel, no ponderous axes rung;*
> *Like some tall palm, the noiseless fabric sprung.*

Perhaps Fontana's exploit of setting on end the obelisk in front of St Peter's in Rome suggested the possibility of causing a tower and spire complete to be suddenly seen rising above the roof of the Yorkville St Paul's.[10] On an humble scale we have Fontana's arrangements reproduced. While in the men at the gin-poles working in obedience to signs, we have the old Egyptians over again—a very small detachment of them indeed—as seen in the old sculptures on the banks of the Nile.

The original St Paul's, before it acquired in this singular manner the dignified appurtenance of a steeple, was a long, low, barn-like, wooden building. Mr Howard otherwise improved it, enlarging it by the addition of an aisle on the west side. When some twenty years later—viz., in 1861—the new stone church was

---

10 Domenico Fontana was the architect of Pope Sixtus V, who ordered the obelisk moved to its present position in 1586.

erected, the old wooden structure was removed bodily to the
west side of [i.e., west of] Yonge Street, together with the tower
—curtailed, however, of its spire.[11]

We have been informed that the four fine stems, each eighty-
five feet long, which formed the interior frame of the tower and
spire of 1841, were a present from Mr Allan of Moss Park; and
that the Rev. Charles Mathews, occasionally officiating in St
Paul's, gave one hundred pounds in cash towards the expense
of the ornamental addition now made to the edifice.

The history of another of Mr Howard's erections on Yonge
Street, which we are perambulating, illustrates the rapid advance and expansion of architectural ideas amongst us. In the
case now referred to it was no shell of timber and deal-boards
that was taken down, but a very handsome solid edifice of cut-
stone, which might have endured for centuries. The Bank of
British North America, built by Mr Howard at the corner of
Yonge Street and Wellington Street in 1843, was deliberately
taken down block by block in 1871 and made to give place to a
structure which should be on a par in magnificence and altitude
with the buildings put up in Toronto by the other banks. Mr
Howard's building, at the time of its erection, was justly regarded as a credit to the town. Its design was preferred by the
directors in London to those sent in by several architects there.
Over the principal entrance were the Royal Arms, exceedingly
well carved in stone on a grand scale and wholly disengaged
from the wall; and conspicuous over the parapet above was the
great scallop shell, emblem of the gold digger's occupation, introduced by Sir John Soane in the architecture of the Bank of
England. (The Royal Arms of the old building have been
deemed worthy of a place over the entrance to the new Bank.[12])

The cemetery, the gates and keeper's lodge of which, after
crossing the concession road [Bloor Street] and advancing on our
way northward, we used to see on the left, was popularly known

---

[11] It then became the first Church of the Redeemer and, like the present
church, was situated at the north-east corner of Bloor Street and Avenue
Road.

[12] This was an often-quoted story, but photographs show that the two coats
of arms, though similar, were different in detail.

as 'The Potter's Field'—'a place to bury strangers in'. Its official style was 'The York General or Strangers' Burying Ground'. In practice it was the Bunhill Fields of York—the receptacle of the remains of those whose friends declined the use of the St James' churchyard and other early burial-plots.

Walton's *Directory* for 1833 gives the following information which we transfer hither, as well for the slight degree of quaintness which the narrative has acquired as also on account of the familiar names which it contains. 'This institution', Walton says, 'owes its origin to Mr Carfrae, junior. It comprises six acres of ground, and has a neat sexton's house built close by the gate. The name of the sexton is John Wolstencroft, who keeps a registry of every person buried therein. Persons of all creeds and persons of no creed are allowed burial in this cemetery: fees to the sexton, 5s. It was instituted in the fall of 1825, and incorporated by Act of Parliament, 30th January, 1826. It is managed by five trustees, who are chosen for life; and in case of the death of any of them, a public meeting of the inhabitants is called, when they elect a successor or successors in their place. The present trustees (1833) are Thomas Carfrae, jun., Thomas D. Morrison, Peter Paterson, John Ewart, Thomas Helliwell.'[13]

(Mr Carfrae was for some years [1835-41] the collector of Customs of the Port of York. The other trustees named were respectively the medical man, iron-merchant, builder, and brewer, so well known in the neighbourhood.)

A remote sequestered piece of ground in 1825, the Potter's Field in 1845 was more or less surrounded by buildings and regarded as an impediment in the way of public improvement. Interments were accordingly prohibited. To some extent it has been cleared of human remains and in due time will be built over. Its successor and representative is the Toronto Necropolis, the trustees of which are empowered, after the lapse of twenty-one years, to sell the old burying-ground.

The singular *Hôtel de Ville* which in modern times distinguishes Yorkville has a Flemish look. It might have strayed hither from Ghent. Nevertheless, as seen from numerous points of

---

[13] This is the beginning of the present Toronto General Burying Grounds.

view it cannot be characterized as picturesque or in harmony with its surroundings. The shield of arms sculptured in stone and set in the wall above the circular window in the front gable presents the following charges arranged quarterly: a Beer-barrel with an s below; a Brick-mould with an A below; and Anvil, with a w below; and a Jackpine, with a D below. In the centre, in a shield of pretence, is a Sheep's head with an H below. These symbols commemorate the first five Councillors or Aldermen of Yorkville at the time of its incorporation in 1853, and their trades or callings, the initials being those respectively of the surnames of Mr John Severn, Mr Thomas Atkinson, Mr James Wallis, Mr James Dobson, and Mr Peter Hutty. Over the whole, as a crest is the Canadian Beaver.[14]

The road which enters from the west [Davenport], a little way on, calls up memories of Russell-hill, Davenport, and Spadina, each of them locally historic. We have already spoken of them in our journey along Front Street and Queen Street when, in crossing Brock Street, Spadina-house in the distance caught the eye. It is a peculiarity of this old by-road that, instead of going straight as most of our highways monotonously do, it meanders a little, unfolding a number of pretty suburban scenes. The public school on the land given to Yorkville by Mr Ketchum is visible up this road.

In this direction were the earliest public ice-houses established in our region, in rude buildings of slab thickly thatched over with pine branches. Spring-water ice, gathered from the neighbouring mill-ponds, began to be stored here in quantities by an enterprising man of African descent, Mr Richards, five-and-thirty years ago.

On the east side of Yonge Street, near the northern toll-gate, stood Dr R. C. Horne's house, the lurid flames arising from which somewhat alarmed the town in 1837 when the malcontents of the north were reported to be approaching with hostile intent. Of Dr Horne we have already spoken in connection with the early press of York.

---

14 The building was built in 1859 and demolished in 1942.

XIII

YONGE
STREET
FROM
YORKVILLE
TO
HOGG'S
HOLLOW

Of long standing is the group of buildings on the right after
passing the Davenport Road. It is the brewery and malting-
house of Mr Severn, settled here since 1835. The main building
overlooks a ravine which, as seen by the passer-by on Yonge
Street, retains to this day in its eastern recess a great deal of
natural beauty, although the stream below attracted manufacturers at an early period to its borders at numerous points.
There is a picturesque irregularity about the outlines of Mr
Severn's brewery. The projecting galleries round the domestic
portion of the building pleasantly indicate that the adjacent
scenery is not unappreciated: nay, possibly enjoyed on many a
tranquil autumn evening.

Further on a block-house of two storeys—both of them rectangular, but the upper turned half round on the lower, built
in consequence of the troubles of 1837 and supposed to command the great highway from the north—overhung a high bank
on the right. (Another of the like build was placed at the eastern
extremity of the First Concession Road. It was curious to
observe how rapidly these two relics acquired the character and
even the look, grey and dilapidated, of age. With many, they
dated at least from the War of 1812.)

A considerable stretch of striking landscape here skirts our route on the right. Rosedale-house, the old extra-mural home, still existent and conspicuous, of Mr Stephen Jarvis, Registrar of the Province in the olden time, afterwards of his son the Sheriff, of both of whom we have had occasion to speak repeatedly, was always noticeable for the romantic character of its situation on the crest of a precipitous bank overlooking deep winding ravines. Set down here while yet the forest was but little encroached on, access to it was of course for a long time, difficult and laborious.

The memorable fancy-ball given here at a comparatively late period [c. 1839], but during the Sheriff's lifetime, recurs as we go by. On that occasion, in the dusk of evening, and again probably in the grey dawn of morning, an irregular procession thronged the highway of Yonge Street and toiled up and down the steep approaches to Rosedale-house—a procession consisting of the simulated shapes and forms that usually revisit the glimpses of the moon at masquerades—knights, crusaders, Plantagenet, Tudor, and Stuart princes, queens, and heroines; all mixed up with an incongruous ancient and modern canaille, a Tom of Bedlam, a Nicholas Bottom 'with amiable cheeks and fair large ears', an Ariel, a Paul Pry, a Pickwick, &c., &c., not pacing on with some verisimilitude on foot or respectably mounted on horse, ass, or mule, but borne along most prosaically on wheels or in sleighs.

This pageant, though only a momentary social relaxation, a transient but still not unutilitarian freak of fashion, accomplished well and cleverly in the midst of a scene literally a savage wild only a few years previously, may be noted as one of the many outcomes of precocity characterizing society in the colonies of England.

Rosedale is a name of pleasant sound. We are reminded thereby of another of the same genus, but of more recent application in these parts—Hazeldean, the pretty title given by Chief Justice Draper to his rural cottage which overhangs and looks down upon the same ravines as Rosedale but on the opposite side.

The perils and horrors encountered every spring and autumn

by travellers and others in their ascent and descent of the precipitous sides of the Rosedale ravine, at the point where the primitive Yonge Street crossed it, were a local proverb and byword: perils and horrors ranking for enormity with those associated with the passage of the Rouge, the Credit, the Sixteen, and a long list of other deeply ploughed watercourses intersected of necessity by the two great highways of Upper Canada.

The ascent and descent of the gorge were here spoken of collectively as the 'Blue Hill' [above Davenport Rd]. Certain strata of bluish clay had been remarked at the summit on both sides. The waggon track passed down and up by two long wearisome and difficult slopes cut in the soil of the steep sides of the lofty banks. After the autumnal rains and during the thaws at the close of winter, the condition of the route here was indescribably bad. At the period referred to, however, the same thing for many a year was to be said of every rood of Yonge Street throughout its thirty miles of length.

Nor was Yonge Street singular in this respect. All our roads were equally bad at certain seasons every year. We fear we conveyed an impression unfavourable to emigration many years ago when walking with two or three young English friends across some flat clayey fields between Cambridge and Gogmagogs. It chanced that the driftways for the farmers' carts—the holls, as they are locally called if we remember rightly—at the sides of the ploughed land were mire from end to end. Under the impulse of the moment, pleased in fact with a reminder of home far distant, we exclaimed, 'Here are Canadian roads!' The comparison was altogether too graphic; and our companions could never afterwards be got to entertain satisfactory notions of Canadian civilization.

The mode of extricating a vehicle from a slough or mudhole when once in may be gathered from a passage in McTaggart's *Three Years in Canada*, ii., 205. The time referred to is 1829: 'There are few roads,' McTaggart says, 'and these are generally excessively bad, and full of mudholes in which if a carriage fall, there is great trouble to get it out again. The mail coaches or waggons are often in this predicament, when

the passengers instantly jump off, and having stripped rails
off the fence, they lift it up by sheer force. Coming up brows they
sometimes get in; the horses are then taken out, and yoked to
the stern instead of the front; and it is drawn out backwards.'

The county between York and Lake Huron was, as we have
already seen, first explored by Governor Simcoe in person in
1793. It was also immediately surveyed and in some measure
occupied; and so early as 1794, we read in a *Gazette* the following notice: 'Surveyor-General's Office, Upper Canada, 15th July,
1794. Notice is hereby given that all persons who have obtained
assignments for land on Dundas Street, leading from the head
of Burlington Bay to the upper forks of the River Thames, and
on Yonge Street leading from York to Lake Simcoe, that unless
a dwelling-house shall be built on every lot under certificate of
location, and the same occupied within one year from the date
of their respective assignments, such lots will be forfeited on the
said Roads. D. W. SMITH, *Acting Surveyor-General.*'

All the conditions required to be fulfilled by the first settlers
were these: 'They must within the term of two years, clear fit
for cultivation and fence, ten acres of the lot obtained; build a
house 16 by 20 feet of logs or frame, with a shingle roof; also
cut down all the timber in front of and the whole width of the
lot (which is 20 chains, 133 feet wide), 33 feet of which must be
cleared smooth and left for half of the public road.' To issue
injunctions for the performance of such work was easy. To do
such work, or to get such work effectually done, was, under the
circumstances of the times, difficult. Hence Yonge Street continued for some years after 1794 to be little more than a rambling forest wheel-track through the woods.

In 1794 Mr William Berczy brought over from the Pulteney
Settlement on the south side of Lake Ontario sixty German
families and conducted them to the township of Markham,
north-east of York, where lands had been assigned them. In
effecting this first lodgment of a considerable body of colonists
in a region entirely new, Mr Berczy necessarily cut out by the
aid of his party, and such other help as he could obtain, some
kind of track through the forest along the line of Yonge Street.
He had already once before successfully accomplished a similar

work. He had, we are told, hewn out a waggon road for emigrants through trackless woods all the way from Philadelphia to the Genesee country where the Pulteney Settlement was.

In 1795 Mr Augustus Jones, a Deputy Provincial Surveyor who figures largely in the earliest annals of Upper Canada, was directed by the Lieutenant-Governor to survey and open in a more effective manner the route which Mr Berczy and his emigrants had travelled. A detachment of the Queen's Rangers was at the same time ordered to assist.

On the 24th December 1795, Mr Jones writes to D. W. Smith, Acting Surveyor-General:—'His Excellency was pleased to direct me, previous to my surveying the township of York, to proceed on Yonge Street, to survey and open a cart-road from the harbour at York to Lake Simcoe, which I am now busy at (*i. e.* I am busily engaged in the preparations for this work.) Mr Pearse is to be with me in a few days' time with a detachment of about thirty of the Queen's Rangers, who are to assist in opening the said road.'

The survey and opening of the Street from York bay to the Landing occupied forty-three days (January 4 to February 16). Three days sufficed for the return of the party to the place of beginning. The memoranda of these three days, and the following one, when Mr Jones presented himself before the Governor in the Garrison at York, runs thus: 'Wednesday, 17th, returned back to a small Lake at the twenty-first mile tree; pleasant weather, light winds from the west. Thursday, 18th, came down to five mile tree from York, pleasant weather. Friday, 19th, came to the town of York, busy entering some of my field notes; weather as before. Saturday, 20th, went to Garrison, York, and waited on His Excellency the Governor, and informed him that Yonge Street is opened from York to the Pine Fort Landing, Lake Simcoe, As there is no provision to be had at the place,' Mr Jones proceeds, 'His Excellency was pleased to say that I must return to Newark, and report to the Surveyor General, and return with him in April next, when the Executive will sit, and that my attendance would be wanted. Pleasant weather, light winds from the west.'

Just beyond the Blue Hill ravine, on the west side, stood for a long while a lonely unfinished frame building with gable towards the street and windows boarded up. The inquiring stage passenger would be told good-humouredly by the driver that it was Rowland Burr's Folly. It was, we believe, to have been a Carding or Fulling Mill, worked by peculiar machinery driven by the stream in the valley below; but either the impracticability of this from the position of the building or the as yet insignificant quantity of wool produced in the country made the enterprise abortive.

Mr Burr was an emigrant to these parts from Pennsylvania in 1803, and from early manhood was strongly marked by many of the traits which are held to be characteristic of the speculative and energetic American. Unfortunately in some respects for himself, he was in advance of his neighbours in a clear perception of the capabilities of things as seen in the rough, and in a strong desire to initiate works of public utility, broaching schemes occasionally beyond the natural powers of a community in its veriest infancy. A canal to connect Lake Ontario with the Georgian Bay of Lake Huron, via Lake Simcoe and the valley of the Humber, was pressed by him as an immediate necessity years ago; and at his own expense he minutely examined the route and published thereon a report which has furnished to later theorizers on the same subject much valuable information.

Mr Burr was a born engineer and mechanician, and at a more auspicious time, with proper opportunities for training and culture, he would probably have become famed as a local George Stephenson. He built on his own account, or for others, a number of mills and factories, providing and getting into working order the complicated mechanism required for each, and this at a time when such undertakings were not easy to accomplish, from the unimproved condition of the country and the few facilities that existed for importing and transporting inland heavy machinery. The mills and factories at Burwick in Vaughan originated with him, and from him that place takes its name.

The early tramway on Yonge Street of which we have already spoken was suggested by Mr Burr, and when the cutting down of the Blue Hill was decided on, he undertook and effected the work.

It is now some forty years since the peculiar clay of the Blue Hill began to be turned to useful account. In or near the brick-fields, which at the present time are still to be seen on the left, Messrs James and William Townsley burnt kilns of white brick, a manufacture afterwards carried on here by Mr Nightingale, a family connection of the Messrs Townsley. Mr Worthington also for a time engaged on the same spot in the manufacture of pressed brick and drain tiles. The Rossin House [Prince George] Hotel in Toronto and the Yorkville Town Hall were built of pressed brick made here.

Chestnut Park, which we pass on the right, the residence now of Mr McPherson, is a comparatively modern erection put up by Mr Mathers, an early merchant of York, who, before building here, lived on Queen Street near the Meadows, the residence of Mr J. Hillyard Cameron. Oaklands, Mr John McDonald's residence, of which a short distance back we obtained a passing glimpse far to the west, and Rathnally, Mr McMaster's palatial abode beyond, are both modern structures put up by their respective occupants. Woodlawn, still on the left, the present residence of Mr Justice Morrison, was previously the home of Mr. Chancellor Blake and was built by him.

Summer Hill, seen on the high land far to the right and commanding a noble view of the wide plain below, including Toronto with its spires and the lake view along the horizon, was originally built by Mr Charles Thompson whose name is associated with the former travel and postal service of the whole length of Yonge Street and the Upper Lakes. In Mr Thompson's time, however, Summer Hill was by no means the extensive and handsome place into which it has developed since becoming the property and the abode of Mr Larratt Smith.

The primitive waggon track of Yonge Street ascended the hill at which we now arrive, a little to the west of the present line of road. It passed up through a narrow excavated notch. Across this depression or trench a forest tree fell without being broken and there long remained. Teams, in their way to and from town, had to pass underneath it like captured armies of old under the yoke. To some among the country folk it suggested the beam of the gallows-tree; hence sprang an ill-omened name [Gallows Hill] long attached to this particular spot.

Near here, at the top of the hill, were formerly to be seen, as we have understood, the remains of a rude windlass or capstan, used in the hauling up of the North West Company's boats at this point of the long portage from Lake Ontario to Lake Huron.

So early as 1799 we have it announced that the North West Company intended to make use of this route. In the Niagara *Constellation* of August 3, 1799, we read: 'We are informed on good authority that the North-West company have it seriously in contemplation to establish a communication with the Upper Lakes by way of York, through Yonge Street to Lake Simcoe, a distance of about 33 miles only.' The *Constellation* embraces the occasion to say also, 'That the government has actually begun to open that street for several miles, which example will undoubtedly be no small inducement to persons who possess property on that street and its vicinity to exert themselves in opening and completing what may be justly considered one of the primary objects of attention in a new country, a good road.'

The *Gazette* of March 9 in this year (1799) had contained an announcement that 'The North-West Company has given twelve thousand pounds towards making Yonge Street a good road, and that the North-West commerce will be communicated through this place (York): an event which must inevitably benefit this country materially, as it will not only tend to augment the population but will also enhance the present value of landed property.'

Bouchette, writing in 1815, speaks of improvements on Yonge Street, 'of late effected by the North-West Company'. 'This route', he says in his Topographical description, 'being of much more importance, has of late been greatly improved by the North-West Company for the double purpose of shortening the distance to the Upper Lakes, and avoiding any contact with the American frontiers.'

As stated already in another connection, we have conversed

with those who had seen the cavalcade of the North West Company's boats, mounted on wheels, on their way up Yonge Street. It used to be supposed by some that the tree across the notch through which the road passed had been purposely felled in that position as a part of the apparatus for helping the boats up the hill.

The tableland now attained was long known as the Poplar Plains. A pretty rural byroad that ascends this same rise near Rathnally, Mr McMaster's house, is still known as the Poplar Plains road.

A house, rather noticeable, to the left but lying slightly back and somewhat obscured by fine ornamental trees that overshadow it, was the home for many years of Mr J. S. Howard, sometime Postmaster of York and afterwards Treasurer of the counties of York and Peel: an estimable man and an active promoter of all local works of benevolence. He died in Toronto in 1866, aged 68.

This house used to be known as Olive Grove and was originally built by Mr Campbell, proprietor and manager of the Ontario House Hotel in York, once before referred to; eminent in the Masonic body, and father of Mr Steadman Campbell, a local barrister of note, who died early.

Mashquoteh to the left, situated a short distance in, on the north side of the road which enters Yonge Street here, is a colony transplanted from the neighbouring Spadina, being the home of Mr W. Augustus Baldwin, son of Dr W. W. Baldwin, the builder of Spadina. 'Mashquoteh' is the Ojibway for 'meadow'. We hear the same sounds in Longfellow's 'Mushkodasa', which is, by interpretation, 'prairie-fowl'.

Deer Park, to the north of the road that enters here but skirting Yonge Street as well, had that name given it when the property of Mrs Heath, widow of Col. Heath of the H[onourable] E[ast] I[ndia] Company's Service. On a part of this property was the house built by Colonel Carthew, once before referred to, and now the abode of Mr Fisken. Colonel Carthew, a half-pay officer of Cornish origin, also made large improvements on property in the vicinity of Newmarket.

Just after Deer Park, to avoid a long ravine which lay in the

line of the direct route northward, the road swerved to the left
and then descended, passing over an embankment, which was
the dam of an adjacent sawmill, a fine view of the interior of
which, with the saw usually in active motion, was obtained by
the traveller as he fared on. This was Michael Whitmore's
sawmill.

Of late years the apex of the long triangle of no man's land
that for a great while lay desolate between the original and
subsequent lines of Yonge Street has been happily utilized by
the erection thereon of a Church, Christ Church, an object
well seen in the ascent and descent of the street. Anciently, very
near the site of Christ Church, a solitary longish wooden building fronting southward was conspicuous, the abode of Mr Hudson, a provincial land surveyor of mark. Looking back southward from near the front of this house, a fine distant glimpse of
the waters of Lake Ontario used to be obtained, closing the
vista made in the forest by Yonge Street.

Before reaching Whitmore's sawmill, while passing along the
brow of the hill overlooking the ravine which was avoided by
the street as it ran in the first instance, there was to be seen at a
little distance to the right, on some rough undulating ground,
a house which always attracted the eye by its affectation of
'Gothic' in the outline of its windows. On the side towards the
public road it showed several obtuse-headed lancet lights. This
peculiarity gave the building, otherwise ordinary enough, a
slightly romantic air; it had the effect, in fact, at a later period
of creating for this habitation, when standing for a considerable
while tenantless, the reputation of being haunted.

This house and the surrounding grounds constituted Springfield Park, the original Upper Canadian home of Mr John Mills
Jackson, an English gentleman, formerly of Downton in Wilt-
shire, who emigrated hither prior to 1806; but finding public
affairs managed in a way which he deemed not satisfactory, he
returned to England, where he published a pamphlet addressed
to the King, Lords and Commons of the United Kingdom of
Great Britain and Ireland entitled *A View of the Political
Situation of the Province* [1809], a brochure that made a stir in

Upper Canada, if not in England, the local House of Assembly voting it a libel.

Our Upper Canadian Parliament partially acquired the habit of decreeing reflections on the local government to be libels. Society in its infancy is apt to resent criticism, even when legitimate. Witness the United States and Mrs Trollope. At the same time critics of infant society should be themselves sufficiently large-minded not to expect in infant society the perfection of society well developed, and to word their strictures accordingly.

In the preface to his pamphlet, which is a well-written production, Mr Jackson gives the following account of his first connection with Canada and his early experience there: 'Having by right of inheritance', he says, 'a claim to a large and very valuable tract of land in the Province of Quebec, I was induced to visit Lower Canada for the purpose of investigating my title; and being desirous to view the immense lakes and falls in Upper Canada, where I had purchased some land previous to my leaving England, I extended my travels to that country, with which I was so much pleased, that I resolved to settle on one of my estates, and expended a considerable sum on its improvement (the allusion is probably to Springfield Park); but considering neither my person nor property secure under the system pursued there, I have been obliged to relinquish the hope of its enjoyment.'

The concluding sentences of his appeal will give an idea of the burden of his complaint. To his mind the colony was being governed exactly in the way that leads finally to revolt in colonies. The principles of the constitution guaranteed by the mother country were violated. One of his grievances was not that a seventh of the public land had been set apart for an established Church, but that 'in seventeen years not one acre had been turned to any beneficial account; not a clergyman, except such as England pays or the Missionary Society sends (only five in number), without glebe, perquisite or parsonage house; and still fewer churches than ministers of an established religion.'

He concludes thus: 'I call upon you to examine the Journals

of the House of Assembly and Legislative Council; to look at the distribution and use made of the Crown Lands; the despatches from the Lieutenant-Governor (Gore); the memorials from the Provincial Secretary, Receiver-General and Surveyor-General; the remonstrances of the Six Nations of Indians; and the letters from Mr Thorpe (Judge Thorpe), myself and others, on the state of the Colony, either to the Lords of the Treasury or to the Secretary of State. Summon and examine all the evidence that can be procured here (England), and, if more should appear necessary, send a commission to ascertain the real state of the Province. Then you will be confirmed in the truth of every representation I have made, and much more which, for the safety of individuals, I am constrained to withhold. Then you will be enabled to relieve England from a great burden, render the Colony truly valuable to the mother country, and save one of the most luxuriant ramifications of the Empire. You will perform the promise of the crown; you will establish the law and liberty directed by the (British) Parliament; and diffuse the Gospel of Christ to the utmost extremity of the West. You will do that which is honourable to the nation, beneficial to the most deserving subjects, and lovely in the sight of God.'

This pamphlet is of interest as an early link (its date is 1809) in the catena of protests on the subject of Canadian affairs, from Whiggish and other quarters, culminating at last in Lord Durham's Report. Nevertheless, what the old French trader said of Africa— *'Toujours en maudissant ce vilain pays, on y reviens toujours'*—proved true in respect to Canada in the case of Mr Jackson, as in the case likewise of several other severe critics of Canadian public affairs in later times. He returned and dwelt in the land after all, settling with his family on Lake Simcoe, where Jackson's Point and Jackson's Landing retain his name, and where descendants of his still remain.

Mr Jackson had possessions likewise in the West Indies, and made frequent visits thither, as also to England, where at length he died in 1836. Up to about that date, we observe his name in the Commission of the Peace.

Fifty years ago in Canada English families, whose habits and ideas were more in harmony with Bond Street than with the backwoods, had, in becoming morally acclimatized to the country, a tremendous ordeal to pass through: how they contrived to endure the pains and perils of the process is now a matter of wonder.

One of Mr Jackson's sons, Clifton, is locally remembered as an early example in these parts of the exquisite of the period—the era of the Prince Regent and Lord Byron. By extra-sacrificing to the Graces, at a time when *articles de cosmetique et de luxe* generally were scarce and costly in Canada, he got himself into trouble. In 1822 he had occasion to make his escape from 'durance vile' in York by opening a passage, one quiet Sunday morning, through the roof of the old jail. He was speedily pursued by Mr Parker the warden, and an associate, Mr Garsides; overtaken at Albany in the State of New York; apprehended under the feigned charge; and brought back to York. Among the inhabitants of some of the villages between Albany and Youngstown, a suspicion arose that a case of kidnapping was in progress, and Messrs Parker and Garsides were exposed to risk of personal violence before they could reach the western bank of the Niagara river with their prey. By a happy turn of affairs, a few years later Mr Clifton Jackson obtained a situation in the Home Colonial Office with a good salary.

As we reach again the higher land, after crossing the dam of Whitmore's mill, and returning into the more direct line of the street, some rude pottery works met the eye. Here in the midst of woods, the passer-by usually saw on one side of the road a one-horse clay-grinding machine laboriously in operation; and on the other, displayed in the open air on boards supported by wooden pins driven into the great logs composing the wall of the low windowless building, numerous articles of coarse brown ware, partially glazed, pans, crocks, jars, jugs, demijohns, and so forth; all which primitive products of the plastic art were ever pleasant to contemplate. These works were carried on by Mr John Walmsley.

A tract of rough country was now reached, difficult to clear and difficult to traverse with a vehicle. Here a genuine corduroy causeway was encountered, a long series of small saw-logs laid side by side over which wheels jolted deliberately. In the wet season portions of it, being afloat, would undulate under the weight of a passing load; and occasionally a horse's leg would be entrapped, and possibly snapped short by the sudden yielding or revolution of one of the cylinders below.

We happen to have a very vivid recollection of the scene presented along this particular section of Yonge Street, when the woods, heavy pine chiefly, after having been felled in a most confused manner, were being consumed by fire, or rather while the effort was being made to consume them. The whole space from near Mr Walmsley's potteries to the rise beyond which Eglinton is situated was, and continued long, a chaos of blackened timber most dismaying to behold.

To the right of this tract was one of the Church glebes so curiously reserved in every township in the original laying out of Upper Canada—one lot of two hundred acres in every seven of the same area—in accordance with a public policy which at the present time seems sufficiently Utopian. Of the arrangement alluded to, now broken up, but expected when the Constitutional Act passed in 1791 to be permanent, a relic remained down to a late date in the shape of a wayside inn, on the right near here, styled on its sign the 'Glebe Inn'—a title and sign reminding one of the 'Church Stiles' and 'Church Gates' not uncommon as village ale-house designations in some parts of England.

Hitherto the general direction of Yonge Street has been north, sixteen degrees west. At the point where it passes the road marking the northern limit of the third concession from the bay, it swerves seven degrees to the eastward. In the first survey of this region there occurred here a jog or fault in the lines. The portion of the street proposed to be opened north failed by a few rods to connect in a continuous right line with the portion of it that led southward into York. The irregularity was afterwards corrected by slicing off a long narrow angular piece from three lots on the east side and adding like quantity of land to the opposite lot—it happening just here that the lots on the east side lie east and west while those on the west side lie north and south. After the third concession, the lots along the street lie uniformly east and west.

With young persons in general perhaps, at York in the olden time, who ever gave the cardinal points a thought, the notion prevailed that Yonge Street was 'north'. We well remember our own slight perplexity when we first distinctly took notice that the polar star, the dipper, and the focus usually of the northern lights, all seemed to be east of Yonge Street. That an impression existed in the popular mind at a late period to the effect that Yonge Street was north was shown when the pointers indicating east, west, north, and south came to be affixed to the apex of a spire on Gould Street. On that occasion several compasses had to be successively taken up and tried before the workmen could be convinced that 'north' was so far 'east' as the needle of each instrument would persist in asserting.

The first possessor of the lot on the west side, slightly augmented in the manner just spoken of, was the Baron de Hoen, an officer in one of the German regiments disbanded after the United States Revolutionary War. His name is also inscribed in the early maps of the adjacent lot to the north, known as No. 1 in the township of York, west side.

At the time of the capture of York in [April] 1813, Baron de Hoen's house on lot No. 1 proved a temporary refuge to some ladies and others, as we learn from a manuscript narrative taken down from the lips of the late venerable Mrs Breakenridge by her daughter, Mrs Murney. That record well recalls the period and the scene. 'The ladies settled to go out to Baron de Hoen's farm,' the narrative says. 'He was a great friend', it then explains, 'of the Baldwin family, whose real name was Von Hoen; and he had come out about the same time as Mr St George and had been in the British army. He had at this time a farm about four miles up Yonge Street and on a lot called No. 1. Yonge Street was then a corduroy road immediately after leaving King Street and passing through a dense forest. Miss Russell (sister of the late President Russell) loaded her phaeton with all sorts of necessaries so that the whole party had to walk. My poor old grandfather (Mr [Robert] Baldwin [Sr], the father of Mrs Breakenridge) by long persuasion at length consented to give up fighting and accompany the ladies. Aunt Baldwin (Mrs Dr Baldwin) and her four sons, Major Fuller, who was an invalid under Dr Baldwin's care, Miss Russell, Miss Willcox, and the whole cavalcade sailed forth: the youngest boy, St George, a mere baby, my mother (Mrs Breakenridge) carried on her back nearly the whole way.

'When they had reached about half way out,' the narrative proceeds, 'they heard a most frightful concussion, and all sat down on logs and stumps, frightened terribly. They learned afterwards that this terrific sound was occasioned by the blowing up of the magazine of York Garrison when five hundred Americans were killed, and at which time my uncle, Dr Baldwin, was dressing a soldier's wounds; he was conscious of a strange sensation: it was too great to be called a sound, and he found a shower of stones falling all around him, but he was quite unhurt. The family at length reached Baron de Hoen's log house consisting of two rooms, one above and one below. After three days Miss Russell and my mother walked into town just in time to prevent Miss Russell's house from being ransacked by the soldiers.

'All now returned to their homes and occupations,' the narrative goes on to say, 'except Dr Baldwin, who continued dressing wounds and acting as surgeon until the arrival of Dr Hackett, the surgeon of the 8th Regiment. Dr Baldwin said it was most touching to see the joy of the poor wounded fellows when told that their own doctor was coming back to them.' It is then added: 'My mother (Mrs Breakenridge) saw the poor 8th Grenadiers come into town on the Saturday, and in church on Sunday, with the handsome Captain McNeil at their head, and the next day they were cut to pieces to a man. My father (Mr Breakenridge) was a student at law with Dr Baldwin, who had been practising law after giving up medicine as a profession, and had been in his office about three months, when he went off like all the rest to the battle of York.'

The narrative then gives the further particulars: 'The Baldwin family all lived with Miss Russell after this, as she did not like being left alone. When the Americans made their second attack about a month after the first, the gentlemen all concealed themselves, fearing to be taken prisoners like those at Niagara. The ladies received the American officers: some of these were very agreeable men, and were entertained hospitably; two of them were at Miss Russell's; one of them was a Mr Bookes, brother-in-law of Archdeacon Stuart of Kingston. General Sheaffe had gone off some time before, taking every surgeon with him. On this account Dr Baldwin was forced, out of humanity, to work at his old profession again, and take care of the wounded.'

Lot No. 1 was afterwards the property of an English gentleman, Mr Hervey Price, a member of our Provincial Government as Commissioner of Crown Lands, whose conspicuous residence, castellated in character and approached by a broad avenue of trees, was a little further on. In 1820 No. 1 was being offered for sale in the following terms, in the *Gazette* of March 25th: 'That well known farm No. 1, west side of Yonge Street, belonging to Captain de Hoen, about four or five miles from York, 210 acres. The land is of excellent quality, well-wooded with about forty acres cleared, a never failing spring of excellent water, barn and farm house. Application to be made to the subscriber at York.—W. W. BALDWIN.'

Baron de Hoen was second to Mr Attorney-General White, killed in the duel with Mr Small in 1800 (January 3rd). In the contemporary account of that incident in the Niagara *Constellation,* the name is phonetically spelt *De Hayne.* In the above-quoted MS. the name appears as de Haine.

In our progress northward we now traverse ground which, as having been the scene of a skirmish and some bloodshed during the troubles of 1837, has become locally historic. The events alluded to have been described from different points of view at sufficient length in books within reach of everyone. We throw over them here the mantle of charity, simply glancing at them and passing on.

Upper Canada, in miniature and in the space of a half century, curiously passed through conditions and processes, physical and social, which old countries on a large scale and in the course of long ages passed through. Upper Canada had, in little, its primæval and barbaric but heroic era, its mediæval and high-prerogative era, and then, after a revolutionary period of a few weeks, its modern, defeudalized, democratic era. Without doubt the introduction here in 1790 of an 'exact transcript' of the contemporary constitution of the mother country, as was the boast at the time, involved the introduction here also of some of the spirit which animated the official administrators of that constitution in the mother country itself at the period—the time of the Third George.

We certainly find from an early date, as we have already seen, a succession of intelligent, observant men, either casual visitors to the country or else intending settlers and actual settlers, openly expressing dissatisfaction at some of the things which they noted, experienced, or learned, in respect of the management of Canadian public affairs. These persons for the most part were themselves perhaps only recently become alive to the changes which were inevitable in the governmental principles of the mother country; and so were peculiarly sensitive, and even, it may be, petulant in regard to such matters. But however well-meaning and advanced in political wisdom they may have been, they nevertheless, as we have before intimated, exhibited narrowness of view themselves and some ignorance of mankind in expecting to find in a remote colonial out-station of the empire a state of things better than that which at the moment existed at the heart of the empire; and in imagining that strictures on their part, especially when acrimonious, would under the circumstances be amiably and submissively received by the local authorities.

The early rulers of Canada, Upper and Lower, along with the members of their little courts, were not to be lightly censured. They were but copying the example of their royal Chief and his circle of Kew, Windsor, or St James'. Of the Third George, Thackeray says: 'He did his best; he worked according to his lights; what virtue he knew he tried to practise; what knowledge he could master he strove to acquire.' And so did they. The same fixity of idea in regard to the inherent dignity and power of the Crown that characterized him characterized them, together with a like sterling uprightness which commanded respect even when a line of action was adopted that seemed to tend, and did in reality tend, to a popular outbreak.

All men, however, now acquiesce in the final issue. The

social turmoil which for a series of years agitated Canada, from whatever cause arising; the explosion which at length took place, by whatever instrumentality brought on, cleared the political atmosphere of the country and hastened the good time of general contentment and prosperity which Canadians of the present day are enjoying. After all, the explosion was not a very tremendous one. Both sides after the event have been tempted to exaggerate the circumstances of it a little, for effect.

The recollections which come back to us as we proceed on our way are for the most part of a date anterior to those associated with 1837, although some of the latter date will of course occasionally recur.

The great conspicuous wayside inn, usually called Montgomery's, was at the time of its destruction by the Government forces in 1837 in the occupation of a landlord named Lingfoot. The house of Montgomery, from whom the inn took its name, he having been a former occupant, was on a farm owned by himself, beautifully situated on rising ground to the left, subsequently the property and place of abode of Mr James Lesslie, of whom already.

Mr Montgomery had once had a hotel in York named 'The Bird in Hand', on Yonge Street, a little to the north of Elliot's. We have this inn named in an advertisement to be seen in the *Canadian Freeman* of April 17, 1828, having reference to the 'Farmer's Store Company'. 'A general meeting of the Farmer's Storehouse Company', says the advertisement, 'will be held on the 22nd of March next, at 10 o'clock, a.m., at John Montgomery's tavern, on Yonge Street, "The Bird in Hand". The farmers are hereby also informed that the storehouse is properly repaired for the accommodation of storage, and that every possible attention shall be paid to those who shall store produce therein. JOHN GOESSMANN, *clerk.*'

The Farmer's Store was at the foot of Nelson [Jarvis] Street. Mr Goessmann was a well-known Deputy Provincial Surveyor, of Hanoverian origin. In an address published in the *Weekly Register* of July 15, 1824, on the occasion of his retiring from a contest for a seat in the House as representative for the counties of York and Simcoe, Mr Goessmann alluded as follows to his nationality: 'I may properly say', he observed, 'that I was a born British subject before a great number of you did even draw breath; and have certainly borne more oppressions during the late French war than any child of this country, that never peeped beyond the boundary even of this continent, where only a small twig of that all-crushing war struck. Our sovereign has not always been powerful enough to defend all his dominions. We, the Hanoverians, have been left the greater part during that contest, to our own fate; we have been crushed to yield our privileges to the subjection of Bonaparte, his greatest antagonist,' &c.

Eglinton, through which at the present day Yonge Street passes hereabout, is a curious stray memorial of the Tournament in Ayrshire which made a noise in 1839. The passages of arms on the farther side of the Atlantic that occasionally suggest names for Canadian villages are not always of so peaceful a character as that in the Earl of Eglinton's grounds in 1839, although it is a matter of some interest now to remember that even in that a Louis Napoleon figured, who at a later period was engaged in jousts of a rather serious kind, promoted by himself.[1]

We now speedily arrived at the commencement of the difficult descent into the valley of the great west branch of the Don [Hogg's Hollow]. Yonge Street here made a grand detour to the east and failed to regain the direct northerly course for some time. As usual, wherever long inclined planes were cut in the steep sides of lofty clay banks, the condition of the roadway hereabout was, after rain, indescribably bad. After reaching the stream and crossing it on a rough timber bridge, known anciently sometimes as Big Creek bridge and sometimes as Heron's bridge, the track ascended the further bank, at first by means of a narrow hogsback, which conveniently sloped down to the vale; afterwards it made a sweep to the northward

---

[1] Archibald, 13th Earl of Eglinton, held a mock medieval tournament at Eglinton Castle in August 1839 which cost £30-40,000 and received wide publicity. Louis Napoleon, the future Napoleon III of France (1852-70), was one of the participants.

along the brow of some broken hills, and then finally turned westward until the direct northern route of the street was again touched.

The banks of the Don are here on every side very bold, divided in some places into two stages by an intervening plateau. On a secondary flat thus formed, in the midst of a grass-grown clearing, to the left, as the traveller journeyed from York, there was erected at an early date the shell of a place of worship appertaining to the old Scottish Kirk, put up here through the zeal of Mr James Hogg, a member of that communion and the owner, for a time at least, of the flour mills in the valley near the bridge. From him this locality was popularly known as Hogg's Hollow, despite the postal name of the place, York Mills.

Mr Hogg was of Scottish descent and a man of spirit. He sent a cartel in due form in 1832 to Mr Gurnett, editor of the *Courier*. An article in that paper had spoken in offensive terms of supposed attempts on the part of a committee in York to swell the bulk of a local public meeting [on March 23] by inviting into town persons from the rural parts. 'Every wheel of their well-organized political machine was set in motion', the *Courier* asserted, 'to transmute country farmers into citizens of York. Accordingly about nine in the morning, groups of tall, broad-shouldered, hulking fellows were seen arriving from Whitby, Pickering and Scarborough, some crowded in waggons, and others on horseback; and Hogg, the miller, headed a herd of the swine of Yonge Street, who made just as good votes at the meeting as the best shopkeepers in York.' No hostile encounter, however, took place, although a burlesque account of an 'affair of honour' was published, in which it was pretended that Mr Hogg was saved from a mortal wound by a fortunate accumulation, under the lapel of his coat, of flour, in which his antagonist's bullet buried itself.

Mr Hogg died in 1839. Here is an extract from the sermon preached by the Rev. Mr Leach on the occasion of his funeral: 'He was faithful to his word and promise,' the preacher said, 'and when surrounded with danger and strongly instigated, and tempted to a departure from public faith by the enemies of his country his determination expressed in his own words, was "I will die a Briton." Few men had all the veins of nature more clearly and strongly developed; and few men had a better sense of what is due to God.'

The circuit of the hills overhanging the mills below was always tedious; but several good bits of scenery were caught sight of. On the upland, after escaping the chief difficulties, on the left hand a long low wooden building was seen, with gable and door towards the road. This was an early place of worship of the Church of England, an outpost of the mission at York [St John's York Mills]. The long line of its roof was slightly curved downwards by the weight of a short chimney built at its middle point for the accommodation of an iron stove within. Just before arriving at the gate of the burying-ground attached to this building, there were interesting glimpses to the left down into deep woody glens, all of them converging southward on the Don. In some of them were little patches of pleasant grassland. But along here, for the most part, the forest long remained undisturbed.

The church or chapel referred to was often served by divinity students sent out from town, and frequently, no doubt, had its walls echoed with prentice-attempts at pulpit oratory. Gourlay says that this chapel and the Friends' Meeting House near Newmarket were the only two places of public worship on Yonge Street in 1817, 'a distance of nearly forty miles'. A notice of it is inserted in *A Visit to the Province of Upper Canada in 1819, by James Strachan* (the Bishop's brother), a work published at Aberdeen in 1820.

'My brother', Mr Strachan says, 'had, by his exertions and encouragement among the people, caused a chapel to be built about eight miles from York, where he officiates once a month, one of the young students under his care reading the service and a sermon on the intermediate Sundays. On his day of doing duty,' Mr S. continues, 'I went with him and was highly gratified. The chapel is built in a thick wood. . . . The dimensions are 60 by 30 feet; the pews are very decent, and what was much better, they were filled with an attentive congregation. As you see very few inhabitants on your way out, I could not conceive where all the people came from.' A public baptism of five adults is then described.

Some six and twenty years later (in 1843), the foundation stone of a durable brick church was laid near the site of the old frame chapel.[2] On that occasion Dr Strachan, now Bishop Strachan, named as especial promoters of the original place of worship Mr Seneca Ketchum and Mr Joseph Shepard, 'the former devoting much time and money in the furtherance of the work, and the latter giving three acres of land as a site, together with a handsome donation in cash.' A silver medal which had been deposited under the old building was now transferred to a cavity in the foundation stone of its proposed successor. It bore on the obverse, 'Francis Gore, Esq., Lieutenant-Governor, 1816,' and on the reverse, 'Fifty-sixth of George Third.' To it were now added a couple of other medals of silver; one bore on the obverse 'John Strachan, D.D., Bishop of Toronto; Alexander Sanson, Minister, 1843' and on the reverse, 'Sixth of Victoria'. The other had inscribed on it the name of the architect, Mr J. G. Howard, with a list of other churches erected in Upper Canada under his direction.

Among the persons present during the ceremony were Chief Justice Robinson, Vice-Chancellor Jameson, the Hon. and Rev. A. Cavendish, and the Rev. G. Mortimer of Thornhill. Prior to the out-door proceedings, a remarkable scene had been witnessed within the walls of the old building. Four gentlemen received the rite of confirmation at the hands of the Bishop, all of them up to a recent date non-conformists: three of them non-conformist ministers of mark, Mr Townley, Mr Leach (whom we heard just now pronouncing an eulogy on Mr Hogg), and Mr Ritchie; the fourth, Mr Sanson, not previously a minister but now in Holy Orders of the Church of England and the minister appointed to officiate in the new church.

At the present day Yonge Street crosses Hogg's Hollow in a direct line on a raised embankment which the ancient Roman road-makers would have deemed respectable—a work accomplished about the year 1835 before the aid of steam power was

2 This structure forms the nave of the present church.

procurable in these parts for such purposes. Mr Lynn was the engineer in charge here at that time. The picturesque character of the valley has been considerably interfered with. Nevertheless a winding road over the hills to the right leading up to the church (St John's) has still some sylvan surroundings. In truth, were a building or two of the chalet type visible, the passer-by might fancy himself for a moment in an upland of the High Alps, so Swiss-like is the general aspect.

It may be added that the destruction of the beautiful hereabout has to some extent a set-off in the fine geological studies displayed to the eye in the sides of the deep cuts at both ends of the great causeway. Lake Ontario's ancient floor here lifted up high and dry in the air exhibits, stratum super stratum, the deposits of successive periods long ago. (The action of the weather, however, has at the present time greatly blurred the interesting pictures of the past formerly displayed on the surface of the artificial escarpments at Hogg's Hollow.)

XIV

THE

HARBOUR:

ITS

MARINE,

1793-1834

The first formal survey of the harbour of Toronto was made by Joseph Bouchette in 1793. His description of the bay and its surroundings at that date is, with the historians of Upper Canada, a classic passage. For the completeness of our narrative it must be produced once more. 'It fell to my lot,' says Bouchette, 'to make the first survey of York Harbour in 1793.' And he explains how this happened. 'Lieutenant-Governor, the late Gen. Simcoe, who then resided at Navy Hall, Niagara [-on-the-Lake], having', he says, 'formed extensive plans for the improvement of the colony, had resolved upon laying the foundations of a provincial capital. I was at that period in the naval service of the Lakes, and the survey of Toronto (York) Harbour was entrusted by his Excellency to my performance.'

He then thus proceeds—writing, we may observe, in 1831: 'I still distinctly recollect the untamed aspect which the country exhibited when first I entered the beautiful basin, which thus became the scene of my early hydrographical operations. Dense and trackless forests lined the margin of the lake and reflected their inverted images in its glassy surface. The wandering savage had constructed his ephemeral habitation beneath their luxuriant foliage—the group then consisting of two families of Mississagas—and the bay and neighbouring marshes were the hitherto uninvaded haunts of immense coveys of wild fowl. Indeed, they were so abundant,' he adds, 'as in some measure to annoy us during the night.' The passage is to be found in a note at p. 89 of volume one of the quarto edition of *The British Dominions in North America*, published in London in 1831.

Joseph Bouchette in 1793 must have been under twenty years of age. He was born in 1774. He was the son of Commodore Bouchette who in 1793 had command of the Naval Force on Lake Ontario. When Joseph Bouchette first entered the harbour of Toronto, as described above, he was not without associates. He was probably one of an exploring party which set out from Niagara in May 1793. It would appear that the Governor himself paid his first visit to the intended site of the capital of his young province on the same occasion.

In the *Gazette* of Thursday, May 9th, 1793, published at Newark or Niagara [-on-the-Lake], we have the following record: 'On Thursday last (this would be May the 3rd) his Excellency the Lieutenant-Governor, accompanied by several military gentlemen, set out in boats for Toronto, round the Head of the Lake Ontario, by Burlington Bay; and in the evening his Majesty's vessels the *Caldwell* and *Buffalo*, sailed for the same place.' Supposing the boats which proceeded round the head of the Lake to have arrived at the cleared spot where the French stockaded trading-post of Toronto had stood, on Saturday the 4th the inspection of the harbour and its surroundings by the Governor and 'military gentlemen' occupied a little less than a week; for we find that on Monday the 13th they are back again in safety at Niagara. The *Gazette* of Thursday, the 16th of May, thus announces their return: 'On Monday (the 13th) about 2 o'clock, his Excellency the Lieut.-Governor and suite arrived at Navy Hall from Toronto; they returned in boats round the Lake.'

It is probable that Bouchette was left behind, perhaps with the *Caldwell* and *Buffalo*, to complete the survey of the harbour. (In the work above named is a reduction of Bouchette's chart of the harbour with the soundings and bottom; also with lines shewing 'the breaking of the ice in the spring'. His minute delineation of the pinion-shaped peninsula of sand which forms the outer boundary of Toronto bay enables the observer to see very clearly how, by long-continued drift from the east, that barrier was gradually thrown up; as also how inevitable were the marshes at the outlet of the Don.)

The excursion from Niagara just described was the Governor's first visit to the harbour of Toronto, and we may suppose the *Caldwell* and the *Buffalo* to have been the first sailing-craft of any considerable magnitude that ever stirred its waters. In April 1793 the Governor had not yet visited Toronto. We learn this from a letter dated the 5th of that month, addressed by him to Major-General Clarke at Quebec. Gen. Clarke was the Lieut.-General in Lower Canada. Lord Dorchester, the Governor-General himself, was absent in England. 'Many American officers', Gen. Simcoe says to Gen. Clarke on the 5th of April, 'give it as their opinion that Niagara should be attacked and that Detroit must fall of course. I hope by this autumn,' he continues, 'to show the fallacy of this reasoning, by opening a safe and expeditious communication to La Tranche [the Thames River]. But on this subject I reserve myself till I have visited Toronto.'

The safe and expeditious communication referred to was the great military road, Dundas Street, projected by the Governor to connect the port and arsenal at Toronto with the Thames and Detroit.[1] It was in the February and March of this very same year, 1793, that the Governor had made, partly on foot and partly in sleighs, his famous exploratory tour through the woods from Niagara to Detroit and back with a view to the establishment of this communication.

On the 31st of May he is writing again to Gen. Clarke at Quebec. He has now, as we have seen, been at Toronto; and he speaks warmly of the advantages which the site appeared to him to possess. 'It is with great pleasure that I offer to you', he says, 'some observations upon the Military strength and Naval convenience of Toronto (now York), which I propose immediately to occupy. I lately examined the harbour,' he continues,

---

[1] Detroit at that time was still in British hands and Simcoe's objective in laying out Dundas Street was to prevent American interruption of communications to the west in case of war. Only the section of Dundas Street from Dundas itself to the site of Paris was laid out while Simcoe was governor.

'accompanied by such officers, naval and military, as I thought most competent to give me assistance therein, and upon minute investigation I found it to be, without comparison, the most proper situation for an arsenal, in every extent of that word, that can be met with in this Province.'

The words 'now York' appended here and in later documents to 'Toronto' show that an official change of name had taken place. The alteration was made between the 15th and 31st of May. No proclamation, however, announcing its change is to be found either in the local *Gazette* or in the archives at Ottawa.

Nor is there any allusion to the contemplated works at York either in the opening or closing speech delivered by the Governor to the houses of parliament, which met at Niagara for their second session on the 28th of May and were dismissed to their homes again on the 9th of the following July. We may suppose the minds of the members and other persons of influence otherwise prepared for the coming changes, chiefly perhaps by means of friendly conferences.

Soon after the prorogation, July the 9th, steps preparatory to a removal to York began to be taken. Troops, for example, were transported across to the north side of the Lake. 'A few days ago,' says the *Gazette* of Thursday, August the 1st, 1793, 'the first Division of his Majesty's Corps of Queen's Rangers left Queenston for Toronto—now York (it carefully added), and proceeded in batteaux round the head of the Lake Ontario by Burlington Bay. And shortly afterwards another division of the same regiment sailed in the King's vessels, the *Onondago* and *Caldwell*, for the same place.'

It is evident the Governor, as he expressed himself to Gen. Clarke in the letter of May 31st, is about 'immediately to occupy' the site which seemed to him so eligible for an arsenal and strong military post. Accordingly, having thus sent forward two divisions of the regiment whose name is so intimately associated with his own, to be a guard to receive him on his own arrival, and to be otherwise usefully employed, we find the Governor himself embarking for the same spot. 'On Monday evening (this would be Monday, the 29th of July),' the *Gazette* just quoted informs us, 'his Excellency the Lieutenant-Governor left Navy

Hall and embarked on board his Majesty's schooner, the *Missis-saga*, which sailed immediately with a favourable gale for York, with the remainder of the Queen's Rangers.' On the following morning, July 30, 1793, they would, with the aid of the 'favourable gale', be at anchor in the harbour of York.

We should have been glad of a minute account of each day's proceedings on the landing of the troops at York, and the arrival there of the Governor and his suite. But we can readily imagine the Rangers establishing themselves under canvas on the grassy glade where formerly stood the old French trading-post [Fort Rouillé]. We can imagine them landing stores—a few cannon and some other munitions of war—from the ships; landing the parts and appurtenances of the famous canvas-house which the Governor had provided for the shelter of himself and his family, and which, as we have before noted, was originally constructed for the use of Captain Cook in one of the scientific expeditions commanded by that celebrated circumnavigator.

It was known that hostilities were going on between the allied forces of Europe and the armies of Revolutionary France. And now came intelligence that the English contingent on the continent had contributed materially to a success over the French in Flanders on the 23rd of May last. Now this contingent, 10,000 men, was under the command of the Duke of York, the King's son. A happy thought strikes the Governor. What could be more appropriate than to celebrate the good news in a demonstrative manner on a spot which in honour of that Prince had been named YORK.

Accordingly on the 26th of August we find the following General Order issued: 'York, Upper Canada, 26th of August, 1793. His Excellency the Lieutenant-Governor having received information of the success of his Majesty's arms, under His Royal Highness the Duke of York, by which Holland has been saved from the invasion of the French armies,—and it appearing that the combined forces have been successful in dislodging their enemies from an entrenched camp supposed to be impregnable, from which the most important consequences may be expected; and in which arduous attempts His Royal Highness the Duke of York and His Majesty's troops supported the national glory:—It is His Excellency's orders that on the rising of the Union Flag at twelve o'clock to-morrow a Royal Salute of twenty-one guns is to be fired to be answered by the shipping in the Harbour, in respect to His Royal Highness and in commemoration of the naming this Harbour from his English title, YORK. E. B. LITTLEHALES, *Major of Brigade.*'

These orders, we are to presume, were punctually obeyed; and we are inclined to think that the running up of the Union Flag at noon on Tuesday, the 27th day of August, and the salutes which immediately after reverberated through the woods and rolled far down and across the silvery surface of the lake, were intended to be regarded as the true inauguration of the Upper Canadian YORK.

The rejoicing, indeed, as it proved, was somewhat premature. The success which distinguished the first operations of the royal duke did not continue to attend his efforts. Nevertheless, the report of the honours rendered in this remote portion of the globe would be grateful to the fatherly heart of the King.

On the Saturday after the Royal Salutes, the first meeting of the Executive Council ever held in York took place in the garrison—in the canvas-house, as we may suppose. 'The first Council,' writes Mr W. H. Lee from Ottawa, 'held at the garrison, York, late Toronto, at which Lieutenant-Governor Simcoe was present, was on Saturday, 31st August, 1793.' It transacted business there, Mr Lee says, until the following fifth of September when the Government returned to Navy Hall. Still, the Governor and his family passed the ensuing winter at York. Bouchette speaks of his inhabiting the canvas-house 'through the winter'; and under date of York, on the 23rd of the following February (1794), we have him writing to Mr Secretary Dundas.

In the dispatch of the day just named, after a now-prolonged experience of the newly established post, the Governor thus glowingly speaks of it: 'York', he says, 'is the most important and defensible situation in Upper Canada, or that I have seen', he even adds, 'in North America. I have, sir,' he continues, 'formerly entered into a detail of the advantages of this arsenal of Lake Ontario. An interval of Indian land of six and thirty miles divides this settlement from Burlington Bay, where that of Niagara commences. Its communication with Lake Huron is very easy in five or six days, and will in all respects be of the most essential importance.'

Before the channel at the entrance of the harbour of York was visibly marked or buoyed, the widespread shoal to the west and south must have been very treacherous to craft seeking to approach the new settlement. In 1794 we hear of the Commodore's vessel, 'the *Anondaga*, of 14 guns', being stranded here and given up for lost. We hear likewise that the Commodore's son, Joseph Bouchette, the first surveyor of the harbour, distinguished himself by managing to get the same *Anondaga* off after she had been abandoned; and we are told of his assuming the command and sailing with her to Niagara, where he is received amidst the cheers of the garrison and others assembled on the shores to greet the rescued vessel.

This exploit, of which he was naturally proud, and for which he was promoted on the 12th of May 1794 to the rank of Second Lieutenant, Bouchette duly commemorates on his chart of York Harbour by conspicuously marking the spot where the stranded ship lay, and appending the note—'H. M. Schooner *Anondaga*, 14 guns, wrecked, but raised by Lieutenant Joseph Bouchette and brought to.' (A small two-masted vessel is seen lying on the north-west bend of the great shoal at the entrance of the harbour.) A second point is likewise marked on the map 'where she again grounded but was afterwards brought to'. (Here again a small vessel is seen lying at the edge of the shoal, but now towards its northern point.) The Chart, which was originally engraved for Bouchette's octavo book, *A Topographical Description of Canada, &c.* published in 1815, is repeated with the marks and accompanying notes, from the same plate, in the quarto work of 1831—*The British Dominions of North America.* The *Anondaga* of the Bouchette narrative is, as we suppose, the *Onondago* of the *Gazette* which, as we have seen, helped to take over the Rangers in August 1793.

Bouchette was possibly recalling the commencement of the Public Buildings in 1794 when in his second work, published in 1831, he inserted the note which has given rise, in the minds of some, to a slight doubt as to whether 1793 or 1794 was the year

of the founding of York. The *Gazettes*, as we have seen, shew
that 1793 was the year. The *Gazettes* also shew that the so-
called Public Buildings—i.e., the Parliamentary Buildings—
were not begun until 1794. Thus in the *Gazette* of July 10, 1794,
we read the advertisement: 'Wanted: Carpenters for the Public
Buildings to be erected at York. Application to be made to
John McGill, Esq., at York, or to Mr Allan MacNab at Navy
Hall.'

In 1796 Governor Simcoe was ordered to the West Indies. He
met his Parliament at Newark on the 16th of May and prorogued it on the 3rd of June after assenting to seven Acts.

In the *Gazette* of Sept. 11, 1796, a proclamation from Peter
Russell announces that 'His most gracious Majesty has been
pleased to grant his royal leave of absence to his Excellency
Major General Simcoe,' and that consequently the government
pro tem. had devolved upon himself.

In the November following, Mr Russell, now entitled President, comes over from Niagara on the *Mohawk*. The *Gazette*
of Nov. 4, 1796 (still published at Niagara) announces: 'Yesterday (Nov. 3), his Honour the President of the Province and
family sailed in the *Mohawk* for York. On his departure he was
saluted with a discharge of cannon at Fort George, which was
answered by three cheers from on board.' (Fort George, afterwards famous in Canadian annals and whose extensive remains
are still conspicuous, had now been constructed, on the west
side of the river close by Newark or Niagara, as a kind of
counterpoise to the French Fort on the east side of the river
immediately opposite, which had just been surrendered to the
United States.)

It is briefly noted in the *Gazette* of the 26th of January in the
following year (1797) that the President's new house at York had
been destroyed by fire. This may account for his being at
Niagara in May (1797) and sailing over again in the *Mohawk* to
York, apparently to open Parliament. The *Gazette* of the 31st of
May 1797 says: 'On Saturday last, sailed in the *Mohawk* for
York, his Honour the Administrator, and several members of
the Parliament of the Province.'

In August 1799 Governor Hunter, lately appointed, arrived

in York Harbour in the *Speedy*. The Niagara *Constellation* of Aug. 23, 1799, gives us the information. It says: 'His Excellency, Governor Hunter, arrived at York on Friday morning last in the *Speedy*. On landing', we are told, 'he was received by a party of the Queen's Rangers; and at one o'clock p.m. was waited on at his Honour's the President's, by the military officers, and congratulated on his safe arrival and appointment to the government of the Province.'

Under date of York, Saturday, Sept. 14th, 1799, we have mention made in the *Gazette* of a new vessel. 'The *Toronto Yacht*, Capt. Baker,' the *Gazette* announces, 'will in the course of a few days be ready to make her first trip. She is', the *Gazette* says, 'one of the handsomest vessels of her size that ever swam upon the Ontario; and if we are permitted to judge from her appearance, and to do her justice, we must say she bids fair to be one of the swiftest sailing vessels. She is admirably calculated for the reception of passengers, and can with propriety boast of the most experienced officers and men. Her master-builder', it is subjoined, 'was a Mr Dennis, an American, on whom she reflects great honour.' This was Mr Joseph Dennis; and the place where the vessel was built was a little way up the Humber. (The name Dennis is carelessly given in the *Gazette* as Dennison.)

In the *Gazette* of Aug. 29th in this year (1801) we have the appointment of Mr Allan to the collectorship for the harbour of York. Thus runs the announcement: 'To the Public.—His Excellency the Lieutenant-Governor has been pleased to appoint the subscriber Collector of Duties at this Port, for the Home District: as likewise Inspector of Pot and Pearl Ashes and Flour. Notice is hereby given that the Custom House for entry will be held at my store-house at the water's edge, and that I will attend accordingly, agreeably to the Act. w. ALLAN, *York, 25th Aug., 1801*.'

In the *Gazette* of April [1802] a boat is advertised as about to make trips between York and the Head of the Lake. This is the advertisement: 'The subscriber will run a boat from York to the Head of the Lake once a week. The first departure will be

from York the 31st instant (on Wednesday), and from the Head
of the Lake on Saturday, every week. Any commands left with
Messrs Miles and Playter, and Mr Beman at York, and at the
Government House, Mr Bates; and Richard Beasly, Esq., at the
Head of the Lake, will be attended to with confidence and des-
patch. LEVI WILLARD, *York, 30th March, 1802.*'

The disappointment occasioned to merchants sometimes by
the uncertainty of communication between York and the outer
world in the stormy season may be conceived of from a postscript to an advertisement of Mr Quetton St George's in the
Gazette of Dec. 10, 1803. It says: 'Mr St George is very sorry, on
account of his customers, that he has not received his East
India Goods and Groceries: he is sure they are at Oswego; and
should they not arrive this season, they may be looked for early
in the spring.' It was tantalizing to suppose they were so near
York as Oswego and yet could not be had until the spring.

The principal incident connected with the marine of the
harbour of York in 1804 was the loss of the *Speedy*. We give the
contemporary account of the disaster from the *Gazette* of Saturday, Nov. 3, 1804.

'The following', the *Gazette* says, 'is as accurate an account of
the loss of the schooner *Speedy*, in His Majesty's service on
Lake Ontario, as we have been able to collect. The *Speedy*,
Capt. Paxton, left this port (York)[2] on Sunday evening, the 7th
of October last, with a moderate breeze from the north-west, for
Presqu'ile [off Brighton], and was descried off that island on the
Monday following before dark, where preparations were made
for the reception of the passengers, but the wind coming round
from the north-east, blew with such violence as to render it
impossible for her to enter the harbour; and very shortly after
she disappeared. A large fire was then kindled on shore as a
guide to the vessel during the night; but she has not since been
seen or heard of; and it is with the most painful sensations we
have to say, we fear is totally lost. Inquiry, we understand, has
been made at almost every port of the Lake, but without effect;
and no intelligence respecting the fate of this unfortunate ves-

---

[2] The *Gazette* had moved from Niagara-on-the-Lake to York in 1798.

sel could be obtained. It is, therefore, generally concluded that she has either upset or foundered. It is also reported by respectable authority that several articles, such as the compass-box, hencoop and mast, known to have belonged to this vessel, have been picked up on the opposite side of the Lake.—The passengers on board the ill-fated *Speedy*, as near as we can recollect,' the narrative goes on to say, 'were Mr Justice Cochrane; Robert I. D. Gray, Esq., Solicitor-General, and Member of the House of Assembly; Angus Macdonell, Esq., Advocate, Member of the House of Assembly; Mr Jacob Herchmer, Merchant; Mr John Stegman, Surveyor; Mr George Cowan, Indian Interpreter; James Ruggles, Esq.; Mr Anderson, Student in the Law; Mr John Fisk, High Constable, all of this place. The above-named gentlemen were proceeding to the District of Newcastle, in order to hold the Circuit, and for the trial of an Indian (also on board the *Speedy*) indicted for the murder of John Sharp, late of the Queen's Rangers. It is also reported, but we cannot vouch for its authenticity, that exclusive of the above passengers, there were on board two other persons, one in the service of Mr Justice Cochrane, and the other in that of the Solicitor-General; as also two children of parents whose indigent circumstances necessitated them to travel by land. The crew of the *Speedy*, it is said, consisted of five seamen (three of whom have left large families) exclusive to Captain Paxton, who also had a very large family. The total number of souls on board the *Speedy* is computed to be about twenty. A more distressing and melancholy event has not occurred to this place for many years; nor does it often happen that such a number of persons of respectability are collected in the same vessel. Not less than nine widows, and we know not how many children, have to lament the loss of their husbands and fathers, who, alas, have, perhaps in the course of a few minutes, met with a watery grave. It is somewhat remarkable', the *Gazette* then observes, 'that this is the third or fourth accident of a similar nature within these few years, the cause of which appears worthy the attention and investigation of persons conversant in the art of ship-building.'

We hear of the *Toronto Yacht* in 1805 casually. A boat puts off from her to the rescue of some persons in danger of drowning, near the Garrison at York, in November of that year. 'On Sunday last, the 10th,' says the *Gazette* of Nov. 16th, 1805, 'a boat from the River Credit for this place (York), containing four persons, and laden with salmon and country produce, over- set near the Garrison, at the entrance of this harbour; and not- withstanding the most prompt assistance rendered by a boat from the *Toronto Yacht*, we are sorry to add that one person was unfortunately drowned, and a considerable part of the cargo lost.' At this date the *Toronto Yacht* was under the com- mand of Capt. Earl.

In the *Gazette* of Oct. 11th, 1806, it is noted that Governor Gore crossed from York to Niagara in little more than four hours. The vessel is not named. Probably it was the *Toronto Yacht*.

The *Gazette* of October 31st, 1807, speaks of the incon- veniences to itself arising from the irregularity in the commun- ication between York and Niagara. 'The communication with Niagara by water,' it says, 'from being irregular lately, has prevented us receiving our papers this week. The Indian Express', the *Gazette* then adds, 'having commenced its regular weekly route, our publishing day will be changed to Wednesday. We have nothing of moment or interest. Should anything occur we will give an extra sheet.' On the 18th of November the *Gazette* appears printed on blue paper, such as used to be seen on the outside of pamphlets and magazines. An apology is offered. 'We have to apologize to our readers for the necessity of publishing this week on an inferior quality of paper, owing to the non-arrival of our expected supply.' The same kind of paper is used in a succession of numbers. It is curious to observe that the effect of time has been to produce less disfigurement in the bright appearance of the pages and print of the blue numbers of the *Gazette* than in the ordinary white paper numbers, which have now assumed a very coarse, dingy, inferior aspect.

In 1808 the important announcement is made in the *Gazette* of March 16th that a lighthouse is about to be immediately established on Gibraltar Point, at the entrance of York Harbour.[3] 'It is with pleasure we inform the public,' the *Gazette* says, 'that the dangers to vessels navigating Lake Ontario will in a great measure be avoided by the erection of a Lighthouse on Gibraltar Point, which is to be immediately completed, in compliance with an Address of the House of Assembly to the Lieutenant-Governor.'

We have understood that a lighthouse was begun at the point of York peninsula before the close of the last century; that the *Mohawk* was employed in bringing over stone for the purpose from Queenston; and that Mr John Thompson, still living in 1873, was engaged in the actual erection of the building. It was perhaps then begun [c. 1798]. In 1803 an Act passed by the Provincial Legislature for the establishment of lighthouses 'on the south-western-most point of a certain island called Isle Forest, situated about three leagues from the town of Kingston, in the Midland District; another upon Mississaga point, at the entrance of the Niagara river, near to the town of Niagara; and the other upon Gibraltar point.' It was probably not practicable to carry the Act fully into effect before 1806. According to the Act a fund for the erection and maintenance of such lighthouses was to be formed by levying three-pence per ton on every vessel, boat, raft, or other craft of ten tons' burthen and upwards doubling the point named, inward bound. That lighthouse duty should be levied at ports where there was no lighthouse became a grievance, and in 1818 it was enacted that 'no vessel, boat, raft or other craft of the burthen of ten tons and upwards shall be liable to pay any Lighthouse Duty at any port where there shall be no lighthouse erected, any law or usage to the contrary notwithstanding.'

In June 1808 Governor Gore departs from York for a tour in the western part of the Province. The *Gazette* seems mildly to rebuke him for having swerved from his first design in regard to this tour. He had intended to proceed *via* Lake Huron; that is, by the Yonge Street route, but he had finally preferred to go *via* Lake Ontario. 'His Excellency the Lieut.-Governor left this

---

[3] This is the lower portion of the lighthouse that still may be seen on the Island. It was remodelled and its height increased in 1832.

place, York', the *Gazette* announces, 'on the 15th instant, on a visit to Sandwich, etc. We are sorry', the editor then ventures to observe, 'that he did not, as he originally destined, proceed by Lake Huron, according to his amiable intention and view of promoting the first interests of this province.'

A postal notice issued in the *Gazette* of Jan. 4th in the following year, 1809, is interesting now. It reads thus: 'For General Information. The winter mail will be dispatched from Quebec for Upper Canada on the following days: Monday, 2nd Jan., 1809: do. 6th Feb.: do. 6th March: do. 3rd April. Each mail may be looked for here (York) from 16 to 18 days after the above periods. The Carrier from Kingston (the Indian Express) [the mail stage] is to go on to Niagara without making any stay (unless found necessary) at this place; so that any persons will have time to prepare their letters by the time he returns from Kingston again. w. ALLAN, *Deputy* P. M., *York, 2nd Jan. 1809.*' The mail between Montreal and Kingston was carried on the back of one Anderson. Between these two places the postage was nine-pence.

Between 1809 and 1812 we do not light upon many notices of vessels frequenting York Harbour. In 1810 a schooner called the *Lady Gore* or the *Bella Gore*, commanded by Captain Sanders and plying to Kingston, was a well-known vessel. (It may be noted that in 1811 Governor Gore left York for England, on leave of absence, and was away during the four eventful years that followed.) In 1812 and previously a sloop commanded by Captain Conn was running between York and Niagara. From some peculiarity in her contour, she was popularly spoken of as 'Captain Conn's Coffin'. Another sloop, commanded by Captain Grace, was plying between York, Niagara, and Kingston about the same time.

The government vessels with whose names we have become familiar were now either unseaworthy or wrecked. The *Mohawk,* the *Onondaga,* the *Caldwell,* the *Sophia,* the *Buffalo,* are no longer heard as passing in and out of the harbour of York. It had been the fate of the *Toronto Yacht,* while under the command of Capt. Fish, to run on the sands at Gibraltar Point through a mistake as to the position of the light. Her skeleton was long a conspicuous object, visited by ramblers on the Island. This incident occurred just before the outbreak of the war.

Most of the vessels which had been engaged in the ordinary traffic of the Lake were, during the war, employed by the government in the transport service.

The *Moira* was lying off the Garrison at York when the *Simcoe* transport came in sight filled with prisoners taken on Queenston Heights [1812], and bringing the first intelligence of the death of General Brock. We have heard the Rev. Dr Richardson of Toronto, who at the time was Sailing Master of the *Moira* under Captain Sampson, describe the scene. The approaching schooner was recognized at a distance as the *Simcoe*: it was a vessel owned and commanded, at the moment, by Dr Richardson's father, Captain James Richardson. Mr Richardson accordingly speedily put off in a boat from the *Moira* to learn the news. He was first startled at the crowded appearance of the *Simcoe's* deck and at the unwonted guise of his father who came to the gangway conspicuously girt with a sword. A great battle had been fought, he was told, on Queenston Heights. The enemy had been beaten. The *Simcoe* was full of prisoners of war, to be transferred instanter to the *Moira* for conveyance to Kingston. General Brock was killed! Elated with the first portion of the news, Dr Richardson spoke of the thrill of dismay which followed the closing announcements as something indescribable and never to be forgotten.

Among the prisoners on board the *Simcoe* was Windfield Scott, an artillery officer, afterwards the distinguished General Scott. He was not taken to Kingston but with others released on parole.

The year following (1813), York Harbour was visited by the United States fleet, consisting of sixteen vessels. The result other pages will tell. It has been again and again implied in these papers. The government vessel named the *Prince Regent* narrowly escaped capture. She had left port only a few days before the arrival of the enemy. The frames of two ships on the stocks were destroyed, but not by the Americans. At the command of General Sheaffe, they were fired by the royal troops when beginning the retreat in the direction of Kingston. A schooner, the *Governor Hunter*, belonging to Joseph Kendrick, was caught in the harbour and destroyed; but as we have understood, the American commander paid a sum of money to the owner by way of compensation. At the taking of York, Captain Sanders, whom we have seen in command of the *Bella Gore*, was killed. He was put in charge of the dockyardmen who were organized as a part of the small force to be opposed to the invaders.

Soon after the close of the war with the United States in 1814, the era of steam navigation on Lake Ontario opens. The first steamer, the *Frontenac*, was launched at Ernesttown on the Bay of Quinté in 1816. Her trips began in 1817. The length of her deck was 170 feet; the breadth 32 feet; her burden 700 tons; her cost £15,000; her commander, Capt. James McKenzie, a retired officer of the Royal Navy.

In successive numbers of the Kingston *Chronicle*, the advertisement of the *Frontenac*, occupying the width of two columns, conspicuously appears with a large rude woodcut of a steamer with two smoke-pipes at the top. For the sake of the fares and other particulars, we copy this document (from the *Chronicle* of April 30, 1819). 'The Steamboat *Frontenac*, James McKenzie, Master, will in future leave the different ports on the following days: viz., Kingston for York, on the 1st, 11th and 21st days of each month. York for Queenston, 3rd, 13th and 23rd days of each month. Niagara for Kingston, 5th, 15th and 25th days of each month. Rates of Passages: From Kingston to York and Niagara, £3. From York to Niagara, £1. Children under three years of age, half-price; above three, and under ten, two-thirds. A Book will be kept for entering the names of passengers, and the berths which they may choose at which time the passage money must be paid. Passengers are allowed sixty pounds weight of baggage; surplus baggage to be paid for at the usual rate. Gentlemen's servants cannot sleep or eat in the Cabin. Deck passengers will pay fifteen shillings, and may either bring their own provisions, or be furnished by the Steward. For each dog brought on board, five shillings. All application for passage to be made to Capt. McKenzie, on board. Freight will be transported to and from the above places at the rate of four shilling per barrel bulk, and Flour at the customary rate delivered to the different consignees. A list of their names will be put in a conspicuous place on board, which must be deemed a sufficient notice; and the Goods, when taken from the Steamboat will be considered at the risk of the owners. For each small parcel 2s. 6d., which must be paid on delivery. *Kingston, April 28th, 1819.'*

In 1820 a Traveller, whose journal is quoted by Willis in Bartlett's *Canadian Scenery* (ii. 48), was six days in accomplishing the journey from Prescott to York by water. 'On the 3rd of September,' he says, 'we embarked for York at Prescott, on board a small schooner called the *Caledonia*. We performed this voyage, which is a distance of 250 miles, in six days.' In 1818 Mr M. F. Whitehead of Port Hope was two days and a half in crossing from Niagara to York. 'My first visit to York', Mr Whitehead says in a communication to the writer, 'was in September, 1818, crossing the Lake from Niagara with Dr Baldwin—a two-and-a-half days' passage. The Doctor had thoughtfully provided a leg of lamb, a loaf of bread, and a bottle of porter: all our fare', adds Mr Whitehead, 'for two days and a-half.' We have ourselves more than once in former days experienced the horrors of the middle passage between Niagara and York, having crossed and re-crossed in very rough weather in the Kingston packet or *Brothers*, and having been detained on the Lake for a whole night and a good portion of a day in the process. The schooners for Niagara and elsewhere used to announce the time of their departure from the wharf at York in primitive style by repeated blasts from a long tin horn, so called, sounded at intervals previous to their casting loose and at the moment of the start. Fast and large steamers have of course now reduced to a minimum the miseries of a voyage between the north and south shores; but these miseries are still not slight at the stormy seasons, when Lake Ontario often displays a mood by no means amiable—

> *Outrageous as a sea, dark, wasteful, wild*
> *Up from the bottom turned by furious winds*
> *And surging waves.*

Again, the mode in which the first lake steamers were made to
near the landing-place in the olden time was something which
would fill a modern steamboat captain with amazement. Accustomed as we are every day to see huge steamers guided without any ado straight up to the margin of a quay or pier, the
process of putting in seems a simple affair. Not so was it, however, in practice to the first managers of steamboats. When the
Frontenac or *William IV* was about to approach the warf at
York, the vessel was brought to a standstill some way out in the
harbour. From near the fore and after gangways, boats were
then lowered bearing hawsers; and by means of these, when
duly landed, the vessel was solemnly drawn to shore. An agitated multitude usually witnessed the operation.

In the *Gazette* of July 20, 1820, we have the information that
'on Saturday evening, a schooner of about sixty tons, built for
Mr Oates and others, was launched in this port (York). She
went off', the *Gazette* says, 'in very fine style, until she reached
the water, where, from some defect in her ways, her progress was
checked; and from the lateness of the hour, she could not be
freed from the impediment before the next morning, when she
glided into the Bay in safety. Those who are judges say that it
is a very fine vessel of the class. It is now several years', continues
the *Gazette*, 'since any launch has been here; it therefore,
though so small a vessel, attracted a good deal of curiosity.' This
was the *Duke of Richmond* packet, afterwards a favourite on the
route between York and Niagara. The *Gazette* describes the
Richmond somewhat incorrectly as a schooner and likewise
understates the tonnage. She was a sloop of the Revenue cutter
build, and her burthen was about one hundred tons. Of Mr
Oates we have had occasion to speak in our perambulation of
King Street.

In an *Observer* of 1820 we have the first advertisement of the
Richmond. It reads thus: 'The *Richmond* Packet, Edward
Oates, commander, will commence running between the Ports
of York and Niagara on Monday, the 24th instant (July), as a
regular Packet. She will leave York on Mondays, Wednesdays
and Fridays, at 9 o'clock a.m., precisely; and Niagara on Tues-
days, Thursdays and Saturdays, at 10 a.m., to the 24th of Sep-

tember, when the hour of departure will be made known to the
Public. The *Richmond* has excellent accommodations for
Ladies, Gentlemen and other Passengers, and nothing will be
omitted to make her one of the completest and safest passage
vessels of the class in America, being manned with experienced
mariners. Rates of passage: after Cabin, 10s.; Fore Cabin, 6s. 3d.
Children under twelve years, half-price. Sixty pounds baggage
allowed to each passenger; above that weight, 9d. per cwt., or
2s. per barrel bulk. For freight or passage apply to John Crooks,
Esq., Niagara; the Captain on board; or at the Subscriber's store.
ED. OATES, *York, July 17, 1820.'*

Captain Vavassour, commandant at Fort George, presented
Capt. Oates with a gun and a set of colours. The former used to
announce to the people of York the arrival and departure of the
Richmond; and a striped signal-flag found among the latter was
hoisted at the lighthouse on Gibraltar Point whenever the *Richmond* Packet hove in sight. (For a considerable period all vessels were signalized by a flag flying from the lighthouse.)

As the *Richmond* packet filled an important place in the
early marine of the harbour, it will be of interest to mention
her ultimate fate. While engaged in 1826 in conveying a cargo
of salt from Oswego, she was wrecked near Brighton, on the
bay of Presqu'île, towards the eastern part of Lake Ontario.
The Captain, no longer Mr Oates, losing his presence of mind
in a gale of wind, cut the cable of his vessel and ran her ashore.
The remains of the wreck, after being purchased by Messrs
Willman, Bailey and Co., were taken to Wellington on the
south side of the peninsula of Prince Edward county, where the
cannon which had ornamented the deck of the defunct packet,
and had for so many years daily made the harbour of York re-
sound with its detonations, did duty in firing salutes on royal
birthdays and other public occasions up to 1866, when, being
overcharged, it burst, the fragments scattering themselves far
and wide in the waters round the wharf at Wellington.

Just as the *Richmond* disappears, another favourite vessel, for
some years distinguished in the annals of York Harbour and
commanded by a man of note, comes into the field of view. 'The
new steamer *Canada'*, says the *Loyalist* of June 3, 1826, 'was

towed into port this week by the *Toronto*, from the mouth of
the river Rouge, where she was built during the last winter.
She will be shortly fitted up for her intended route, which, we
understand, will be from York and Niagara round the head of
the lake, and will add another to the increasing facilities of
conveyance in Upper Canada.' The *Loyalist* then adds: 'Six
steamboats now navigate the St Lawrence and Lake Ontario, in
this Province, besides the *Canada*, and a boat nearly ready for
launching at Brockville.' We shall presently hear much of the
career of the *Canada* and her commander.

The *Toronto* (Capt. Shaw), named above as towing the
Canada into the harbour, was a steam-packet of peculiar make,
built at York. She was constructed without any difference of
shape at the bow and stern, and without ribs. She was a shell of
successive layers of rather thin boards placed alternately lengthwise and athwart, with coatings between of stout brown paper
pitched. She proved a failure as a vessel for the Lake traffic, and
was speedily taken down the river, where she was also unfortunate. We hear of her in the *Loyalist* of June 17, 1826. 'By
a letter', the Editor says, 'received from Kingston we are sorry
to hear that the steamboat *Toronto*, on her first trip from that
place to Prescott, had unfortunately got aground several times,
and that in consequence it had been found necessary to haul
her out of the water at Brockville, to be repaired. The damage
is stated not to be very great, but the delay, besides occasioning
inconvenience, must be attended with some loss to the proprietors.'

The *Frontenac* is still plying to York. In 1826 she brings up
the Lieut.-Governor, Sir Peregrine Maitland, from Kingston.
The following week she brings over from Niagara Col. Mc-
Gregor and the 70th Regiment. The *Loyalist* of June 10, 1826,
thus speaks. 'We have much pleasure in announcing the arrival
in this place of the Head Quarter Division of the 70th Regiment, under the command of Lieut.-Col. McGregor. They
landed from the steamboat *Frontenac* yesterday morning and
marched into the York Garrison.' It was on this occasion that
many of the inhabitants of York beheld for the first time the
impressive sight of a Highland regiment, wearing the kilt and

the lofty plumed cap. A full military band, too, which accompanies only Head Quarter Divisions, was a novelty at York; as previous to this year Niagara and not York, was regarded as Military headquarters. The Pipers increased the excitement. The band of the 70th displayed, moreover, at this period further accessories of pomp and circumstance in the shape of Negro cymbal players and a magnificent oriental-looking standard of swaying tails surmounted by a huge glittering crescent bearing small bells.

In the *Loyalist* [August 12, 1826] we hear again of Capt. Richardson's new steamboat, the *Canada*. We read of her first passage across from York to Niagara thus: 'The new steamboat *Canada*, Capt. Richardson, made her first trip to Niagara on Monday last, and went out of the harbour in fine style. Her appearance reflects much credit on her builder, Mr Joseph Dennis; and the machinery, manufactured by Messrs Wards of Montreal, is a specimen of superior workmanship. The combined excellence of the model and machinery of this boat is such', says the *Loyalist*, 'as will render her what is usually termed "a fast boat". The trip to Niagara was performed in four hours and some minutes. Her present route, we observe, is advertised from York to Niagara and the Head of the Lake. In noticing this first trip of another steamboat,' continues the *Loyalist*, 'we cannot help contrasting the present means of conveyance with those ten years ago. At that time only a few schooners navigated the Lake, and the passage was attended with many delays and much inconvenience. Now there are five steamboats, all affording excellent accommodation, and the means of expeditious travelling. The routes of each are so arranged that almost every day of the week the traveller may find opportunities of being conveyed from one extremity of the Lake to the other in a few hours. The *Niagara* and *Queenston* from Prescott, and the *Frontenac* from Kingston once a week, and the *Canada* and *Martha Ogden* between York and Niagara and the Head of the Lake every day, afford facilities of communication which the most sanguine could scarcely have anticipated at the period we speak of. Independent of these boats, it must be mentioned that the *Cornwall* on Lake St Louis makes a trip every day from Côteau du Lac to Cornwall; the *Dalhousie* runs between Prescott and Kingston twice a week and conveys the mail; the *Charlotte* and *Toronto* once a week from Prescott to the Head of the Bay of Quinté; thus affording to every part of the country the same advantages of convenient intercourse. These are some of the evidences of improvement among us during the last few years which require no comment. They speak for themselves, and it must be pretty evident from such facts as these, that those who cannot, or will not, see the progress we are making, must be wilfully blind.' (The closing remark was of course for the benefit of contemporary editors at York and elsewhere who from their political view of things gave their readers the impression that Canada was a doomed country, going rapidly to perdition.)

In the *Loyalist* for May 5, 1827, we have the following notice: 'The *Canada* British Steam-Packet, Capt. Hugh Richardson, leaves Niagara daily for York at 7 o'clock in the morning, and starts from York for Niagara every day at 2 o'clock in the afternoon. The *Canada* crosses the Lake in the short space of four hours and a half, and affords travellers arriving at the Falls an expeditious and convenient opportunity of visiting the Capital of Upper Canada. Fare: Cabin passage, two dollars; Deck and Fore Cabin, one dollar. Passengers returning immediately with the boat will only pay half of the above prices for the return. HUGH RICHARDSON, *Managing Owner, York, April 21, 1827.*'

On December 1st, the *Loyalist* announces that 'the *Canada* Steam Boat made her last trip from Niagara on Tuesday, and is now laid up for the winter.' In the following spring, on the 27th of March, she takes over Sir Peregrine Maitland. 'His Excellency the Lieutenant-Governor and family left York,' says the *Loyalist* of March 29, 1828, 'on Thursday morning for Stamford. His Excellency embarked on board the *Canada* Steam Packet under a salute from the Garrison.' A communication from the Captain appears in the *Loyalist* of the 12th of April, having reference to this trip. He replies to some strictures [by Mackenzie] in the *Colonial Advocate* on some alleged exclusiveness exhibited by Sir Peregrine while crossing the Lake in the *Canada*. 'Having observed in the *Colonial Advocate* of the 3rd of

April, under the head of Civilities, that His Excellency the Lieutenant-Governor engaged the whole of the two cabins of the *Canada* for himself and family, and would not allow even the Members of Assembly who were returning home to go over that day, except as deck passengers, I have to declare the same an impudent falsehood. His Excellency having condescended to intimate to me his desire to remove his family and household as early as possible, I hastened the equipment of the *Canada* expressly on His Excellency's account, contrary to my intentions, and the requisite delay for outfit until 1st April. To all applications for passage on the day fixed for His Excellency's embarkation I replied, I considered the vessel at His Excellency's orders. The moment His Excellency came on board, and understood that I was excluding passengers, I received His Excellency's orders to take on board every passenger that wished to embark. The only further intimation I received of His Excellency's pleasure was, on my application to know if I should stop at Niagara, I received for answer that His Excellency had no desire to stop there, but if I wished it, it could make no difference to His Excellency. Born and bred under a Monarchical Government, educated in the discipline of a British seaman, I have not yet learned the insolence of elbowing a desire (in right, an order) of the Representative of my Sovereign, by an impertinent wish of my own. I have only to say that as long as I command the *Canada*, and have a rag of colour to hoist, my proudest day will be when it floats at her mast-head indicative of the presence and commands of the Representative of my King. HUGH RICHARDSON, *Master and Managing Owner of the* Canada *Steam-Packet. April 11th, 1828.* P.S. Perhaps Dr Lefferty being a Member on the right side, who embarked on board the *Canada*, and who did me the honour of a call a night or two before, for information, may confirm this.'

Captain Richardson, as we can see, was a man of chivalrous temperament. His outward physique, moreover, corresponded with his character. His form was lithe, graceful, and officer-like. It was not alone when the Governor of the Province happened to be present that established distinctions in society were required to be observed on board the *Canada* steam-packet. At all times he was particular on this point. This brought him into collision occasionally with democratically disposed spirits, especially from the opposite side of the Lake; but he did not scruple to maintain his rules by main force when extreme measures were necessary, calling to his aid the stout arms of a trusty crew.

In the *Loyalist* of June 28, 1828, the arrival in York Harbour of the steamer lately launched at Niagara as successor to the *Frontenac* is noticed. She is named the *Alciope*. Alciope is a singular name, taken as we suppose from the Greek mythology, betokening, it may have been thought, one of the Nereids, although we are not aware that the name occurs on the roll of that very large family. One of the several wives of the mighty Hercules was a daughter of Alciopus; she consequently may be conceived to have been an Alciope. But how Mr Hamilton, of Queenston, or Captain McKenzie, came to think of such a *recherché* name for the new steamer is a mystery which we wish we could clear up. It is certain that the selection led to mispronunciations and misconceptions on the part of the general public. By the unlearned she was usually spoken of as the *Alciope*, of course. By a kind of antagonism among the unwashed she was the *All-soap*. In a similar way, Captain McIntosh's vessel, the *Eunice*, which frequented the harbour at an early period, was almost always popularly and excusably termed the *Euneece*.

From the *Loyalist* of September 27, 1828, we learn that Mr George Savage has been appointed to the Collectorship of the port of York.[4] He himself announces the fact to the public in the following advertisement: 'His Excellency the Lieutenant-Governor having been pleased to appoint me to the Collectorship of Customs for this port, I beg leave to acquaint the merchants, shipowners, and others having business to transact with this branch of the revenue after the first day of October next, that I have temporarily established an office in part of the premises fronting on Duke Street, occupied by Mr Columbus.

---

4 Succeeding William Allan who had held the post for twenty-seven years.

GEORGE SAVAGE, *Collector. York, 26th September, 1828.'* Bulky in form and somewhat consequential in manner, Mr Savage was a conspicuous figure in York down to the time of his death in 1835, when he was succeeded by Mr Thos. Carfrae. Mr Savage was, as his office required him to be, vigilant in respect of the dues leviable at the Port of York. But the contrabandists were occasionally too adroit for him. We have heard of a number of kegs or barrels, supposed to contain spirits, confidentially reported to him as sunk in the depths of the bay near one of the wharves, which kegs or barrels, when carefully fished up and conveyed to Mr Mosley's rooms to be disposed of by auction, were found on being tapped to contain harmless water; but while Mr Savage and his men were busily engaged in making this profitless seizure, the real wares—teas, spirits, and so on—which were sought to be illicitly introduced, were landed without molestation in Humber Bay. The practice of smuggling was, we believe, rather rife in and about the harbour of York in the olden time. In a *Gazette* of 1820 (Nov. 30), we observe the schooner *Industry* advertised for sale by the Custom House authorities as having been taken in the act; and on the 17th of October 1821, Mr Allan reports to the magistrates at Quarter Sessions that he had seized ten barrels of salt in which were found concealed kegs of tobacco to the value of five pounds and upwards, brought to York from the United States in an American schooner, called the *New Haven*, A. Johnson, master. The Magistrates declared the whole forfeited to the 'King'.

It was in 1834 the grand old name Toronto was recovered by the harbour and town, whose early marine we have sought in some degree to recall.

HOC OPUS EXEGI; FESSÆ DATE SERTA CARINÆ
CONTIGIMUS PORTUM, QUO MIHI CURSUS ERAT.

[THIS WORK I'VE ENDED; GRANT THE WEARY SHIP TO BE WITH GARLANDS CROWNED; WE'VE REACHED THE HAVEN WHITHER I WAS BOUND.]

APPENDIX I:
THE
PIONEERS

In 1869, the survivors of the early occupants of York, Upper
Canada, formed themselves into a Society entitled The Pioneers, for the joint purpose of mutual conference and of gathering together and preserving whatever memorials of the local
past might be found to be yet extant. The names of the members of this Association are subjoined, all of whom were resident at York, customably, or occasionally, at some period prior
to March 6th, 1834, when the name of the town was changed to
Toronto. The date which precedes each group shows the year
in which the members included in the group became identified
with York, whether by birth or otherwise. In numerous instances, the father of the individual named in the following list,
having been the establisher of a family in these parts and its
first breadwinner here, was the true pioneer. (By a change in
the original constitution of the Society, the sons and descendants of the first members of the Association and of all the first
grantees or occupants of land in the county of York, as defined
in 1798, are, on their attaining the age of 40 years, eligible to
be members.)

1794—EDWARD SIMCOE WRIGHT, Toronto.—ISAAC WHITE, do.

1795—Lieut FRANCIS BUTTON, Buttonville.

1797—JOHN THOMPSON, Toronto.

1798—Hon. W. B. ROBINSON, Toronto.—JOHN BRIGHT, do.

1799—JOHN W. GAMBLE, Pine Grove, Vaughan.

1800—ANDREW HERON, Toronto.—CORNELIUS VAN NOSTRAND,
Yonge Street.

1801—ROBERT BRIGHT, Toronto.

1805—JOHN MURCHISON, Toronto.

1806—Hon. H. J. BOULTON, Toronto.—WILLIAM CAWTHRA,
do.—JOHN RIDOUT, do.

1808—Rev. SALTERN GIVINS, Toronto.—ALLAN MACDONELL, do.—JOSEPH GOULD, ex-M.P.P., Uxbridge.—JAMES MARSHALL, Youngstown, N.Y.

1809—Judge G. S. JARVIS, Cornwall.—WILLIAM ROE, Newmarket.

1810—Rev. WILLIAM MACMURRAY, D.D., Niagara.—RICHARD P. WILLSON, Holland Landing.

1811—GEORGE BOSTWICK, Yorkville.—JOSEPH LAWRENCE, Collingwood.—Rev. D. McMULLEN, Picton.

1812—FRANCIS H. HEWARD, Toronto.—WILLIAM DOUGALL, Picton.

1813—R. E. PLAYTER, Toronto.—GEORGE SNIDER, M.P.P., Owen Sound.—Capt. THOMAS G. ANDERSON, Cobourg.

1814—Lieut.-Col. RICHARD L. DENISON, Toronto.—HENRY B. HEWARD, do.

1815—R. G. ANDERSON, Toronto.—GEORGE MONRO, do.—Dr GEORGE CRAWFORD, do.

1816—Col. GEORGE T. DENISON, Toronto.—Ven. Archdeacon FULLER, do.—Lieut.-Col. W. M. BUTTON, Buttonville.—Capt. ROBERT BROCK PLAYTER, Queenston.—THOMAS MONTGOMERY, Etobicoke.

1817—R. H. OATES, Toronto.—CHARLES STOTESBURY, do.—Sheriff B. W. SMITH, Barrie.—ROBERT PETCH, Toronto.—J. W. DRUMMOND, do.—ALEX. STEWART, do.—JAMES STAFFORD, do.

1818—JAMES BEATY, M.P., Toronto.—J. O. BOUCHIER, Georgina.—JOHN DOEL, senior, Toronto.—JOHN DOEL, junior, do.—JAMES GEDD, do.—THOMAS HUMPHREY, do.—JOHN HARPER, do.—JOHN MOORE, do.—WILLIAM REYNOLDS, do.—JAMES SPARKS, do.

1819—W. B. PHIPPS, Toronto.—GRANT POWELL, Ottawa.—F. H. MEDCALF, Toronto, ex-Mayor.—ROBERT H. SMITH, Newmarket.—JOHN RAPER, Toronto.—JOHN B. BAGWELL, Hamilton.

1820—W. J. COATES, Toronto.—ALEXANDER HAMILTON, do.—CLARKE GAMBLE, do.—Hon. J. G. SPRAGGE, do.—W. H. LEE, Ottawa.—Dr JOHN TURQUAND, Woodstock.—CHARLES L. HELLIWELL, Stayner.—WILLIAM HELLIWELL, Highland Creek.—EDWARD MUSSON, Toronto.—THOMAS J. WALLIS, do.

1821—Lieut.-Col. ROBERT B. DENISON, Toronto.—WILLIAM BARBER, M.P.P., Springfield.—HENRY SPROATT, Toronto.—JOHN EASTWOOD, Port Elgin.—EDWARD C. FISHER, Humber.—WILLIAM DUNCAN, York Township.—JONATHAN SCOTT, Toronto.—CHARLES SCADDING, do.— Rev. Dr SCADDING, do.

1822—Lieut.-Col. FREDERICK WELLS, Davenport.—STEPHEN M. JARVIS, Toronto.—JOHN HELLIWELL, do.

1823—Hon. DAVID REESOR, Markham.—Major JOHN PAUL, Weston.—JOHN SMALL, M.D., Toronto.—JAMES McMULLEN, do. —Alderman ADAMSON, do.—JAMES DUNCAN, York Township.

1824—Rev. Dr RICHARDSON, Toronto.—MATTHEW TEEFY, Richmond Hill.—JOHN BELL, Toronto.—CHARLES LOUNT, do.— ROBERT YOUNG, Georgetown.—RUFUS SKINNER, Toronto.

1825—ALLAN McLEAN HOWARD, Toronto.—D. O. BROOKE, do.—THOMAS HELLIWELL, do.—THOMAS ARMSTRONG, do.—JAMES TAYLOR, Eglinton.

1826—JAMES STITT, Toronto.—ISHMAEL IREDALE, do.—DAVID BURNS, do.—ALEX. CAIRD, Weston.

1827—Col. KINGSMILL, Toronto.—STEPHEN HEWARD, do.— WILLIAM HEWITT, do.—H. B. HOLLAND, do.—GEO. LESLIE, Leslieville.—W. L'ESTARGE, Toronto.—THOMAS J. PRESTON, do.— WILLIAM H. DOEL, do.—ANDREW SIEBER, do.

1828—JAMES BARKER, Georgetown.—H. R. CORSON, Markham. —MATTHEW DREW, Toronto.—G. B. HOLLAND, do.—THOMAS A. MILNE, Markham.—Dr OGDEN, Toronto.—JAMES R. ARMSTRONG, do.—C. P. REID, do.—

1829—THOMAS D. HARRIS, Toronto.—Hon. JOSEPH C. MORRISON, do.—THOMAS MEREDITH, do.—ARCHIBALD BARKER, Markham.—W. R. HARRIS, Toronto.—ROBERT DEFRIES, do.—Capt. ROBERT KERR, do.—R. B. MILLER, do.—Capt. JOHN McGANN, do.—J. MERRITT, St Catharines.—SAMUEL PLATT, Toronto.—J. C. SMALL, do.—WILLIAM QUIGLEY, do.—ALEX. RENNIE, Hamilton.—JOHN KITSON, Toronto.—ROBERT HILL, do.

1830—Hon. W. P. HOWLAND, Lieut.-Governor, Toronto.— JOHN WALLIS, do.—PETER HUTTY, Yorkville, do.—PHILIP ARMSTRONG, Yorkville.—G. M. HAWKE, Toronto.—Alderman SPENCE, do.—ALEX. MUNRO, do.—THOMAS METCALF, do.—JAMES FARREL, do.—THOMAS STORM, do.—W. G. STORM, do.—DUNCAN MACDONNELL, Montreal.—EDWARD COPPING, Toronto.

1831—JAMES G. WORTS, Toronto.—SAMUEL SWINARTON, ex M.P.P., Coventry.—JAMES ACHESON, Toronto.—GEORGE HENDERSON, do.—SAMUEL ROGERS, do.—JOHN SMALL, do.—JOHN NIXON, do.—ALFIO DE GRASSI, do.—FREDERICK MILLIGAN, do.— GEORGE BALFOUR, do.—JEREMIAH IREDALE, do.—JAMES ASHFIELD, do.—ROBERT FOWLER, do.—JOHN JACQUES, do.—ANDREW T. McCORD, do.—JOHN ARGUE, do.—NOAH L. PIEPER, do.

1832—Sir FRANCIS HINCKS, Ottawa.—WILLIAM GOODERHAM, senior, Toronto.—ISAAC GILMOUR, do.—JOHN PATERSON, do.—SAMUEL BOWMAN, do.—JOHN BROWN, do.—JOHN CARR, do.—Capt. C. G. FORTIER, do.—GEORGE GRAHAM, do.—JOHN G. HOWARD, Humber Bay.—A. K. BOOMER, Toronto.—THOMAS LAILEY, do.—THOMAS MARA, do.—WILLIAM OSBORNE, do.—WM. ROWLAND, do.—WM. STEERS, Stratford.—JOHN BUGG, Toronto. —C. W. COOPER, do.—JAMES SEVERS, do.—ARTHUR CRAWFORD, do.—THOMAS CLARKSON, do.—ROBERT DODDS, do.—JOHN EVANS, Montreal.—WILLIAM FREELAND, Toronto.—GEORGE PRICE, do. —DAVID KENNEDY, do.

1833—WILLIAM ARTHURS, Toronto.—ROBERT BEEKMAN, do.—THOMAS BURGESS, do.—JOHN DILL, do.—EDWARD DACK, do.—WM. HENDERSON, do.—ROBERT HORNBY, M.D., do—W. M. JAMIESON, do.—WM. LEA, Don, York Township.—JOHN LAWDER, Eglinton.—JOHN P. SMITH, Toronto.—JOHN SHANKLIN, do. —SAMUEL THOMPSON, do.—ALFRED WILSON, do.—ALEX. MUIR, Newmarket.—JOHN GARTSHORE, Toronto.—SAMUEL WESTMAN, do.—THOMAS DEWSON, Bradford.—W. BARCHARD, Toronto.—JOHN WATSON, York Townshsip.—WILLIAM GRUBBE, Weston.—J. A. DONALDSON, Toronto.—JOHN LEVS, do.

Under recent By-law.—HENRY QUETTON ST GEORGE, Toronto. —Hon. Member, Dr CANNIFF, Toronto.

APPENDIX II: LIEUTENANT-GOVERNORS[1] OF UPPER CANADA 1791-1841

JOHN GRAVES SIMCOE, 1791-1799
PETER RUSSELL, *Administrator*, 1796-1799

PETER HUNTER, 1799-1805
ALEXANDER GRANT, *Administrator*, 1805-1806

FRANCIS GORE, 1806-1817
SIR ISAAC BROCK, *Administrator*,[2] 1811-1812

SIR ROGER HALE SHEAFFE, *Administrator*, 1812-1813

BARON FRANCIS DE ROTTENBURG, *Administrator*, 1813

SIR GORDON DRUMMOND, *Administrator*, 1813-1815

SIR GEORGE MURRAY,
Provisional Lieutenant-Governor, 1815

SIR FREDERICK P. ROBINSON,
Provisional Lieutenant-Governor, 1815

SAMUEL SMITH, *Administrator*, 1817-1818

SIR PEREGRINE MAITLAND, 1818-1828
SAMUEL SMITH, *Administrator*, 1820[3]

SIR JOHN COLBORNE, later BARON SEATON, 1828-1836

SIR FRANCIS BOND HEAD, 1836-1838

SIR GEORGE ARTHUR, 1838-1841

---

[1] In the absence of the lieutenant-governor, the head of state was the administrator or president.

[2] Brock and his three successors were also commanders of the troops in Upper Canada during the War of 1812. Gore was on leave of absence in England from 1811 to 1815.

[3] Maitland was Administrator of Lower Canada for some months in 1820 and Smith took his place in Upper Canada.

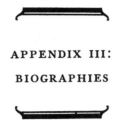

APPENDIX III:

BIOGRAPHIES

This biographical appendix cannot, unfortunately, claim to be comprehensive because many of the people connected with the early history of Toronto who are mentioned by Scadding have been so completely forgotten that a biographical entry would add no information to what he gives in his text. As some of the early biographical works consulted were compiled by amateurs and were often based on inadequate information, complete accuracy is also impossible.

For further information on the more important people mentioned in the index, the reader is referred to Henry J. Morgan, *Sketches of Prominent Canadians* (1862), John Charles Dent, *The Canadian Portrait Gallery* (4 vols, 1880-1), and W. S. Wallace, *The Macmillan Dictionary of Canadian Biography* (1963). Edith G. Firth's *The Town of York, 1793-1815* (1962) contains valuable biographical footnotes on many less prominent people. For genealogical information, by far the most useful work is E. J. Chadwick, *Ontarian Families* (2 vols, 1894-8).

ADDISON, ROBERT (1754?-1829)
He came to Canada as a missionary in 1791 and the next year became rector of Niagara, holding that post until his death.

ALLAN, WILLIAM (1770-1853)
The financial genius of the Family Compact and probably the wealthiest man in Upper Canada, he was the first president of the Bank of Upper Canada and a member of the Legislative Council (1825-41) and the Executive Council (1836-41).

ALEXANDER, SIR JAMES EDWARD
A British officer who toured North America about 1830 and was stationed in Canada for several years after 1841. He wrote two books on his experiences: *Transatlantic*

sketches (1833) and *L'Acadie, or Seven years' exploration in British America* (1849).

ALLCOCK, HENRY (d. 1808)
An English lawyer who became a judge of the court of the King's Bench in Upper Canada in 1798, chief justice in 1802, and chief justice of Lower Canada in 1805.

ANGELL, EDWARD (*fl.* 1820s)
As well as being builder of the two bridges over the Don, he was a land agent in the 1820s. After 1825 he went to England where he opposed the Canada Company.

APPLETON, THOMAS
A Yorkshireman who arrived in Canada in 1819 and became master of the Common School at York in 1820.

ARMOUR, SAMUEL (1785-1853)
Born in Ireland, he became an
M.A. at the University of Glasgow
in 1807 and emigrated to Canada
in 1820. He taught at the Home
District School, was ordained by
James Stewart (q.v.) in 1826, and
was the Anglican clergyman at
Peterborough and, after 1832, at
Cavan.

ARMSTRONG, JOHN
An axe-maker by profession, he
was a Reformer in politics and was
elected to the city council as an
alderman for the Reform faction
in 1835. He left Toronto before
the end of the year.

ASHBRIDGE, JOHN (1761-1843)
He migrated from Philadelphia
in 1793 and purchased land on
Ashbridge's Bay.

BABY, JAMES or JACQUES
(1763-1833)
A member of a prominent Quebec
family who had settled in Detroit,
he became a fur trader. He was
appointed to both the Executive
and Legislative Councils of Upper Canada in 1792 and held
these posts until his death. In
1816 he was appointed inspector-
general of public accounts (minister of finance), a post he held
until his death, and moved from
Sandwich to York. He was one of
the most influential members of
the Family Compact.

BABY, RAYMOND (1808 -1840)
Son of Jacques Baby, he became
sheriff of the Western District in
1839.

BAGOT, SIR CHARLES (1781-1843)
An English diplomat who negoti-
ated the Rush-Bagot convention
with Washington in 1817 and
the Canadian-Russian (Alaska)
boundary in 1825. In 1841 he was
appointed governor of Canada
and is best known for bringing
the French Canadians into the
government.

BALDWIN FAMILY
The originators of the idea of
responsible government in the
British Empire. Robert Baldwin
of County Cork came to Upper
Canada in 1798 and three of his
sons became prominent in the life
of the province: William Warren,
Augustus, and John Spread
(qq.v.). A daughter, Barbara,
married Daniel Sullivan and became the mother of Robert Baldwin Sullivan (q.v.), the second
mayor of Toronto. William Warren Baldwin's son Robert (q.v.)
was the man who successfully inaugurated responsible government. John Spread Baldwin was
Henry Scadding's father-in-law
and the father of Maurice Baldwin (1836-1904) who became
bishop of Huron in 1883.

BALDWIN, AUGUSTUS ['Admiral Baldwin'] (1776-1866)
He entered the navy in 1794 and
retired to settle in York in 1817.
He was a member of the Legislative Council from 1831 to 1841
and a member of the Executive
Council after 1836. In 1846 he
received the rank of admiral.

BALDWIN, JOHN SPREAD (1787-1843)
He became a partner in the Quetton St George (q.v.) business in
1814. After St George returned to
France in 1815, Baldwin and Jules
Quesnel ran the business until
1832. He was also a leading figure
in all main Toronto financial operations. His daughter Harriet
(d. 1843) married Henry Scadding.

BALDWIN, QUETTON ST GEORGE
(1810-1829)
Son of William Warren Baldwin
(q.v.).

BALDWIN, ROBERT, Sr (d. 1816)
Father of William Warren, Augustus, and John Spread Baldwin
(qq.v.), he came to Canada in
1798 after suffering financial difficulties in Cork. He settled first
in Clarke Township, then joined

his son Dr W. W. Baldwin at York.

BALDWIN, ROBERT, Jr (1804-1858)
Born in York, he was the son of William Warren Baldwin (q.v.), and a leading moderate Reformer prior to the Union of the Provinces in 1841. His recommendations on responsible government were embodied in Lord Durham's *Report* of 1839. With Louis H. Lafontaine he served as joint leader of the government in 1842-3, and again in the first responsible government in 1848-51.

BALDWIN, WILLIAM AUGUSTUS (1808-1883)
Son of William Warren Baldwin (q.v.), he married Isabella, the daughter of James Buchanan, the British consul in New York.

BALDWIN, WILLIAM WARREN ['Dr Baldwin'] (1775-1844)
Doctor, lawyer, architect, and the probable originator of the theory of responsible government in the colonies. Born in Ireland, he graduated from Edinburgh University as an M.D. in 1796, came to Canada with his father in 1798, settled in York in 1802, and later became wealthy through his wife's inheritance of the lands of Peter Russell (q.v.). In politics he was one of the leading moderate Reformers. He was a member of the Legislative Assembly in 1828-30 and was appointed to the Legislative Council in 1843.

BARBER, GEORGE ANTHONY (d. 1874)
An assistant in the Home District Grammar School 1825-9, he then became the first English master of Upper Canada College. He edited the Toronto *Commercial Herald* in the early 1840s.

BARTLETT, WILLIAM HENRY (1809-1854)
An English artist who travelled widely in Europe, in the near east, and in North America preparing illustrations for at least twenty-

one works. These included the two-volume sets, *American Scenery* (1840) and *Canadian Scenery* (1842). All his pictures from Constantinople to Cobourg have the same romantic atmosphere.

BAXTER, PETER *or* JAMES (d. 1832)
Peter Baxter was a brother-in-law of William Lyon Mackenzie with whom he was associated in Mackenzie's newspaper work as publisher of the *Colonial Advocate*. When he died, his father James (Mackenzie's father-in-law) came to York from Pittsburgh to take his place.

BEARD, JOSHUA GEORGE (1797-1866)
He owned considerable property in the city, including an iron foundry and a hotel. He sat on the city council for St Lawrence Ward for many years and became mayor in 1854. He was also clerk to the sheriff of York.

BEATY, JAMES Sr (1807?-1865)
A grocer and capitalist, he was the founder of the *Leader* in 1852 and represented St Lawrence Ward as a common councilman in 1836 and as an alderman, 1846-9.

BEIKIE, JOHN (1767?-1839)
Sheriff of the Home District (1810-15) and Clerk of the Executive Council (1832-9). He was also a member of the Legislative Assembly (1812-16).

BELCOUR, FRANÇOIS (d. 1808)
He came to York about 1804 and opened a bakery.

BEMAN, ELISHA (d. 1822)
An emigrant from New York State who became an innkeeper at York and, after 1806, a miller at Newmarket. In 1805 he married, as his second wife, the widow of Christopher Robinson.

BENNETT, JOHN (1756?-1824)
He learned the printing trade in Quebec and became King's Printer of Upper Canada and editor of the *Upper Canada Gazette*, 1801-7.

BERCZY, WILLIAM VON MOLL (1748-1813)
He attempted to found a German settlement at Markham in 1794. After this failed to develop, he moved to Montreal in 1805 where he supported himself by portrait painting.

BERTHON, GEORGE THEODORE (1806-1892)
A Viennese portrait painter who came to Canada in 1841, settling in Toronto. He painted the portraits of many officials and considered the portrait of Sir John Beverley Robinson (q.v.) in Osgoode Hall to be his masterpiece.

BIDWELL, BARNABAS (1763-1833)
Father of Marshall Spring Bidwell (q.v.). A graduate of Yale University (1785), he became attorney-general of Massachusetts. He fled to Upper Canada in 1810 after he had been accused of malversation of funds, settling first in Bath, then in Kingston. In 1821 he was elected to the Legislative Assembly for Lennox and Addington. His expulsion as a former American and because of the malversation charge set off the alien rights controversy. He died at Kingston, and was never a regular resident of York.

BIDWELL, MARSHALL SPRING (1799-1872)
He came to Canada with his father Barnabas Bidwell (q.v.) in 1810, and was called to the bar in 1821. In 1822 he was elected to the Legislative Assembly for Lennox and Addington when his father was declared ineligible but was not allowed to sit until he was re-elected in 1825 under a new electoral law that admitted some former Americans. The leader of the moderate Reformers, he held his seat until 1836. He was elected speaker in both of the Legislative Assemblies that the Reformers dominated: 1828-30 and 1834-6.

Forced to flee after the Rebellion of 1837, he settled in Albany, N.Y., and became a leading member of the bar.

BILLINGS, THEODORE F. or FRANCIS T. (1778?-1867)
Both Christian names appear on old lists. Billings probably moved to York about 1823 and became treasurer of the Home District. He died in Oshawa.

BLAKE, WILLIAM HUME (1809-1870)
Educated at Trinity College, Dublin (B.A., 1830), he came to Canada in 1832 and three years later settled in York. He opened a law office in 1838. After holding the solicitor-generalship, he became chancellor of Upper Canada (1849-62) and later a judge of appeal.

BLOOR, JOSEPH (1788-1862)
He came to Canada from Staffordshire and opened a hotel in York in 1819. Later he moved north of the town and was responsible with Sheriff (W.B.) Jarvis (q.v.) for opening a new development at Yorkville, near his own well-known brewery. Bloor Street is named after him.

BONNYCASTLE, SIR RICHARD HENRY (1791-1847)
An officer of the Royal Engineers who served in Canada on several occasions. He commanded the Royal Engineers in Upper Canada at the time of the Rebellion of 1837 and was knighted for the part he played. He wrote four books on British North America, including one on Newfoundland.

BOSTWICK, LARDNER (1774-1834)
He emigrated to York from the United States in 1810 and became a wheelwright. He was a reformer in politics and was elected to the first City Council in 1834, but died shortly afterwards in the cholera epidemic.

BOUCHETTE, JEAN BAPTISTE (1736-1804)
He served in the Canadian Militia in the Seven Years' War and became commander of the naval forces on Lake Ontario in 1794. Father of Joseph Bouchette (q.v.).

BOUCHETTE, JOSEPH (1774-1841)
Surveyor-general of Lower Canada (1804-41) and author of various works including *The British Dominions in North America* (1831).

BOULTON FAMILY
One of the wealthiest and most socially prominent families in Scadding's Toronto. D'Arcy Sr came to York from England in 1797. He and three of his sons—D'Arcy Jr (1785-1846), Henry John (q.v.), and George S. (1797-1865)—were all prominent lawyers, and George S. was a member of the Legislative Council from 1847 to 1867. D'Arcy Jr's son, William Henry (1812-74), was mayor of Toronto in 1845-7 and represented the city in the Legislative Assembly. The Boulton family home, the Grange, was a centre of social life from the time it was built in 1818 until the death of Professor Goldwin Smith (who had married William Henry's widow) in 1910. It is now part of the Art Gallery of Toronto.

BOULTON, D'ARCY, Sr ['Mr Justice Boulton'] (1759-1834)
Arriving at York in 1797, he became solicitor-general in 1805 and attorney-general in 1814. In 1818 he became a judge of assize. He wrote *Sketch of His Majesty's Province of Upper Canada* (1805).

BOULTON, HENRY JOHN (1790-1870)
The second son of D'Arcy Boulton Sr (q.v.), he was called to the English bar in 1815 and shortly afterwards began to practise in York. He became solicitor-general in 1818, attorney-general in 1829, and from 1833 to 1838 was chief justice of Newfoundland. He later sat in the Legislative Assembly (1841-4, 1848-51). He was the author of *A Short Sketch of the Province of Upper Canada* (1826).

BOYLE, ROBERT EDWARD
Son of the 8th Earl of Cork, he became a lieutenant in the Coldstream Guards.

BREAKENRIDGE, JOHN (1789-1828)
A lawyer at Niagara-on-the-Lake who married Mary Warren Baldwin (1791-1871), sister of William Warren Baldwin (q.v.), in 1816.

BROCK, SIR ISAAC (1769-1812)
A British officer who fought in the Napoleonic Wars, he was transferred to Canada in 1802. He was put in command of the forces in Upper Canada in 1810 and became administrator of the province in 1811. He captured Detroit in the War of 1812 but fell in the battle of Queenston Heights.

BUCHANAN, ISAAC (1810-1883)
One of the leading merchants of Upper Canada. He arrived at York in 1830 and was soon head of a large wholesale business. He was a member of the Legislative Assembly for Toronto from 1841 to 1844 and for Hamilton from 1857 to 1865. He was a member of the cabinet briefly in 1864.

BURNS, DAVID (d. 1806)
A surgeon who received minor appointments in York under John Graves Simcoe (q.v.).

BURNSIDE, ALEXANDER (1780?-1854)
An American who was admitted to practise medicine in York in 1822. Noted for his charitable activities, he supported the Mechanics' Institute and left bequests to the General Hospital and to Trinity College.

BURWELL, MAHLON (1783-1846)
Employed as a surveyor by the provincial government from 1809 to 1840, he surveyed a large part of Western Ontario including London. He was a member of the Legislative Assembly for Middlesex, 1812-24, and for London, 1836-41.

BUTTON, JOHN (1772-1861)
A cooper, he came to Upper Canada in 1798 and settled in Markham township. He commanded a troop of cavalry during the War of 1812.

CALDICOTT, THOMAS FORD (1804-1869)
He came to Canada as a tutor in 1824 and by 1833 had settled in York and opened a school. He was active in Baptist circles and was later ordained in the United States where he preached for some years before returning to Toronto as the minister of Bond Street Baptist Church in 1860.

CAMERON, DUNCAN (1765?-1838)
A merchant of York from at least 1801, he became provincial secretary in 1817 and held that office until his death.

CAMERON, JOHN (1776?-1815)
A merchant who, from 1807 until his death, was King's Printer and editor of the *Upper Canada Gazette*.

CAMERON, JOHN HILLYARD (1817-1876)
A leading lawyer and conservative politician, he rivaled Sir John A. Macdonald for leadership of the party in the mid-1850s. Though a member of Parliament for many years, he never held cabinet office after 1848. In 1859 he became Grand Master of the Orange Order.

CAMPBELL, STEADMAN B. (1818?-1868)
Son of hotel proprietor William Campbell, he became a solicitor in Toronto.

CAMPBELL, SIR WILLIAM (1758-1834)
He served in the Royal Navy until 1784 and then retired to Nova Scotia until he was appointed attorney-general of Cape Breton in 1804. In 1811 he became a judge of the King's Bench in Upper Canada and in 1825 chief justice. He retired in 1829 and was knighted.

CAMPBELL, WILLIAM (1781?-1847)
He emigrated to York from New England and became one of the leading hotel proprietors in the town.

CAREY, JOHN (*fl.* 1819-1841)
An Irishman who published the *Observer*, the first unofficial newspaper in York, from 1820 to 1831. He made two later attempts to establish papers in the city.

CARFRAE, THOMAS Jr (1796-1841)
A leading York merchant who became an alderman in the first city council and Collector of Customs in 1835.

CARLETON, SIR GUY, 1ST BARON DORCHESTER (1724-1808)
He entered the army in 1742 and went with Wolfe to Quebec in 1759. In 1766 he became lieutenant-governor and in 1768 governor of Quebec. He was the originator of the Quebec Act. He retired in 1778 but in 1782 was made commander-in-chief of British North America, in which capacity he arranged the transportation of the Loyalists from the town of New York. As Baron Dorchester he was again governor of Quebec from 1786 to 1796 when he retired to his English estates.

CASSELS, ROBERT (1815-1882)
An English banker who emigrated to Canada and was connected with various banking operations in Halifax, Quebec, Montreal, and Toronto.

CAWTHRA, JOSEPH (1759-1842)
An early general storekeeper who laid the basis of a family fortune during the War of 1812. He was a moderate Reformer prior to 1837.

CAWTHRA, WILLIAM (1801-1880)
Son of Joseph Cawthra (q.v.), he was associated with his father in his business enterprises and was probably the richest man in Ontario at the time of his death.

CAYLEY, FRANK (1807-1890)
Builder of 'Drumsnab' near Castle Frank.

CHALÛS, JEAN LOUIS, VICOMTE DE
Scion of an old family of Maine in France, he fought in Brittany as a royalist, and then with his brother, René Augustin, Comte de Chalûs, joined the unsuccessful French settlement north of Toronto in 1798. He was back in France by 1815.

CHEWETT, JAMES GRANT (1793-1862)
Son of William Chewett (q.v.), he was educated by John Strachan (q.v.) at Cornwall and spent thirty years in the surveyor-general's office, rising to become deputy surveyor-general. He retired at the union of the provinces in 1841. He built various buildings in York, including part of the Legislature of 1829.

CHEWETT, WILLIAM (1753-1849)
He emigrated to Canada in 1771 and became deputy surveyor-general of Upper Canada in 1791 and joint acting surveyor-general with Thomas Ridout (q.v.) in 1799.

CLARKE, SIR ALURED (1745?-1832)
He joined the British army in 1759, fought in the American Revolution, and became governor of Jamaica (1782-90). From 1791 to 1796 he was lieutenant-governor of Lower Canada and brought the Constitutional Act into force in that province. He was later commander-in-chief in India (1798-1801). He was knighted in 1797 and promoted to field-marshal in 1830.

CLINKENBROOMER, CHARLES. See KLINGENBRUMMER, CHARLES

COCHRANE, THOMAS (1777-1804)
Appointed puisne judge of the court of the King's Bench in 1803, he was drowned in the wreck of the *Speedy* a year later.

COFFIN, NATHANIEL (d. 1846)
Brother-in-law of Sir Roger H. Sheaffe (q.v.), he entered the army in 1783 and was appointed a provincial aide-de-camp and lieutenant-colonel in 1812 when Sheaffe was administrator. In 1815 he became adjutant-general of the Upper Canada Militia. He died in Toronto.

COLBORNE, SIR JOHN (1778-1863)
He fought in the Napoleonic Wars and afterwards became governor of Guernsey (1825-8), of Upper Canada (1828-36), and then commander-in-chief of the forces in Canada, in which capacity he put down the rebellions in Lower Canada in 1837 and 1838. He was administrator of Canada both before and after Lord Durham's mission in 1838, and in 1839 became governor-in-chief. At the end of the year he returned to England and was raised to the peerage as Baron Seaton.

COLLINS, FRANCIS (1801-1834)
Emigrating to York from Ireland in 1818, he established the Reform newspaper, *Canadian Freeman*, in 1825 and published it until his death.

COLUMBUS, ISAAC (d. 1846)
A blacksmith, locksmith, and gunsmith who probably came from an Isle d'Orléans family.

COOPER, WILLIAM (1761?-1840)
He settled in York in 1793 and later claimed to have built the first house there. He owned various enterprises including a tavern, mills on the Humber, and a wharf at the foot of York Street.

CRAIG, JOHN (fl. 1830-1850)
A house and portrait painter who was a Tory member of the City Council from 1834 until he resigned in 1849.

CROOKSHANK, GEORGE (1773-1859)
He came to York in 1796 and entered the commissary department, where his brother-in-law John McGill (q.v.) was in charge.

CUMBERLAND, FREDERIC (1821-1881)
Born in England where he studied engineering and architecture, he came to Toronto in 1847. He was responsible for many of the most beautiful buildings in the city, including St James' Cathedral, Osgoode Hall, and University College. In 1860 he gave up architecture and became managing director of the Northern Railway.

DALTON, THOMAS (1792-1840)
Born in Birmingham, Eng., he came to Canada about 1812 and in 1828 founded *The Patriot and Farmer's Monitor*, a weekly, in Kingston. In 1832 he moved the paper to York where it was published semi-weekly after 1833. Dalton's political outlook became progressively more Tory.

DALY, CHARLES (1808-1864)
Born in Ireland and educated in Belgium and France, he first worked as a librarian in the London Athenaeum and then emigrated to Canada. In 1835 he became second city clerk of Toronto and held that office until his death.

DANFORTH, ASA (1746-1836)
Born in Massachusetts, he supervised many developmental projects in the United States and in York where in 1799 he was contracted to build the Danforth Road.

DE BLAQUIÈRE, PETER BOYLE (1784-1860)
Son of the first Lord de Blaquière, he emigrated to Toronto from Ireland in 1837 and two years later was appointed to the Legislative Council. He was reappointed to the new Legislative Council at the union of the provinces in 1841 and sat till his death in 1860. He was chancellor of the University of Toronto, 1850-2.

DE HOEN, FREDERICK, BARON (b. 1764?)
A British officer who farmed, not too successfully, a lot at the northwest corner of Yonge Street and Eglinton Avenue. He returned to Baden, in his native Germany, in 1817.

DENISON FAMILY
Descended from John Denison (q.v.) and his wife Sophia who emigrated from England in 1792, the Denisons have been active in Toronto political and military activities from the first, and have had more members on the city council than any other family.

DENISON, GEORGE TAYLOR I (1783-1853)
Son of John Denison (q.v.), he served in the militia in the War of 1812 and in the Rebellion of 1837. In 1833 he founded 'Denison's Horse', a militia regiment. He was one of the first aldermen of Toronto.

DENISON, GEORGE TAYLOR III (1839-1925)
Grandson of George Taylor Denison I (q.v.), he became a lawyer and senior police magistrate of Toronto (1877-1923). He was also connected with the family regiment and wrote several books, including two influential works on cavalry.

DENISON, JOHN (1755-1824)
He emigrated from Yorkshire in 1792 and came to York in 1796 where he managed Petersfield, the Russell farm, and generally received the patronage of that family.

DENISON, ROBERT BRITTAIN (1821-1900)
Son of George Taylor Denison I (q.v.), he played a leading part in Toronto military affairs, becoming a lieutenant-colonel in 1861 and acting as deputy adjutant-general, 1881-6. He was an alderman in 1848-9.

DENNIS, JOHN
A Loyalist who came to York in 1796, he was a shipbuilder and built the government yacht *Toronto*.

DICKSON, WILLIAM (1769-1846)
He settled at Niagara-on-the-Lake in 1792 and in 1815 purchased the township of Dumfries and settled it. He was a member of the Legislative Council from 1815 to 1841.

DIEHL, PETER (1787-1868)
Born at Quebec, he studied medicine first in Montreal and then at Edinburgh. After practising in Montreal, he moved to York in 1828 and was in partnership with Dr Christopher Widmer (q.v.) until 1835. He served in the army in 1837 and, after practising in Kingston, retired to Toronto in 1855. He married Ann, daughter of Dr James Macaulay (q.v.), in 1829.

DIXON, ALEXANDER (1792-1855)
He came to York in 1830 and set up business as a saddler and hardware merchant. He sat on the city council for the St Lawrence Ward as a common councilman in 1835 and as an alderman from 1837 to 1844.

DOEL, JOHN (1790?-1871)
He settled in York about 1818 and became one of the leading brewers in the town. He was a Reformer in politics.

DORCHESTER, BARON. *See* CARLETON, SIR GUY.

DRAPER, WILLIAM HENRY (1801-1877)
Born in England, he came to Upper Canada in 1820 and was called to the bar in 1828. He was a member of the Legislative Assembly for Toronto from 1836 to 1841. In 1836 he was also appointed to the Executive Council, was made solicitor-general in 1837, and became attorney-general for Canada West in 1841. When the provinces united he was leader of the government in 1841-2, and again from 1843 to 1847 when he was appointed to the bench of Canada West. He was chief justice of Upper Canada, 1863-9, and president of the Court of Error and Appeal, 1869-77.

DRUMMOND, SIR GORDON (1771-1854)
Born in Quebec, he became a lieutenant-general in the British army. He was appointed second-in-command to Sir George Prevost (q.v.) in 1813 and distinguished himself in the War of 1812. From 1813 to 1815 he was administrator of Upper Canada and in 1815-16 administrator of Canada.

DUFFERIN, FREDERICK, EARL OF (1826-1902)
One of the most brilliant members of Queen Victoria's civil service, he was governor-general of Canada, 1872-8, and viceroy of India, 1884-8. He was also ambassador at St Petersburg, Constantinople, Rome, and Paris. He was created Marquis of Dufferin and Ava in 1888.

DUGGAN, GEORGE, Sr (1783-1863)
A merchant and coroner of the Home District, he sat on the city council as an alderman in 1834 and 1835.

DUGGAN, GEORGE, Jr (1813-1876)
A lawyer and member of the Legislative Assembly for the second riding of York county, 1841-7. He was afterwards recorder of Toronto and from 1868 senior judge of the county of York. He sat on the city council as an alderman from 1838 to 1840 and from 1843 to 1850.

DUNDAS, HENRY (1742-1811)
Home secretary, 1791-4, and secretary of war, 1794-1801, he was a friend of Governor Simcoe (q.v.). Dundas Street was named in his honour.

DUNLOP, WILLIAM (1792-1848)
A Scottish surgeon who came to Upper Canada first in 1813 during the War of 1812 and again with the Canada Company in 1826. He sat in the Legislative Assembly from 1841 to 1846 and was well known as an author. Nicknamed 'Tiger' Dunlop because of his hunting triumphs in India, he was one of the most colourful figures in the province.

DUNN, ALEXANDER ROBERTS (1833-1868).
Son of J. H. Dunn (q.v.), he participated in the charge of the Light Brigade in 1856 (winning the Victoria Cross) and later became colonel of the Royal Canadian Regiment. He was killed accidently in Abyssinia during the war against King Theodore.

DUNN, JOHN HENRY (1794-1854)
He came to Canada in 1820 as receiver-general of Upper Canada and member of the Executive Council and the Legislative Council. At the Union of 1841 he was elected M.P. for Toronto and continued as receiver-general and as a member of the executive. He gave up all offices at the end of 1843 and later returned to England.

DURAND, CHARLES (1811-1905)
Born near the site of Hamilton,

Ont., he is chiefly noted for the publication of his *Reminiscences* in 1897.

DUTCHER, FREDERICK R.
He set up a cupola furnace at King and Yonge Streets in 1828 after moving from Dundas Street. He had many partners: William A. Dutcher, Samuel Andrus, William B. Sheldon, and B. and J. Van Norman. By the mid-1830s the business had reached a considerable size, but it disappeared between 1836 and 1843. James Good may have taken it over.

ELGIN AND KINCARDINE, JAMES, 8TH EARL OF (1811-1863)
He married Lady Mary, daughter of the Earl of Durham, in 1846 and shortly afterwards was appointed governor-general of British North America with instructions to bring in responsible government. He held the office with great distinction until 1854. He became viceroy of India in 1862.

ELMSLEY, JOHN, Sr (1762-1805)
Called to the English bar in 1796, he was appointed chief justice of Upper Canada in 1796 and was transferred to the same office in Lower Canada in 1802.

ELMSLEY, JOHN, Jr (1801-1863)
Son of John Sr (q.v.), he was a member of the Executive Council (1831-3 and 1836-8) and of the Legislative Council (1831-41). Both before and after his conversion to Catholicism in 1833, he gave liberally to various church organizations.

EWART, JOHN (1788-1856)
A Scottish emigrant who became a leading contractor in York. Among his buildings were the Court House, Parliament Buildings, and Osgoode Hall. He was also the first president of the Mechanics' Insititute in 1831 and became the father-in-law of Sir Oliver Mowat.

FENTON, JOHN
He came to Canada as a Wesleyan missionary in 1819 and was an assistant in the Common School of York and the parish clerk of St James' Church. He eventually emigrated to the United States and became an Episcopalian clergyman.

FITZGIBBON, JAMES (1780-1863)
Born in Ireland, he came to Canada with the 49th Regiment in 1801 and then served in the Napoleonic Wars. He received the surrender of the American forces at Beaver Dams in 1813. He was acting adjutant-general at the time of the Rebellion of 1837 and led the forces that defeated William Lyon Mackenzie at Montgomery's Tavern. He was appointed clerk of the House of Assembly in 1827. He went to live in England in 1846 and was appointed a military Knight of Windsor in 1850.

FOTHERGILL, CHARLES (1782-1840)
He was King's Printer and editor of the *Upper Canada Gazette*, 1822-6. With his son he published the *Palladium of British America and Upper Canada Mercantile Advertiser* from 1837 to 1839. He was one of the first naturalists in the province.

GALT, JOHN (1779-1839)
A Scottish novelist who was responsible for the establishment of the Canada Company in 1825 and was its first superintendent in Canada until he was dismissed in 1829, partly because he disagreed with John Strachan (q.v.). He founded Guelph in 1827. Later he interested himself in a similar enterprise in Lower Canada.

GAMBLE, CLARKE (1808-1902)
Youngest son of John Gamble (q.v.), he became a lawyer and was city solicitor of Toronto, 1840-63. He was also solicitor for the British America Assurance Co. and promoter of the Toronto and Lake Huron Railway Co.

GAMBLE, JOHN (1755-1811)
Born in Ireland, he studied medicine at Edinburgh University. He immigrated to New York in 1774 and fought with the Queen's Rangers in the Revolutionary War. He then settled in Saint John, N.B., and became assistant surgeon to the reconstituted Queen's Rangers at York in 1796. Later he settled in Kingston and died there. His widow, Isabella (1767-1859), moved to York in 1820, establishing the family there.

GAMBLE, WILLIAM (1800?-1882?)
Son of John Gamble (q.v.), he became one of the first wholesalers in Toronto and later established 'Milton Mills, Etobicoke', one of the largest flour mills in the province.

GIVINS, JAMES (1759?-1846)
A fur trader who served with John Graves Simcoe (q.v.) and fought in the War of 1812. He was chief superintendent of Indian affairs for Upper Canada in 1827-42.

GOODERHAM, GEORGE (1830-1905)
The son of William Gooderham (q.v.), he became president of the family firm and also of the Bank of Toronto in 1882. He was an enthusiastic yachtsman, and built the magnificent mansion that still stands at the north-east corner of Bloor and St George Streets (the York Club).

GOODERHAM, WILLIAM (1790-1881)
He served in the army in the West Indies and emigrated to York in 1832. Almost immediately, with his brother-in-law James Worts (q.v.), he founded a flour mill which became a distillery in 1837. He provided most of the financial backing for the business and was the leading person in it after his brother-in-law died.

GORDON, JAMES (d. 1865)
A member of the Legislative Council of Upper Canada, 1829-41, and of the United Canadas, 1845-65.

GORE, FRANCIS (1769-1852)
Lieutenant-governor of Bermuda (1804-6) and Upper Canada (1806-17, on leave 1811-15). It was under his administration that the Reform opposition first appeared in the Legislative Assembly.

GOURLAY, ROBERT FLEMING (1778-1863)
A -Scottish agitator whose first brief residence in Upper Canada in 1817-19 was marked by constant turmoil that grew out of his criticisms of the Family Compact and was a factor in the consolidation of the Reform party. He was arrested as a seditious alien, tried, found guilty, and banished. Back in Scotland he published a valuable *Statistical Account of Upper Canada* (1822). His sentence was rescinded in 1842 and he returned to Canada for four years in 1856.

GRANT, ALEXANDER (1734-1813)
He came to America in 1757. After serving as an officer in the navy, he was appointed to the Executive and Legislative Councils in 1792. He was administrator of Upper Canada, 1805-6.

GRASETT, HENRY (1808-1882)
A graduate of Cambridge University (1834), he became assistant at St James' Church in 1835, rector in 1847, and first dean in 1867. He is buried in the same vault as Bishop Strachan in the chancel.

GRAY, ROBERT ISAAC DAY (1772?-1804)
He came to Canada with his parents at the beginning of the American Revolution. He practised law in Cornwall and in 1794 was appointed solicitor-general of Upper Canada. He was elected to the Legislative Assembly in 1796 and was drowned when the *Speedy* sank in Lake Ontario in 1804.

GURNETT, GEORGE (1792?-1861)
Born in England, he came to Upper Canada from Virginia. From 1827 to 1828 he published the *Gore Gazette* at Ancaster and in 1829 founded in York the *Courier of Upper Canada*, which he continued to publish until 1837, the year he became mayor of Toronto. He was mayor four times in all.

GZOWSKI, SIR CASIMIR (1813-1898)
A Polish engineer who fled to Canada after the suppression of the revolt of 1830. He settled in Toronto in 1841 and became a leading contractor, his work including the building of the Grand Trunk Railway from Toronto to Sarnia.

HALE, ELIPHALET (d. 1807)
He came to York in 1799 and engaged in various building trades until 1806 when he became high constable.

HAMILTON, ROBERT (1750-1809)
One of the first great merchants of Upper Canada, he came to Upper Canada during the American Revolutionary War. He lived near Kingston, then moved west and founded Queenston. He was appointed to the Legislative Council in 1792. The city of Hamilton was named after his son George.

HARRIS, JOSEPH HEMINGTON (1800-1881)
A doctor of divinity of Clare College, Cambridge, he was brought to York in 1829 by Sir John Colborne (q.v.) as first principal of Upper Canada College, a post he held until 1838 when he returned to England.

HARRIS, THOMAS DENNIE (1803-1873)
Ironmonger, hardware dealer, and in his time one of the leading merchants of the city, he was chief engineer of the fire brigade from 1838 to 1841 and harbour master,

1870-2. He was also active at St James' Church where he was a warden, 1841-64.

HARRISON, SAMUEL BEALY (1802-1867)
An English lawyer who emigrated to Canada just before the Rebellion of 1837, he was private secretary to Sir George Arthur and then provincial secretary, 1841-3. In 1845 he became a judge.

HELLIWELL, THOMAS, Sr (1769-1825?) and THOMAS, Jr (1796?-1862)
Father and son who founded a flourishing brewery and various mills on the Don River.

HELLIWELL, WILLIAM (1811-1897)
Another son of Thomas Helliwell Sr (q.v.), he became a partner in the family brewery in 1832 and manager in 1833. Later he operated a grist mill at Highland Creek.

HENRY, WALTER (1791-1860)
An English army doctor who was stationed in various locations in Canada from 1827, he attended Sir William Campbell (q.v.), the former chief justice, in his last illness in 1834. From 1852 to 1856 he was inspector-general of hospitals. He was the author of *Trifles from my Portfolio* (1839).

HERCHMER (HERKIMER), JACOB
A Loyalist and a nephew of General Nicholas Herkimer of the Revolutionary Army, he became a fur trader and merchant in York and at Rice Lake and was drowned in the loss of the *Speedy* in 1804.

HEWARD, HUGH
There were two Hugh Hewards in early Toronto. The first died in 1803 at Niagara; the second, his son, held various minor government posts.

HEWARD, STEPHEN (1777?-1828)
A militia captain, he took part in the defence of York in 1813. He held various minor government posts such as the clerkship of the peace of the Home District. He married Mary, a sister of Sir John Beverley Robinson (q.v.).

HIGGINS, WILLIAM
Chief constable or high bailiff of Toronto in 1834.

HINCKS, SIR FRANCIS (1807-1885)
Arriving in York from Belfast in 1830, he became a merchant and in 1835 a banker. He was a moderate Reformer and founded the *Examiner*, the first Reform newspaper after the Rebellion, in 1838. Elected to the first Legislative Assembly of United Canada in 1841, his political career reached its height when he was premier from 1851 to 1854. He was governor of Barbados, 1855-62, of British Guiana, 1862-9, and ended his political career as Canadian finance minister, 1869-73. He was knighted in 1869.

HODGES, EDWARD
He received his doctorate in music at Cambridge University and was briefly organist of St James' Church before moving to New York where he was organist of Trinity Church, 1839-59.

HOGG, JAMES (d. 1839)
A Scottish settler who owned extensive mills in what is now Hogg's Hollow on North Yonge Street. In 1832 he challenged George Gurnett (q.v.) to a duel.

HORNE, ROBERT CHARLES (d. 1845)
A member of the Royal College of Surgeons, he came to York about 1815 or 1816. He edited the *Upper Canada Gazette* from 1817 to 1821. Though he served on various medical boards, he did not built up a practice in York but worked for the Bank of Upper Canada.

HORNER, THOMAS
A member of the Legislative Assembly for Oxford from about 1820 to 1834.

HOWARD, JAMES SCOTT (1798-1866)
He emigrated to Canada about
1819 and became assistant postmaster, and in 1828 postmaster of
York. He was fired by Sir Francis
Bond Head in 1837 for supposed
sympathy with the rebels, but
from about 1842 on was treasurer
of the Home District (after 1850
the counties of Peel and York).

HOWARD, JOHN GEORGE (1803-1890)
An English architect and surveyor
who emigrated to Canada in 1832
and played a leading role in civic
affairs, being city engineer for
many years. His house, Colborne
Lodge, is still standing in High
Park, his estate which he willed to
the city in return for a moderate
pension in his old age.

HUDSON, JOSEPH
An Englishman who resided in
Canada from 1826 to 1836, holding various posts; he was chaplain
to the York Garrison and assistant
to Dr John Strachan (q.v.).

HUNTER, PETER (1746-1805)
Born in Scotland, he was a lieutenant-general in the British army.
He was appointed commander-in-
chief of all the troops in Canada
and lieutenant-governor of Upper
Canada in 1799. His military
duties necessitated his absence
from York during most of his
tenure of office. He died at Quebec in 1805.

JACKSON, JOHN MILLS (1764?-1836)
An English emigrant who came to
Upper Canada about 1806, he
published a critical account of the
government in 1809. His daughter
married Admiral Augustus Baldwin (q.v.).

JAMESON, ANNA (1794-1860)
The author of *Characteristics of
Women* (1832) and of several
books of art criticism, in 1836 she
visited Upper Canada where her
husband, Robert Jameson (q.v.),
was attorney-general. She returned to England in 1838 and published her *Winter Studies and
Summer Rambles in Canada*
(1838), one of the finest descriptions of the province.

JAMESON, ROBERT (d. 1854)
An English lawyer who came to
Upper Canada in 1833 as attorney-general after being a judge
in Dominica. From 1837 until his
death he was vice-chancellor of
the Court of Equity. His wife was
Anna Jameson (q.v.).

JARVIS FAMILY
The Toronto Jarvises are descended from two grandsons of Samuel
Jarvis (1698-1779) of Norwalk,
Conn.: William (q.v.), who came
to Upper Canada when Simcoe
became governor, and Stephen
(q.v.) who came in 1809. Both
had served in the Queen's Rangers and both had settled first in
New Brunswick.

JARVIS, FREDERICK WILLIAM
(1818-1887)
Grandson of Stephen Jarvis (q.v.),
Frederick William succeeded his
uncle, William Botsford Jarvis
(q.v.), as sheriff in 1864 and held
that office until his death.

JARVIS, GEORGE STEPHEN BENJAMIN
(1797-1878)
Son of Stephen Jarvis (q.v.), he
fought in the War of 1812 and
was admitted to the bar in 1823.
He settled in Cornwall and from
1834 was a county judge.

JARVIS, SAMUEL PETERS, Sr
(1792-1857)
Son of William Jarvis (q.v.), he
became a lawyer, clerk of the
crown in chancery, and later chief
superintendent of Indian affairs.

JARVIS, SAMUEL PETERS, Jr
(1820-1905)
Son of Samuel Peters Jarvis (q.v.),
the superintendent of Indian Affairs. He entered the army and served in the Indian Mutiny, 1857-9.
Later he was adjutant-general of
the Militia of Canada, commanded the Ontario Rifles in the Red
River Expedition in 1870, and
became commandant of the garrison at Fort Garry.

JARVIS, STEPHEN ['The Registrar']
(1756-1840)
A Loyalist and cousin of William
Jarvis (q.v.), he served on the British side in the American Revolution and then, after living in New
Brunswick, moved to York in
1809. He became registrar of
deeds for the Home District and
in 1833 gentleman usher of the
black rod in the Legislative Assembly.

JARVIS, WILLIAM ['Mr Secretary
Jarvis'] (1756-1817)
Born in Stamford, Conn., he
fought in the Queen's Rangers
under John Graves Simcoe (q.v.)
and came to Upper Canada with
him. He was appointed provincial
secretary in 1791, holding that
post until his death.

JARVIS, WILLIAM BOTSFORD
['Mr Sheriff Jarvis'] (1799-1864)
Son of Stephen Jarvis (q.v.), he
held the office of sheriff of the
Home District from 1827.

JEUNE, FRANCIS (1806-1868)
A graduate of Pembroke College,
Oxford, he became secretary to
Sir John Colborne (q.v.) in 1832.
By 1834 he had returned to Eng-
land and later was Master of
Pembroke College (1843-64) and
Bishop of Peterborough (1864-8).

JONES, AUGUST (1763?-1836)
A New York Loyalist who became
a deputy surveyor in 1788 and
prepared several surveys of the
town and township of York.

JORDAN, JOHN
A baker and keeper of Jordan's
York Hotel, the most popular
hotel in York for many years.

KANE, PAUL (1810-1871)
Son of Michael Kane, he came to
York from Ireland with his family
about 1818. A self-taught portrait
painter, he studied art in Italy
and France and returned to Canada in 1845. He then travelled
widely in western Canada, painting his famous Indian pictures,
many of which are now in the
Royal Ontario Museum. He is the
author of *Wanderings of an Artist among the Indians of North
America* (1859).

KETCHUM, JESSE (1782-1867)
He moved to Toronto from New
York State in 1799 and made a
fortune in the tanning business.
He sat in the Assembly for York
County (Reform) from 1830 to
1834. In 1845 he retired to Buffalo. Both there and in Toronto
he was an outstanding philanthropist.

KETCHUM, JOSEPH (1718-1803)
An uncle of Jesse Ketchum (q.v.),
he emigrated to Canada with Seneca Ketchum (q.v.). He settled
first in Kingston in 1792, then
moved to Scarborough in 1796.
He received a land patent in 1798.

KETCHUM, SENECA (1772-1850)
The elder brother of Jesse Ketchum (q.v.), he came to Canada in
1792 and settled at Eglinton on
Yonge Street about 1804. He was
one of the leading figures in the
founding of St John's York Mills.

KLINGENBRUMMER, CHARLES
(1799?-1881)
A watchmaker, he was believed to
be the oldest inhabitant of Toronto at his death.

KLINGER, or CLINGER, PHILIP
(1755?-1827)
A blacksmith who is first noted
in York in 1804. He spelled his
name with a 'C', though Scadding
uses a 'K'.

LA ROCHEFOUCAULD-LIANCOURT,
FRANÇOIS ALEXANDRE FRÉDÉRIC,
DUC DE (1747-1827)
An exile from the French Revolution who travelled in the United
States and Canada, 1795-7. He returned to France in 1799 and
published several volumes on his
journeys.

LEACH, WILLIAM TURNBULL
(1805-1886)
Educated at Edinburgh University (M.A. 1827), he was ordained a minister of the Church of Scotland in 1831. He came to Canada a year later, becoming minister of St Andrew's Church in Toronto until 1841 when he became an Anglican. He then moved to Montreal where he later became archdeacon.

LEE, WILLIAM (1763?-1833)
A regimental doctor who retired to York in 1807 and later became secretary of the Medical Board, he was Gentleman Usher of the Black Rod to the Legislative Council from 1816.

LEFFERTY or LAFFERTY, JOHN JOHNSTON (1877?-1842)
A doctor, farmer, and member for Lincoln, 1826-34.

LESSLIE, EDWARD (1764?-1828)
He migrated to Dundas, Ont., from Dundee in 1823 and was associated with his sons in the family business which had branches in York and Kingston.

LESSLIE, JAMES (1800-1885)
Son of Edward Lesslie (q.v.), he was a leading figure in Toronto business circles, a Reformer, and an alderman for St David's Ward in 1834. He was general manager of the Bank of the People, 1835-40, and proprietor of the *Examiner*, 1844-55.

LIANCOURT, DUC DE. See LA ROCHEFOUCAULD-LIANCOURT, DUC DE.

LITTLEHALES, SIR EDWARD BAKER
(d. 1825)
Military secretary of John Graves Simcoe (q.v.) in Upper Canada. He became a baronet in 1802.

LORING, ROBERT ROBERTS
(1790?-1848)
He fought in the War of 1812, became aide-de-camp to Sir Roger Sheaffe (q.v.), and was taken prisoner at Lundy's Lane.

McCAUL, JOHN (1807-1886)
An Anglican clergyman who came to Canada as principal of Upper Canada College in 1839 and in 1842 joined the university staff. From 1853 to 1880 he was president of the University of Toronto.

MACAULAY, JAMES (1759-1822)
Born in Scotland, he was an army surgeon who came to Upper Canada with John Graves Simcoe (q.v.). He was appointed deputy-inspector of hospitals. From 1819 to 1821 he was president of the newly formed Medical Board of Upper Canada. His was the first park-lot north-west of Queen and Yonge which later developed into the first suburb of Toronto and was called Macaulaytown.

MACAULAY, SIR JAMES BUCHANAN
(1793-1859)
Son of Dr James Macaulay (q.v.), he was called to the bar in 1822 and became a judge in 1829 and chief justice of the Court of Common Pleas, 1849-56. He was later made a judge of appeal and was knighted just before his death.

MACAULAY, JOHN SIMCOE ['Capt. Macaulay'] (1791-1855)
Son of Dr James Macaulay (q.v.), he became an officer of the Royal Engineers and a legislative councillor of Upper Canada, 1839-41. He retired to England in 1843.

MACAULAY, WILLIAM (1794-1874)
Educated by John Strachan (q.v.) at Cornwall, he was rector at Hallowell (Picton) from 1827 until his death. He was also chaplain to the Legislative Assembly for many years.

MACDONALD, JOHN (1824-1890)
A founder of one of the largest dry-goods businesses in Toronto in 1849, he was a Liberal member of Parliament for some years and later was appointed to the Senate by Sir John A. Macdonald—the only Liberal thus appointed.

MACDONELL or McDONELL, A.
Scadding's reference is either to Angus (d. 1804), first clerk of the Legislative Assembly (1792-1801) and member of the Assembly for Simcoe (1801-4) who was drowned on the *Speedy*; or to his brother Alexander (1762-1842), sheriff of the Home District (1792-1805) and later member of the Assembly for Glengarry.

MACDONELL, ALEXANDER (1762-1840)
The Roman Catholic bishop of Kingston, 1826-40, his diocese included all of Upper Canada. He was appointed to the Legislative Council in 1831.

MACDONELL, JOHN (1785-1812)
Attorney-General of Upper Canada (1812), he was aide-de-camp to Isaac Brock (q.v.) and fell with him at Queenston Heights.

MACDOUGALL, PETER
A French Canadian who came to York from Niagara about 1820 and became a merchant.

McGILL, JOHN ['Capt. McGill']
(1752-1834)
He fought as a captain in the Queen's Rangers under John Graves Simcoe (q.v.) in the American Revolution and later settled in New Brunswick. He came to Upper Canada in 1792. He was appointed to the Executive Council in 1796 and to the Legislative Council in 1797. He was inspector-general, 1801-13, receiver-general, 1813-22, and then retired on a pension.

McGILL, PETER (1789-1860)
A nephew of John McGill (q.v.). he changed his name from McCutcheon to inherit an uncle's estate. From 1834 to 1860 he was president of the Bank of Montreal and from 1841 a member of the Legislative Council.

MACKENZIE, WILLIAM LYON
(1795-1861)
Born in Scotland, he came to Upper Canada in 1820. He was the leader of the radical wing of the Reformers in the Legislative Assembly and the first mayor of Toronto in 1834. Largely responsible for the Rebellion of 1837 in Upper Canada, he fled to the United States where he stayed until 1849. His *Colonial Advocate* (1824-34) was one of the most influential Reform papers in the province.

MACLEAN, ALLAN (1752-1847)
A Kingston lawyer and member of the Legislative Assembly for Frontenac, 1804-24, he was speaker of the House in the sixth parliament (1812-16).

McLEAN, ARCHIBALD (1791-1865)
A pupil of John Strachan (q.v.) at Cornwall, he was admitted to the bar in 1815 and represented Stormont in the Legislative Assembly, 1820-36. He was then appointed to the Legislative Council and a year later to the bench. In 1862-3 he was chief justice of the Queen's Bench, and from 1863 to 1865 president of the Court of Appeal.

McMAHON, EDWARD
A civil secretary to Isaac Brock (q.v.), he became chief clerk in the Government Office.

McMASTER, WILLIAM (1811-1887)
An Irish immigrant who became a prominent Toronto dry-goods merchant and the first president of the Canadian Bank of Commerce, 1867-86, he was elected to the Legislative Council in 1862 and later became a senator. He founded McMaster University and left the bulk of his estate to its endowment fund.

MACNAB, ALEXANDER (d. 1815)
Born in Virginia, he was the son of a surgeon who served in Major McAlpin's Corps of Loyalists. In 1797 he was appointed confidential clerk to the Executive Council. He became an ensign in the Queen's Rangers in 1800 and entered a British regiment after the Rangers' disbandment. He was killed at Waterloo.

MACNAB, ALLAN (1768-1830)
Sergeant-at-arms of the House of Assembly from 1815 to 1830 and the father of Sir Allan MacNab.

MACNAB, ARCHIBALD ['The Chief'] (1781?-1860)
The 13th hereditary chieftain of the clan MacNab, he was possibly the most obnoxious personality in early Ontario history. He fled his creditors in Scotland in 1823 and received the Township of MacNab on the Ottawa River which he settled with Highlanders whom he exploited unmercifully. He was finally ousted in 1843 and returned to Scotland. He died in the south of France, a pensioner of his estranged wife.

MAITLAND, SIR PEREGRINE (1777-1854)
He fought in the Napoleonic Wars from 1792 to Waterloo. He was appointed lieutenant-governor of Upper Canada in 1818 and held that office for ten years. He later attained the rank of general, and was governor or commander-in-chief in Nova Scotia, the Madras Presidency, and the Cape of Good Hope.

MAITLAND, LADY SARAH (d. 1873)
Daughter of the Duke of Richmond, she married Sir Peregrine Maitland (q.v.) in 1815 and from 1818 to 1828 was the centre of society in York.

MANNING, ALEXANDER (1819-1903)
Alderman for the St Lawrence Ward for many years and mayor of Toronto in 1873 and 1885, he was a contractor and built the Normal School and parts of the parliament buildings in Ottawa. He also worked on the Welland Canal, 1842-3.

MARIAN, PAUL (d. 1808)
A Frenchman, he was the first baker in York, where he lived from 1799.

MARKLAND, GEORGE HERKIMER (1790?-1862)
A pupil and protégé of John Strachan (q.v.), he sat on the Legislative Council, 1820-41, and on the Executive Council, 1822-36. He was inspector-general from 1833 to 1838 when he was forced to resign on embezzlement charges after defalcations were discovered in his accounts. He retired to Kingston in 1841.

MATTHEWS, CHARLES STEPHENS (1800-77)
A graduate of Cambridge University (M.A. 1828), he became an original member of the staff of Upper Canada College. He was also Rector of St John's York Mills and assisted at St Paul's. In 1843 he retired to the Island of Guernsey and remained there until his death.

MERCER, ANDREW (d. 1871)
He came to Canada with chief justice Thomas Scott (q.v.) and went into partnership in a general store with Samuel S. Ridout (q.v.). His estate passed to the crown and was used to establish the Mercer Reformatory.

MILES, ABNER (1752?-1806)
One of the earliest tavern keepers in York, he moved in 1802 to Richmond Hill where he kept a tavern and general store.

MONRO, GEORGE (1799?-1882)
He immigrated to Canada in 1814 and became one of the leading wholesalers. He was known as the 'A. T. Stewart' of Toronto after the great New York merchant. He sat on the City Council as an alderman for the St Lawrence Ward from 1834 to 1845, except for 1836, and was mayor in 1841. He retired from business in 1857.

MONRO, JOHN (1788?-1830)
Brother of George Monro (q.v.), he was associated with him in his business before 1824, but afterwards had his own store.

MONTGOMERY, JOHN (1783-1879)
Born in New Bruswick, he came to Upper Canada in time to serve in the War of 1812 and then operated the famous tavern on Yonge Street above Eglinton which became the rebel headquarters in 1837. He was sentenced to transportation but escaped from Fort Henry and in 1843 returned to Canada under the Amnesty Act, becoming postmaster at Davidtown. He died in Barrie, Ont.

MORRISON, JOSEPH CURRAN (1816-1885)
A prominent politician of the Union period and law partner of William Hume Blake (q.v.). He held various cabinet posts between 1853 and 1862 when he was elevated to the bench. He was chancellor of the University of Toronto, 1863-76.

MORRISON, THOMAS DAVID (1796?-1856)
Born in Quebec, he settled in York in 1816 and became a doctor in 1824. A prominent Reformer, he was mayor of Toronto in 1836. He was arrested for treason after the Rebellion of 1837 but was acquitted. He fled the country, however, remaining in the United States until 1843.

MORTIMER, GEORGE (1784-1844)
A graduate of Cambridge (M.A. 1815), he was ordained in the Church of England in 1811. After spending some years as a vicar in England, he came to Canada and took over the parish of Thornhill in 1832.

MOSLEY, THOMAS
A warehouse keeper and auctioneer in York who received his training in London.

MOUNT, ROSWELL (1797-1834)
Son of a Loyalist, he was a member of the Assembly for Middlesex, 1830-4.

MURCHISON, JOHN (1778?-1870)
Son of a Loyalist, he began tailoring in Montreal and moved to York in 1808.

MURRAY, ALEXANDER
He worked as a clerk for William Proudfoot (q.v.) and later was in partnership with James Newbigging (d. 1838) and then Lewis Moffat.

NICHOL, ROBERT (1774?-1824)
He served in the War of 1812 as quartermaster-general of the militia and represented Norfolk in the Legislative Assembly, 1812-21. He was afterwards a judge at Niagara-on-the-Lake.

NIGHTINGALE, THOMAS (b. 1828
He came to Canada as a child and first turned to farming; then in 1858 he began a brick-making business.

OATES, EDWARD (1772-1827)
A relative of Peter Russell (q.v.), he settled at York in 1817 after serving in the British navy. In 1820 he built the *Richmond* which ran from York to Niagara.

O'GRADY, WILLIAM JOHN (d. 1840)
An Irish priest who was given the charge of York in 1828. He became a Reformer, quarreled with the bishop, and was suspended in 1832. He then founded the Reform *Correspondent* which merged with William Lyon Mackenzie's *Colonial Advocate* in 1834 and was sold to Charles Fothergill (q.v.) in 1837. He died at Whitby.

PATERSON, PETER, Sr (d. 1846)
He came to Canada from Scotland in 1819 and established a hardware business in the Market Square of York. His sons David, John, and Peter (q.v.) were associated in some of his enterprises and the business eventually passed on to a third generation.

PATERSON, PETER, Jr (1808?-1883)
A leading dry-goods and hardware merchant who carried on the business of his father (see above).

PAXTON, THOMAS (1754-1804)
A native of Newcastle-on-Tyne who entered the Marine Department on Lake Ontario in 1787, he was lost with his ship, the *Speedy*, in 1804.

PERRY, PETER (1793-1851)
A Reform leader of Loyalist descent, he was joint member of the Legislative Assembly for Lennox and Addington with Marshall Spring Bidwell (q.v.) from 1824 to 1836. After storekeeping for some years on the site of Whitby which he founded, he re-entered politics in 1849 as one of the founders of the Clear Grit Party and was elected to the legislature for York.

PETERS, SAMUEL (1735-1826)
A Connecticut Loyalist who moved to England, he attempted unsuccessfully to obtain an appointment as Bishop of Nova Scotia and later of Upper Canada. He was the father-in-law of Secretary William Jarvis (q.v.).

PHILLIPS, THOMAS (1781-1849)
A graduate of Cambridge in 1805, he became an Anglican clergyman. He was principal of the Home District Grammar School, 1825-30. When Upper Canada College was established he became vice-principal, holding that office until 1834 when he retired to become rector of Weston.

PINHEY, HAMNET
A member of the Legislative Assembly for Carleton, 1830-4, and of the Legislative Council, 1847-57.

PLAYTER, ELY (b. 1775)
Son of George Playter (q.v.), he was a tavern-keeper and later a farmer who served in the transport service in the War of 1812 and represented York County and Simcoe in the Legislative Assembly from 1824 to 1828, though he lived in Buffalo from 1826.

PLAYTER, GEORGE (1736-1822)
A Loyalist who came to Kingston and then to York where he settled above Castle Frank on the west side of the Don. He left many descendants.

PLAYTER, JAMES (1776?-1809)
A son of George Playter (q.v.), he was associated with his brother Ely as a tavern-keeper and later farmed near Richmond Hill.

PLAYTER, JOHN (b. 1774?)
A son of George Playter (q.v.), he settled across the Don River from his father.

POST, JORDAN (1767-1845)
A watchmaker and landowner in York who moved to Scarborough in 1834 and built a sawmill on Highland Creek.

POWELL, GRANT (1779-1838)
A son of William Dummer Powell (q.v.), he studied medicine and settled in York in 1812. He retired from medical practice in 1817 and held various government offices, including the clerkship of the Legislative Council.

POWELL, WILLIAM DUMMER (1755-1834)
Born in Boston, he studied law in England before coming to Canada in 1779. He began his law practice in Montreal. In 1789 he was appointed one of the first judges when a court system was set up in Upper Canada. In 1794 he became a judge of the King's Bench and from 1816 to 1825 was chief justice.

POWER, MICHAEL (1804-1847)
The first Roman Catholic Bishop of Toronto, 1841-7.

PREVOST, SIR GEORGE (1767-1816)
He entered the British army in 1784 and was governor of St Lucia, Dominica, and of Nova Scotia before becoming governor-in-chief of Canada in 1811. He was also commander-in-chief during the War of 1812 and was recalled from both posts in 1815.

PRICE, JAMES HERVEY (1797-1882)
Arriving in Canada in 1828, he was admitted to the bar in 1833. A Reformer, he became the first city clerk of Toronto in 1834 but soon left the post. He was a member of Parliament, 1841-51, and commissioner of crown lands, 1848-51, when he returned to England.

PROUDFOOT, WILLIAM
Emigrating from Scotland shortly after 1815, he first worked for D'Arcy Boulton Jr, then became a merchant on his own from 1825. From 1835 to 1860 he was president of the Bank of Upper Canada.

PUISAYE, JOSEPH GENEVIÈVE, COMTE DE (1755-1827)
The leader of an unsuccessful settlement of French emigrés in the years 1798-1802. Settlements were attempted in the townships of Markham and Vaughan.

QUETTON DE ST GEORGE, LAURENT.
See ST GEORGE, LAURENT QUETTON DE.

RADDISH, THOMAS
The first clergyman in York, he arrived in 1796 to shepherd the Anglican congregation but left Canada six months later.

RANDALL, ROBERT (1766-1834)
Born in Maryland, he came to Upper Canada in 1798 and settled at Niagara Falls. He engaged in various developmental projects and was a Reformer in politics. He was a member of the Legislative Assembly for Lincoln, 1820-34.

REES, WILLIAM (fl. 1819-1869)
He first came to York in 1829 after being trained in medicine in England and practising in Quebec. He was involved in many wild schemes, some of them in association with Charles Fothergill. He was first superintendent of the Provincial Asylum, 1841-4. He also built Rees's Wharf near the old Parliament Buildings.

RICHARDSON, HUGH (1784-1870)
He came to Canada in 1820 and became a leading captain on Lake Ontario. He built his own steamship, the Canada, and did much to improve Toronto harbour. He was Harbour Master, 1850-69.

RICHARDSON, JAMES (1791-1875)
He served in the War of 1812 and lost an arm at Sackett's Harbour. He became a Methodist preacher, editor of the Christian Guardian, and in 1858 bishop of the Methodist Episcopal Church of Canada.

RICHMOND, CHARLES, 4TH DUKE OF (1764-1819)
He was appointed governor-in-chief of Canada in 1818 because he was in financial difficulties and his brother-in-law was Colonial Secretary Lord Bathurst. He had previously been a success as lord-lieutenant of Ireland (1807-13), but his governorship in Canada led to a deterioration of English-French relations.

RIDOUT FAMILY
One of the prominent families of early Toronto, the Ridouts originally came from Sherborne in Dorsetshire, England. The Toronto Ridouts were all descended from George Ridout (1702-79) whose son Thomas (q.v.) was brought to Canada from Maryland by Indians and whose grandson George (nephew of Thomas) emigrated later.

RIDOUT, GEORGE (1791-1871)
A son of Thomas Ridout (q.v.), he was a lawyer who practised in Toronto and Clinton.

RIDOUT, GEORGE PERCIVAL (1807-1873)
A son of George Ridout (q.v.) and a prominent Toronto merchant.

RIDOUT, JOHN (1799-1817)
Son of Thomas Ridout (q.v.), he fought in the War of 1812 and was killed in a duel with Samuel Peters Jarvis Sr.

RIDOUT, JOSEPH DAVIS (1808-1884)
Son of George Ridout (q.v.) and a prominent Toronto merchant.

RIDOUT, SAMUEL SMITH (1778-1855)
The eldest son of Thomas Ridout (q.v.), he ran a general store, then became sheriff of the Home District (1815-27) and then registrar.

RIDOUT, THOMAS ['The Surveyor-General'] (1754-1829)
Associated with the surveyor-general's office, he became joint acting surveyor-general in 1799 and surveyor-general in 1810. He sat in the Assembly from 1812 to 1816 and became a Legislative Councillor in 1825.

RIPLEY, WILLIAM HONYWOOD (1815?-1849)
The first rector of 'little' Trinity Church, 1843-9, and a teacher at Upper Canada College.

RITCHEY (RITCHIE, RICHEY), JOHN (1796-1866)
A leading builder and contractor who came to York from Ireland in 1819. He built the Church of St George the Martyr, the east wing of Osgoode Hall, the Court House, and many other buildings.

ROBINSON FAMILY
The Robinsons were one of the first families of Virginia where they settled about 1670, before becoming one of the first families of Upper Canada. John Robinson was the President of the Council and acting governor of Virginia when he died in 1759. His elder son John (1704-66) was Treasurer of Virginia from 1738 until his death, and his younger son Beverley (1722-92) was one of the greatest landowners of New York State at the time of the Revolution. Christopher Robinson (1764-98), the son of the Treasurer, came to Upper Canada in 1792 and to York in 1798. Christopher's three sons Peter (q.v.), Sir John Beverley (q.v.), and William (1797-1873), played leading roles in Upper Canada politics.

ROBINSON, SIR JOHN BEVERLEY (1791-1863)
Born in Berthier, Quebec, the second son of Christopher Robinson, he studied under John Strachan (q.v.) and fought in the War of 1812. He became solicitor-general in 1815, attorney-general in 1818, and chief justice in 1829, holding this office until 1862 when he became president of the Court of Error and Appeal. Possessor of one of the most brilliant minds in the Family Compact, he played a leading role in the Legislative Assembly and later in the Legislative Council. He was created a baronet in 1854; it is one of the few surviving Canadian titles.

ROBINSON, PETER (1785-1838)
The eldest son of Christopher Robinson, he served in the War of 1812 and in 1824-5 was responsible for settling Irish immigrants in the Peterborough area which was named for him. From the late 1820s to 1836 he was a member of both the Executive and Legislative Councils and Commissioner of Crown Lands.

ROGERS, JOSEPH (1787?-1873)
A prominent merchant, Scadding refers to him as a furrier, but he was possibly best known as the leading hatter of the city.

ROLPH, JOHN (1793-1870)
He studied law and medicine in England and practised both in

Canada after 1821. He settled in York in 1831, founded the Toronto School of Medicine, and sat in the Legislative Assembly for several years, becoming one of the Reform leaders. He sat on the Executive Council for two weeks in 1836. He joined the rebellion and was exiled from Canada until the amnesty of 1843. He was a member of the Hincks-Morin government, 1851-4.

ROLPH, THOMAS (1820?-1883)
An English doctor who came to Ancaster in 1833 and became Emigration Agent a few years later. He returned to England permanently about 1844 and settled in Portsmouth. He published a statistical account of the province in 1836.

ROY, LOUIS (d. 1799)
A printer who established the *Upper Canada Gazette* at Niagara-on-the-Lake in 1793 but after two years moved to Montreal and founded the bilingual Montreal *Gazette*. He moved to New York in 1797.

RUSSELL, ELIZABETH (1754-1822)
The half-sister of Peter Russell (q.v.), she lived with him from 1786 and inherited his lands in 1808, which she in turn left to her cousins Maria Willcocks and Phoebe Willcocks Baldwin (Mrs W. W.).

RUSSELL, PETER (1733-1808)
He came to Canada from England as receiver-general of Upper Canada in 1792, and the next year he was appointed to both the Executive and Legislative Councils. From 1796 to 1799 he was administrator of the province, and the large land holdings he acquired passed to his half-sister Elizabeth (q.v.) and then to the Baldwin family.

ST GEORGE, LAURENT QUETTON DE (1771-1821)
After fighting against the Republic in France he came to Canada with the Comte de Puisaye (q.v.) in 1798. In 1802 he opened a store in York and soon had branches from Kingston to Amherstburg. He returned to France in 1815 and became a Chevalier of the Order of St Louis.

SANDERS, MATTHIAS (d. 1813)
A carpenter, shipbuilder, and commander of the *Bella Gere*, he was killed in the explosion of the magazine during the capture of York.

SANSOM, ALEXANDER (1819-1904)
Educated in Scotland at Edinburgh University and ordained as an Anglican clergyman, he was rector of St John's York Mills until 1842 and then transferred to Trinity Church, Toronto, in 1852, where he remained until his death.

SAVAGE, GEORGE (1777?-1835)
Collector of customs in York from 1828. By profession he was a watchmaker, coming originally from Manchester and then working sixteen years in London.

SCADDING, JOHN (1754-1824)
Father of Henry Scadding, he came to York in 1793 and received a 253-acre land grant on the east bank of the Don River. He returned to England in 1796 to manage the estates of John Graves Simcoe (q.v.) and did not come back to Canada until 1818. His wife was Melicent Triggs (1768-1860). See also the Editor's Introduction.

SCARLETT, JOHN (1766-1864?)
An English settler who owned mills and a distillery on the Humber River. He was very active in the lumber trade.

SCORESBY, WILLIAM (1789-1857)
An arctic navigator who became an Anglican clergyman in 1834 and held various rectories in England.

SCOTT, THOMAS (1746-1824)
An English lawyer who became attorney-general of Upper Canada (1800-6), and chief justice (1806-16), with seats on the Executive and Legislative Councils.

SCOTT, WINDFIELD (1786-1866)
Usually known as 'Old Fuss and Feathers', he trained at West Point, fought in the War of 1812, and was responsible for pacifying the Canadian border after the *Caroline* crisis. He became general-in-chief of the United States army in 1841 and fought successfully against Mexico, but retired shortly after the Civil War began in 1861.

SEATON, BARON. *See* COLBORNE, SIR JOHN

SELKIRK, THOMAS, 5TH EARL OF (1771-1820)
The Scottish philanthropist and financier who founded three settlements in British North America on Prince Edward Island, in Baldoon (Upper Canada), and in the Red River valley. The Red River colony involved him ruinously in a conflict between the Hudson's Bay Company, in which he had a controlling interest with his brother-in-law, and the North West Company.

SHADE, ABSALOM (1793?-1862)
A native of Pennsylvania who was employed by the Hon. William Dickson of Niagara about 1816 to settle the township of North Dumfries which he owned. Shade is mainly remembered as the founder of Galt.

SHANK, DAVID (d. 1831)
A Loyalist who had served in John Graves Simcoe's first Queen's Rangers and came to Canada in 1792 as second in command when the Rangers were re-constituted. He returned to England in 1799.

SHAW, AENEAS (d. 1815)
A Scotsman, he served in the Queen's Rangers during the American Revolution, settled in New Brunswick, and then came to Upper Canada in 1792 and was appointed to the Legislative and Executive Councils in 1794. He became a major-general in 1811. During the War of 1812 he was adjutant-general of the militia.

SHEAFFE, SIR ROGER HALE (1763-1851)
He had a long military career in Canada before he succeeded Isaac Brock (q.v.) as administrator of Upper Canada when Brock was killed at Queenston Heights in 1812. In 1813 he was dismissed for the loss of York. He was created a baronet for his part in the battle at Queenston Heights.

SHEPARD, HARVEY
An early iron worker and axe maker after whom Sheppard Street was named.

SHEPARD, JOSEPH (d. 1837)
An Indian trader and radical Reformer who settled on Yonge Street at Sheppard Avenue, which was named after him.

SHERWOOD, LEVIUS PETERS (1777-1850)
Admitted to the bar in 1803, he practised law in Brockville and represented Leeds in the Legislative Assembly. He was a judge of the King's Bench from 1825 to 1841 and a member of the Legislative Council from 1842.

SIBBALD, WILLIAM
A captain in the 1st Royal Regiment, he came to Canada in 1833. He established the *Canadian Magazine* just after his arrival.

SICOTTE, LOUIS VICTOR (1812-1889)
A Reform politician who was co-premier in 1862-3 and afterwards a judge of the Superior Court of Quebec until 1887.

SIMCOE, ELIZABETH POSTHUMA (1766-1850)
The daughter of Col. Thomas Gwillim, she married John Graves Simcoe (q.v.) in 1782 and lived with her husband in Upper Canada from 1792 to 1796. A considerable heiress, she purchased their Wolford estate in Devonshire in 1784. She made many water-colour sketches during her stay in Upper Canada and kept a diary, the most recent edition of which was published in 1965.

SIMCOE, FRANCIS GWILLIM (1791-1812)
A son of John Graves Simcoe (q.v.), he became a lieutenant in the 27th Foot and was killed at the battle of Badajoz in Spain, 6 April 1812.

SIMCOE, JOHN GRAVES (1752-1806)
The first lieutenant-governor of Upper Canada from 1791 to 1798, though he resided in the province only until 1796. Earlier he had fought in the American Revolutionary War, commanding the Queen's Rangers, and had been a member of Parliament for Cornwall. He founded York in 1793. After he left Upper Canada, he was briefly commander-in-chief at San Domingo, and just before he died he was appointed commander-in-chief for India.

SMALL, CHARLES (1800-1864)
A son of John Small (q.v.), he succeeded to his father's office of clerk of the Crown and Pleas in 1825.

SMALL, JAMES EDWARD (d. 1869)
A son of John Small (q.v.), he was born in York before 1800 and called to the bar in 1821. He was the counsel for William Lyon Mackenzie (q.v.) in the printing-press case in 1826. He was a member of the Legislative Assembly for York County, 1839-49, and solicitor-general, 1840-3. From 1849 until his death he was county judge for Middlesex.

SMALL, JOHN (1746-1831)
He came to Canada from England in 1792 and from 1793 until his death was clerk of the Executive Council.

SMITH, SIR DAVID WILLIAM (1764-1837)
He came to Canada from England in 1790 and was elected a member of the Legislative Assembly in 1792, 1796, and 1800. He was speaker in 1797-9 and 1801-4, appointed to the Executive Council in 1796, and was made surveyor-general in 1800. He returned to England in 1804 but continued to receive a pension— an emolument that was one of William Lyon Mackenzie's chief subjects of complaint. He wrote a topographical survey of the province which appeared in 1799. He was created a baronet in 1821.

SMITH, MICHAEL (fl. 1808-1814)
A Pennsylvania Baptist minister who came to Upper Canada in 1808 but left after the War of 1812 began. He published a geographic survey in 1813.

SMITH, SAMUEL (1756-1826)
Born in New York State, he served in the Queen's Rangers during the American Revolution. He became a member of the Executive Council in 1813 and was administrator in 1817-18 and again in 1820.

SMITH, WILLIAM (d. 1819)
Born in Nottinghamshire, Eng., he came to Niagara-on-the-Lake in 1792 and spent the summer of 1793 in York. He was a builder and was responsible for many of the early buildings in York.

SPRAGGE, JOHN GODFREY (1806-1884)
Son of Joseph Spragge (q.v.), he was called to the bar in 1828. He was made vice-chancellor in 1851, chancellor in 1869, and chief justice of Ontario in 1881.

SPRAGGE, JOSEPH (1775-1848)
Born in Canterbury, Eng., he
came to Canada in 1820 as master
of the York Central School, holding this office for most of the period up to 1844.

STANTON, ROBERT (1794-1866)
Son of William Stanton (q.v.), he
was educated by John Strachan
(q.v.), was King's Printer and editor of the *Upper Canada Gazette*
from 1826 to 1843, and then Collector of Customs for Toronto
from 1843 to 1849. Afterwards he
was an officer of the courts at
Osgoode Hall.

STANTON, WILLIAM (1756-1833)
He settled at York after some
years in the Royal Navy and held
minor government posts in Toronto and Amherstburg.

STEGMAN(N), JOHN (1754-1804)
An early land surveyor.

STEWART, ALEXANDER (d. 1840)
Educated at Edinburgh University, he came to Canada in 1818.
He was the first teacher at the
York Common School in 1819-19.
He later taught in Toronto township, became a land agent, and
then a Baptist minister at York,
1829-36.

STEWART, CHARLES JAMES
(1775-1837)
A Scottish missionary who came
to Canada in 1808 and became
the second Anglican bishop of
Quebec in 1825. Though he spent
most of his time in Lower Canada,
his diocese included Upper Canada.

STOYELL, THOMAS (1760?-1832)
A non-practising American doctor
who had settled in York by 1799.
He first kept a tavern and after
1812 became a brewer. His property was left to the Methodist
Conference.

STRACHAN, JOHN (1778-1867)
Born in Aberdeen, Scotland, and
educated there and at St Andrew's University, he emigrated to
Kingston in 1799 and became the
outstanding personality in Upper
Canada, probably standing next
to John Graves Simcoe (q.v.) in
his influence on its early development. In 1803 he took Anglican
orders and was made rector of
Cornwall and master of the leading school there, to which many
prominent Upper Canadian families sent their sons. In 1812 he
was transferred to York as rector,
in time to play a leading role
during the American occupation
of 1813. He sat on the Executive
Council from 1818 to 1836, on
the Legislative Council from 1820
to 1841, and during much of this
time was the most influential person in the Family Compact. He
became archdeacon of York in
1827 and first bishop of Toronto
in 1839. He was president of
King's College from 1827 to
1840; when it was secularized in
1850 he founded Trinity College
in 1851. A strong supporter of an
'established church', and of the
Clergy Reserves, he fought a long
series of battles with dissenting
denominations and against se-
cularization in all forms.

STUART, GEORGE OKILL (1776-1862)
Born and brought up in the
United States, a graduate of Har-
vard (1801), he was rector of
York from 1801 to 1812, and of
Kingston from 1812 until his
death. He became archdeacon of
Upper Canada in 1821.

SULLIVAN, AUGUSTUS (1814-1868)
Brother of R. B. Sullivan (q.v.),
he became a barrister.

SULLIVAN, ROBERT BALDWIN
(1802-1853)
Born in Ireland, the son of Barbara Baldwin, a sister of William

Warren Baldwin (q.v.), he came to Canada in 1819 and became a lawyer in 1828. He was the second mayor of Toronto in 1835 and was appointed to the Executive Council in 1836 and the Legislative Council in 1839. After the Union of 1841 he was reappointed to both councils, sitting on the Executive Council until 1843 and on the Legislative Council until 1851. He was made provincial secretary in the first responsible government in 1848. From 1848 on he was a judge.

SYDENHAM AND TORONTO, CHARLES POULETT THOMSON, 1ST BARON (1799-1841)
A member of a wealthy English merchant family, he was elected to Parliament and became president of the Board of Trade in 1830. In 1839 he was sent to Canada as governor to carry out Lord Durham's recommendations for the union of Upper and Lower Canada. He died an accidental death at Kingston.

TALBOT, THOMAS (1771-1853)
Born in Ireland, he first came to Canada in 1790 with the 24th Regiment and from 1792 until he returned to England in 1794 was secretary to John Graves Simcoe (q.v.). He came back to Canada in 1803 and achieved his real fame by opening up a vast area along the north shore of Lake Erie and establishing and ruling the Talbot settlement there until 1837.

TAYLOR, JOHN FENNINGS (1817-1882)
He came to Canada from England in 1836 and was clerk of the Legislative Council and, in 1867, of the Senate. He wrote several books.

TERRY, PARSHALL (1756-1808)
Born in Orange County, N.Y., he came to Canada as a Loyalist.

After living in Kingston and Niagara, he settled on the east bank of the Don River where he built a sawmill. He was a member of the first Legislature.

THORPE, ROBERT (fl. 1781-1820)
An Irish lawyer who was admitted to the bar in 1781, he later became a protégé of Lord Castlereagh. He was chief justice of Prince Edward Island (1802-5) and a justice of the King's Bench of Upper Canada (1805-7). He made himself leader of the anti-government forces and was dismissed by Governor Gore. From 1808 to 1815 he was chief justice of Sierra Leone where he again became involved in a series of quarrels and was dismissed.

TIERS (TIERCE), DANIEL
He was a German from Pennsylvania who settled in Berczy's (q.v.) Markham settlement before 1798. By 1808 he had become a tavern keeper in York and later ran the Red Lion Inn in Yorkville, on Yonge Street north of Bloor.

TIFFANY, GIDEON (1774-1854)
The printer of the *Upper Canada Gazette* at Niagara 1794-7 and of the *Canada Constellation*, 1799-1800. He later became a farmer in Middlesex county.

TIFFANY, SILVESTER (1758-1811)
Brother of Gideon Tiffany (q.v.), he was associated with him at Niagara in editing the *Canada Constellation* and then edited the *Niagara Herald* until 1802 when he moved to the United States.

TOWNSLEY, WILLIAM (1827-1877)
He came to Canada as a child, and began manufacturing bricks and brick-making machines in 1855 at Yorkville.

TURNER, ENOCH (1790?-1866)
A brewer and philanthropist whose schoolhouse still stands behind 'Little' Trinity.

TURQUAND, BERNARD (1790-1848)
An Englishman of Huguenot descent who emigrated to Upper Canada in 1820 and worked in the receiver-general's department, rising to the post of deputy receiver-general. From 1822 to 1842 he was grand secretary of the provincial Masonic Lodge. He died in Montreal.

VANSITTART, HENRY (1779-1844)
An English naval officer who became a rear-admiral in 1830 and a vice-admiral in 1841. He settled on an estate near Woodstock in 1834.

VAN ZANTE, JOHN
An emigrant from Pennsylvania who carried on a tannery business on Yonge Street for some years. When the War of 1812 broke out, he was forced to sell the business to Jesse Ketchum (q.v.) and leave the country because he had remained an American citizen.

WALTON, GEORGE
He flourished at York in various capacities in the early 1830s but is best known as the publisher of the 1833 and 1837 directories.

WASHBURN, SIMON E. (1793?-1837)
He studied law under William Warren Baldwin and then practised in York. He was clerk of the peace for the Home District, 1828-37, and an alderman for St David's Ward in 1837. He married Margaret FitzGibbon, sister of James FitzGibbon (q.v.), in 1821.

WATSON, RICHARD (d. 1849)
He was King's Printer and editor of the *Upper Canada Gazette* from 1843 until his death.

WEEKES, WILLIAM (d. 1806)
An Irishman who studied law in the United States. He came to York in 1798 and was elected to the Legislative Assembly in 1805. He was killed in a duel with William Dickson (q.v.).

WELLER, WILLIAM (1799?-1863)
A resident and sometime mayor of Cobourg, he was the leading stage-coach operator in Upper Canada in the days before the railways.

WELLS, JOSEPH (1773-1853)
A Peninsular War veteran who retired to York in 1815 and became a member of the Legislative (1820-41) and Executive (1829-36) Councils. He was bursar of King's College, 1827-39.

WHITE, JOHN (d. 1800)
He studied at the Inner Temple from 1777 and was admitted to the bar in 1785. He lived in Jamaica for a time and in 1792 was appointed attorney-general of Upper Canada, which office he held until he was killed in a duel. He was also a member of the Legislative Assembly for Leeds and Frontenac, 1792-6.

WIDMER, CHRISTOPHER (1780-1858)
Born in England, he was the father of surgery in Upper Canada. After fighting in the Peninsular Wars he came to York late in 1814 and was at first the only practising physician there. He was a member of the Legislative Council from 1843.

WILLCOCKS, CHARLES (1762-1826)
The only son of William Willcocks (q.v.), he came to Upper Canada in 1797 with his sisters.

WILLCOCKS, JOSEPH (d. 1814)
Born in Ireland, he came to York in 1799 because of his distant connection with Peter Russell (q.v.). He was sheriff of the Home District, 1803-7. A critic of government, he was a member of the Legislative Assembly, 1808-12, and eventually joined the Americans on whose side he was killed while fighting at Fort Erie.

WILLCOCKS, WILLIAM (1736-1813)
A first cousin of Peter Russell (q.v.), he came to Canada from Cork in 1792. After an unsuccessful attempt to settle Whitby Township in 1795-7, he moved to York where he became the first postmaster and a merchant. He had three children: Phoebe, who married W. W. Baldwin (q.v.) in 1803, Maria, and Charles (q.v.).

WILLIS, JOHN WALPOLE (1793-1877)
An English equity lawyer who was appointed a judge of the King's Bench in 1827 but who soon quarrelled with almost everyone and was dismissed by Sir Peregrine Maitland in 1828.

WILLIS, LADY MARY
The wife of John Walpole Willis (q.v.), she was the daughter of the Earl of Strathmore. She demanded precedence over Lady Sarah Maitland (q.v.), wife of the lieutenant-governor, during the brief period her husband was a judge in Upper Canada (1827-8). The Willis marriage was dissolved in 1838.

WILLSON, DAVID (1778?-1866)
He emigrated to Canada from New York State in 1801 and by 1812 had founded a religious sect called the 'Children of Peace' which he led until his death. His temple is still standing at Sharon.

WINNIETT, JAMES
He became resident superintendent of Indian Affairs on the Grand River in 1832.

WOOD, ALEXANDER (1772?-1844)
Born in Scotland, he came to Kingston about 1793 and by 1797 had opened a store in York in partnership with William Allan (q.v.). After 1801 he was on his own until he gradually retired after 1812. He was active as a magistrate and in charitable work. He died in Scotland.

WORTS, JAMES (1792?-1834)
The brother-in-law of William Gooderham (q.v.), he had been engaged in milling for many years in England before coming to Canada in 1831 to establish the family flour-mill business.

WORTS, JAMES GOODERHAM (1818-1882)
He came from England with his parents and from 1845 on was an active member of the family business (see above). He was a supporter of Trinity Church and was Harbour Commissioner for a time.

WRAGG, JOHN
Wragg & Co. were Montreal ironmongers who opened a branch of their business in York in 1826 and another in Kingston called John Wragg & Co.

WRIGHT, EDWARD GRAVES SIMCOE (1794-1860s)
The son of one of the earliest settlers and possibly the first child of European parents born in York. His Greenland Fisheries Tavern at the north-west corner of Front and John Streets was one of the most famous taverns in the city. He was alderman for St George's Ward in 1834.

YONGE, SIR GEORGE (1731-1812)
A friend of John Graves Simcoe (q.v.), he was a member for Honiton (where Simcoe's Wolford Lodge was located), 1763-96, Secretary of War (1782-94), Master of the Mint (1794-9), and Governor of the Cape (1799-1801). Yonge Street was named in his honour.

YOUNG, THOMAS (d. 1860)
An English architect and draftsman, he came to Upper Canada in 1836. He was made the first city engineer of Toronto in 1840 and was the architect of King's College.

Appendix IV
Changes in Street Names

Unlike the urban centres in many European nations, Canadian cities have fortunately never been subjected to the wholesale name changes that can follow political upheavals. Still, in the process of growth and development the nomenclature of Toronto's streets has undergone considerable revision, particularly during the middle years of the last century. Probably the most frequent cause of changing names has been the North American fixation on having only one designation for an entire street, rather than letting it change name every few blocks. As extensions of streets in the Town of York often had different names, regularizing them required considerable change. Also, some early streets had no generally accepted names, or, in some cases, no name at all. The Scadding family themselves have suffered from this process of change. Amelia Street still commemorates the Canon's wife; but Wellesley Street East has been extended to include Charles Street, named in honour of of the the Canon's brother, which was earlier called Frank Street after the Scadding's summer retreat, which had itself been named after Henry and Amelia's son Frank. Scadding Street is now the south end of Broadview Avenue.

By the 1840s, with the rapid growth of the city, street names were beginning to cause considerable confusion, and sometimes seemed to lack appropriate dignity for a burgeoning metropolis. To sort matters out, in 1844 the City Council passed By-law #84 "An Act to establish names of Certain Streets in the City of Toronto". The act began by raising Lot Street, a name chosen because it was the base line for the park or farm lots of the wealthy which stretched north from it, to the dignity of Queen Street in honour of the young Victoria. In 1845, a second By-law, #89, made more changes and others have followed since. Some of the amendments, though properly enacted, never came into force. For instance, Temperance Street never became Alfred Street despite the 1845 legal change, thus preserving a bit of colour in the city's nomenclature. Other changes made to improve the tone of a street failed in the desired result of cleaning up the neighbourhood; the prostitutes who frequented it did not care what March-Stanley-Lombard Street was called and their clients were still able to find their way. Fortunately, a modern attempt to have Jarvis Street renamed for the same reason was never carried through.

The following list, which does not attempt completeness, shows the major changes that have taken place in the names of early Toronto streets. In many cases, the earlier names only covered a part of the present thoroughfare. Some names were used for more than one street at different times. Unless noted otherwise, all were designated "Street".

Present Name	Former Name
Albert	- Macaulay Lane
Adelaide	- Newgate Street - Duke Street east of Jarvis
Bathurst	- Crookshank's Lane north of Queen
Bay	- Teraulay, north of Queen to College - Vincent, Chapel and North between College and Bloor
Bloor	- 2nd Concession Road - St. Paul's Road - Sydenham Road
Berkeley	- Parliament, south end
Chesnut	- Sayer
Colborne	- Market Lane
Dundas	- originally ran north from Queen West as the south part of Denison and then

turned west. It was gradually extended east from Denison incorporating a large number of streets including: St. Patrick's, Agnes and Wilton Avenue

Esplanade

- The Mall

Front

- Palace east of Jarvis

Granby

- Ann

Henrietta

- a lane near present King Edward Hotel

Jarvis

- first New
- later Nelson

Kingston Road

- Road to Quebec

Lombard

- first March
- later Stanley

Market (West)

- Francis, south part
- Stuart's Lane north of King

Queen

- Lot

Richmond

- Simcoe west of Spadina
- Hospital from Yonge to Spadina
- Dutchess east of Jarvis

St. Patrick

- Dummer
- William

Sherbourne

- Caroline south of Queen

Simcoe

- Graves south of Queen
- William north of Queen

Spadina Avenue   - Brock below Queen

University Avenue   - College Avenue
                           - University (these ran beside each other)

Victoria   - Upper George south of Queen
                           (not connected with Lower
                           George, now George)

Wellington   - Market

Further Reference

For further references on the origins and changes in the names of Toronto streets see:

Arthur, Eric, *Toronto No Mean City!* 3rd Edition (Toronto, 1986 revised by Stephen Otto) — Appendix on "The Origin of Street names in Toronto", pp 272-93.

Robertson, John Ross, *Landmarks of Toronto* Vol. 1 (Toronto, 1894) — Chapter CLXXVII "Street Nomenclature" pp 516-28.

BIBLIOGRAPHY

1. BIBLIOGRAPHIC SOURCES

Armstrong, Frederick H., Alan F.J. Artibise, and Melvin Baker. *Bibliography of Canadian Urban History. Part 1V: Ontario*, in Vance Bibliographies. (Monticello, Ill., 1980)

Artibise, Alan F.J., and Gilbert A. Stelter. *Canada's Urban Past; A Bibliography to 1980 and a Guide to Canadian Urban Studies.* (Vancouver, 1981).

Bishop, Olga B. *Bibliography Of Ontario History, 1867-1976.* (2 vols., Toronto, 1980)

2. GENERAL WORKS

Adam, Graeme Mercer. *Toronto: Old and New.* (Toronto, 1891, reprinted 1972)

Armstrong, Frederick H. *Toronto: The Place of Meeting* . (Los Angelos, 1983)

Careless, J.M.S. *Toronto to 1918: An Illustrated History.* (Toronto, 1984)

Firth, Edith G. *The Town of York,1793-1834.* (2 vols.,Toronto, 1962-1966)

Glazebrook, George P. de T. *The Story of Toronto.* (Toronto, 1971)

Goheen, Peter G. *Victorian Toronto 1850-1890.* (Chicago, 1970)

Illustrated Historical Atlas of the County of York. (Toronto, 1878, reprinted 1969)

Kerr, Donald and Jacob Spelt. *The Changing Face of Toronto.* (Toronto, 1965)

Kyte, Ernest C., ed. *Old Toronto: A Selection of Excerpts from "Landmarks of Toronto" by John Ross Robertson.* (Toronto, 1970)

Masters, Donald C. *The Rise of Toronto, 1850-1890.* (Toronto, 1974)

Middleton, Jesse E. *The Municipality Of Toronto, A History.* (3 vols., Toronto, 1923)

Mulvany, Charles Pelham. *Toronto, Past and Present* . (Toronto, 1884, reprinted 1970)

Pearson, William H. *Recollections and Records of Toronto of Old.* (Toronto, 1914)

Robertson, John Ross. *Landmarks of Toronto.* (6 vols., Toronto, 1894-1914, reprints Vol. 1, 1976, Vol. 3, 1974)

Robinson, Percy C. *Toronto During The French Régime, 1715-1793* . (Toronto, 1933, reprinted 1965)

Scadding, Henry and John Charles Dent. *Toronto, Past and Present.* (Toronto, 1884)

Spelt, Jacob. *Toronto.* (Toronto, 1973)

_____ . *Urban Development in South-Central Ontario.* (Assen, the Netherlands, 1955, reprinted 1972)

West, Bruce. *Toronto* . (Toronto, 1967)

3. SPECIAL STUDIES

Arthur, Eric. Toron*to: No Mean CIty!* (Toronto, 1964)

Dendy, William. *Lost Toronto* . (Toronto, 1978)

Martyn, Lucy Booth. *Aristocratic Toronto: Nineteenth Century Grandeur.* (Toronto, 1980)

_____ . *The Face of Early Toronto: An Architectural Record: 1797-1936.* (Sutton West, 1982)

_____ . *Toronto 100 Years of Grandeur: The Inside Story Of Toronto's Great Homes.* (Toronto, 1978)

St. Lawrence Hall. (Toronto, 1969)

Thom, Ron, and others. *Exploring Toronto*. (Toronto, 1972)

Thompson, Austin Seton. *Jarvis Street: a Story of Triumph and Tragedy*. (Toronto, 1980)

_____ . *Spadina: A Story of Old Toronto*. (Toronto, 1975)

Toronto Board of Education, Centennial Story, 1850-1950. (Toronto, 1950)

Transit in Toronto: The Story of Public Transportation in Metropolitan Toronto. (Toronto, 1982)

Wallace, William Stewart. *A History of the University of Toronto, 1827-1927*. (Toronto, 1927)

Zerker, Sally F. *The Rise and Fall of the Toronto Typographical Union, 1832-1972: A Case Study of Foreign Domination*. (Toronto, 1982)

4. MUNICIPAL POLITICAL FIGURES

Flint, David. *William Lyon Mackenzie: Rebel Against Authority*. (Toronto, 1971)

Kilbourn, William. *The Firebrand*. (Mackenzie) . (Toronto, 1956)

Russell, Victor L. *Mayors of Toronto, Vol. 1, 1834-1899*. (Toronto, 1982; the second volume will appear shortly.)

In addition to the above, the completed volumes of the *Dictionary of Canadian Biography* for the 19th century, Vols. IV, V, VI, VIII, IX, X, and XI, covering the period 1801 to 1835 and 1851 to 1890 contain biographies of many Torontonians who died during those years.

INDEX

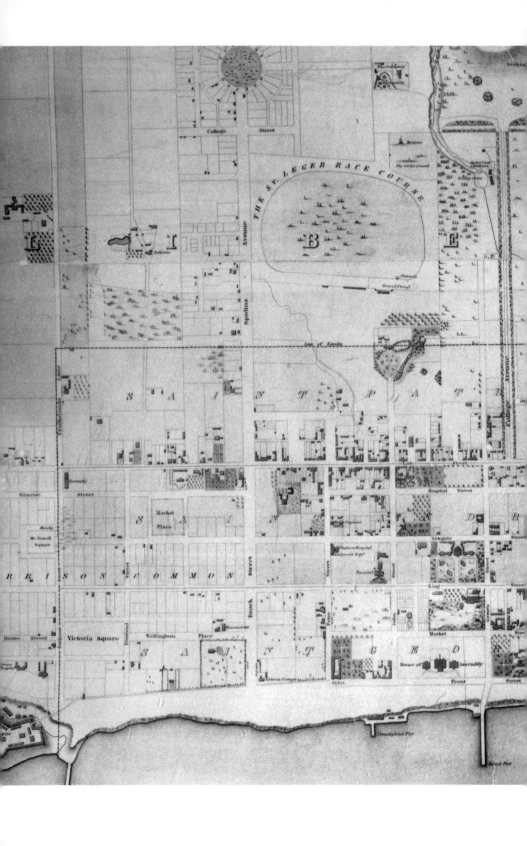

Printed in Canada